Data Analytics for Accounting

Vernon J. Richardson
University of Arkansas,
Xi'an Jiaotong Liverpool University

Ryan A. Teeter
University of Pittsburgh

Katie L. Terrell
University of Arkansas

Mc
Graw
Hill
Education

DATA ANALYTICS FOR ACCOUNTING

Published by McGraw-Hill Education, 2 Penn Plaza, New York, NY 10121. Copyright © 2019 by McGraw-Hill Education. All rights reserved. Printed in the United States of America. No part of this publication may be reproduced or distributed in any form or by any means, or stored in a database or retrieval system, without the prior written consent of McGraw-Hill Education, including, but not limited to, in any network or other electronic storage or transmission, or broadcast for distance learning.

Some ancillaries, including electronic and print components, may not be available to customers outside the United States.

This book is printed on acid-free paper.

2 3 4 5 6 7 8 9 LKV 21 20 19 18

ISBN 978-1-260-28840-7
MHID 1-260-28840-4

Cover Image: © *SUNSHADOW/Shutterstock*

Dedications

My wonderful eldest daughter, Alison.

—Vernon Richardson

My wife, Erin, and children, Sylvia
and Theodore.

—Ryan Teeter

My husband, Kevin. Thank you for your
support and patience along the way!

—Katie Terrell

Preface

Data Analytics is changing the business world—data simply surrounds us! With so much data available about each of us (i.e., how we shop, what we read, what we buy, what music we listen to, where we travel, whom we trust, etc.), arguably, there is the potential for analyzing those data in a way that can answer fundamental business and accounting questions and create value.

According to the results of 18th Annual Global CEO Survey conducted by PwC, many CEOs put a high value on Data Analytics, and 80 percent of them place data mining and analysis as the second-most important strategic technology for CEOs. In fact, per PwC's 6th Annual Digital IQ survey of more than 1,400 leaders from digital businesses, the area of investment that tops CEOs' list of priorities is business analytics.[1]

This text addresses what we believe will be a similar impact of Data Analytics on accounting and auditing. For example, we argue that Data Analytics will play an increasingly critical role in the future of audit. In a recent *Forbes* Insights/KPMG report, "Audit 2020: A Focus on Change," the vast majority of survey respondents believe:

1. Auditors must better embrace technology.
2. Technology will enhance the quality, transparency, and accuracy of the audit.

No longer will auditors simply check for errors, misstated accounts, fraud, and risk in the financial statements or merely report their findings at the end of the audit. Through the use of Data Analytics, audit professionals will collect and analyze the company's data similar to the way a business analyst would help management make better business decisions. In our text, we emphasize audit data analytics and all the testing that can be done to perform audit testing.

Data Analytics also potentially has an impact on financial reporting. With the use of so many estimates and valuations in financial accounting, some believe that employing Data Analytics may substantially improve the quality of the estimates and valuations. Likewise, the use of XBRL data gives accountants access to more timely and more extensive accounting data for financial analysis.

This text recognizes that accountants don't need to become data scientists—they may never need to build a data repository or do the real hard-core Data Analytics or machine learning. However, we do emphasize seven skills that we believe analytic-minded accountants should have:

1. An analytics mindset—recognize when and how Data Analytics can address business questions.
2. Data scrubbing and data preparation—comprehend the process needed to clean and prepare the data before analysis.
3. Data quality—recognize what is meant by data quality, be it completeness, reliability, or validity.
4. Descriptive data analysis—perform basic analysis to understand the quality of the underlying data and their ability to address the business question.
5. Data analysis through data manipulation—demonstrate ability to sort, rearrange, merge, and reconfigure data in a manner that allows enhanced analysis.
6. Problem solving through statistical data analysis—identify and implement an approach that will use statistical data analysis to draw conclusions and make recommendations on a timely basis.
7. Data visualization and data reporting—report results of analysis in an accessible way to each varied decision maker and his or her specific needs.

[1]PwC, "Data Driven: What Students Need to Succeed in a Rapidly Changing Business World," https://www.pwc.com/us/en/faculty-resource/assets/pwc-data-driven-paper-feb2015.pdf posted February 2015, extracted December 14, 2017.

Consistent with these skills we desire in all accountants, we recognize that Data Analytics is a process. The process begins by identifying business questions that can be addressed with data and then testing the data, refining our testing, and finally, communicating those findings to management. We describe our Data Analytics process by using an established data analytics model called the IMPACT cycle, by Isson and Harriott:[2]

1. Identify the question
2. Master the data
3. Perform test plan
4. Address and refine results
5. Communicate insights
6. Track outcomes

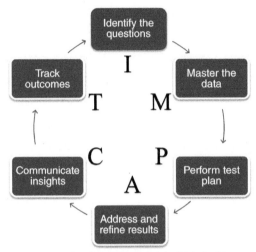

Adapted from *Win with Advanced Business Analytics: Creating Business Value from Your Data,* by Jean Paul Isson and Jesse S. Harriott.

We describe the IMPACT cycle in the first four chapters and then illustrate the process in audit, managerial accounting, and financial reporting in the final four chapters.

We also emphasize hands-on practice. Students will be provided hands-on learning (click-by-click instructions, screenshots, etc.) on datasets within the chapter; within the end-of-chapter materials; and in the four to eight hands-on labs at the end of each chapter, where students identify questions, download data, perform testing, and then communicate the results of that testing. We highlight the use of real-world data from **LendingClub, College Scorecard, Dillard's, the State of Oklahoma,** as well as other data from our labs.

We also emphasize the tools students will use. In this text, we emphasize data analysis using Excel, Access (including SQL), Tableau (free student license), IDEA (free student license), and Weka (free student license). Students will compare and contrast the different tools to determine which one is best suited for the necessary data analysis, data visualization, and communication of the insights gained—for example, which tool is easiest for internal controls testing, which is best for big datasets or big SQL queries, and so on.

[2] Jean Paul Isson and Jesse S. Harriott, *Win with Advanced Business Analytics: Creating Business Value from Your Data* (Hoboken, NJ: Wiley, 2013).

About the Authors

Vernon J. Richardson is a Distinguished Professor of Accounting and the G. William Glezen Chair in the Sam M. Walton College of Business at the University of Arkansas and a Research Fellow at Xi'an Jiaotong Liverpool University. He received his BS, Master of Accountancy, and MBA from Brigham Young University and a PhD. in accounting from the University of Illinois at Urbana-Champaign. He has taught students at the University of Arkansas, University of Illinois, Brigham Young University, Aarhus University, and University of Kansas and internationally at the China Europe International Business School (Shanghai), Xi'an Jiaotong Liverpool University, and the University of Technology Sydney.

Dr. Richardson is a member of the American Accounting Association. He has served as president of the American Accounting Association Information Systems section. He previously served as an editor of *The Accounting Review* and is currently an editor at *Accounting Horizons.* He has published articles in *The Accounting Review, Journal of Information Systems, Journal of Accounting and Economics, Contemporary Accounting Research, MIS Quarterly, International Journal of Accounting Information Systems, Journal of Management Information Systems, Journal of Operations Management,* and *Journal of Marketing.*

Ryan A. Teeter is a Clinical Assistant Professor of Accounting in the Katz Graduate School of Business at the University of Pittsburgh. He teaches accounting information systems, auditing, and accounting data analytics. Prior to receiving his PhD. in accounting information systems from Rutgers University, he worked at Google in Mountain View, California. He has since worked with internal audit organizations at Siemens, Procter & Gamble, Alcoa/Arconic, and FedEx, helping to develop robotic process automation programs and data analytic solutions.

Dr. Teeter is a member of the American Accounting Association and has published articles in the *Journal of Strategic Technologies in Accounting* and *Issues in Accounting Education.* He has received grant funding for data analytics research from PwC.

Katie L. Terrell is an instructor in the Sam M. Walton College of Business at the University of Arkansas. She received her BA degrees in English literature and in the Spanish language from the University of Central Arkansas and her MBA from the University of Arkansas. She expects a doctoral degree by 2019. She has taught students at the University of Arkansas; Soochow University (Suzhou, China); the University College Dublin (Ireland); and Duoc UC, a branch of the Catholic University of Chile (Viña del Mar, Chile).

She is a member of the American Accounting Association and has published a Statement on Management Accounting for the Institute of Management Accountants on managing organizational change in operational change initiatives. She has recently been recognized for her innovative teaching by being the recipient of the Mark Chain/FSA Teaching Award for innovative graduate-level accounting teaching practices in 2016. She has worked with Tyson Foods, where she held various information system roles, focusing on business analysis, project management for ERP implementations and upgrades, and organizational change management.

Acknowledgments

Our sincere thanks to all who helped us on this project.

Our biggest thanks to the awesome team at McGraw-Hill Education, including Steve Schuetz, Tim Vertovec, Allie Kukla, Fran Simon, Kevin Moran, and Shawntel Schmitt.

Our thanks also to each of the following:

The Walton College Enterprise Team (Paul Cronan, Ron Freeze, Michael Gibbs, Michael Martz, Tanya Russell) for their work helping us get access to the Dillard's data.

Lucas Hoogduin from KPMG for reviewing the textbook and providing comments.

Shane Lunceford from LendingClub for helping gain access to LendingClub data.

Julie Peters from PwC for her support and feedback on this project.

Ali Saeedi of University of Minnesota Crookston, for his accuracy check and review of the manuscript.

In addition, the following reviewers and classroom testers who provided ideas and insights for this edition. We appreciate their contributions.

Amelia Annette Baldwin
University of South Alabama

Andrea S. Kelton
Middle Tennessee State University

Ali Saeedi
University of Minnesota Crookston

Drew Sellers
Kent State University

Dereck Barr-Pulliam
University of Wisconsin-Madison

Elizabeth Felski
State University of New York at Geneseo

Heather Carrasco
Texas Tech University

Joe Shangguan
Robert Morris University

Kathy Nesper
University at Buffalo

Karen Schuele
John Carroll University

Lorrie A. Metzger
University at Buffalo

Margarita Maria Lenk
Colorado State University

Marcia Watson
University of North Carolina at Charlotte

Partha Mohapatra
California State University, Sacramento

Sharon M. Lightner
National University

Uday Murthy
University of South Florida

Vincent J. Shea
St. John's University

Vernon Richardson
Ryan Teeter
Katie Terrell

Key Features

- **Emphasis on Skills:** Working through the IMPACT cycle framework, students will learn problem assessment, data preparation, data analysis, data visualization, control contesting, and more.
- **Emphasis on Hands-On Practice:** Students will be provided hands-on learning (click-by-click instructions with screenshots) on datasets within each chapter, within the end-of-chapter materials, and in the labs and comprehensive cases.
- **Emphasis on Datasets:** To illustrate data analysis techniques and skills, multiple practice datasets (audit, financial, and managerial data) will be used in every chapter. Students gain real-world experience working with data from **LendingClub, Dillard's, College Scorecard, the State of Oklahoma,** as well as financial statement data (via XBRL) from *Fortune* 100 companies.
- **Emphasis on Tools:** Students will learn how to conduct data analysis using Excel Access (including SQL), Tableau (free student license), IDEA (free student license), and Weka (free student license). Students will compare and contrast the different tools to determine which are best suited for basic data analysis and data visualization, which are easiest for internal controls testing, which are best for SQL queries, and so on.

Total Products Sold by State

© OpenStreetMap contributors

Total Products Sold

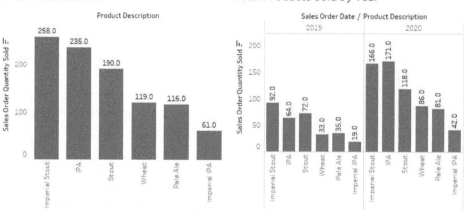

Total Products Sold by Year

Main Text Features

Chapter Maps

These maps provide a guide of what we're going to cover in the chapter as well as a guide of what we've just learned and what's coming next.

Chapter-Opening Vignettes

Because companies are facing the new and exciting opportunities with their use of Data Analytics to help with accounting and business decisions, we detail what they're doing and why in our chapter-opening vignettes.

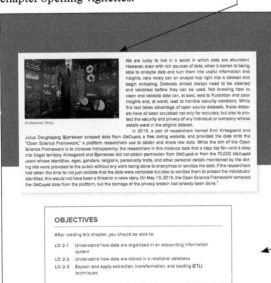

Chapter 2
Data Preparation and Cleaning

A Look at This Chapter

This chapter provides an overview of the types of data that are used in the accounting cycle and common data that are stored in a relational database. The chapter addresses *mastering the data*, the second step of the IMPACT cycle. We will describe how data are requested and *extracted* to answer business questions and how to *transform* data for use via data preparation, validation, and cleaning. We conclude with an explanation of how to *load* data into the appropriate tool in preparation for analyzing data to make decisions.

A Look Back

Chapter 1 defined Data Analytics and explained that the value of Data Analytics is in the insights it provides. We described the Data Analytic Process using the IMPACT cycle model and explained how this process is used to address both business and accounting questions. We specifically emphasized the importance of identifying appropriate questions that data analytics might be able to address.

A Look Ahead

Chapter 3 describes how to go from defining business problems to analyzing data, answering questions, and addressing business problems. We make the case for three data approaches we argue are most relevant to accountants and provide examples of each.

We are lucky to live in a world in which data are abundant. However, even with rich sources of data, when it comes to being able to analyze data and turn them into useful information and insights, very rarely can an analyst hop right into a dataset and begin analyzing. Datasets almost always need to be cleaned and validated before they can be used. Not knowing how to clean and validate data can, at best, lead to frustration and poor insights and, at worst, lead to horrible security violations. While this text takes advantage of open source datasets, these datasets have all been scrubbed not only for accuracy, but also to protect the security and privacy of any individual or company whose details were in the original dataset.

In 2015, a pair of researchers named Emil Kirkegaard and Julius Daugbjerg Bjerrekaer scraped data from OkCupid, a free dating website, and provided the data onto the "Open Science Framework," a platform researchers use to obtain and share raw data. While the aim of the Open Science Framework is to increase transparency, the researchers in this instance took a step too far—and a step into illegal territory. Kirkegaard and Bjerrekaer did not obtain permission from OkCupid or from the 70,000 OkCupid users whose identities, ages, genders, religions, personality traits, and other personal details maintained by the dating site were provided to the public without any work being done to anonymize or sanitize the data. If the researchers had taken the time to not just validate that the data were complete but also to sanitize them to protect the individuals' identities, this would not have been a threat or a news story. On May 13, 2015, the Open Science Framework removed the OkCupid data from the platform, but the damage of the privacy breach had already been done.[1]

Shutterstock / Wichy

OBJECTIVES

After reading this chapter, you should be able to:

LO 2-1   Understand how data are organized in an accounting information system

LO 2-2   Understand how data are stored in a relational database

LO 2-3   Explain and apply extraction, transformation, and loading (ETL) techniques

Learning Objectives

We feature learning objectives at the beginning of each chapter. Having these learning objectives provides students with an overview of the concepts to be taught in the chapter and the labs.

Progress Checks

Periodic progress check questions are posed to the students throughout each chapter. These checks provoke the student to stop and consider the concepts presented.

✓ PROGRESS CHECK

1. Referring to Exhibit 2-1, locate the relationship between the Employee and Purchase Order tables. What is the unique identifier of each table? (The unique identifier attribute is called the primary key—more on how it's determined in the next learning objective.) Which table contains the attribute that creates the relationship? (This attribute is called the foreign key—more on how it's determined in the next learning objective.)

2. Referring to Exhibit 2-1, review the attributes in the Suppliers table. There is a foreign key in this table that doesn't relate to any of the tables in the diagram. Which table do you think it is? What type of data would be stored in that table?

End-of-Chapter Materials

Answers to Progress Checks

Allow students to evaluate if they are on track with their understanding of the materials presented in the chapter.

Multiple Choice Questions

Quickly assess student's knowledge of chapter content.

Multiple Choice Questions

1. Mastering the data can also be described via for:
   a. Extract, total, and load data.
   b. Enter, transform, and load data.
   c. Extract, transform, and load data.
   d. Enter, total, and load data.
2. The goal of the ETL process is to:
   a. Identify which approach to data analytics s
   b. Load the data into a relational database fo
   c. Communicate the results and insights fou

Discussion Questions

Provide questions for group discussion.

Discussion Questions

1. The advantages of a relational database include limiting the amount of r that are stored in a database. Why is this an important advantage? What when redundant data are stored?
2. The advantages of a relational database include integrating business p is it preferable to integrate business processes in one information syste store different business process data in separate, isolated databases?
3. Even though it is preferable to store data in a relational database, stori separate tables can make data analysis cumbersome. Describe three re worth the trouble to store data in a relational database.
4. Among the advantages of using a relational database is enforcing busine on your understanding of how the structure of a relational database help redundancy and other advantages, how does the primary key/foreign k

Problems

Challenge the student's ability to see relationships in the learning objectives by employing higher-level thinking and analytical skills.

Problems

The following problems correspond to the College
to answer each question by just looking at the
DataDictionary.pdf) included in Appendix A, but if yo
free to do so (CollegeScorecard_RawData.txt).

1. Which attributes from the College Scorecard da
   attendance across types of institutions (public, p

2. Which attributes from the College Scorecard d
   scores across types of institutions (public, privat

3. Which attributes from the College Scorecard da
   diversity across types of institutions (public, priv

4. Which attributes from the College Scorecard da
   tion   across types of institutio   ublic, pr

Labs

Give students hands-on experience working with different types of data and the tools used to analyze them. Students will conduct data analysis using Excel, Access (including SQL), Tableau, IDEA, XBRL, and Weka.

Lab 2-1   Create a Request for Data Extra

One of the biggest challenges you face with data analysis is getting the rig
may have the best questions in the world, but if there are no data available to
hypothesis, you will have difficulty providing value. Additionally, there are
which the IT workers may be reluctant to share data with you. They may se
data, the wrong data, or completely ignore your request. Be persistent, and yo
look for creative ways to find insight with an incomplete picture.

Company summary

Sláinte is a fictional brewery that has recently gone through big changes. Sláin
ferent products. The brewery has only recently expanded its business to distribu
state to nine states, and now its business has begun stabilizing after the expans

Comprehensive Cases

Use a real-life Big Data set based on **Dillard's** actual company data from 2014 to 2016. This dataset allows students to build their skills and test their conclusions across concepts covered in each chapter. The Comprehensive Cases can be followed continuously from the first chapter or picked up at any later point in the book; enough information is provided to ensure students can get right to work.

Lab 2-8   Comprehensive Case: Dillard's S
Connecting Excel to a SQL Data

Company summary

Dillard's is a department store with approximately 33
is in Little Rock, Arkansas. You can learn more about
com (Ticker symbol = DDS) and the Wikipedia sit
William T. Dillard II is an accounting grad of the Ur
College of Business, which may be why he shared tran
for this lab and labs throughout this text.

Data

Connect for Data Analytics for Accounting

With **Connect** for Data Analytics in Accounting, your students receive proven study tools and hands-on assignment materials as well as an adaptive eBook. All of the following assets are assignable in Connect.

SmartBook: SmartBook provides adaptive reading assignments that require students to answer questions; it then provides feedback to direct a student learning and ensure mastery of concepts.

Orientation Videos: Video-based tutorial assignments are designed to train students via an overview video followed by a quiz for each of the assignment types they will find in Connect.

Multiple Choice Questions: The multiple choice questions from the end-of-chapter materials are assignable in Connect, providing students with instant feedback on their answers.

Test Bank: The test bank includes auto-graded multiple choice and true/false assessment questions. It is available in Connect and TestGen.

Problems: Select problems from the text are available for assignment in Connect to ensure students are building an analytical skill set.

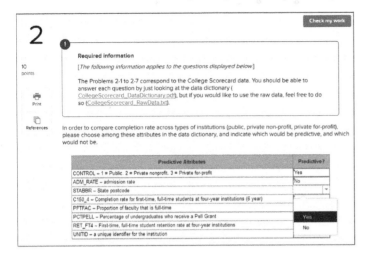

Labs: Select labs are assignable in Connect but will require students to work outside of Connect to complete the lab. Once completed, students go back into Connect to answer questions designed to ensure they completed the lab and understood the key skills and outcomes from their lab work.

Comprehensive Cases: Select comprehensive labs/cases are assignable in Connect but will require students to work outside of Connect to complete the lab using the Dillard's real-world Big Data set. Once students complete the comprehensive lab, they will go back into Connect to answer questions designed to ensure they completed the lab and understood the key skills and outcomes from their lab work.

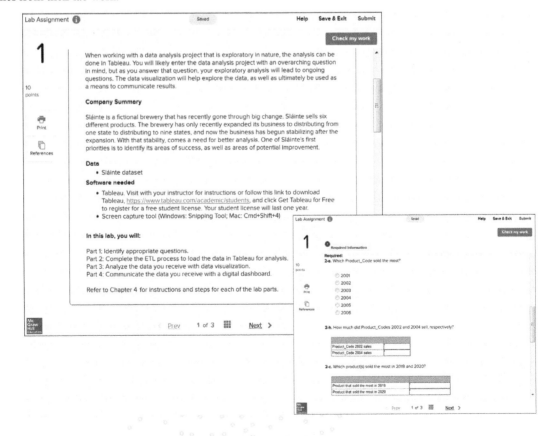

McGraw-Hill Connect® is a highly reliable, easy-to-use homework and learning management solution that utilizes learning science and award-winning adaptive tools to improve student results.

Homework and Adaptive Learning

- Connect's assignments help students contextualize what they've learned through application, so they can better understand the material and think critically.

- Connect will create a personalized study path customized to individual student needs through SmartBook®.

- SmartBook helps students study more efficiently by delivering an interactive reading experience through adaptive highlighting and review.

Connect's Impact on Retention Rates, Pass Rates, and Average Exam Scores

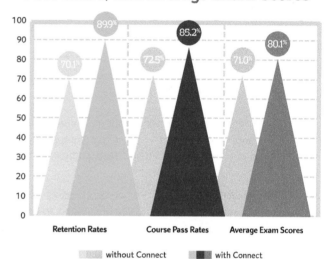

without Connect   with Connect

Over **7 billion questions** have been answered, making McGraw-Hill Education products more intelligent, reliable, and precise.

Using **Connect** improves retention rates by **19.8** percentage points, passing rates by **12.7** percentage points, and exam scores by **9.1** percentage points.

73% of instructors who use **Connect** require it; instructor satisfaction **increases** by 28% when **Connect** is required.

Quality Content and Learning Resources

- Connect content is authored by the world's best subject matter experts, and is available to your class through a simple and intuitive interface.

- The Connect eBook makes it easy for students to access their reading material on smartphones and tablets. They can study on the go and don't need internet access to use the eBook as a reference, with full functionality.

- Multimedia content such as videos, simulations, and games drive student engagement and critical thinking skills.

Robust Analytics and Reporting

- Connect Insight® generates easy-to-read reports on individual students, the class as a whole, and on specific assignments.

- The Connect Insight dashboard delivers data on performance, study behavior, and effort. Instructors can quickly identify students who struggle and focus on material that the class has yet to master.

- Connect automatically grades assignments and quizzes, providing easy-to-read reports on individual and class performance.

©Hero Images/Getty Images

Impact on Final Course Grade Distribution

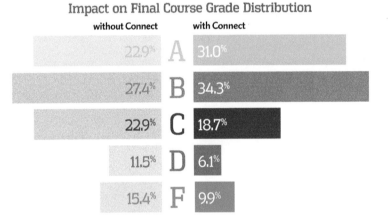

without Connect		with Connect
22.9%	A	31.0%
27.4%	B	34.3%
22.9%	C	18.7%
11.5%	D	6.1%
15.4%	F	9.9%

More students earn **As** and **Bs** when they use **Connect**.

Trusted Service and Support

- Connect integrates with your LMS to provide single sign-on and automatic syncing of grades. Integration with Blackboard®, D2L®, and Canvas also provides automatic syncing of the course calendar and assignment-level linking.

- Connect offers comprehensive service, support, and training throughout every phase of your implementation.

- If you're looking for some guidance on how to use Connect, or want to learn tips and tricks from super users, you can find tutorials as you work. Our Digital Faculty Consultants and Student Ambassadors offer insight into how to achieve the results you want with Connect.

Brief Table of Contents

Detailed TOC

Chapter 1
Data Analytics in Accounting and Business 2

A Look at This Chapter 2
A Look Ahead 2
Data Analytics 4
How Data Analytics Affects Business 4
How Data Analytics Affects Accounting 5
- *Auditing* 5
- *Financial Reporting* 6
- *Taxes* 7

The Data Analytics Process Using the IMPACT Cycle 8
- *Step 1: Identify the Question (chapter 1)* 8
- *Step 2: Master the Data (chapter 2)* 8
- *Step 3: Perform Test Plan (chapter 3)* 9
- *Step 4: Address and Refine Results (chapter 4)* 11
- *Steps 5 and 6: Communicate Insights and Track Outcomes (chapter 4 and each chapter thereafter)* 11
- *Back to Step 1* 12

Data Analytic Skills Needed by Analytic-Minded Accountants 12
Hands-On Example of the IMPACT Model 13
- *Identify the Question* 13
- *Master the Data* 13
- *Perform Test Plan* 15
- *Address and Refine Results* 17
- *Communicate Insights* 19
- *Track Outcomes* 19

Summary 20
Key Words 20
Answers to Progress Checks 21
Multiple Choice Questions 23
Discussion Questions 24
Problems 24
Answers to Multiple Choice Questions 26
Lab 1-0 How to Complete Labs in This Text 27
Lab 1-1 Data Analytics in Financial Accounting 28
Lab 1-2 Data Analytics in Managerial Accounting 31
Lab 1-3 Data Analytics in Auditing 33
Lab 1-4 Comprehensive Case: Dillard's Store Data 34

Chapter 2
Data Preparation and Cleaning 38

A Look at This Chapter 38
A Look Back 38
A Look Ahead 38
How Data Are Used and Stored in the Accounting Cycle 40
Data And Relationships in a Relational Database 41
- *Columns in a Table: Primary Keys, Foreign Keys, and Descriptive Attributes* 41

Data Dictionaries 43
Extraction, Transformation, and Loading (ETL) of Data 44
Extraction 44
- *Step 1: Determine the Purpose and Scope of the Data Request* 45
- *Step 2: Obtain the Data* 45

Transformation 48
- *Step 3: Validating the Data for Completeness and Integrity* 48
- *Step 4: Cleaning the Data* 49

Loading 50
- *Step 5: Loading the Data for Data Analysis* 50

Summary 50
Key Words 51
Answers to Progress Checks 51
Multiple Choice Questions 52
Discussion Questions 53
Problems 54
Appendix A: College Scorecard Dataset 55
Answers to Multiple Choice Questions 55
Lab 2-1 Create a Request for Data Extraction 57
Lab 2-2 Use PivotTables to Denormalize and Analyze the Data 59
Lab 2-3 Resolve Common Data Problems in Excel and Access 67
Lab 2-4 Generate Summary Statistics in Excel 71
Lab 2-5 College Scorecard Extraction and Data Preparation 73
Lab 2-6 Comprehensive Case: Dillard's Store Data: How to Create an Entity-Relationship Diagram 74

Data Analytics for Accounting

Chapter 1

Data Analytics in Accounting and Business

A Look at This Chapter

Data Analytics is changing the business world. In this chapter, we define it and explain its impact on business and the accounting profession, noting that the value of Data Analytics is in the insights it provides. We also describe how to develop an analytics mindset. We describe the Data Analytic Process using the IMPACT cycle model and explain how this process is used to address both business and accounting questions. We specifically emphasize the importance of identifying appropriate questions that Data Analytics might be able to address.

A Look Ahead

Chapter 2 provides a description of how data are prepared and scrubbed to be ready for analysis to answer business questions. We explain how to extract, transform, and load data and then how to validate and normalize the data. In addition, we explain how data standards are used to facilitate the exchange of data between senders and receivers.

Alibaba.com

The Chinese e-commerce company, **Alibaba**, is perhaps the biggest online commerce company in the world. Using its three main websites, Taobao, Tmall, and Alibaba.com, it hosts millions of businesses and hundreds of millions of users with $248 billion in sales last year (more than **eBay** and **Amazon** combined!). With so many transactions and so many users, **Alibaba** has worked to capture fraud signals directly from its extensive database of user behaviors and its network, and then analyzes them in real time using machine learning to accurately sort the bad users from the good ones. **Alibaba** has developed five stages of fraud detection for each user: (1) account check, (2) device check, (3) activity check, (4) risk strategy, and (5) manual review. These stages all combine to develop a risk score for each user. This fraud risk prevention score is so valuable to **Alibaba** and others, **Alibaba** shares and sells it to external customers, developing a risk score for each current and potential customer. What will Data Analytics do next?

Sources: J. Chen, Y. Tao, H. Wang, and T. Chen, "Big Data Based Fraud Risk Management at Alibaba," *The Journal of Finance and Data Science* 1, no. 1 (2015), pp. 1–10; and K. Pal, "How to Combat Financial Fraud by Using Big Data," 2016, http://www.kdnuggets.com/2016/03/combat-financial-fraud-using-big-data.html.

OBJECTIVES

After reading this chapter, you should be able to:

LO 1-1 Define Data Analytics

LO 1-2 Understand why Data Analytics matters to business

LO 1-3 Explain why Data Analytics matters to accountants

LO 1-4 Describe the Data Analytics Process using the IMPACT cycle

LO 1-5 Describe the skills needed by accountants

LO 1-6 Explain how to translate common business questions into fields and values

LO 1-1

Define Data
Analytics

DATA ANALYTICS

Data surrounds us! By the year 2020, about 1.7 megabytes of new information will be created every second for every human being on the planet. In fact, more data have been created in the last 2 years than in the entire previous history of the human race.[1] With so much data available about each of us (i.e., how we shop, what we read, what we've bought, what music we listen to, where we travel, whom we trust, etc.), arguably, there is the potential for analyzing those data in a way that can answer fundamental business questions and create value.

We define **Data Analytics** as the process of evaluating data with the purpose of drawing conclusions to address business questions. Indeed, effective Data Analytics provides a way to search through large structured and unstructured data to discover unknown patterns or relationships.[2] In other words, Data Analytics often involves the technologies, systems, practices, methodologies, databases, statistics, and applications used to analyze diverse business data to give organizations the information they need to make sound and timely business decisions.[3] That is, the process of Data Analytics aims to transform raw data into knowledge to create value.

Sometimes another term for data analytics is used, called **Big Data** which refers to datasets that are too large and complex for businesses' existing systems to handle utilizing their traditional capabilities to capture, store, manage, and analyze these datasets. Another way to describe Big Data is by use of 3 Vs: its Volume (the sheer size of the dataset), Velocity (the speed of data processing), and Variety (the number of types of data). While sometimes *Data Analytics* and *Big Data* are terms used interchangeably, we will use the term *Data Analytics* throughout and focus on the ability to turn data into knowledge and knowledge into value.

 PROGRESS CHECK

1. How does having more data around us translate into value for a company?
2. Banks know a lot about us, but they have traditionally used externally generated credit scores to assess creditworthiness when deciding whether to extend a loan. How would you suggest a bank use Data Analytics to get a more complete view of its customers' creditworthiness? Assume the bank has access to a customer's loan history, credit card transactions, deposit history, and direct deposit registration. How could it assess whether a loan might be repaid?

LO 1-2

Understand why
Data Analytics
matters to
business

HOW DATA ANALYTICS AFFECTS BUSINESS

There is little question that the impact of data analytics on business is overwhelming. In fact, in PwC's 18th Annual Global CEO Survey, 86 percent of chief executive officers (CEOs) say they find it important to champion digital technologies and emphasize a clear vision of using technology for a competitive advantage, while 85 percent say they put a high value on Data Analytics. According to the same survey, many CEOs put a high value on Data Analytics, and 80 percent of them place data mining and analysis as the second-most important strategic technology for CEOs. In fact, per PwC's 6th Annual Digital IQ survey

[1] http://www.forbes.com/sites/bernardmarr/2015/09/30/big-data-20-mind-boggling-facts-everyone-must-read/#2a3289006c1d (accessed November 10, 2016).
[2] Roger S. Debreceny and Glen L. Gray, "IT Governance and Process Maturity: A Multinational Field Study," *Journal of Information Systems* 27, no. 1 (Spring 2013), pp. 157–188.
[3] H. Chen, R. H. L. Chiang, and V. C. Storey, "Business Intelligence Research," *MIS Quarterly* 34, no. 1 (2010), pp. 201–203.

of more than 1,400 leaders from digital businesses, the area of investment that tops CEOs' list of priorities is business analytics.[4]

A recent study from McKinsey Global Institute estimates that Data Analytics could generate up to $3 trillion in value per year in just a subset of the total possible industries affected.[5] Data Analytics could very much transform the manner in which companies run their businesses in the near future. The real value of data comes from Data Analytics. With a wealth of data on their hands, companies use Data Analytics to discover the various buying patterns of their customers, investigate anomalies that were not predicted, forecast future possibilities, and so on. For example, with insight provided through Data Analytics, companies could do more directed marketing campaigns based on patterns observed in their data, giving them a competitive advantage over companies that do not use this information to improve their marketing strategies. Patterns discovered from past archives enable businesses to identify opportunities and risks and better plan for the future. In addition to producing more value externally, studies show that Data Analytics affects internal processes, improving productivity, utilization, and growth.[6]

✓ PROGRESS CHECK

3. Let's assume a brand manager at **Samsung** identifies that an older demographic might be concerned with the use of an iPhone and the radiation impact it might have on the brain. How might **Samsung** use Data Analytics to assess if this is a problem?

4. How might Data Analytics assess the higher cost of paying employees to work overtime? Consider how Data Analytics might be helpful in reducing a company's overtime direct labor costs in a manufacturing setting.

HOW DATA ANALYTICS AFFECTS ACCOUNTING

> **LO 1-3**
>
> Explain why Data Analytics matters to accountants

Data Analytics is expected to have dramatic effects on auditing, financial reporting, and tax and managerial accounting. We detail how we think this might happen in each of the following sections.

Auditing

Data Analytics plays an increasingly critical role in the future of audit. In a recent *Forbes Insights*/KPMG report, "Audit 2020: A Focus on Change," the vast majority of survey respondents believe both that:

1. Audit must better embrace technology.
2. Technology will enhance the quality, transparency, and accuracy of the audit.

Indeed, "As the business landscape for most organizations becomes increasingly complex and fast-paced, there is a movement toward leveraging advanced business analytic techniques to

---

[4]"Data Driven: What Students Need to Succeed in a Rapidly Changing Business World," PwC, http://www.pwc.com/us/en/faculty-resource/assets/PwC-Data-driven-paper-Feb2015.pdf, February 2015 (accessed January 9, 2016).

[5]"Open Data: Unlocking Innovation and Performance with Liquid Information," McKinsey Global Institute, http://www.mckinsey.com/insights/business_technology/open_data_unlocking_innovation_and_performance_with_liquid_information, October 2013 (accessed September 7, 2015).

[6]Joseph Kennedy, "Big Data's Economic Impact," https://www.ced.org/blog/entry/big-datas-economic-impact, December 3, 2014 (accessed January 9, 2016).

refine the focus on risk and derive deeper insights into an organization."[7] Many auditors believe that auditor data analytics will, in fact, lead to deeper insights that will enhance audit quality. This sentiment of the impact of Data Analytics on the audit has been growing for several years now and has given many public accounting firms incentives to invest in technology and personnel to capture, organize, and analyze financial statement data to provide enhanced audits, expanded services, and added value to their clients. As a result, Data Analytics is expected to be the next innovation in the evolution of the audit and professional accounting industry.

Given the fact that operational data abound and are easier to collect and manage, combined with CEOs' desires to utilize these data, the accounting firms may now approach their engagements with a different mindset. No longer will they be simply checking for errors, material misstatements, fraud, and risk in financial statements or merely be reporting their findings at the end of the engagement. Now, audit professionals will be collecting and analyzing the company's data similar to the way a business analyst would to help management make better business decisions. This means that, in many cases, external auditors will stay engaged with clients beyond the audit. This is a significant paradigm shift. The audit process will be changed from a traditional process toward a more automated one, which will allow audit professionals to focus more on the logic and rationale behind data queries and less on the gathering of the actual data.[8] As a result, audits will not only yield important findings from a financial perspective, but also information that can help companies refine processes, improve efficiency, and anticipate future problems.

> "It's a massive leap to go from traditional audit approaches to one that fully integrates big data and analytics in a seamless manner."[9]

Data Analytics also expands auditors' capabilities in services like testing for fraudulent transactions and automating compliance-monitoring activities (like filing financial reports to the SEC or to the IRS). This is possible because Data Analytics enables auditors to analyze the complete dataset, rather than the sampling of the financial data done in a traditional audit. Data Analytics enables auditors to improve its risk assessment in both its substantive and detailed testing.

Financial Reporting

Data Analytics also potentially has an impact on financial reporting. With the use of so many estimates and valuations in Financial Accounting, some believe that employing Data Analytics may substantially improve the quality of the estimates and valuations. Data from within an enterprise system and external to the company and system might be used to address many of the questions that face financial reporting. Many financial statement accounts are just estimates and so accountants often ask themselves questions like this to evaluate those estimates:

1. How much of the accounts receivable balance will ultimately be collected? What should the allowance for loan losses look like?
2. Is any of our inventory obsolete? Should our inventory be valued at market or cost (applying the lower-of-cost-or-market rule)? When will it be out of date? Do we need to offer a discount on it now to get it sold?

---

[7] Deloitte, "Adding Insight to Audit: Transforming Internal Audit through Data Analytics," http://www2 .deloitte.com/content/dam/Deloitte/ca/Documents/audit/ca-en-audit-adding-insight-to-audit.pdf (accessed January 10, 2016).

[8] PwC, "Data Driven: What Students Need to Succeed in a Rapidly Changing Business World," http://www .pwc.com/us/en/faculty-resource/assets/PwC-Data-driven-paper-Feb2015.pdf, posted February 2015 (accessed January 9, 2016).

[9] EY, "How Big Data and Analytics Are Transforming the Audit," https://eyo-iis-pd.ey.com/ARC/documents/ EY-reporting-issue-9.pdf, posted April 2015 (accessed January 27, 2016).

3. Has our goodwill been impaired due to the reduction in profitability from a recent merger company? Will it regain value in the near future?

4. How should we value contingent liabilities like warranty claims or litigation? Do we have the right amount?

Data Analytics may also allow an accountant or auditor to assess the probability of a goodwill write-down, warranty claims or the collectability of bad debts based on what customers, investors, and other stakeholders are saying about the company in blogs and in social media (like Facebook and Twitter). This information might help the firm determine both its optimal response to the situation and appropriate adjustment to its financial reporting.

It may be possible to use Data Analytics to scan the environment—that is, scanning Google searches and social media (such as Instagram and Facebook) to identify potential risks and opportunities to the firm. For example, in a business intelligence sense, it may allow a firm to monitor its competitors and its customers to better understand opportunities and threats around it. For example, are its competitors, customers, or suppliers facing financial difficulty, etc., that might affect the company's interactions with them and open up opportunities that otherwise it wouldn't have considered?

Taxes

Traditionally, tax work dealt with compliance issues based on data from transactions that have already taken place. Now, however, tax executives are charged with sophisticated tax planning capabilities that assist the company to minimize its taxes and do it in such a way as to either avoid or prepare for a potential audit. Arguably, one of the things that Data Analytics does best is predictive analytics—predicting the future! This shift in focus makes tax data analytics valuable for its ability to help tax staffs to predict what will happen rather than reacting to what just did happen. An example of how tax data analytics might be used is the capability to predict the potential tax consequences of a potential international transaction, R&D investment, or proposed merger or acquisition.

One of the issues of performing predictive Data Analytics is the efficient organization and use of data stored across multiple systems on varying platforms that were not originally designed for the tax department. Organizing tax data into a data warehouse to be able to consistently model and query the data is an important step toward developing the capability to perform tax data analytics. This issue is exemplified by the 29 percent of tax departments that find the biggest challenge in executing an analytics strategy is integration with the IT department and the available technology tools.[10]

✓ PROGRESS CHECK

5. How could the use of internal audit data analytics find the pattern that one accountant enters the majority of the journal entries each quarter? Why might this be an issue that would need addressing?

6. How specifically will Data Analytics change the way a tax staff does its taxes?

---

[10] Deloitte, "The Power of Tax Data Analytics," http://www2.deloitte.com/us/en/pages/tax/articles/top-ten-things-about-tax-data-analytics.html (accessed October 12, 2016).

LO 1-4

Describe the Data
Analytics Process
using the IMPACT
cycle

THE DATA ANALYTICS PROCESS
USING THE IMPACT CYCLE

Data Analytics is a process—identifying business questions and problems that can be addressed with data. We start to describe our Data Analytics Process by using an established Data Analytics model called the IMPACT cycle, by Isson and Harriott (as shown in Exhibit 1-1).

We explain the full IMPACT cycle briefly here, but in more detail in later in chapter 1 and then also in chapters 2, 3, and 4. We use its approach throughout this textbook.

EXHIBIT 1-1

The IMPACT Cycle

Source: J. P. Isson and
J. S. Harriott, *Win with
Advanced Business Analytics:
Creating Business Value from
Your Data* (Hoboken, NJ:
Wiley, 2013).

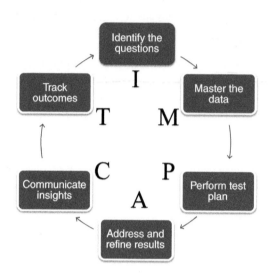

Step 1: Identify the Questions (chapter 1)

It all begins with understanding a business problem that needs addressing. Questions can arise from many sources from how to better attract customers, to how to price a product, to how to find errors or fraud. Having a concrete, specific question that is potentially answerable by Data Analytics is an important first step.

Accountants and auditors might be interested in questions like the following:

- Are employees circumventing internal controls over payments?
- Are there any suspicious travel and entertainment expenses?
- How can we increase the amount of add-on sales of additional goods to our customers?
- Are our customers paying us in a timely manner?
- How can we predict the allowance for loan losses for our bank loans?
- How can we find transactions that are risky in terms of accounting issues?
- Who authorizes checks above $100,000?
- How can errors be identified?

Step 2: Master the Data (chapter 2)

Mastering the data requires one to know what data are available and whether those data might be able to help address the business problem. We need to know everything about the data, including how to access, availability, reliability (if there are errors), and what time periods are covered to make sure the data coincide with the timing of our business problem, etc.

In addition, to give us some idea of the data questions, we may want to consider the following:

- Review data availability in a firm's internal systems (including those in the financial reporting system or ERP systems that might occur in its accounting cycles—financial, procure-to-pay, production, order-to-cash, human resources).
- Review data availability in a firm's external network, including those that might already be housed in an existing data warehouse.
- Data dictionaries and other contextual data—to provide details about the data.
- Extraction, transformation, and loading.
- Data validation and completeness—to provide a sense of the reliability of the data.
- Data normalization—to reduce data redundancy and improve data integrity.
- Data preparation and scrubbing—Data Analytics professionals estimate that they spend between 50 and 90 percent of their time cleaning data so the data can be analyzed.[11]

Step 3: Perform Test Plan (chapter 3)

After mastering the data (in step 2) and after the data are ready, we are prepared for analysis. With the data ready for analysis, we need to think of the right approach to the data to be able to answer the question.

In Data Analytics, we work to extract knowledge from the data to address questions and problems. We take from all available data and see if we can identify a relationship between the **response or dependent variables** and those items that affect the response (also called **predictor, explanatory, or independent variables**). To do so, we'll generally make a model, a simplified representation of reality to address this purpose.

An example might be helpful here. Let's say we are trying to predict each of your classmates' performance on their next intermediate accounting exam. The response or dependent variable will be the score on the next exam. What helps predict the performance of each exam will be our predictor, explanatory, or dependent variables. Variables such as study time, score on last exam, IQ, and standardized test scores (ACT, SAT, etc.), as well as student enjoyment of accounting, might all be considered. Perhaps given your experience you can name other predictor variables to include in our model predicting exam performance.

The research question, the model, the data availability, and the expected statistical inference may all suggest the use of different data approaches. Provost and Fawcett[12] detail eight different approaches to data analytics depending on the question. We will discuss the most applicable ones to accounting more formally in chapter 3 and highlight accounting questions that they might address. The eight different approaches include the following:

- **Classification**—An attempt to assign each unit (or individual) in a population into a few categories. An example classification might be, of all the loans this bank has offered, which are most likely to default? Or which loan applications are expected to be approved? Or which transactions would a credit card company flag as potentially being fraudulent and deny payment?
- **Regression**—An attempt to estimate or predict, for each unit, the numerical value of some variable using some type of statistical model. An example regression analysis might be, given a balance of total accounts receivable held by a firm, what is the appropriate level of allowance for doubtful accounts for bad debts?

---

[11]"One-Third of BI Pros Spend Up to 90% of Time Cleaning Data," http://www.eweek.com/database/one-third-of-bi-pros-spend-up-to-90-of-time-cleaning-data.html, posted June 2015 (accessed March 15, 2016).

[12]Foster Provost and Tom Fawcett, *Data Science for Business: What You Need to Know about Data Mining and Data-Analytic Thinking* (Sebastopol, CA: O'Reilly Media, Inc.), 2013.

- **Similarity matching**—An attempt to identify similar individuals based on data known about them. The opening vignette mentioned **Alibaba** and its attempt to identify seller and customer fraud based on various characteristics known about them to see if they were similar to known fraud cases.
- **Clustering**—An attempt to divide individuals (like customers) into groups (or clusters) in a useful or meaningful way. In other words, identifying groups of similar data elements and the underlying drivers of those groups. For example, clustering might be used to segment a customer into a small number of groups for additional analysis and marketing activities.
- **Co-occurrence grouping**—An attempt to discover associations between individuals based on transactions involving them. **Amazon** might use this to sell another item to you by knowing what items are "frequently bought together" or "Customers who bought this item also bought . . ." as shown in Exhibit 1-2.

EXHIBIT 1-2

Example of Co-occurrence Grouping on Amazon.com

©Amazon Inc.

- **Profiling**—An attempt to characterize the "typical" behavior of an individual, group, or population by generating summary statistics about the data (including mean, standard deviations, etc.). By understanding the typical behavior, we'll be able to more easily identify abnormal behavior. When behavior departs from that typical behavior—which we'll call an anomaly—then further investigation is warranted. Profiling might be used in accounting to identify fraud or just those transactions that might warrant some additional investigation (e.g., travel expenses that are three standard deviations above the norm).
- **Link prediction**—An attempt to predict a relationship between two data items. This might be used in social media. For example, because an individual might have 22 mutual Facebook friends with me and we both attended Brigham Young University, is there a chance we would like to be Facebook friends as well? Exhibit 1-3 provides an example of this used in Facebook. Link prediction in an accounting setting might work to use social media to look for relationships between related parties that are not otherwise disclosed.

EXHIBIT 1-3
Example of Link
Prediction on Facebook
©Facebook Inc.

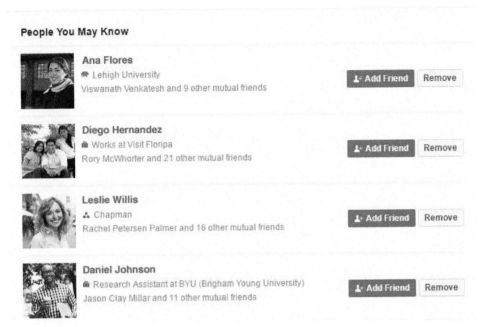

People You May Know

Ana Flores
Lehigh University
Viswanath Venkatesh and 9 other mutual friends
Add Friend   Remove

Diego Hernandez
Works at Visit Floripa
Rory McWhorter and 21 other mutual friends
Add Friend   Remove

Leslie Willis
Chapman
Rachel Petersen Palmer and 16 other mutual friends
Add Friend   Remove

Daniel Johnson
Research Assistant at BYU (Brigham Young University)
Jason Clay Millar and 11 other mutual friends
Add Friend   Remove

- **Data reduction**—A data approach that attempts to reduce the amount of information that needs to be considered to focus on the most critical items (i.e., highest cost, highest risk, largest impact, etc.). It does this by taking a large set of data (perhaps the population) and reducing it with a smaller set that has the vast majority of the critical information of the larger set. An example might include the potential to use these techniques in auditing. While auditing has employed various random and stratified sampling over the years, Data Analytics suggests new ways to highlight which transactions do not need the same level of vetting as other transactions.

Step 4: Address and Refine Results (chapter 4)

After the data have been analyzed (in step 3 of the IMPACT cycle), the fourth step is to address and refine results. Data analysis is iterative. We slice and dice the data, find correlations, ask ourselves further questions, ask colleagues what they think, and revise and rerun the analysis. But once that is complete, we have the results ready to communicate to interested stakeholders.

Chapter 4 discusses ways to communicate results, including the use of static reports, digital dashboards, and data visualizations. Data Analytics is especially interested in reporting results that help decision makers see the data in an all-new way to develop insights that help answer business questions. Digital dashboards and data visualizations are particularly helpful in communicating results.

Steps 5 and 6: Communicate Insights and Track Outcomes (chapter 4 and each chapter thereafter)

Once the results have been determined (in step 4 of the IMPACT cycle), insights are formed by decision makers and are communicated (the "C" in the IMPACT cycle) to others. Some outcomes will be continuously tracked (the "T" in the IMPACT cycle) perhaps via monthly reports or a digital dashboard. These portions of the IMPACT cycle will be covered in the remaining chapters.

Back to Step 1

Of course, the IMPACT cycle is iterative, so once insights are gained and outcomes are tracked, new questions emerge and the IMPACT cycle begins anew.

 PROGRESS CHECK

7. Let's say we are trying to predict how much money college students spend on fast food each week. What would be the response, or dependent, variable? What would be examples of independent variables?

8. How might a data reduction approach be used in auditing to spend time and effort on the most important items?

LO 1-5

Describe the skills needed by accountants

DATA ANALYTIC SKILLS NEEDED BY ANALYTIC-MINDED ACCOUNTANTS

While we don't believe that accountants need to become data scientists—they may never need to build a data repository or do the real, hardcore Data Analytics—they must know how to do the following:

- Clearly articulate the business problem the company is facing,
- Communicate with the data scientists about specific data needs and understand the underlying quality of the data.
- Draw appropriate conclusions to the business problem based on the data and make recommendations on a timely basis.
- Present their results to individual members of management (CEOs, audit managers, etc.) in an accessible manner to each member.

Consistent with that, in this text, we emphasize seven skills that analytic-minded accountants should have:

1. Develop an analytics mindset—recognize when and how data analytics can address business questions.
2. Data scrubbing and data preparation—comprehend the process needed to clean and prepare the data before analysis.
3. Data quality—recognize what is meant by data quality, be it completeness, reliability, or validity.
4. Descriptive data analysis—perform basic analysis to understand the quality of the underlying data and its ability to address the business question.
5. Data analysis through data manipulation—demonstrate ability to sort, rearrange, merge and reconfigure data in a manner that allows enhanced analysis.
6. Define and address problems through statistical data analysis—identify and implement an approach that will use statistical data analysis to draw conclusions and make recommendations on a timely basis.
7. Data visualization and data reporting—report results of analysis in an accessible way to each varied decision maker and his or her specific needs.

We address these seven skills throughout the first four chapters in the text in hopes that the analytic-minded accountant will develop and practice these skills to be ready to address business questions. We then demonstrate these skills in the labs and hands-on analysis throughout the rest of the book.

HANDS-ON EXAMPLE OF THE IMPACT MODEL

LO 1-6

Explain how to translate common business questions into fields and values

Here we provide a complete, hands-on example of the IMPACT model to show how it could be implemented for a specific situation.

Let's suppose I am trying to get a loan to pay off some credit card debt and my friend has told me about a new source of funds that doesn't involve a bank. In recent years, facilitated by the Internet, peer-to-peer lenders allow individuals to both borrow and lend money to each other. While there are other peer-to-peer lenders, in this case, we will specifically consider the **LendingClub**.

My question is whether I will be able to get a loan, given my prior loan history (poor), credit score, and the like. According to our approaches mentioned above, this would be an example of a classification approach because we are attempting to predict whether a person applying for a loan will be approved and funded or whether she will be denied a loan.

Identify the Questions

Stated specifically, our question is, "Given my borrower profile, can I expect the **LendingClub** to extend a loan to me?"

Master the Data

LendingClub is a U.S.-based, peer-to-peer lending company, headquartered in San Francisco, California. **LendingClub** facilitates both borrowing and lending by providing a platform for unsecured personal loans between $1,000 and $35,000. The loan period is for either 3 or 5 years. There is information available that allows potential investors to search and browse the loan listings on the **LendingClub** website and select loans in which they would like to invest. The available information includes information supplied about the borrower, amount of the loan, loan grade (and related loan interest rate), and loan purpose. Investors invest in the loans and make money from interest. **LendingClub** makes money by charging borrowers an origination fee and investors a service fee. Since 2007, hundreds of thousands of borrowers have obtained more than $20 billion in loans via **LendingClub**.[12]

Some basic statistics are included on the LendingClub Statistics website (Exhibit 1-4).

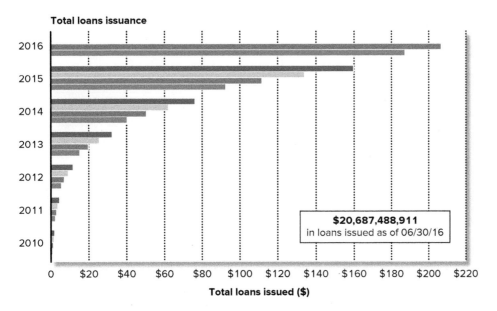

Total loans issued ($)

EXHIBIT 1-4
LendingClub Statistics

Source: https://www.lendingclub.com/info/statistics.action (accessed October 6, 2016).

---

[12]https://www.lendingclub.com/ (accessed September 29, 2016).

Borrowers borrow money for a variety of reasons, including refinancing other debt and paying off credit cards, as well as borrowing for other purposes (Exhibit 1-5).

EXHIBIT 1-5

LendingClub Statistics by Reported Loan Purpose

59.65% of LendingClub borrowers report using their loans to refinance existing loans or pay off their credit cards as of 06/30/16.

Source: https://www .lendingclub.com/info/ statistics.action (accessed October 6, 2016).

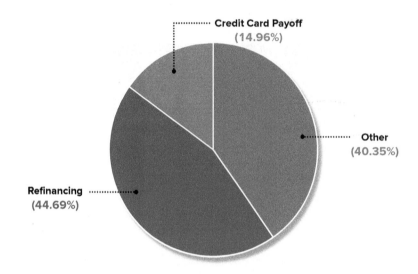

LendingClub actually provides datasets: data on the loans they approved and funded as well as data for the loans that were declined. In this chapter, we will emphasize the rejected loans and the reasons they were rejected.

The datasets and the data dictionary are available at https://www.lendingclub.com/info/download-data.action.

As we learn about the data, it is important to know what is available to us. To that end, there is a **data dictionary** that provides descriptions for all of the data attributes of the dataset. A cut-out of the data dictionary for the rejected stats file (i.e., the statistics about those loans rejected) is included in the data files as shown in Exhibit 1-6.

EXHIBIT 1-6

2007–2012 LendingClub Data Dictionary for Declined Loan Data

Source: Available at https://www.lendingclub.com/ info/download-data.action (accessed October 13, 2016)

RejectStats File	Description
Amount Requested	The total amount requested by the borrower
Application Date	The date which the borrower applied
Loan Title	The loan title provided by the borrower
Risk_Score	For applications prior to November 5, 2013 the risk score is the borrower's FICO score. For applications after November 5, 2013 the risk score is the borrower's Vantage score.
Debt-To-Income Ratio	A ratio calculated using the borrower's total monthly debt payments on the total debt obligations, excluding mortgage and the requested LC loan, divided by the borrower's self-reported monthly income.
Zip Code	The first 3 numbers of the zip code provided by the borrower in the loan application.
State	The state provided by the borrower in the loan application
Employment Length	Employment length in years. Possible values are between 0 and 10 where 0 means less than one year and 10 means ten or more years.
Policy Code	publicly available policy_code=1 new products not publicly available policy_code=2

We could also take a look at the data files available for both the funded loan data. However, for our analysis in the rest of the chapter, we use the Excel file "RejectStatsA Ready," which has rejected loan statistics from 2007 to 2012. It is a cleaned-up file ready for analysis. We'll learn more about data scrubbing in chapter 2.

Exhibit 1-7 provides a cut-out of the 2007–2012 "Approved Loan" dataset provided.

Amount R	Application D	Loan Title	Risk_Score	Debt-To-I	Zip Code	State	Employm	Policy Code
1000	5/26/2007	Wedding	693	10%	481xx	NM	4 years	0
1000	5/26/2007	Consolida	703	10%	010xx	MA	< 1 year	0
11000	5/27/2007	Want to cc	715	10%	212xx	MD	1 year	0
6000	5/27/2007	waksman	698	38.64%	017xx	MA	< 1 year	0
1500	5/27/2007	mdrigo	509	9.43%	209xx	MD	< 1 year	0
15000	5/27/2007	Trinfiniti	645	0%	105xx	NY	3 years	0
10000	5/27/2007	NOTIFYi Ir	693	10%	210xx	MD	< 1 year	0
3900	5/27/2007	For Justin.	700	10%	469xx	IN	2 years	0
3000	5/28/2007	title?	694	10%	808xx	CO	4 years	0
2500	5/28/2007	timgerst	573	11.76%	407xx	KY	4 years	0
3900	5/28/2007	need to cc	710	10%	705xx	LA	10+ years	0
1000	5/28/2007	sixstrings	680	10%	424xx	KY	1 year	0
3000	5/28/2007	bmoore51	688	10%	190xx	PA	< 1 year	0
1500	5/28/2007	MHarkins	704	10%	189xx	PA	3 years	0
1000	5/28/2007	Moving	694	10%	354xx	AL	< 1 year	0
8000	5/28/2007	Recent Co	708	10%	374xx	TN	< 1 year	0
12000	5/29/2007	Founders(	685	10%	770xx	TX	3 years	0
1000	5/29/2007	UChicago2	698	10%	207xx	MD	3 years	0

EXHIBIT 1-7
2007–2012 Declined
Loan Applications
(RejectStatsA)
Dataset

Available at: https://www
.lendingclub.com/info/
download-data.action.
Accessed 10/6/2016

Perform Test Plan

Considering our question, "Will I receive a loan from **LendingClub**?" and the available data, we will do three analyses to predict whether we will receive a loan, including:

1. The debt-to-income ratios and number of rejected loans.
2. The length of employment and number of rejected loans.
3. The credit (or risk) score and number of rejected loans.

Because **LendingClub** collects this information, we believe it will give **LendingClub** an idea if the borrower will be able to pay back the loan and give us an idea if our loan will be approved or rejected.

The first analysis we perform considers the *debt-to-income ratio.* That is, how big is the debt compared to the size of the annual income earned?

To consider the debt-to-income ratio in our analysis, three buckets (labeled DTI bucket) are constructed for each grouping of the debt-to-income ratio. These three buckets include the following:

1. High (debt is greater than 20 percent of income).
2. Medium ("mid") (debt is between 10 and 20 percent of income).
3. Low (debt is less than 10 percent of income).

Once those buckets are constructed, we are ready to analyze the breakdown in rejected loan applications by the debt-to-income ratio.

The Excel PivotTable is an easy way to make comparisons between the different levels of DTI. When we run a PivotTable analysis, we highlight the loans, which count the number of loans applied for and rejected, and the DTI bucket (see Exhibit 1-8). The PivotTable counts the number of loan applications in each of the three DTI buckets: high, medium (mid), and low. This suggests that because the high DTI bucket has the highest number of loan applications, perhaps the applicant asked for a loan that was too big given his or her income. **LendingClub** might have seen that as too big of a risk and chosen to not extend the loan to the borrower using the debt-to-income ratio as an indicator.

EXHIBIT 1-8

LendingClub Declined Loan Applications by DTI (Debt-to-Income) DTI bucket includes high (debt > 20 percent of income), medium ("mid") (debt between 10 and 20 percent of income), and low (debt < 10 percent of income).

Source: Microsoft Excel 2016

Row Labels ▾	Count of Rejected Loans
High	312,986
Low	171,228
Mid	161,200
Grand Total	**645,414**

PivotTable Fields

Choose fields to add to report:

- ☑ **Rejected Loans**
- ☐ Amount Requested
- ☐ Application Date
- ☐ Loan Title
- ☐ Risk_Score
- ☐ Risk Score Bucket
- ☐ Debt-To-Income Ratio
- ☑ **DTI Bucket**
- ☐ Zip Code
- ☐ State
- ☐ Employment Length
- ☐ EmploymentNum

The second analysis was on the length of employment and its relationship with rejected loans (see Exhibit 1-9). Arguably, the longer the employment, the more stable of a job and income stream you will have to ultimately repay the loan. LendingClub reports the number of years for each of the rejected applications. The PivotTable analysis lists the number of loans by the length of employment. Almost 77 percent (495,109 out of 645,414) out of the total rejected loans had worked at a job for less than 1 year, suggesting potentially an important reason for rejecting the requested loan. Perhaps some had worked a week, or just a month, and still want a big loan?

EXHIBIT 1-9

LendingClub Declined Loan Applications by DTI (Debt-to-Income) DTI bucket includes high (debt > 20 percent of income), medium ("mid") (debt between 10 and 20 percent of income), and low (debt < 10 percent of income).

Source: Microsoft Excel 2016

Row Labels ▾	Count of Rejected Loans
< 1 year	495,109
1 year	20,732
2 years	21,987
3 years	17,487
4 years	13,848
5 years	12,865
6 years	9,829
7 years	7,221
8 years	6,652
9 years	5,083
10+ years	34,601
Grand Total	**645,414**

PivotTable Fields

Choose fields to add to report:

- ☑ **Rejected Loans**
- ☐ Amount Requested
- ☐ Application Date
- ☐ Loan Title
- ☐ Risk_Score
- ☐ Risk Score Bucket
- ☐ Debt-To-Income Ratio
- ☐ DTI Bucket
- ☐ Zip Code
- ☐ State
- ☑ **Employment Length**
- ☐ EmploymentNum

The third analysis we perform is to consider the credit or risk score of the applicant. As noted in Exhibit 1-10, risk scores are typically classified in this way with those in the excellent and very good category receiving the lowest possible interest rates and best terms with a credit score above 750. On the other end of the spectrum are those with very bad credit (with a credit score less than 600).

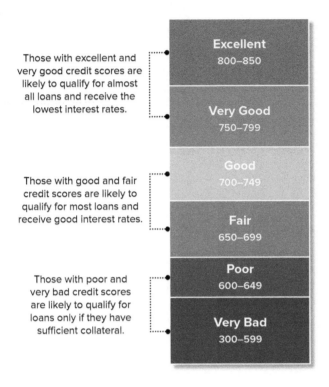

EXHIBIT 1-10

Breakdown of Customer Credit Scores (or Risk Scores)

Source: Cafecredit.com

Another predictor of loan repayment is the credit score that the borrower has. We classify the sample according to this breakdown into excellent, very good, good, fair, poor, and very bad credit according to their credit score noted in Exhibit 1-10.

Address and Refine Results

After performing a PivotTable analysis (as seen in Exhibit 1-11), we count the number of rejected loan applications by credit (risk) score. We'll note in the rejected loans that nearly 82 percent [(167,379 + 151,716 + 207,234)/645,414] of the applicants have either very bad, poor, or fair credit ratings, suggesting this might be a good reason for a loan rejection. We also note that only 0.3 percent (2,494/645,414) of those rejected loan applications had excellent credit.

So, if these are the applications that were all rejected, the question is how many of these that might apply for a loan not only had excellent credit, but also had worked more than 10 years and had asked for a loan that was less than 10 percent of their income (in the high DTI bucket)? Use of a PivotTable (as shown in Exhibit 1-12) allows us to consider this three-way interaction to and the question and suggests an answer of 89 out of 645414 (0.014 percent of the total). This might suggest that the use of these three metrics is reasonable at predicting loan rejection because the number who have excellent credit, worked more than 10 years, and requested a loan that was less than 10 percent of their income was such a small percentage of the total.

Row Labels ▾	Count of Rejected Loans
Excellent	2,494
Very Good	20,036
Good	96,555
Fair	207,234
Poor	151,716
Very Bad	167,379
Grand Total	**645,414**

PivotTable Fields

Choose fields to add to report:

- ☑ **Rejected Loans**
- ☐ Amount Requested
- ☐ Application Date
- ☐ Loan Title
- ☐ Risk_Score
- ☑ **Risk Score Bucket**
- ☐ Debt-To-Income Ratio
- ☐ DTI Bucket
- ☐ Zip Code
- ☐ State
- ☐ Employment Length
- ☐ EmploymentNum

MORE TABLES...

EXHIBIT 1-11   The Count of LendingClub Rejected Loan Applications by Credit or Risk Score Classification Using PivotTable Analysis

Source: Microsoft Excel 2016

Row Labels ▾	Count of Rejected Loans
⊟Excellent	2,494
⊟High	762
< 1 year	543
1 year	14
10+ years	89
2 years	26
3 years	16
4 years	16
5 years	14
6 years	20
7 years	10
8 years	7
9 years	7

PivotTable Fields

Choose fields to add to report:

- ☑ **Rejected Loans**
- ☐ Amount Requested
- ☐ Application Date
- ☐ Loan Title
- ☐ Risk_Score
- ☑ **Risk Score Bucket**
- ☐ Debt-To-Income Ratio
- ☑ **DTI Bucket**
- ☐ Zip Code
- ☐ State
- ☑ **Employment Length**
- ☐ EmploymentNum

MORE TABLES...

EXHIBIT 1-12   The Count of LendingClub Declined Loan Applications by Credit Score, Debt-to-Income, and Employment Length Using PivotTable Analysis (highlighting added)

Source: Microsoft Excel 2016

Perhaps those with excellent credit just asked for too big of a loan given their existing debt and that is why they were rejected. Exhibit 1-13 shows the PivotTable analysis. The analysis shows those with excellent credit asked for a larger loan (16.2 percent of income) given the debt they already had as compared to any of the others, suggesting a reason even those potential borrowers with excellent credit were rejected.

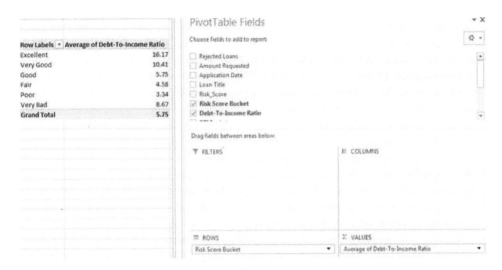

EXHIBIT 1-13   The Average Debt-to-Income Ratio (shown as a percentage) by Credit (Risk) Score for LendingClub Declined Loan Applications Using PivotTable Analysis

Source: Microsoft Excel 2016

Communicate Insights

Certainly further and more sophisticated analysis could be performed, but at this point we have a pretty good idea of what **LendingClub** uses to decide whether to extend a loan. We can communicate these insights either by showing the PivotTables or stating what three of the determinants are.

Track Outcomes

There are a wide variety of outcomes that could be tracked. But in this case, it might be best to see if we could predict future outcomes. For example, the data we analyzed was from 2007–2012. We could make our predictions for subsequent years based on what we had found in the past and then test and see how accurate we are with those predictions. We could also change our prediction model when we learn new insights and additional data become available.

In this chapter, we discussed how businesses and accountants derive value from Data Analytics. We gave some specific examples of how Data Analytics is used in business, auditing, managerial accounting, financial accounting, and tax accounting.

We introduced the IMPACT model and explained how it is used. And then talked specifically about the importance of identifying the question. We walked through the first few steps of the IMPACT model and introduced eight data approaches. We also discussed the data analytic skills needed by analytic-minded accountants.

We followed this up by looking at the case of why **LendingClub** rejected loans for a set of its customers using the IMPACT model. We performed this analysis using various filtering and PivotTable tasks.

PROGRESS CHECK

9. Doing your own analysis, download the rejected loans dataset titled "RejectStatsA Ready" and perform an Excel PivotTable analysis by state and figure out the number of rejected applications for the state of California. That is, count the loans by state and see what percentage of the rejected loans came from California. How close is that to the relative proportion of the population of California as compared to that of the United States?

10. Doing your own analysis, download the rejected loans dataset titled "RejectStatsA Ready" and run an Excel PivotTable by risk (or credit) score classification and DTI bucket to determine the number of rejected loans requested by those rated as having an excellent credit score.

Summary

- With data all around us, businesses and accountants are looking to Data Analytics to extract the value that the data might possess.
- Data Analytics is changing the audit and the way that accountants look for risk. Now, auditors can consider 100 percent of the transactions in their audit testing. It is also helpful in finding the anomalous or unusual transactions. Data Analytics is also changing the way financial accounting, managerial accounting, and taxes are done at a company.
- The IMPACT cycle is a means of doing Data Analytics that goes all the way from identifying the question, to mastering the data, to performing data analyses and communicating results. It is recursive in nature, suggesting that as questions are addressed, new important questions may emerge that can be addressed in a similar way.
- Eight data approaches address different ways of testing the data: classification, regression, similarity matching, clustering, co-occurrence grouping, profiling, link prediction, and data reduction. These are explained in more detail in chapter 3.
- Data analytic skills needed by analytic-minded accountants are specified and are consistent with the IMPACT cycle, including the following:
  - Develop an analytics mindset.
  - Data scrubbing and data preparation.
  - Data quality.
  - Descriptive data analysis.
  - Data analysis through data manipulation.
  - Define and address problems through statistical data analysis.
  - Data visualization and data reporting.

Key Words

Big Data (4) Datasets that are too large and complex for businesses' existing systems to handle utilizing their traditional capabilities to capture, store, manage, and analyze these datasets.

classification (9) A data approach that attempts to assign each unit in a population into a few categories potentially to help with predictions.

clustering (10) A data approach that attempts to divide individuals (like customers) into groups (or clusters) in a useful or meaningful way.

co-occurrence grouping (10)   A data approach that attempts to discover associations between individuals based on transactions involving them.

Data Analytics (4)   The process of evaluating data with the purpose of drawing conclusions to address business questions. Indeed, effective Data Analytics provides a way to search through large structured and unstructured data to identify unknown patterns or relationships.

data dictionary (14)   Centralized repository of descriptions for all of the data attributes of the dataset.

data reduction (11)   A data approach that attempts to reduce the amount of information that needs to be considered to focus on the most critical items (i.e., highest cost, highest risk, largest impact, etc.).

link prediction (10)   A data approach that attempts to predict a relationship between two data items.

profiling (10)   A data approach that attempts to characterize the "typical" behavior of an individual, group, or population by generating summary statistics about the data (including mean, standard deviations, etc.).

predictor (or independent or explanatory) variable (9)   A variable that predicts or explains another variable, typically called a predictor or independent variable.

response (or dependent) variable (9)   A variable that responds to, or is dependent on, another.

regression (9)   A data approach that attempts to estimate or predict, for each unit, the numerical value of some variable using some type of statistical model.

similarity matching (10)   A data approach that attempts to identify similar individuals based on data known about them.

✓ ANSWERS TO PROGRESS CHECKS

1. The plethora of data alone does not necessarily translate into value. However, if we carefully use the data to help address critical business problems and questions, the data may create value.

2. Banks could certainly use credit scores from companies like **Experian**, **TransUnion**, and **Equifax**, but if they have access to all of the banking information of their clients, arguably they could make more informed decisions. We would know how much money they have and how they spend it. We would know if they had prior loans and if they were paid in a timely manner. We would know where they work and their monthly income via the direct deposits. All of these combined, in addition to a credit score, might be used to assess creditworthiness to gain a better evaluation of customers' creditworthiness when they would like a loan. It might also give us needed information for a marketing campaign to target potential creditworthy customers.

3. The brand manager at **Samsung** might use Data Analytics to see what is being said about its phones on social media websites (such as Snapchat, Instagram, and Facebook), particularly those that attract an older demographic. This will help them to assess if there is a problem with the perceptions of its phones.

4. Data Analytics might be used to collect information on the amount of overtime. Who worked overtime? What were they working on? Do we actually need more full-time employees to reduce the level of overtime (and its related costs to the company and to the employees)? All of these questions could be addressed by looking at recent overtime records.

5. Data Analytics could tabulate the number of journal entries by an accountant to see who entered the most journal entries. This might be an issue if there was a perception of a problem in risk, such as segregation of duties in having one person enter so many journal entries or just how the accounting workload is distributed across accounting staff.

6. The tax staff would become much more adept at efficiently organizing data stored across multiple systems across an organization and performing Data Analytics to help with tax planning to structure transactions in a way that might minimize taxes.

7. The dependent variable could be the amount of money spent on fast food. Independent variables could be proximity of the fast food, ability to cook own food, discretionary income, socioeconomic status, etc.

8. The data reduction approach might help auditors spend more time and effort on the riskiest transactions or on those that might be anomalous in nature. This will help them more efficiently spend their time on items that may well be of highest importance.

9. An analysis of the rejected loans suggests that 85,793 of the total 645,414 rejected loans were from the state of California. That represents 13.29 percent of the total rejected loans. This is greater than the relative population of California to the United States as of the 2010 census, of 12.1 percent (37,253,956/308,745,538).

Row Labels ▼	Count of Rejected Loans
AK	1,608
AL	10,959
AR	7,868
AZ	13,830
CA	85,793
CO	11,697
CT	10,589
DC	1,524
DE	2,287
FL	49,620
GA	23,774
HI	3,715

PivotTable Fields

Choose fields to add to report:

- ☑ **Rejected Loans**
- ☐ Amount Requested
- ☐ Application Date
- ☐ Loan Title
- ☐ Risk_Score
- ☐ Risk Score Bucket
- ☐ Debt-To-Income Ratio
- ☐ DTI Bucket
- ☐ Zip Code
- ☑ **State**

Source: Microsoft Excel 2016

10. A PivotTable analysis of the rejected loans suggests that more than 30.5 percent (762/2,494) of those in the excellent risk/credit score range asked for a loan with a debt-to-income ratio of more than 20 percent.

Row Labels ▼	Count of Rejected Loans
⊟ **Excellent**	**2,494**
High	762
Mid	393
Low	1,339
⊟ **Very Good**	**20,036**
High	9,593
Mid	4,022
Low	6,421
⊟ **Good**	**96,555**
High	59,241
Mid	18,291
Low	19,023

PivotTable Fields

Choose fields to add to report:

- ☑ **Rejected Loans**
- ☐ Amount Requested
- ☐ Application Date
- ☐ Loan Title
- ☐ Risk_Score
- ☑ **Risk Score Bucket**
- ☐ Debt-To-Income Ratio
- ☑ **DTI Bucket**
- ☐ Zip Code
- ☐ State

Source: Microsoft Excel 2016

■connect

Multiple Choice Questions

1. Big Data is often described by the three Vs, or
   a. Volume, velocity, and variability.
   b. Volume, velocity, and variety.
   c. Volume, volatility, and variability.
   d. Variability, velocity, and variety.

2. Which approach to Data Analytics attempts to assign each unit in a population into a small set of classes where the unit belongs?
   a. Classification
   b. Regression
   c. Similarity matching
   d. Co-occurrence grouping

3. Which approach to Data Analytics attempts to identify similar individuals based on data known about them?
   a. Classification
   b. Regression
   c. Similarity matching
   d. Data reduction

4. Which approach to Data Analytics attempts to predict relationship between two data items?
   a. Profiling
   b. Classification
   c. Link prediction
   d. Regression

5. Which of these terms is defined as being a central repository of descriptions for all of the data attributes of the dataset?
   a. Big Data
   b. Data warehouse
   c. Data dictionary
   d. Data Analytics

6. Which skills were *not* emphasized that analytic-minded accountants should have?
   a. Develop an analytics mindset
   b. Data scrubbing and data preparation
   c. Classification of test approaches
   d. Define and address problems through statistical data analysis

7. Which skills were *not* emphasized that analytic-minded accountants should have?
   a. Data quality
   b. Descriptive data analysis
   c. Data visualization
   d. Data and systems analysis and design

8. The IMPACT cycle includes all *except* the following process:
   a. Visualize the data.
   b. Identify the questions.
   c. Master the data.
   d. Track outcomes.

9. The IMPACT cycle includes all *except* the following process:
    a. Communicate insights.
    b. Data preparation.
    c. Address and refine results.
    d. Perform test plan.
10. By the year 2020, about 1.7 megabytes of new information will be created every:
    a. Week.
    b. Second.
    c. Minute.
    d. Day.

Discussion Questions

1. Define Data Analytics and explain how a university might use its techniques to recruit and attract potential students.
2. Give an example of how Data Analytics creates value for businesses.
3. Give an example of how Data Analytics creates value for accounting.
4. How might Data Analytics be used in financial reporting? And how might it be used in doing tax planning?
5. Describe the IMPACT cycle. Why does its order of the processes and its recursive nature make sense?
6. Why is identifying the question such a critical first step in the IMPACT process cycle?
7. What is included in mastering the data as part of the IMPACT cycle described in the chapter?
8. In the chapter, we mentioned eight different data approaches. Which data approach was used by **Alibaba**, as mentioned in the chapter-opening vignette?
9. What data approach mentioned in the chapter might be used by Facebook to find friends?
10. Auditors will frequently use the data reduction approach when considering potentially risky transactions. Provide an example of why focusing on a portion of the total number of transactions might be important for auditors to assess risk.
11. Which data approach might be used to assess the appropriate level of the allowance for doubtful accounts?
12. Why might the debt-to-income attribute included in the declined loans dataset considered in the chapter be a predictor of declined loans? How about the credit (risk) score?
13. To address the question "Will I receive a loan from **LendingClub**?" we had available data to assess the relationship among (1) the debt-to-income ratios and number of rejected loans, (2) the length of employment and number of rejected loans, and (3) the credit (or risk) score and number of rejected loans. What additional data would you recommend to further assess whether a loan would be offered? Why would it be helpful?

Problems

1. Download and consider the data dictionary file "LCDataDictionary," specifically the LoanStats tab. This represents the data dictionary for the loans that were funded. Seeing all of the data attributes listed there, which attributes do you think might predict which loans will go delinquent and which will ultimately be fully repaid? How could we test that?

2. Download and consider the rejected loans dataset of **LendingClub** data titled "RejectStatsA Ready." Given the analysis performed in the chapter, what three items do you believe would be most useful in predicting loan acceptance or rejection? What additional data do you think could be solicited either internally or externally that would help you predict loan acceptance or rejection?

3. Download the rejected loans dataset of **LendingClub** data titled "RejectStatsA Ready" from the Connect website and do an Excel PivotTable by state; then figure out the number of rejected applications for the state of Arkansas. That is, count the loans by state and compute the percentage of the total rejected loans in the USA that came from Arkansas. How close is that to the relative proportion of the population of Arkansas as compared to the overall U.S. population (per 2010 census)?

4. Download the rejected loans dataset of **LendingClub** data titled "RejectStatsA Ready" from the Connect website and do an Excel PivotTable by state; then figure out the number of rejected applications for each state. Reorder these and make a graph ordering the states and the number of rejected loans from highest to lowest. Is there a lot of variability among states?

   For Problems 5, 6, and 7, we will be cleaning a data file in preparation for subsequent analysis.

   The analysis performed on **LendingClub** data in the chapter was for the years 2007–2012. For this and subsequent problems, please download the declined loans table for 2013–2014 from the Connect website, https://www.lendingclub.com/info/download-data.action.

5. Consider the 2013 declined loan data from **LendingClub** titled "RejectStatsB2013" from the Connect website. Similar to the analysis done in the chapter, let's scrub the risk score data. First, because our analysis requires risk scores, debt-to-income data, and employment length, we need to make sure each of them has valid data.

   a. Open the file in Excel.

   b. Sort the file based on risk score and remove those observations (the complete row or record) that have a missing score or a score of zero.

   c. Assign each risk score to a risk score bucket similar to the chapter. That is, classify the sample according to this breakdown into excellent, very good, good, fair, poor, and very bad credit according to their credit score noted in Exhibit 1-10. Classify those with a score greater than 850 as "Excellent". Consider using if-then statements to complete this. Or sort the row and manually input.

   d. Run a PivotTable analysis that shows the number of loans in each risk score bucket. Which group had the most rejected loans (biggest count)? Which group had the least rejected loans (smallest count)? This is the deliverable. Is it similar to Exhibit 1-11 performed on years 2007–2012?

6. Consider the 2013 declined loan data from **LendingClub** titled "RejectStatsB2013." Similar to the analysis done in the chapter, let's scrub the debt-to-income data. Because our analysis requires risk scores, debt-to-income data, and employment length, we need to make sure each of them has valid data.

   a. Sort the file based on debt-to-income and remove those observations (the complete row or record) that have a missing score, a score of zero, or a negative score.

   b. Assign each valid debt-to-income ratio into three buckets (labeled DTI bucket) by classifying each debt-to-income ratio into high (>20 percent), medium (10–20 percent), and low (<10 percent) buckets. Consider using if-then statements to complete this. Or sort the row and manually input.

   c. Run a PivotTable analysis that shows the number of loans in each DTI bucket. Any interpretation of why these loans were declined based on debt-to-income ratios?

7. Consider the 2013 declined loan data from **LendingClub** titled "RejectStatsB2013." Similar to the analysis done in the chapter, let's scrub the employment length. Because our analysis requires risk scores, debt-to-income data, and employment length, we need to make sure each of them has valid data.

a. Sort the file based on employment length and remove those observations (the complete row or record) that have a missing score ("NA") or a score of zero.

b. Sort the file based on debt-to-income and remove those observations (the complete row or record) that have a missing score, a score of zero, or a negative score.

c. Sort the file based on risk score and remove those observations (the complete row or record) that have a missing score or a score of zero.

d. There should now be 669,993 observations. Any thoughts on what biases are imposed when we remove observations? Is there another way to do this?

e. Run a PivotTable analysis to show the number of Excellent Risk Scores but High DTI Bucket loans in each Employment year bucket. Any interpretation of why these loans were declined based on employment length?

Answers to Multiple Choice Questions

1. B
2. A
3. C
4. C
5. C
6. C
7. D
8. A
9. B
10. B

Lab 1-0 How to Complete Labs in This Text

The labs in this book will provide valuable hands-on experience in generating and analyzing accounting problems. Each lab will provide a company summary with relevant facts, techniques that you will use to complete your analysis, software that you'll need, and an overview of the lab steps.

When you've completed your lab, you will submit a lab report showing your thought process with written responses and validating that you've completed specific checkpoints by taking screenshots along the way. This lab will demonstrate how to use basic lab tools.

In this lab, you will:

Part 1: Create a Word document on OneDrive.

Part 2: Take a screenshot of your document.

Part 3: Add another screenshot and submit your document.

Submit two screenshots.

Part 1: Create a New Word Document on OneDrive

On Office.com

1. Open your web browser and go to www.office.com.
2. Click OneDrive and log in using your university or personal e-mail address and password.
3. Click **+ New > Word document**. A new window will open with a new blank document.
4. Type "Lab 1-0 Data Analytics Lab Overview [Your name] [Your university email address]" in the first line (e.g., *Lab 1-0 Data Analytics Lab Overview Ryan Teeter rteeter@pitt.edu*).
5. Click **File > Save As > Save As** and name the document "*Lab 1-0 Data Analytics Lab Overview Ryan Teeter rteeter@pitt.edu.*" (You can also click the document name in the title bar (e.g., Document2) and change it there.
6. Because your document is in the cloud, changes are saved automatically and you won't lose your document when you log out of a lab computer.
7. Keep your document open and go to the next part of the lab.

Part 2: Take a Screenshot of Your Document

In Windows

1. Click the **Start** button and Search for "Snipping Tool."
2. Click **New** (**Rectangular Snip**) and draw a rectangle across your screen that includes your entire window.
3. A preview window with your screenshot will appear.
4. Press **Ctrl + C** to copy your screenshot.
5. Go to your Word document and press **Ctrl + V** to paste the screenshot into your document.
6. Keep your document open and go the next part of the lab.

On a Mac

1. Press **Cmd + Shift + 4** and draw a rectangle across your screen that includes your entire window.
2. Your screenshot will be saved in your Desktop folder.
3. Drag the screenshot file into your Word document.
4. Keep your document open and go the next part of the lab.

Part 3: Add Another Screenshot and Submit Your Document

1. Open a new web browser window and go to mhhm.com.
2. Take a screenshot of your results (label it 1-0A) of the page and paste it into your lab document.
3. Save your document and submit it to your instructor. If you're using Word Online on OneDrive, click **File > Save As > Download a Copy**.

End of Lab

Lab 1-1   Data Analytics in Financial Accounting

Let's see how we might use financial accounting data to perform some simple Data Analytics. The purpose of this lab is to help you identify relevant questions that may be answered using Data Analytics.

Company summary

You were just hired as an analyst for a credit rating agency that evaluates publicly listed companies in the United States. The company already has some Data Analytics tools that it uses to evaluate financial statements and determine which companies have higher risk and which companies are growing quickly. The company uses these analytics to provide ratings that will allow lenders to set interest rates and determine whether to lend money in the first place. As a new analyst, you're determined to make a good first impression.

Technique

- Some experience with spreadsheets and basic formulas is helpful here.

Software needed

- Word processor
- Web browser
- Screen capture tool (Windows: Snipping Tool; Mac: Cmd + Shift + 4)

In this lab, you will:

Part 1: Identify appropriate questions, and develop a hypothesis for each question.
Part 2: Translate questions into target fields and value in a database.
Part 3: Perform a simple analysis.

Part 1: Identify the Questions

Think about ways that you might analyze data from a financial statement. You could use a horizontal analysis to view trends over time, a vertical analysis to show account proportions, or ratios to analyze relationships.

1. Create a new word processing document and name the file **"Lab 1-1 Data Analytics in Financial Accounting Lab–[Your name] [Your email address]."**
2. Use what you know about financial statement analysis (or search the web if you need a refresher) to generate three different metrics for evaluating financial performance.

For example, if you wanted to evaluate a company's profit margin from one year to the next your question might be, "Has [Company X's] gross margin increased in the last three years?" **Type your three questions in your document.**

3. Next to each question **generate a hypothetical answer to the question** to help you identify what your expected output would be. You may use some insight or intuition or search for industry averages to inform your hypothesis. For example: "Hypothesis: Apple Inc's gross margin has increased slightly in the past 3 years."

4. Save your document.

Part 2: Master the Data

To answer your questions, you'll need to evaluate specific account values or financial statement paragraphs. As an analyst, you have access to the Security and Exchange Commission's (SEC's) EDGAR database of XBRL financial statements as well as a list of XBRL tags from the Financial Accounting Standards Board (FASB). XBRL stands for eXtensible Business Reporting Language and is used to make the data in financial statements machine-readable. Public companies have been preparing XBRL reports since 2008. While there are some issues with XBRL data, such data have become a useful means for comparing and analyzing financial statements. Every value, date, and paragraph is "tagged" with a label that identifies what each specific value represents, similar to assigning attributes in a database. Because companies tag their financial statements with XBRL tags, you can use those tags to identify specific data that you need to answer your questions from Part 1.

Analyze your questions:

5. **Evaluate each question from Part 1.** There are specific data attributes that will help you find the answer you're looking for. For example, if your question was "Has [Company X's] gross margin increased in the last 3 years?" and the expected answer is "Apple Inc's gross margin has increased slightly in the past 3 years," this tells you what attributes (or fields) to look for: *company name, gross margin (sales revenues – cost of goods sold), year.*

6. For each of your questions, **identify the account or data attribute you need** to answer your question. Then use FASB's XBRL taxonomy (see next section for instructions) to identify the specific XBRL tags that represent those accounts. For example:

   Company name = EntitySectorIndustryClassificationPrimary

   Gross margin = GrossProfit

   Sales revenues = SalesRevenueNet

   Cost of goods sold = CostOfGoodsAndServicesSold

   Year = DocumentPeriodEndDate

7. Save your document.

   Identify XBRL tags from the FASB's taxonomy:

8. Open a web browser, and go to xbrlview.fasb.org.
9. Click the + next to US GAAP (2016-01-31).
10. Click the **ALL (Main/Entire)** option, and then click **Open** to load the taxonomy.
11. Navigate through the financial statements to determine which accounts you need to answer your questions from Part 1. The name of the XBRL tag is found in the properties pane next to "Name." For example, the tag for Total Assets can be found by clicking + Statement of Financial Position [Abstract], + Statement [Table], + Statement [Line Items], + Assets [Abstract], + Assets, Total, as shown in Exhibit 1-1A. You may also use the search function.

Note: Be careful when you use the search function. The tag you see in the results may appear in the wrong statement. Double-click the tag to expand the tree and show where the account appears.

LAB EXHIBIT 1-1A
Browse the XBRL
Taxonomy for Financial
Fact Tags Needed for
Your Analysis

Source: Google

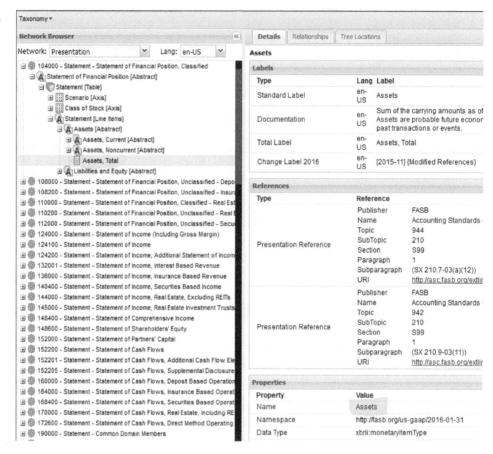

Part 3: Perform the Analysis

Now that you've identified your questions and the data sources, you can build your model and perform your analysis. Because XBRL data are dynamic, we'll use a tool that pulls live data based on your inputs.

12. In your web browser, click on the eBook via Connect to locate the table of contents where you will find **Additional Student Resources > Financial Statement Analysis** or Click Here.
13. Log into your Google Account.
14. Click **File > Make a Copy. . .**
15. In your new document, **add your tags** from Part 2 under the Financial Facts header, similar to Exhibit 1-1B.
16. Under the Analysis header, **use formulas to create your analysis** from Part 1. You may enhance your output by using conditional formatting or other visualizations that will be covered in chapter 4.
17. Take a screenshot (label it 1-1A) of your analysis and paste it into your lab document.
18. Save your document and submit it to your instructor.

End of Lab

Financial Statement Analysis

LAB EXHIBIT 1-1B
Add Your Tags to
Perform a Simple
Analysis Using XBRL
Data

Source: Google

Main Company Ticker	AAPL	(e.g. MSFT)	EntitySectorIndustryClassificationPrimary
Most Recent Year	2016	(e.g. 2014)	DocumentPeriodEndDate
Period	FY	(e.g. FY or Q2)	
Round to	100,000	(e.g. 100,000)	

Apple Inc

Financial Facts	2013	2014	2015	2016
SalesRevenueNet	$ 1,709,100	$ 1,827,950	$ 2,337,150	$ 2,156,390
CostOfGoodsAndServicesSold	$ 1,066,060	$ 1,122,580	$ 1,400,890	$ 1,313,760
GrossProfit	$ 643,040	$ 705,370	$ 936,260	$ 842,630
OperatingIncomeLoss	$ 489,990	$ 525,030	$ 712,300	$ 600,240
[Add XBRL Tag Here]	#ERROR!	#ERROR!	#ERROR!	#ERROR!
[Add XBRL Tag Here]	#ERROR!	#ERROR!	#ERROR!	#ERROR!

Analysis

	2013	2014	2015	2016
Sales Revenue - Cost of Goods Sold	$ 643,040	$ 705,370	$ 936,260	$ 842,630
Increase (Decrease) from previous year		9.69%	32.73%	-10.00%

Lab 1-2   Data Analytics in Managerial Accounting

Let's see how we might use customer data to understand some simple data analytics. The purpose of this lab is to help you identify relevant questions that may be answered using data analytics.

Company summary

LendingClub is a U.S.-based, peer-to-peer lending company, headquartered in San Francisco, California. **LendingClub** facilitates both borrowing and lending by providing a platform for unsecured personal loans between $1,000 and $35,000. The loan period is for either 3 or 5 years. You have been brought in to help managers improve their loan application process.

Technique

- Some critical and creative thinking is helpful here.

Software needed

- Word processor

In this lab, you will:

Part 1: Identify appropriate questions and develop a hypothesis for each question.
Part 2: Identify fields and values in a database that are relevant to your questions.

Part 1: Identify the Questions

LendingClub currently assigns a risk score to all loan applicants. This risk score is used to determine (1) whether a loan is accepted and (2) what interest rate approved loans will receive. The risk score has been used for the past 5 years, but **LendingClub** thinks there may be better ways to evaluate this given that the number of defaulted loans has increased in the past 2 years. It would like you to propose a model that would help it potentially assign a risk score to loan applicants.

1. Create a new word processing document and name the file **"Lab 1-2 Data Analytics in Managerial Accounting Lab – [Your name] [Your email address]."**
2. Use what you know about loan risk (or search the web if you need a refresher) to identify three different questions that might influence risk. For example, if you suspect risky customers live in a certain location, your question might be "Where do the customers live?" **Type your three questions in your document.**
3. Next to each question, **generate a hypothetical answer to each question** to help you identify what your expected output would be. You may use some insight or intuition or search the Internet for ideas on how to inform your hypothesis. For example: "Hypothesis: Risky customers likely live in coastal towns."
4. Finally, identify the data that you would need to answer each of your questions. For example, to determine customer location, you might need the city, state, and zip code. Additionally, if you hypothesize a specific region, you'd need to know which cities, state, and/or zip codes belong to that region. **Add your required data sources to each question in your document.**
5. **Save** your document.

Part 2: Master the Data

To answer your questions, you'll need to evaluate specific data that LendingClub collects. It has provided a listing of fields that it collects in Table 1-2A:

LAB TABLE 1-2A
Names and Descriptions of Selected Data Attributes Collected by LendingClub

Attribute	Description
id	Loan identification number
member_id	Membership id
loan_amnt	Requested loan amount
emp_length	Employment length
issue_d	Date of loan issue
loan_status	Fully paid or charged off
pymnt_plan	Payment plan: yes or no
purpose	Loan purpose: e.g., wedding, medical, debt_consolidation, car
zip_code	Zip code
addr_state	State
dti	Debt-to-income ratio
delinq_2y	Late payments within the past two years
earliest_cr_line	Oldest credit account
inq_last_6mnths	Credit inquiries in the past 6 months
open_acc	Number of open credit accounts
revol_bal	Total balance of all credit accounts
revol_util	Percentage of available credit in use
total_acc	Total number of credit accounts
application_type	Individual or joint application

6. Evaluate each question from Part 1. Do the data you identified in your questions exist in the table provided? **Write the applicable fields next to each question in your document.**

7. Are there data values you identified that don't exist in the table? **Write where else you might look to collect the missing data or how you might suggest collecting those it.**

8. Save your document and submit to your instructor.

End of Lab

Lab 1-3　Data Analytics in Auditing

The purpose of this lab is to help you identify relevant questions that may be answered using data analytics in auditing. Let's evaluate how we might use master and transaction data from an enterprise resource planning system to perform some simple data analytics to assist the financial statement audit.

Company summary

ABC Company is a large retailer that collects its order-to-cash data in a large ERP system that was recently updated to comply with the AICPA's audit data standards. ABC Company currently collects all relevant data in the ERP system and digitizes any contracts, orders, or receipts that are completed on paper. The credit department reviews customers who request credit. Sales orders are approved by managers before being sent to the warehouse for preparation and shipment. Cash receipts are collected by a cashier and applied to a customer's outstanding balance by an accounts receivable clerk.

You have been assigned to the audit team that will perform the internal controls audit of ABC Company.

Technique

- Familiarity with database structure and primary-foreign key relationships may be helpful.

Software needed

- Word processor
- Web browser
- Screen capture tool (Windows: Snipping Tool; Mac: Cmd + Shift + 4)

In this lab, you will:

Part 1: Identify appropriate questions and develop a hypothesis for each question.

Part 2: Translate questions into target fields and value in a database and perform a simple analysis.

Part 1: Identify the Questions

Your audit team has been tasked with identifying potential internal control weaknesses within the order-to-cash processes.

1. Create a new word processing document and name the file **"Lab 1-3 Data Analytics in Auditing Lab – [Your name] [Your email address]."**
2. Use what you know about internal controls over the order-to-cash process (or search the web if you need a refresher) to identify three different questions that might indicate internal control weakness. For example, if you suspect that a manager may be delaying approval of shipments sent to customers, your question might be "Are any shipping managers approving shipments more than 2 days after they are received?" **Type your three questions in your document.**
3. Next to each question **generate a hypothetical answer to each question** to help you identify what your expected output would be. You may use some insight or intuition or search the Internet for ideas on how to inform your hypothesis. For example: "Hypothesis: Only 1 or 2 shipping managers are approving shipments more than 2 days after they are received."
4. Finally, identify the data that you would need to answer each of your questions. For example, to determine the timing of approval and who is involved, you might need the approver id, the order date, and the approval date. **Add your required data sources to each question in your document.**
5. **Save** your document.

Part 2: Master the Data

To answer your questions, you'll need to evaluate the data that are available in the audit data standards.

6. Open your web browser and search for "Audit data standards order to cash." Follow the link to the "Audit Data Standards Library—AICPA," then look for the "Audit Data Standard—Order to Cash Subledger Standard" PDF document.
7. Quickly scan through the document for fields that relate to each question you identified in Part 1. For example, if you're looking for the shipment timing and approval data, you would need the *Shipments_Made_YYYYMMDD_YYYYMMDD* table and *Approved_By, Entered_Date,* and *Approved_Date* fields. **List the tables and fields from the audit data standard in your document needed for each question.**
8. Identify any data that don't appear in the audit data standard that might also be relevant to your questions.
9. Save your document and submit it to your instructor.

End of Lab

Lab 1-4   Comprehensive Case: Dillard's Store Data

The purpose of this lab is to help you identify relevant questions for **Dillard's Inc.** based on its data.

Company summary

Dillard's is a department store with approximately 330 stores in 29 states. Its headquarters is in Little Rock, Arkansas. You can learn more about **Dillard's** by looking at finance .yahoo.com (ticker symbol = DDS) and the Wikipedia site for DDS. You'll quickly note that William T. Dillard II is an accounting grad of the University of Arkansas and the Walton College of Business, which may be why he shared transaction data with us to make available for this lab and labs throughout this text.

Technique

The data for this lab and other all **Dillard's** labs are available at http://walton.uark.edu/enterprise/. Your instructor will be able to help you gain access when it is needed. From the Walton College website, we note the following:

> The Dillard's Department Store Database contains retail sales information gathered from store sales transactions. The sale process begins when a customer brings items intended for purchase (clothing, jewelry, home décor, etc.) to any store register. A Dillard's sales associate scans the individual items to be purchased with a barcode reader. This populates the transaction table (TRANSACT), which will later be used to generate a sales receipt listing the item, department, and cost information (related price, sale price, etc.) for the customer. When the customer provides payment for the items, payment details are recorded in the transaction table, the receipt is printed, and the transaction is complete. Other tables are used to store information about stores, products, and departments.

This retail sales information, UA_DILLARDS, was provided to the Walton College of Business by **Dillard's Stores Inc.** The information consists of five tables with more than 128 million rows already populated and ready for use.

This is a gifted dataset that is based on real operational data. Like any real database, integrity problems may be noted. This can provide a unique opportunity not only to expose students to real data, but also to illustrate the effects of data integrity problems. [Source: http://walton.uark.edu/enterprise/dillardshome.php (accessed September 25, 2017).]

Software needed

- Word processor
- Web browser
- Screen capture tool (Windows: Snipping Tool; Mac: Cmd + Shift + 4)
- Access to the dataset is available at http://walton.uark.edu/enterprise/dillardshome .php. If you plan on doing additional labs on **Dillard's** data, you must receive permission from the Walton College to access the data before use. Additional access instructions are available from your instructor or on the Connect website.

In this lab, you will:

Part 1: Identify appropriate questions for a retailer.

Part 2: Translate questions into target tables, fields, and values in the **Dillard's** database.

Part 1: Identify the Questions

1. Create a new word processing document and name the file **"Lab 1-4 Comprehensive Case – Dillard's Data [Your name] [Your email address]."**
2. Assume that **Dillard's** wants to improve profitability. Name three questions that could be asked to assess current profitability levels for each product and how profitability could be improved in the near future.

3. Assume that **Dillard's** wishes to improve its online sales and profitability on those sales. What three questions could be asked to see where **Dillard's** stands on its online sales?
4. Save your document.

LAB EXHIBIT 1-4A

Source: http://walton.uark .edu/enterprise/dillardshome .php (accessed September 25, 2017).

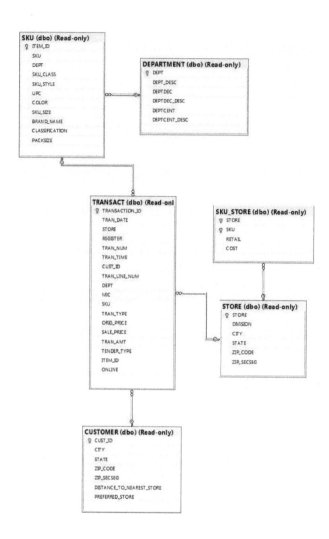

Part 2: Master the Data

To answer your questions and related questions, access the Data Dictionary and Entity Relationship Diagram for the Dillard's Entity Relationship data at http://walton.uark.edu/ enterprise/dillardshome.php or consider the information in Exhibits 1-4A and 1-4B.

5. You're trying to learn about where **Dillard's** stores are located to identify locations for the next additional store. Consider the STORE table. What questions could be asked about store location given data availability?
6. What questions would you have regarding data fields in the SKU table that could be used to help address the cost of shipping? What additional information would be helpful to address this question?
7. What table and fields could address the question of the profit margin (sales price less cost) on each product (SKU) available for sale?

Metadata

LAB EXHIBIT 1-4B

Source: http://walton.uark.edu/enterprise/dillardshome.php (accessed September 25, 2017).

Attribute	Description	Values
AMT	Total amount of the transaction charge to the customer	26.25, 44.00, . . .
BRAND	The brand name of the stock item	TOMMY HI, MARK ECK, . . .
CITY	City where the store is located	ST. LOUIS, TAMPA, . . .
CLASSID	Stock Item Classification	5305, 4505, 8306, . . .
COLOR	The color of the stock item	BLACK, KHAKI, . . .
COST	The cost of the stock item	9.00, 15.00, . . .
DEPT	Department where the stock item belong	800, 801, 1100, . . .
DEPTDESC	Description of the department	CLINIQUE, LESLIE, . . .
INTERID	Internal ID	265005802, 671901998, . . .
MIC	Master Item Code	862, 689, . . .
ORGPRICE	Original price of the item stock	75.00, 44.00, . . .
PACKSIZE	The quantity of item per pack	1, 3, . . .
QUANTITY	Item quantity of the transaction	1, 2, 3, . . .
REGISTER	Register Number of the current transaction	580, 30, 460, . . .
RETAIL	The retail price of the stock item	19.75, 34.00, . . .
SALEDATE	Sale price of the item stock	2005-01-20, 2005-06-02, . . .
SEQ	Sequence number	298100028, 213500030, . . .
SIZE	The size of the stock item	L, 070N, 22, . . .
SKU	Stock Keeping Unit number of the stock item	4757355, 2128748, . . .
SPRICE	Sale price of the item stock	26.25, 65.00, . . .
STATE	State where the store is located	FL, MO, AR, . . .
STORE	Store Number	2, 3, 4, 100, . . .
STYLE	The specific style of the stock item	51 MERU08, 9 126NAO, . . .
STYPE	Type of the transaction (Return or Purchase)	P, R
TRANNUM	Transaction Code	09700, 01800, . . .
UPC	Universal Product Code for the stock item	000400004087945, . . .
VENDOR	The vendor number of the stock item	5511283, 2726341, . . .
ZIP	ZIP Code	33710, 63126, . . .

8. If you're interested in learning which product is sold most often at each store, what tables and fields would you consider?
9. Save your document and submit it to your instructor.

End of Lab

Chapter 2

Data Preparation and Cleaning

A Look at This Chapter

This chapter provides an overview of the types of data that are used in the accounting cycle and common data that are stored in a relational database. The chapter addresses *mastering the data,* the second step of the IMPACT cycle. We will describe how data are requested and *extracted* to answer business questions and how to *transform* data for use via data preparation, validation, and cleaning. We conclude with an explanation of how to *load* data into the appropriate tool in preparation for analyzing data to make decisions.

A Look Back

Chapter 1 defined Data Analytics and explained that the value of Data Analytics is in the insights it provides. We described the Data Analytic Process using the IMPACT cycle model and explained how this process is used to address both business and accounting questions. We specifically emphasized the importance of identifying appropriate questions that data analytics might be able to address.

A Look Ahead

Chapter 3 describes how to go from defining business problems to analyzing data, answering questions, and addressing business problems. We make the case for three data approaches we argue are most relevant to accountants and provide examples of each.

Shutterstock / Wichy

We are lucky to live in a world in which data are abundant. However, even with rich sources of data, when it comes to being able to analyze data and turn them into useful information and insights, very rarely can an analyst hop right into a dataset and begin analyzing. Datasets almost always need to be cleaned and validated before they can be used. Not knowing how to clean and validate data can, at best, lead to frustration and poor insights and, at worst, lead to horrible security violations. While this text takes advantage of open source datasets, these datasets have all been scrubbed not only for accuracy, but also to protect the security and privacy of any individual or company whose details were in the original dataset.

In 2015, a pair of researchers named Emil Kirkegaard and Julius Daugbejerg Bjerrekaer scraped data from **OkCupid**, a free dating website, and provided the data onto the "Open Science Framework," a platform researchers use to obtain and share raw data. While the aim of the Open Science Framework is to increase transparency, the researchers in this instance took that a step too far—and a step into illegal territory. Kirkegaard and Bjerrekaer did not obtain permission from **OkCupid** or from the 70,000 **OkCupid** users whose identities, ages, genders, religions, personality traits, and other personal details maintained by the dating site were provided to the public without any work being done to anonymize or sanitize the data. If the researchers had taken the time to not just validate that the data were complete but also to sanitize them to protect the individuals' identities, this would not have been a threat or a news story. On May 13, 2015, the Open Science Framework removed the **OkCupid** data from the platform, but the damage of the privacy breach had already been done.[1]

OBJECTIVES

After reading this chapter, you should be able to:

LO 2-1 Understand how data are organized in an accounting information system

LO 2-2 Understand how data are stored in a relational database

LO 2-3 Explain and apply extraction, transformation, and loading (ETL) techniques

[1]B. Resnick, "Researchers Just Released Profile Data on 70,000 OkCupid Users without Permission," 2016, http://www.vox.com/2016/5/12/11666116/70000-okcupid-users-data-release (accessed October 31, 2016).

As you learned in chapter 1, Data Analytics is a process, and we follow an established data analytics model called the IMPACT cycle as introduced in chapter 1.[2] The IMPACT cycle begins with identifying business questions and problems that can be, at least partially, addressed with data (the "I" in the IMPACT model). Once the opportunity or problem has been identified, the next step is **mastering the data** (the "M" in the IMPACT model), which requires you to identify and obtain the data needed for solving the problem. Mastering the data requires a firm understanding of what data are available to you and where they are stored, as well as being skilled in the process of extracting, transforming, and loading (ETL) the data in preparation for data analysis. While the extraction piece of the ETL process may often be completed by the information systems team or the database administrator, it is also possible that you will have access to raw data that you will need to extract out of the source database. Both methods of requesting data for extraction and of extracting data yourself are covered in this chapter. The mastering the data step can be described via the ETL process. The ETL process is made up of the following five steps:

Step 1   Determine the purpose and scope of the data request (extract).

Step 2   Obtain the data (extract).

Step 3   Validate the data for completeness and integrity (transform).

Step 4   Sanitize the data (transform).

Step 5   Load the data in preparation for data analysis (load).

This chapter will provide details for each of these five steps.

LO 2-1

Understand how data are organized in an accounting information system

HOW DATA ARE USED AND STORED IN THE ACCOUNTING CYCLE

Before you can identify and obtain the data, you must have a comfortable grasp on what data are available to you and where such data are stored. A basic understanding of accounting processes and its associated data, how those data are organized, and why, can help you request the right data and facilitate that request so that you know exactly where each piece of data is held.

The database schema illustrated in Exhibit 2-1 is a Unified Modeling Language (UML) class diagram. This type of diagram is used to support a relational database, which is the type of database you are most likely to come across when extracting and using accounting and financial data. While it is often preferred to analyze data from a flat file (e.g., in an Excel spreadsheet, in which all the data are stored in one place), when it comes to storing data and maintaining data integrity, a relational database is preferred because of its ability to maintain "one version of the truth" across multiple data elements.

EXHIBIT 2-1
Procure-to-Pay
Database Schema
(Simplified)

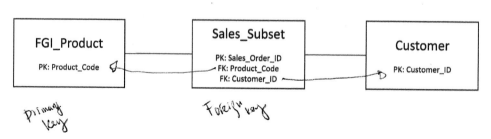

[2] J. P. Isson and J. S. Harriott, *Win with Advanced Business Analytics: Creating Business Value from Your Data* (Hoboken, NJ: Wiley, 2013).

DATA AND RELATIONSHIPS IN A RELATIONAL DATABASE

LO 2-2

Understand how data are stored in a relational database

In this text, we will work with data in a variety of forms, but regardless of the tool we use to analyze data, structured data should be stored in a normalized **relational database**. There are occasions for working with data directly in the relational database, but many times when we work with data analysis, we'll prefer to export the data from the relational database and view it in a more user-friendly form. The benefit of storing data in a normalized database outweighs the downside of having to export, validate, and sanitize the data every time you need to analyze the information.

Storing data in a normalized, relational database instead of a **flat file** ensures that data are complete, not redundant, and that business rules are enforced; it also aids communication and integration across business processes. Each one of these benefits is detailed here:

- *Completeness:* Ensures that all data required for a business process are included in the dataset.
- *No redundancy:* Storing redundant data is to be avoided for several reasons: It takes up unnecessary space (which is expensive), it takes up unnecessary processing to run reports to ensure that there aren't multiple versions of the truth, and it increases the risk of data-entry errors. Storing data in flat files yields a great deal of redundancy, but normalized relational databases require there to be one version of the truth and for each element of data to be stored in only one place.
- *Business rules are enforced:* As will become increasingly evident as we progress through the material in this text, relational databases can be designed to aid in the placement and enforcement of internal controls and business rules in ways that flat files cannot.
- *Communication and integration of business processes:* Relational databases should be designed to support business processes across the organization, which results in improved communication across functional areas and more integrated business processes.[3]

It is valuable to spend some time basking in the benefits of storing data in a relational database because it is not necessarily easier to do so when it comes to building the data model or understanding the structure. It is arguably more complex to normalize your data than it is to throw redundant data without business rules or internal controls into a spreadsheet.

Columns in a Table: Primary Keys, Foreign Keys, and Descriptive Attributes

When requesting data, it is critical to understand how the tables in a relational database are related. This is a brief overview of the different types of attributes in a table and how these attributes support the relationships between tables. It is certainly not a comprehensive take on relational data modeling, but it should be adequate in aiding your knowledge for data requests.

Every column in a table must be both unique and relevant to the purpose of the table. There are three types of columns: primary keys, foreign keys, and descriptive attributes.

Each table must have a **primary key**. The primary key is typically made up of one column, but it can occasionally be made up of a combination of columns. The purpose of the primary key is to ensure that each row in the table is unique, so it is often referred to as a "unique identifier." It is rarely truly descriptive; instead, a collection of letters of simply sequential numbers are often used. As a student, you are probably already very familiar with your unique identifier—your student ID number at the university is the way you as a student

---

[3]G. C. Simsion and G. C. Witt, *Data Modeling Essentials* (Amsterdam: Morgan Kaufmann, 2005).

are stored as a unique record in the university's data model! Other examples of unique identifiers that you are familiar with would be check numbers and driver's license numbers.

One of the biggest differences between a flat file and a relational database is simply how many tables there are—when you request your data into a flat file, you'll receive one big table with a lot of redundancy. While this is ideal for analyzing data, when the data are stored in the database, each group of information is stored in a separate table. Then, the tables that are related to one another are identified (e.g., Supplier and Purchase Order are related; it's important to know which Supplier the Purchase Order is from). The relationship is created by placing a **foreign key** in one of the two tables that are related. The foreign key is another type of attribute, and its function is to create the relationship between two tables. Whenever two tables are related, one of those tables must contain a foreign key to create the relationship.

The other columns in a table are **descriptive attributes**. For example, Supplier Name is a critical piece of data when it comes to understanding the business process, but it is not necessary to build the data model. Primary and foreign keys facilitate the structure of a relational database, and the descriptive attributes provide actual business information.

Refer to Exhibit 2-1, the data schema for a typical procure-to-pay process. Each table has an attribute with the letters "PK" next to them—these are the primary keys for each table. The primary key for Materials is "Item No.," the primary key for Purchase Order is "PO No.," and so on. Several of the tables also have attributes with the letters "FK" next to them—these are the foreign keys that create the relationship between pairs of tables. For example, look at the relationship between Supplier and Purchase Order. The primary key in the supplier table is "Supplier ID." The line between the two tables links the primary key to a foreign key in the Purchase Order table, also named "Supplier ID."

The line items table in Table 2-1 has so much detail in it that it requires two attributes to combine as a primary key. This is a special case of a primary key often referred to as a **composite primary key**, in which the two foreign keys from the tables that it is linking combine to make up a unique identifier. The theory and details that support the necessity of this linking table are beyond the scope of this text—if you can identify the primary and foreign keys, you'll be able to identify the data that you need to request. Table 2-2 shows a subset of the data that are represented by the Purchase Order and Supplier tables. You can see that each of the attributes listed in the class diagram appears as a column, and the data for each purchase order and each supplier are accounted for in the rows.

TABLE 2-1
Line Items Table:
Purchase Order Table

	Purchase Order Table				
PO No.	**Date**	**Created By**	**Approved By**	**Supplier ID**
1787	11/1/2017	1001	1010	1
1788	11/1/2017	1005	1010	2
1789	11/8/2017	1002	1010	1
1790	11/15/2017	1005	1010	1

TABLE 2-2
Line Items Table:
Supplier Table

	Supplier Table		
Supplier ID	**Supplier Name**	**Supplier Address**	**Supplier Type**
1	Northern Brewery Homebrew Supply	6021 Lyndale Ave. S	1
2	Hops Direct LLC	686 Green Valley Road	1
3	The Home Brewery	455 E. Township St.	1
4	The Payroll Company	408 N. Walton Blvd.	2

PROGRESS CHECK

1. Referring to Exhibit 2-1, locate the relationship between the Employee and Purchase Order tables. What is the unique identifier of each table? (The unique identifier attribute is called the primary key—more on how it's determined in the next learning objective.) Which table contains the attribute that creates the relationship? (This attribute is called the foreign key—more on how it's determined in the next learning objective.)

2. Referring to Exhibit 2-1, review the attributes in the Suppliers table. There is a foreign key in this table that doesn't relate to any of the tables in the diagram. Which table do you think it is? What type of data would be stored in that table?

DATA DICTIONARIES

In the previous section, you learned about how data are stored by focusing on the procure-to-pay database schema. Viewing schemas and processes in isolation clarifies each individual process, but it can also distort reality—these schemas do not represent their own separate databases. Rather, each process-specific database schema is a piece of a greater whole, all combining to form one integrated database.

As you can imagine, once these processes come together to be supported in one database, the amount of data can be massive. Understanding the processes and the basics of how data are stored is critical, but even with a sound foundation, it would be nearly impossible for an individual to remember where each piece of data is stored, or what each piece of data represents.

Creating and using a **data dictionary** is paramount in helping database administrators maintain databases and analysts identify the data they need to use. In chapter 1, you were introduced to the data dictionary for the **LendingClub**. The same cut-out of the **LendingClub** data dictionary is provided in Exhibit 2-2 as a reminder.

RejectStats File	Description
Amount Requested	Total requested loan amount
Application Date	Date of borrower application
Loan Title	Loan title
Risk_Score	Borrower risk (FICO) score
Dept-To-Income Ratio	Ratio of borrower total monthly debt payments divided by monthly income.
Zip Code	The first 3 numbers of the borrower zip code provided from loan application.
State	Two digit State Abbreviation provided from loan application.
Employment Length	Employment length in years, where 0 is less than 1 and 10 is greater than 10.
Policy Code	policy_code=1 if publicly available. policy_code=2 if not publicly available

EXHIBIT 2-2
2007–2012
LendingClub Data Dictionary for Declined Load Data

Available at https://www.lendingclub.com/info/download-data.action (accessed October 13, 2016).

Because the **LendingClub** data are provided in a flat file, the only two attributes necessary to describe the data are the attribute name (e.g., Amount Requested) and a description of that attribute. The description ensures that the data in each attribute are used and analyzed in the appropriate way—it's always important to remember that technology will do exactly what you tell it to, so you must be smarter than the computer! If you run analysis on an attribute thinking it means one thing, when it actually means another, you could make some big mistakes and bad decisions even when you're working with great data. It's critical to get to know the data through database schemas and data dictionaries thoroughly before attempting to do any data analysis.

When you are working with data stored in a relational database, you will have more attributes to keep track of in the data dictionary. Table 2-3 provides an example of a data dictionary for a generic Supplier table:

Primary or Foreign Key?	Required	Attribute Name	Description	Data Type	Default Value	Field Size	Notes
PK	Y	Supplier ID	Unique Identifier for Each Supplier	Number	n/a	10	
	N	Supplier Name	First and Last Name	Short Text	n/a	30	
FK	N	Supplier Type	Type Code for Different Supplier Categories	Number	Null	10	1: Vendor 2: Misc

TABLE 2-3   Supplier Data Dictionary

 PROGRESS CHECK

3. What is the purpose of the primary key? A foreign key? A non-key attribute?
4. How do data dictionaries help you understand the data from a database or flat file?

EXTRACTION, TRANSFORMATION, AND LOADING (ETL) OF DATA

Once you have familiarized yourself with the data via data dictionaries and schemas, you are prepared to extract the data from the database manager or extract the data yourself. The ETL process begins with identifying which data you need and is completed when the clean data are loaded in the appropriate format into the tool to be used for analysis.

EXTRACTION

Requesting data is often an iterative practice, but the more prepared you are when requesting data in the first place, the more time you will save for yourself and the database administrators in the long run. Determine exactly what data you need in order to answer your business questions.

Requesting the data involves the first two steps of the ETL extraction process. Each step has questions associated with it that you should try to answer.

Step 1: Determine the Purpose and Scope of the Data Request

- What is the purpose of the data request? What do you need the data to solve? What business problem will they address?
- What risk exists in data integrity (e.g., reliability, usefulness)? What is the mitigation plan?
- What other information will impact the nature, timing, and extent of the data analysis?

Once the purpose of the data request is determined and scoped, as well as any risks and assumptions documented, the next step is to determine whom to ask and specifically what is needed.

Step 2: Obtain the Data

- How will data be requested and/or obtained? Do you have access to the data yourself, or do you need to request a database administrator or the information systems department to provide the data for you?
- If you need to request the data, is there a standard data request form that you should use? From whom do you request the data?
- Where are the data located in the financial or other related systems?
- What specific data are needed (tables and fields)?
- What tools will be used to perform data analytic tests or procedures and why?

Obtaining the Data via a Data Request

Determining not only what data are needed, but also which tool will be used to test and process the data will aid the database administrator in providing the data to you in the most accessible format.

It is also necessary to specify the format in which you would like to receive the data; it is often preferred to receive data in a flat file (i.e., if the data you requested reside in multiple tables or different databases, they should be combined into one file without any hierarchy or relationships built in), with the first row containing column headings (names of the fields requested), and each subsequent row containing data that correspond with the column headings. Subtotals, breaks, and subheadings complicate data cleaning and should not be included.[4]

In a later chapter, you will be provided a deep dive into the audit data standards (ADSs) developed by the American Institute of Certified Public Accountants (AICPA).[5] The aim of the ADSs is to alleviate some of the headaches associated with requesting data for audits by providing a guide to standardize audit data requests and the format in which the data are provided from the company being audited to the auditor. These include the following:

1. Order-to-Cash subledger standards.
2. Procure-to-Pay subledger standards.
3. Inventory subledger standards.
4. General Ledger standards.

While the ADSs provide an opportunity for standardization, they are voluntary. Regardless of whether your request for data will conform to the standards, a **data request form** template can make communication easier between data requestor and provider.

---

[4]T. Singleton, "What Every IT Auditor Should Know about Data Analytics," n.d., from http://www.isaca .org/Journal/archives/2013/Volume-6/Pages/What-Every-IT-Auditor-Should-Know-About-Data-Analytics .aspx#2.

[5]For a description of the audit data standards, please see this website: https://www.aicpa.org/interestareas/ frc/assuranceadvisoryservices/pages/assuranceandadvisory.aspx.

Example Standard Data Request Form:[6]

Requestor Name:	
Requestor Contact Number:	
Requestor Email Address:	
Please provide a description of the information needed (indicate which tables and which fields you require):	
What will the information be used for?	
Frequency (circle one)	One-Off Annually Termly Other:_____
Format you wish the data to be delivered in (circle one):	Spreadsheet Text File Word Document Other: _____
Request Date:	
Required Date:	
Intended Audience:	
Customer (if not requestor):	

Once the data are received, you can move on to the transformation phase of the ETL process. The next step is to ensure that the data that have been extracted are complete and correct.

Obtaining the Data Yourself

If you have direct access to the database or information system that holds all the data you need, you may not need to go through a formal data request process, and you can simply extract the data yourself.

After identifying the goal of the data analysis project in the first step of the IMPACT cycle, you can follow a similar process to how you would request the data if you are going to extract it yourself:

1. Identify the tables that contain the information you need. You can do this by looking through the data dictionary or the relationship model.
2. Identify which attributes, specifically, hold the information you need in each table.
3. Identify how those tables are related to each other.

[6]R&M Data Request Form—Template, Gloucestershire, n.d. Retrieved October 31, 2016, from http://www.gloucestershire.gov.uk/media/word/n/t/datarequestform.doc.

Once you have identified the data you need, you can start gathering the information. There are a variety of methods that you could take to retrieve the data. Two will be explained briefly here—SQL and Excel—and there will be a deep dive into these methods in Labs 2-1 and 2-2 at the end of the chapter using Sláinte data.

1. **SQL:** "Structured Query Language" (SQL, pronounced sequel) can be used to create, update, and delete records and tables in databases, but we will focus on using SQL to extract data—that is, to select the precise attributes and records that fit the criteria of our data analysis goal. Using SQL, we can combine data from one or more tables and organize it in a way that is more intuitive than the way it is stored in the relational database. A firm understanding of the data—the tables, how they are related, and their respective primary and foreign keys—is integral to extracting the data.

    Typically, data should be stored in the database and analyzed in another tool such as Excel or Tableau. However, you can choose to extract only the portion of the data that you wish to analyze via SQL instead of extracting full tables and transforming the data in Excel or Tableau.

    One of the most useful ways to extract data from more than one table in SQL is by using a type of join clause. Joins rely on the structure of normalized relational databases that have tables related through primary keys and foreign keys. If you intend to extract data from two tables that are related, you simply have to identify the two fields that the tables have in common, and create the join based on that relationship. Referencing Exhibit 2-1, the Sláinte Procure-to-Pay Database Schema, if you intended to extract data from both the FGI_Product table and the Sales_Subset table, you would create your join based on the common fields of Product_Code in each table. The code would be written as follows:

```
FROM FGI_Product
INNER JOIN Sales_Subset
ON FGI_Product.Product_Code = Sales_Subset.Product_Code
```

    By inserting the FROM, INNER JOIN, and ON clauses into a SQL query in the pattern described above, you can add any fields that you wish to view from either of the tables to the SELECT clause. The generic pattern of the FROM, INNER JOIN, and ON clauses is as follows:

```
FROM table1
INNER JOIN table2
ON table1.primarykey = table2.foreignkey
```

    There is more description about writing queries and a chance to practice creating joins in Lab 2-2.

    Excel: The tables that contain the data you need can also be extracted in whole into Excel and worked with directly in a spreadsheet. The advantage of this is that further analysis will almost certainly be done in Excel, so it could be beneficial to have all the data readily available for further questions to drill down into once the initial question is answered. Understanding the primary key and foreign key relationships is also integral to working with the data directly in Excel.

    Sometimes, your data are stored directly in Excel instead of a database. In this case, you can also use Excel functions and formulas to combine data from multiple Excel tables into one table, similar to how you can join data with SQL in Access or another relational database. One of Excel's most useful tools for looking up data from two separate tables and matching them based on a matching primary key/foreign key relationship is the

VLookup function. There are a variety of ways that the VLookup function can be used, but for extracting and transforming data it is best used to add a column to a table. Using a similar example from the SQL Join explanation above, assume that your data for the three tables (FGI_Product, Sales_Subset, and Customer_Table) exist in three different spreadsheets of the same Excel workbook. If you wished to view the actual Product_ Description associated with each Product_Code in the Sales_Subset table, you could use VLookup to match the foreign key of Product_Code in the Sales_Subset table to the primary key, Product_Code, in the FGI_Product table, and have the corresponding Product_ Description returned.

When you type the VLookup formula into Excel, the arguments are =VLOOKUP(lookup value, table_array, col_index_num, [range lookup]). In our example, this function would be typed into the spreadsheet holding the Sales_Subset information, and it would be used to look up and return the Product_Description associated with each Product_Code in the Sales_Subset table.

- The **lookup_value** is the foreign key you wish to look up; in our example, you would reference the Product_Code in the Sales_Subset table. This is a single-cell reference.
- The **table_array** is the table that contains the corresponding primary key; in this instance, it is the FGI_Product table. VLookup will always look in the first column of this table_array to find a value that matches the foreign key selected in the lookup_ value argument. This works well when data are well-organized with a primary key situated in the first column of a table. In this example, you would select the entire set of data in the FGI_Product table.
- **Col_Index_Num** refers to the column in your selected table_array that contains the data you wish to view. In other words, if you were to manually match Product_Codes between the two tables, you would look at the foreign key in the Sales_Subset table, navigate to the FGI_Product table to find its match, then run your eyes across the same row to locate the corresponding Product_Description. VLookup will do the very same thing—the first two arguments represent the match, and this argument indicates that you would like the function to return the Product_Description. Product_Description is located in the second column of the FGI_Product table, so you would enter a number 2.
- **[range_lookup]** has two options, either FALSE or TRUE. The default is TRUE, so whenever you want to match data based on an exact match (not an approximate or near match), you need to type in FALSE.

TRANSFORMATION

Step 3: Validating the Data for Completeness and Integrity

Anytime data are moved from one location to another, it is possible that some of the data could have been lost during the extraction. It is critical to ensure that the extracted data are complete (that the data you wish to analyze were extracted fully) and that the integrity of the data remains (that none of the data have been manipulated or tampered with during the extraction). Being able to validate the data successfully requires you to not only have the technical skill to perform the task, but also to know your data well. If you know what to reasonably expect from the data in the extraction (How many records should have been extracted? What are some checksums you can rely on to ensure the data is complete and hasn't been tampered with?), then you have a higher likelihood of identifying any errors or issues from the extraction. The following four steps should be completed to validate the data after extraction:

1. *Compare the number of records* that were extracted to the number of records in the source database. This will give you a quick snapshot into whether any data were skipped or didn't extract properly due to an error or datatype mismatch. This is a critical first step, but it will not provide information about the data themselves other than ensuring that the record counts match.
2. *Compare descriptive statistics for numeric fields:* Calculating the minimums, maximums, averages, and medians will help ensure that the numeric data were extracted completely.
3. *Validate Date/Time fields* in the same way as numeric fields by converting the datatype to numeric and running descriptive statistic comparisons.
4. *Compare string limits for text fields:* Text fields are unlikely to cause an issue if you extracted your data into Excel because Excel allows a maximum character number of 32,767 characters. However, if you extracted your data into a tool that does limit the number of characters in a string, you will want to compare these limits to the source database's limits per field to ensure that you haven't cut off any characters.

If an error is found, depending on the size of the dataset, you may be able to easily find the missing or erroneous data by scanning the information with your eyes. However, if the dataset is large, or if the error is difficult to find, it may be easiest to go back to the extraction and examine how the data were extracted, fix any errors in the SQL code, and re-run the extraction.

Step 4: Cleaning the Data

Once the data have been validated, the data will likely need to be cleaned. The following four items are some of the more common ways that data will need to be cleaned after extraction and validation:

1. *Remove headings or subtotals:* Depending on the extraction technique used and the file type of the extraction, it is possible that your data could contain headings or subtotals that are not useful for analysis. Of course, these issues could be overcome in the extraction steps of the ETL process if you are careful to request the data in the correct format or to only extract exactly the data you need.
2. *Clean leading zeroes and nonprintable characters:* Sometimes data will contain leading zeroes or "phantom" (nonprintable) characters. This will happen particularly when numbers or dates were stored as text in the source database but need to be analyzed as numbers. Nonprintable characters can be white spaces, page breaks, line breaks, tabs, etc., and can be summarized as characters that our human eyes can't see, but that the computer interprets as a part of the string. These can cause trouble when joining data because, while two strings may look identical to our eyes, the computer will read the nonprintable characters and won't find a match.
3. *Format negative numbers:* If there are negative numbers in your dataset, ensure that the formatting will work for your analysis. If your data contain negative numbers formatted in parentheses and you would prefer this formatting to be as a negative sign, this needs to be corrected and consistent.
4. *Correct inconsistencies across data, in general:* If the source database did not enforce certain rules around data entry, it is possible that there are inconsistencies across the data—for example, if there is a state field, Arkansas could be formatted as "AR," "Ark," "Ar.," etc. These will need to be replaced with a common value before you begin your analysis if you are interested in grouping data geographically.

LOADING

Step 5: Loading the Data for Data Analysis

If the extraction and transformation steps have been done well by the time you reach this step, the loading part of the ETL process should be the simplest step. It is so simple, in fact, that if your goal is to do your analysis in Excel and you have already transformed and cleaned your data in Excel, you are finished. There should be no additional loading necessary.

However, it is possible that Excel is not the last step for analysis. The data analysis technique you plan to implement, the subject matter of the business questions you intend to answer, and the way in which you wish to communicate results will all drive the choice of which tool you use to perform your analysis.

Throughout the text, you will be introduced to a variety of different tools to use for analyzing data beyond Access and Excel. These will include Tableau, Weka, and IDEA. As these tools are introduced to you, you will learn how to load data into them.

 PROGRESS CHECK

5. Describe two different methods for obtaining data for analysis.
6. What are four common issues with data that must be fixed before analysis can take place?

Summary

- The first step in the IMPACT cycle is to identify the questions that you intend to answer through your data analysis project. Once a data analysis problem or question has been identified, the next step in the IMPACT cycle is mastering the data, which can be broken down to mean obtaining the data needed and preparing it for analysis.
- In order to obtain the right data, it is important to have a firm grasp of what data are available to you and how that information is stored.
  - Data are often stored in a relational database, which helps to ensure that an organization's data are complete and to avoid redundancy. Relational databases are made up of tables with uniquely identified records (this is done through primary keys) and are related through the usage of foreign keys.
- To obtain the data, you will either have access to extract the data yourself or you will need to request the data from a database administrator or the information systems team. If the latter is the case, you will complete a data request form, indicating exactly which data you need and why.
- Once you have the data, they will need to be validated for completeness and integrity— that is, you will need to ensure that all of the data you need were extracted and that all data are correct. Sometimes when data are extracted, some formatting or sometimes even entire records will get lost, resulting in inaccuracies. Correcting the errors and cleaning the data is an integral step in mastering the data.
- Finally, after the data have been cleaned, there may be one last step of mastering the data, which is to load them into the tool that will be used for analysis. Often, the cleaning and correcting of data occur in Excel and the analysis will also be done in Excel. In this case,

there is no need to load the data elsewhere. However, if you intend to do more rigorous statistical analysis than Excel provides, or if you intend to do more robust data visualization than can be done in Excel, it may be necessary to load the data into another tool following the transformation process.

Key Words

composite primary key (*42*)   A special case of a primary key that exists in linking tables. The composite primary key is made up of the two primary keys in the table that it is linking.

data dictionary (*43*)   Centralized repository of descriptions for all of the data attributes of a dataset.

data request form (*45*)   A method for obtaining data if you do not have access to obtain the data directly yourself.

descriptive attributes (*42*)   Attributes that exist in relational databases that are neither primary nor foreign keys. These attributes provide business information, but are not required to build a database. An example would be "Company Name" or "Employee Address."

ETL (*44*)   The extract, transform, and load process that is integral to mastering the data.

flat file (*41*)   A means of storing data in one place, such as in an Excel spreadsheet, as opposed to storing the data in multiple tables, such as in a relational database.

foreign key (*42*)   An attribute that exists in relational databases in order to carry out the relationship between two tables. This does not serve as the "unique identifier" for each record in a table. These must be identified when mastering the data from a relational database in order to extract the data correctly from more than one table.

mastering the data (*40*)   The second step in the IMPACT cycle; it involves identifying and obtaining the data needed for solving the data analysis problem, as well as cleaning and preparing the data for analysis.

primary key (*41*)   An attribute that is required to exist in each table of a relational database and serves as the "unique identifier" for each record in a table.

relational database (*41*)   A means of storing data in order to ensure that the data are complete, not redundant, and to help enforce business rules. Relational databases also aid in communication and integration of business processes across an organization.

⊘ ANSWERS TO PROGRESS CHECKS

1. The unique identifier of the Employee table is [EmployeeID], and the unique identifier of the Purchase Order table is [PO No.]. The Purchase Order table contains the foreign key.

2. The foreign key attribute that doesn't appear to belong in the Suppliers table is [Supplier Type]. This attribute probably relates to the Supplier Type table. The data in this table will be descriptive, categorical data about the suppliers.

3. The purpose of the primary key is to uniquely identify each record in a table. The purpose of a foreign key is to create a relationship between two tables. The purpose of a descriptive attribute is to provide meaningful information about each record in a table. Descriptive attributes aren't required for a database to run, but they are necessary for people to gain business information about the data stored in their databases.

4. Data dictionaries provide descriptions of the function and data contained in each column (attribute) of a database. Data dictionaries are especially important when databases contain several different tables and many different attributes in order to help analysts identify the information they need to perform their analysis.

5. Depending on the level of security afforded to a business analyst, she can either obtain data directly from the database herself or she can request the data. When obtaining data herself, the analyst must have access to the raw data in the database and a firm knowledge of SQL and data extraction techniques. When requesting the data, the analyst doesn't need the same level of extraction skills, but she still needs to be familiar with the data enough in order to identify which tables and attributes contain the information she requires.

6. Four common issues that must be fixed are removing headings or subtotals, cleaning leading zeroes or nonprintable characters, formatting negative numbers, and correcting inconsistencies across the data.

Mc Graw Hill Education connect

Multiple Choice Questions

1. Mastering the data can also be described via the ETL process. The ETL process stands for:
   a. Extract, total, and load data.
   b. Enter, transform, and load data.
   c. Extract, transform, and load data.
   d. Enter, total, and load data.

2. The goal of the ETL process is to:
   a. Identify which approach to data analytics should be used.
   b. Load the data into a relational database for storage.
   c. Communicate the results and insights found through the analysis.
   d. Identify and obtain the data needed for solving the problem.

3. The advantages of storing data in a relational database include which of the following?
   a. Help in enforcing business rules.
   b. Increased information redundancy.
   c. Integrating business processes.
   d. All of the above are advantages of a relational database.
   e. Only A and B.
   f. Only B and C.
   g. Only A and C.

4. The purpose of transforming data is:
   a. To validate the data for completeness and integrity.
   b. To load the data into the appropriate tool for analysis.
   c. To obtain the data from the appropriate source.
   d. To identify which data are necessary to complete the analysis.

5. Which attribute is required to exist in each table of a relational database and serves as the "unique identifier" for each record in a table?
   a. Foreign key
   b. Unique identifier
   c. Primary key
   d. Key attribute

6. The metadata that describes each attribute in a database is which of the following?

    a. Composite primary key

    b. Data dictionary

    c. Descriptive attributes

    d. Flat file

7. As mentioned in the chapter, which of the following is *not* a common way that data will need to be cleaned after extraction and validation?

    a. Remove headings and subtotals.

    b. Format negative numbers.

    c. Clean up trailing zeroes.

    d. Correct inconsistencies across data.

8. Why is Supplier ID considered to be a primary key for a Supplier table?

    a. It contains a unique identifier for each supplier.

    b. It is a 10-digit number.

    c. It can either be for a vendor or miscellaneous provider.

    d. It is used to identify different supplier categories.

9. What are attributes that exist in a relational database that are neither primary nor foreign keys?

    a. Nondescript attributes

    b. Descriptive attributes

    c. Composite key

    d. Relational table attributes

10. Which of these is *not* included in the five steps of the ETL process?

    a. Determine the purpose and scope of the data request.

    b. Obtain the data.

    c. Validate the data for completeness and integrity.

    d. Scrub the data.

Discussion Questions

1. The advantages of a relational database include limiting the amount of redundant data that are stored in a database. Why is this an important advantage? What can go wrong when redundant data are stored?

2. The advantages of a relational database include integrating business processes. Why is it preferable to integrate business processes in one information system, rather than store different business process data in separate, isolated databases?

3. Even though it is preferable to store data in a relational database, storing data across separate tables can make data analysis cumbersome. Describe three reasons why it is worth the trouble to store data in a relational database.

4. Among the advantages of using a relational database is enforcing business rules. Based on your understanding of how the structure of a relational database helps prevent data redundancy and other advantages, how does the primary key/foreign key relationship structure help enforce a business rule that indicates that a company shouldn't process any purchase orders from suppliers who don't exist in the database?

5. What is the purpose of a data dictionary? Identify four different attributes that could be stored in a data dictionary, and describe the purpose of each.

6. In the ETL process, the first step is extracting the data. When you are obtaining the data yourself, what are the steps to identifying the data that you need to extract?

7. In the ETL process, if the analyst does not have the security permissions to access the data directly, then he or she will need to fill out a data request form. While this doesn't necessarily require the analyst to know extraction techniques, why does the analyst still need to understand the raw data very well in order to complete the data request?

8. In the ETL process, when an analyst is completing the data request form, there are a number of fields that the analyst is required to complete. Why do you think it is important for the analyst to indicate the frequency of the report? How do you think that would affect what the database administrator does in the extraction?

9. Regarding the data request form, why do you think it is important to the database administrator to know the purpose of the request? What would be the importance of the "To be used in" and "intended audience" fields?

10. In the ETL process, one important step to process when transforming the data is to work with NULL, N/A, and zero values in the dataset. If you have a field of quantitative data (e.g., number of years each individual in the table has held a full-time job), what would be the effect of the following?

   a. Transforming NULL and N/A values into blanks

   b. Transforming NULL and N/A values into zeroes

   c. Deleting records that have NULL and N/A values from your dataset

   (*Hint:* Think about the impact on different aggregate functions, such as COUNT and AVERAGE.)

Problems

The following problems correspond to the **College Scorecard** data. You should be able to answer each question by just looking at the data dictionary (CollegeScorecard_ DataDictionary.pdf) included in Appendix A, but if you would like to use the raw data, feel free to do so (CollegeScorecard_RawData.txt).

1. Which attributes from the College Scorecard data would you need to compare cost of attendance across types of institutions (public, private non-profit, or private for-profit)??

2. Which attributes from the College Scorecard data would you need to compare SAT scores across types of institutions (public, private non-profit, or private for-profit)?

3. Which attributes from the College Scorecard data would you need to compare levels of diversity across types of institutions (public, private non-profit, or private for-profit)?

4. Which attributes from the College Scorecard data would you need to compare completion rate across types of institutions (public, private non-profit, or private for-profit)?

5. Which attributes from the College Scorecard data would you need to compare the percentage of students who receive federal loans at universities above and below the median cost of attendance across all institutions (public, private non-profit, or private for-profit)?

6. Which attributes from the College Scorecard data would you need to determine if different regions of the country have significantly different costs of attendance?

7. Use the College Scorecard data to determine if different regions of the country have significantly different costs of attendance (same as Problem 6 above) and fill out a data request form in order to extract the appropriate data. Use the template from the chapter as a guide.

8. If you were analyzing the levels of diversity across public and private institutions using the College Scorecard data, how would you define diversity in terms of the data provided? Would it be beneficial to combine fields?

9. If you were conducting a data analysis in order to compare the percentage of students who receive federal loans at universities above and below the median cost of attendance across all institutions, you would be conducting several steps in your analysis. What question needs to be answered first in order to complete the analysis? Come up with a test plan to address the subsequent questions.

Answers to Multiple Choice Questions

1. C
2. D
3. G
4. A
5. C
6. B
7. C
8. A
9. B
10. D

Appendix A

CollegeScorecard Dataset

Description of Variables/Attributes

UNITID—a unique identifier for the institution

INSTNM—institution name

CITY—city

STABBR—state postcode

CONTROL—1 = Public. 2 = Private nonprofit. 3 = Private for-profit

CCBASIC—Carnegie Classification, basic:

    −2 Not applicable

    0 (Not classified)

    1 Associate's Colleges: High Transfer-High Traditional

    2 Associate's Colleges: High Transfer-Mixed Traditional/Nontraditional

    3 Associate's Colleges: High Transfer-High Nontraditional

    4 Associate's Colleges: Mixed Transfer/Vocational & Technical-High Traditional

    5 Associate's Colleges: Mixed Transfer/Vocational & Technical-Mixed Traditional/Nontraditional

    6 Associate's Colleges: Mixed Transfer/Vocational & Technical-High Nontraditional

    7 Associate's Colleges: High Vocational & Technical-High Traditional

    8 Associate's Colleges: High Vocational & Technical-Mixed Traditional/Nontraditional

    9 Associate's Colleges: High Vocational & Technical-High Nontraditional

    10 Special Focus Two-Year: Health Professions

    11 Special Focus Two-Year: Technical Professions

    12 Special Focus Two-Year: Arts & Design

    13 Special Focus Two-Year: Other Fields

    14 Baccalaureate/Associate's Colleges: Associate's Dominant

    15 Doctoral Universities: Highest Research Activity

    16 Doctoral Universities: Higher Research Activity

    17 Doctoral Universities: Moderate Research Activity

18 Master's Colleges & Universities: Larger Programs

19 Master's Colleges & Universities: Medium Programs

20 Master's Colleges & Universities: Small Programs

21 Baccalaureate Colleges: Arts & Sciences Focus

22 Baccalaureate Colleges: Diverse Fields

23 Baccalaureate/Associate's Colleges: Mixed Baccalaureate/Associate's

24 Special Focus Four-Year: Faith-Related Institutions

25 Special Focus Four-Year: Medical Schools & Centers

26 Special Focus Four-Year: Other Health Professions Schools

27 Special Focus Four-Year: Engineering Schools

28 Special Focus Four-Year: Other Technology-Related Schools

29 Special Focus Four-Year: Business & Management Schools

30 Special Focus Four-Year: Arts, Music & Design Schools

31 Special Focus Four-Year: Law Schools

32 Special Focus Four-Year: Other Special Focus Institutions

33 Tribal Colleges

ADM_RATE – admission rate

SAT_AVG – average equivalent SAT of students admitted

UGDS – enrollment of undergraduate certificate/degree-seeking students

UGDS_WHITE – total share of enrollment of undergraduates who are white

UGDS_BLACK – total share of enrollment of undergraduates who are black

UGDS_HISP – total share of enrollment of undergraduates who are Hispanic

UGDS_ASIAN – total share of enrollment of undergraduates who are Asian

UGDS_AIAN – total share of enrollment of undergraduates who are American Indian/Alaska Native

UGDS_NHPI – total share of enrollment of undergraduates who are Native Hawaiian/Pacific Islander

UGDS_2MOR – total share of enrollment of undergraduates who are two or more races

UGDS_NRA – total share of enrollment of undergraduates who are non-resident aliens

UGDS_UNKN – total share of enrollment of undergraduates whose race is unknown

PPTUG_EF – share of undergraduate degree/certificate-seeking students who are part-time

NPT4_PUB – Average net price for Title IV institutions (public)

NPT4_PRIV – Average net price for Title IV institutions (private for-profit and nonprofit)

COSTT4_A – Average cost of attendance

TUITFTE – Net tuition revenue per full-time equivalent student

INEXPFTE – Instructional expenditures per full-time equivalent student

PFTFAC – Proportion of faculty that is full-time

PCTPELL – Percentage of undergraduates who receive a Pell Grant

C150_4 – Completion rate for first-time, full-time students at four-year institutions (6 year)

PFTFTUG1_EF – Share of undergraduate students who are first-time, full-time, degree seeking undergraduates

RET_FT4 – First-time, full-time student retention rate at four-year institutions

PCTFLOAN – Percent of all federal undergraduates receiving a federal student loan

One of the biggest challenges you face with data analysis is getting the right data. You may have the best questions in the world, but if there are no data available to support your hypothesis, you will have difficulty providing value. Additionally, there are instances in which the IT workers may be reluctant to share data with you. They may send incomplete data, the wrong data, or completely ignore your request. Be persistent, and you may have to look for creative ways to find insight with an incomplete picture.

Company summary

Sláinte is a fictional brewery that has recently gone through big changes. Sláinte sells six different products. The brewery has only recently expanded its business to distributing from one state to nine states, and now its business has begun stabilizing after the expansion. With that stability comes a need for better analysis. You have been hired by Sláinte to help management better understand the company's sales data and provide input for its strategic decisions.

Data

- Data request form
- Sláinte dataset

Technique

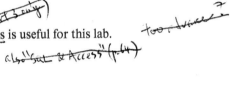

- Some experience with spreadsheets and PivotTables is useful for this lab.

Software needed

- Word processor
- Excel
- Screen capture tool (Windows: Snipping Tool; Mac: Cmd + Shift + 4)

In this lab, you will:

Part 1: Identify appropriate questions and develop a hypothesis for each question.

Part 2: Generate a request for data.

Part 3: Analyze the data you receive.

Part 1: Identify the Questions

One of Sláinte's first priorities is to identify its areas of success as well as areas of potential improvement. Your manager has asked you to focus specifically on sales data at this point. This includes data related to sales orders, products, and customers.

Q1. Given that you are new and trying to get a grasp on Sláinte's operations, **list three questions related to sales** that would help you begin your analysis. For example, *how many products were sold in each state?*

Q2. Now **hypothesize the answers** to each of the questions. Remember, your answers don't have to be correct at this point. They will help you understand what type of data you are looking for. For example: *500 in Missouri, 6,000 in Pennsylvania, 4,000 in New York, etc.*

Q3. Finally, for each question, **identify the specific tables and attributes** that are needed to answer your questions. For example, to answer the question about state sales, you would need the [State] attribute that is most likely located in the [Customer] master table as well as a [Quantity Sold] attribute in a [Sales] table. If you had access to store or distribution center location data, you may also look for a [State] field there as well.

Part 2: Generate a Request for Data

Now that you've identified the data you need for your analysis, complete a data request form.

1. Open the **Data Request Form**.
2. Enter your **contact information**.
3. In the **description field**, identify the tables that you'd like to analyze, along with the time periods (e.g., past month, past year, etc.). *Note:* It's almost always better to ask for complete tables rather than limit your request to specific attributes; there may be useful information that you'll want later.
4. Select a **frequency**. In this case, this is a "One-off request."
5. Enter a **request date** (today) and a **required date** (one week from today).
6. Choose a **format** (spreadsheet).
7. Indicate **what the information will be used for** in the appropriate box (internal analysis).
8. Take a screenshot (label it 2-1A) of your completed form.

Part 3: Perform an Analysis of the Data

After a few days, Rachel, an IT worker, responds to your request. She gives you the following tables and attributes:

LAB EXHIBIT 2-1A

Sales_Subset Table	
Attribute	**Description of Attribute**
Sales_Order_ID (PK)	Unique identifier for each sales order
Sales_Order_Date	The date of the sales order, regardless of the date the order is entered
Sales_Employee_ID (FK)	Unique identifier (from Employee_Listing table) for person who created the record
Customer_ID (FK)	Unique identifier (from Customer_Master_Listing table) of the customer who placed the order
Product_Code (FK)	Unique identifier (from Finished_Good_Products table) for each sales product
Sales_Order_Quantity_Sold	Sales order line quantity
Product_Sale_Price	Sales order line price per unit

FGI_Product Table	
Attribute	**Description of Attribute**
Product_Code (PK)	Unique identifier for each product
Product_Description	Product description (plain English) to indicate the name or other identifying characteristics of the product
Product_Sale_Price	Price per unit of the associated product

Customer Table	
Attribute	**Description of Attribute**
Customer_ID (PK)	Unique identifier for each customer
Business_Name	The name of the customer
Customer_Address	The physical street address of the customer
Customer_City	The physical city where the customer is located
Customer_St	The physical state where the customer is located
Customer_Zip	The zip code of the city where the customer is physically located

You may notice that while there are a few attributes that may be useful in your sales analysis, the list may be incomplete and be missing several values. This is normal with data requests.

Q4. Take a moment and **identify any attributes that you are missing** from your original request.

Q5. **Evaluate your original questions and responses.** How do the data alter the questions? Can you get a similar answer using the data provided by Rachel?

End of Lab

Lab 2-2 Use PivotTables to Denormalize and Analyze the Data

comprehensive, but hard.

Efficient relational databases contain normalized data. That is, each table contains only data that are relevant to the object, and tables' relationships are defined with primary key/foreign key pairs. For example, each record in a customer table is assigned a unique ID (e.g., customer 152883), and the remaining attributes (e.g., customer address) describe that customer. In a sales order table, the only customer data you find is a foreign key pointing to the customer (e.g., customer 152883) we are selling merchandise to. The foreign key value connects the sales order record to the customer record and allows any or all of the linked attributes to appear on the sales order form or report.

With Data Analytics, efficient databases are not as helpful. Rather, we would like to "denormalize" the data or combine all of the related data into one large file that can be easily evaluated for summary statistics or be used to create meaningful PivotTables. Excel calls this the Internal Data Model. In Access, we create a query. This lab will take you through this process. This lab will help you recognize how to create relationships between related spreadsheets in Excel using Excel's Internal Data Model. The Internal Data Model is available in Excel for PC versions from 2013 onward. This lab is in preparation for using the Internal Data Model in future labs to transform data, as well as to aid in understanding of primary and foreign key relationships.

Company summary

Sláinte is a fictional brewery that has recently gone through big changes. Sláinte sells six different products. The brewery has only recently expanded its business to distributing from one state to nine states, and now its business has begun stabilizing after the expansion. With that stability comes a need for better analysis. One of Sláinte's first priorities is to identify its areas of success, as well as areas of potential improvement.

Data

- Sláinte dataset

Technique

(in Part 3 only)

- Some experience with relational databases, spreadsheets, and PivotTables is useful for this lab.

Software needed

- Excel
- Access *(& SQL)* → p. 64 *(can skip)*
- Screen capture tool (Windows: Snipping Tool; Mac: Cmd + Shift + 4)

In this lab, you will:

Part 1: Identify appropriate questions and develop a hypothesis for each question.

Part 2: Master your data and prepare it for analysis in Excel.

Part 3: Perform an analysis using PivotTables.

Part 4: Address and refine your results.

Part 5: Communicate your findings.

Part 1: Identify the Questions

Sláinte has brought you in to help determine potential areas for sales growth in the next year. Additionally, management has noticed that the company's margins aren't as high as they had budgeted and would like you to help identify some areas where they could improve their pricing, marketing, or strategy. Specifically, they would like to know how many of each product were sold.

> Q1. Given Sláinte's request, **identify the data attributes and tables** needed to answer the question.

Part 2: Master the Data: Prepare Data for Analysis in Excel

The requested Sláinte data are available in the Slainte_Subset.xlsx file and include the following tables and fields, presented in a UML diagram:

LAB EXHIBIT 2-2A

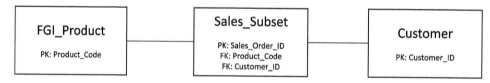

Depending on your desired analysis, there are a few alternative approaches that you could use to prepare the data for analysis.

Alternative 1: Do nothing.

If you are simply trying to calculate statistics or make comparisons using attributes within a **single table**, there is no need to transform the tables. Simply load the table, make sure the data are clean, and proceed to analysis.

For example, to find the total number of each item sold, you would need only the [Sales_Subset] table and its attributes [Product_Code] and [Sales_Order_Quantity_Sold].

> Q2. When would it be a good idea to use a single table?

Alternative 2: Use the Excel Internal Data Model.

For analyses that require **two or more tables**, you need to define the relationships in Excel before you can proceed with your analysis.

For example, if you want to find the total number of each item sold and show the product name instead of just the code, you would need [Sales_Order_Quantity_Sold] from the [Sales_Subset] table and [Product_Description] from the [FGI_Product] table. These two tables are joined together on the [Product_Code] primary/foreign key.

1. Open the **Slainte_Subset.xlsx** file.
2. Click the **Data** tab on the ribbon.
3. Click the **Relationships** button in the **Data Tools** section.
4. In the **Manage Relationships** window, click **New. . .**

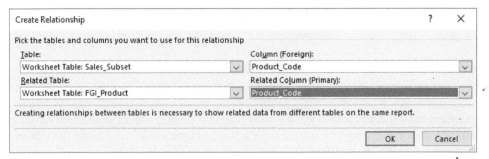

5. Create a relationship between [Sales_Subset] and [FGI_Product] as shown in Exhibit 2-2C. Start with the table that contains the foreign key, then choose the related table that contains the primary key. In this case:
   a. Table: [Sales_Subset]
   b. Related Table: [FGI_Product]
   c. Column (Foreign): [Product_Code]
   d. Related Column (Primary): [Product_Code]
6. Click **OK** to save the relationship. The window will close, and you will return to the **Manage Relationships** window. Click **New...**
7. Now create a relationship between [Sales_Subset] and [Customer]. In this case:
   a. **Table:** [Sales_Subset]
   b. **Related Table:** [Customer]
   c. **Column (Foreign):** [Customer_ID]
   d. **Related Column (Primary):** [Customer_ID]
8. Click **OK** to save the relationship.
9. Take a screenshot (label it 2-2A) of the **Manage Relationships** window with both relationships created.

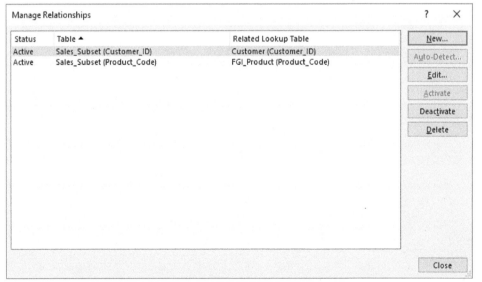

LAB EXHIBIT 2-2C
Complete Relationships
between Sales_Subset,
FGI_Product, and
Customer_Table

Source: Microsoft Excel 2016

10. Click **Close** in the **Manage Relationships** window to return to the spreadsheets. While the spreadsheets do not appear to have changed with the new relationships, we have created a powerful engine for analyzing our data. We will have access to any of the records and related fields in any of the tables without additional work, such as Find and Replace or VLookup.

11. Save your workbook as **Slainte_Relationships.xlsx**.

Q3. How comfortable are you with identifying primary key/foreign key relationships?

Alternative 3: Merging the data into a single table using Excel Query Editor:

While relationships are incredibly useful when dealing with multiple tables, there are times when it is useful to have all of the data together in one table. Both queries and PivotTables are much more straightforward when you don't have to continually define the relationships. The downside to working with a single table is that you must work with a larger file size and there are a lot of redundant data.

1. Create a **new blank spreadsheet** in Excel.
2. Click the **Data** tab on the ribbon.
3. Click the **Get Data** menu in the **Get & Transform Data** section.
4. Choose **From File > From Workbook**.
5. Locate the **Slainte_Subset.xlsx** file on your computer, and click **Open**.
6. In the **Navigator**, check **Select multiple items**, then check the three tables to import, shown in Exhibit 2-2D:
    a. [Customer]
    b. [FGI_Product]
    c. [Sales_Subset]

LAB EXHIBIT 2-2D
Select Multiple Tables to Join

Source: Microsoft Excel 2016

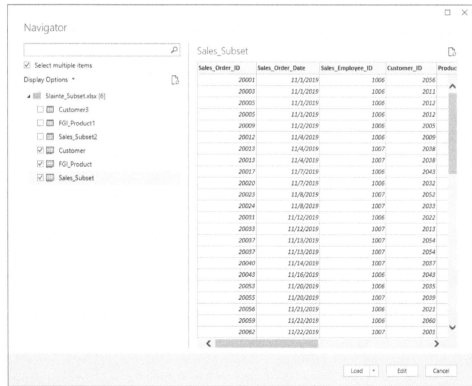

7. Click **Load**. The three tables will appear as queries in the **Queries & Connections** pane on the right side of the screen.
8. Double-click the **[Sales_Subset]** query to open the **Query Wizard**.
9. To merge the tables click the **Home** tab, then choose **Merge Queries** from the **Combine** section. A new **Merge** window will appear.
10. In the **Merge** window, the **[Sales_Subset]** query will appear at the top.

LAB EXHIBIT 2-2E
Select the Primary
and Foreign Keys in
the Merge Window to
Create a Large Table in
Excel's Query Editor

Source: Microsoft Excel 2016

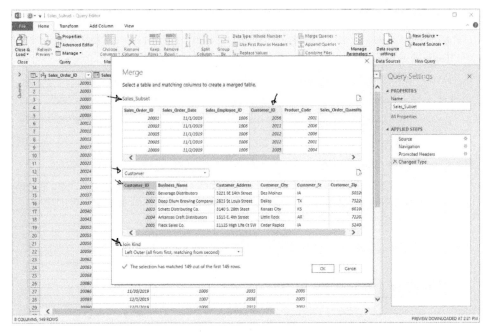

11. To join the **[Sales_Subset]** and **[Customer]** queries, do the following:
    a. Select the **[Customer]** query from the middle drop-down list.
    b. Click the **[Customer_ID]** column in both the **[Sales_Subset]** and **[Customer]** queries.
    c. From the **Join Kind** drop-down list, choose **Left Outer (all from first, matching from second)**. This means **[Sales_Subset].[Customer_ID]** will be identified as the foreign key.
    d. Click **OK** to return to the **Query Editor**.
    e. Double-click the newly added **[NewColumn]** attribute title and rename it **[Customer]**.
    f. Finally, click the **opposing arrows icon** next to the **[Customer]** column title. Select **Expand** and click **OK**. The customer attributes have now been added to the **[Sales_Subset]** query.

12. To join the **[Sales_Subset]** and **[FGI_Product]** queries, do the following:
    a. Select the **[FGI_Product]** query from the middle drop-down list.
    b. Click the **[Product_Code]** column in both the **[Sales_Subset]** and **[FGI_Product]** queries.
    c. From the **Join Kind** drop-down list, choose **Left Outer (all from first, matching from second)**. This means **[Sales_Subset].[Product_Code]** will be identified as the foreign key.
    d. Click **OK** to return to the **Query Editor**.
    e. Double-click the newly added **[NewColumn]** attribute title and rename it **[Product]**.
    f. Finally, click the **opposing arrows icon** next to the **[Product]** column title. Select **Expand** and click **OK**. The product attributes have now been added to the **[Sales_Subset]** query.

13. Maximize the **Query Editor** window, and take a screenshot (label it 2-2B).

14. Click **Close & Load** to return to Excel.

15. In the **Queries & Connections** pane on the right, right-click **[Sales_Subset]** and choose **Load To. . .**

16. In the **Import Data** window that appears, choose **Table** and click **OK**. Your new merged table now appears in your workbook.

17. Rename **[Sheet1]** to **[Sales_Order_Merge]**.

Note: You can also directly load your merged table into a PivotTable if that is the analysis you're going to perform.

18. Save your workbook as **Slainte_Merge.xlsx**.

Q4. Have you used the Query Editor in Excel before? Double-click the [Sales_Subset] query and click through the tabs on the ribbon. Which options do you think will be useful in the future?

Alternative 4: Use SQL queries in Access.

If you're familiar with how to write SQL queries, they can be very efficient. There are also instances where datasets will be too large for Excel, and Access or another query tool will be the only way to analyze the data effectively.

Analytics Tool: SQL Queries

SQL can be used to create tables, delete records, or edit databases, but we will primarily use SQL to query the database—that is, not to edit or manipulate the data, but to create different views of the data to help us answer business questions. There are four key phrases that are used in every query: SELECT fields, FROM table, WHERE criteria, GROUP BY aggregate.

- **SELECT** *indicates which attributes you wish to view. These can be columns that already exist in a table (such as Product_Code), or they can be mathematical expressions that already exist, such as the sum of the quantity sold. Use AS to give your expression a friendly name. For expressions, you write equations similar to an Excel function: SUM(Sales_Order_Quantity_Sold). When you select more than one column, put a comma between them.*

  For example:

  SELECT Product_Code, SUM(Sales_Order_Quantity_Sold)
  SELECT Product_Code, Sales_Order_Quantity_Sold*Product_Sale_Price AS Order_Total

- **FROM** *indicates which table you are pulling the fields in from. If you need to retrieve data from more than one table, you will use another SQL phrase: table JOIN table ON (foreignkey= primarykey).*

  For example:

  FROM Sales_Subset;
  FROM Sales_Subset JOIN Customer ON (Customer_ID=Customer_ID)

- **WHERE** *is used to filter your results on a specific value or range. Commonly, you will compare a field to a specific number (e.g., WHERE Customer_ID=2056) or text value in quotes (e.g., WHERE Product_Description="Pale Ale"). You can also filter on ranges such as dates (e.g., WHERE Sales_Order_Date BETWEEN #1/1/2019# AND #12/31/2019#). Use AND or OR to combine multiple filters*

  For example:

  WHERE Customer_ID=2056 AND Sales_Order_Date BETWEEN #1/1/2019# AND #12/31/2019#

- **GROUP BY** is used anytime you have an aggregate in your SELECT column; this will indicate how you want to categorize, or group, your data. In our example, we intend to group our aggregate by Product_Code. Without the GROUP BY command, you will see duplicate records in the query results.

    For example:

    GROUP BY Product_Code

1. Open the **Slainte_Subset.accdb** file.
2. Open the SQL editor by navigating to the **Create** tab on the ribbon.
3. Click **Query Design** to open the SQL Designer.
4. Click **Close** on the Show Table window.
5. In the top left corner, click **SQL** to open the SQL Editor.
6. The 3 lines of code in the examples of the SQL Key Word Tutorial 1 are the three lines that we will use to execute our report in SQL. In the SQL Editor, type the following lines of code:

    ```
    SELECT Sales_Subset.*, FGI_Product.*, Customer.*
    FROM Customer RIGHT JOIN (FGI_Product RIGHT JOIN Sales_Subset
    ON FGI_Product.Product_Code = Sales_Subset.Product_Code) ON
    Customer.Customer_ID = Sales_Subset.Customer_ID;
    ```

7. Click **Run** from the **Query Tools** > **Design** tab on the Ribbon to view your combined query output.
8. Take a screenshot (label it 2-2C).
9. Save your query as **Slainte_Merge**. From here you can either click **External Data** > **Excel** in Access to export your query as an Excel file OR close your database, open Excel and choose **Data** > **Get Data** > **From Database** > **From Microsoft Access Database**, then navigate to your database and import the query.

Part 3: Perform an Analysis Using PivotTables and Queries

Now that the data have been organized, you're ready for some basic analysis. Given the sales data, management has asked you to prepare a report showing the total number of each item sold each month between January and April 2020. This means that we should create a PivotTable with a column for each month, a row for each product, and the sum of the quantity sold where the two intersect.

Analytics Tool: Excel PivotTables

*PivotTables allow you to quickly summarize large amounts of data. In Excel, click **Insert** > **PivotTable**, choose your data source, then click the checkmark next to or drag your fields to the appropriate boxes in the PivotTable Fields pane to identify filters, columns, rows, or values. You can easily move attributes from one pane to another to quickly "pivot" your data. Here is a brief description of each section:*

- *Rows: Show the main item of interest. You usually want master data here, such as customers, products, or accounts.*
- *Columns: Slice the data into categories or buckets. Most commonly, columns are used for time (e.g., years, quarters, months, dates).*

- **Values:** *This area represents the meat of your data. Any measure that you would like to count, sum, average, or otherwise aggregate should be placed here. The aggregated values will combine all records that match a given row and column.*

- **Filters:** *Placing a field in the Filters area will allow you to filter the data based on that field, but it will not show that field in the data. For example, if you wanted to filter based on a date, but didn't care to view a particular date, you could use this area of the field list. With more recent versions of Excel, there are improved methods for filtering, but this legacy feature is still functional.*

1. From any of the files you created in Part 2, click the **Insert tab** on the ribbon.
2. Click **PivotTable** in the **Tables** section.
3. In the **Create PivotTable** window click **Use this workbook's Data Model**. *Note:* If you have only one table, choose **Select a table or range** and choose your sheet.
4. Click **OK** to create the PivotTable. A **PivotTable Fields** pane appears on the right. *Note:* If at any point while working with your PivotTable, your PivotTable Fields list disappears, you can make it reappear by ensuring that your active cell is within the PivotTable itself. If the Field List still doesn't reappear, navigate to the Analyze tab in the Ribbon, and select Field List.
5. Click the **arrow toggle** next to each table to show the available fields. If you don't see your three tables, click the **All** option directly below the **PivotTable Fields** pane title.
6. Take a screenshot (label it 2-2D).
7. Because you defined relationships or merged the tables in Part 2, you can drag any of the attributes from your list of fields to their respective Filters, Columns, Rows, or Values. Do that now:
   a. **Columns: [Sales_Order_Date] (Month)** from **[Sales_Subset].** *Note*: When you add a date, Excel will automatically try to group the data by Year, Quarter, etc. For now, remove the other options.
   b. **Rows: [Product_Description]** from **[FGI_Products].**
   c. **Values: [Sales_Order_Quantity_Sold]** from **[Sales_Subset].**
   d. **Filters: None.**
8. Finally, to show only the four months from January to April, click the drop-down arrow next to **Column Labels** and uncheck **Nov** and **Dec.**
9. *Optional step:* Clean up your PivotTable. Rename labels and the title of the report to something more useful.
10. Take a screenshot (label it 2-2E).
11. Save a copy of your workbook as **Slainte_Pivot.xlsx.**

To perform a similar, but less flexible analysis in Access, do the following:

1. Open your **Slainte_Subset.accdb** file from Part 2.
2. Click **Create > Query Design**. Close the window that appears.
3. Click **SQL View** in the top-left corner.
4. Enter the following query:

```
SELECT Product_Description, Sum(Sales_Order_Quantity_Sold) AS
Total_Sales
FROM Slainte_Merge
WHERE Sales_Order_Date Between #1/1/2020# And #4/30/2020#
GROUP BY Product_Description;
```

5. Click **Run** to show the results.
6. Take a screenshot (label it 2-2F).
7. Save your query as **Total_Sales_By_Product** and close your database.

Part 4: Address and Refine Your Results

Now that you've completed a basic analysis to answer management's question, take a moment to think about how you could improve the report and anticipate questions your manager might have.

Q5. If the owner of Sláinte wishes to identify which product sold the most, how would you make this report more useful?

Q6. If you wanted to provide more detail, what other attributes would be useful to add as additional rows or columns to your report, or what other reports would you create?

Part 5: Communicate Your Findings

Let's make this easy for others to understand using visualization and explanations.

Q7. Write a brief paragraph about how you would interpret the results of your analysis in plain English. For example, which data points stand out?

Q8. In chapter 4, we'll discuss some visualization techniques. Describe a way you could present these data as a chart or graph.

End of Lab

Lab 2-3   Resolve Common Data Problems in Excel and Access

No Access! optional Python code (p. 70)

There are several issues with this dataset that we'll need to resolve before we can process the data. This will require some cleaning, reformatting, and other techniques.

Company summary

LendingClub is a peer-to-peer marketplace where borrowers and investors are matched together. The goal of LendingClub is to reduce the costs associated with these banking transactions and make borrowing less expensive and investment more engaging. LendingClub provides data on loans that have been approved and rejected since 2007, including the assigned interest rate and type of loan. This provides several opportunities for data analysis.

Data

- LendingClub datasets: ApproveStats

Technique

- Some experience with Excel is useful for this lab.

Software needed

- Excel
- Screen capture tool (Windows: Snipping Tool; Mac: Cmd +Shift + 4)

In this lab, you will:

- Understand and clean the data to enable analysis for various problems.

Part 1: Identify the Questions

You've already identified some analysis questions for **LendingClub** in chapter 1. Here, you'll focus on data quality. Think about some of the common issues with data you receive from other people. For example, is the date field in the proper format? Do number fields contain text or vice versa?

> Q1. What do you expect will be major data quality issues with **LendingClub**'s data?

Part 2: Master the Data

For this lab, you should download the lending data from **LendingClub** and prepare the data for some more advanced analysis in chapter 3. The **LendingClub** data contain two different file types, including LoanStats for approved loans and RejectStats for rejected loans. There are significantly more data available for LoanStats. There are 107 different attributes. To save some time, we've identified 19 of the most interesting in Lab Exhibit 2-3A.

LAB EXHIBIT 2-3A

LoanStatsXXXX.csv

Attribute	Description
id	Loan identification number
member_id	Membership ID
loan_amnt	Requested loan amount
emp_length	Employment length
issue_d	Date of loan issue
loan_status	Fully paid or charged off
pymnt_plan	Payment plan: yes or no
purpose	Loan purpose: e.g., wedding, medical, debt_consolidation, car
zip_code	The first three digits of the applicant's zip code
addr_state	State
dti	Debt-to-income ratio
delinq_2y	Late payments within the past 2 years
earliest_cr_line	Oldest credit account
inq_last_6mnths	Credit inquiries in the past 6 months
open_acc	Number of open credit accounts
revol_bal	Total balance of all credit accounts
revol_util	Percentage of available credit in use
total_acc	Total number of credit accounts
application_type	Individual or joint application

> Q2. Given this list of attributes, what concerns do you have with the data's ability to predict answers to the questions you identified in chapter 1?

Take a moment and familiarize yourself with the data.

1. Open your web browser and go to: https://www.lendingclub.com/info/download-data .action [TRA1].
2. In the **Download Loan Data** section, choose "2014" from the drop-down list, then click **Download**.
3. Locate your downloaded zip files on your computer, and extract the csv files to a convenient location (e.g., desktop or Documents).
4. Open the **LoanStats3c.csv** file in Excel. There should be 235,629 records (ignoring the first two header rows). *Note:* Calculating summary statistics, such as the total number of records, is an important step in data validation. We'll cover that in Lab 2.4.

5. Take a moment and explore the data.

> Q3. Is there anything in the data that you think will make analysis difficult? For example, are there any special symbols, nonstandard data, or numbers that look out of place?

> Q4. What would you do to clean the data in this file?

Let's identify some issues with the data.

- There are many attributes without any data, and that may not be necessary.
- The **[int_rate]** values are written in ##.##%, but analysis will require #.####.
- The **[term]** values include the word "months," which should be removed for numerical analysis.
- The **[emp_length]** values include "n/a", "<", "+", "year", and "years"–all of which should be removed for numerical analysis.
- Dates, including **[issue_d]**, can be more useful if we expand them to show the day, month, and year as separate attributes. Dates cause issues in general because different systems use different date formats (e.g., 1/9/2009, Jan-2009, 9/1/2009 for European dates, etc.), so typically some conversion is necessary.

First, remove the unwanted data:

6. Save your file as "**Loans2007-2011.xlsx**" to take advantage of some of Excel's features.
7. Delete the first row that says "Notes offered by prospectus. . .".
8. Delete the last four rows that include "Total amount funded. . .".
9. Delete columns that have no values, including [id], [member_id], and [url].
10. Repeat for any other blank columns or unwanted attributes.

Next, fix your numbers:

11. Select the **[int_rate]** column.
12. In the **Home** tab, go to the **Number** section and change the number type from **Percentage** to **General** using the drop-down menu.
13. Repeat for any other attributes with percentages.
14. Take a screenshot (label it 2-3A) of your partially cleaned data file.

Then, remove any words from numerical values:

15. Select the **[term]** column.
16. Use **Find & Replace** (**Ctrl+H** or **Home > Editing > Find & Select > Find & Replace**) to find the words "months" and "month" and replace them with a <u>null/blank value</u> "". *Important:* Be sure to include the space before the words and go from the longest variation of the word to the shortest. In this case, if you replaced "month" first, you would end up with a lot of values that still had the letter "s" from "months".
17. Now select the **[emp_length]** column and find and replace the following values:

Original Value	New Value
na or n/a	0
< 1 year	0
1 year	1
2 years	2
3 years	3
4 years	4
5 years	5
6 years	6

Original Value	New Value
7 years	7
8 years	8
9 years	9
10+ years	10
, (comma)	(blank)

18. Take a screenshot (label it 2-5B) of your partially cleaned data file, showing the [term] column.

Analytics Tool: Python

Note: *Finding and replacing 13 values by hand may be tedious, but it is efficient for a one-off analysis and a small file. If you plan to re-perform this analysis multiple times or find and replace dozens of items or you have a file that is larger than Excel can handle, you're better off using a scripting language, such as Python. You can down-load Python free from python.org, and a quick search on Google will help you find tutorials to start with the basics.*

Here's what the script would look like for the find and replace function where you would list the original value as item *and the replacement value as* replacement:

```
import csv


ifile = open(`file', `rb')
reader = csv.reader(ifile,delimiter=`\t')
ofile = open(`file', `wb')
writer = csv.writer(ofile, delimiter=`\t')


s = ifile.read()
for item, replacement in zip(findlist, replacelist):
    s = s.replace(item, replacement)
    s = s.replace(item, replacement)
ofile.write(s)


ifile.close()
ofile.close()
```

Finally, transform those dates:

19. Right-click the column to the right or the **[issue_d]** column, and choose **Insert** to add a blank column.
20. Name the new column **[issue_month]**.
21. Use the =MONTH([column address for issue_d]) formula to extract the month from the date in your new column and copy your formula to the bottom of the sheet. You should see a month number value in each cell. If it still has a date format, change the number format to **General** in the **Home** tab.

22. Now convert the formulas to data values. Select the new **[issue_month]** column that contains your formula.
23. **Copy [Ctrl+C]** and **Paste Special [Ctrl+Alt+V]**. Choose **Values [V]**, then click **OK**.
24. Save your file.
25. Add another blank column and name it **[issue_year]**.
26. Use the =YEAR([column address for issue_d]) formula to extract the month from the date in your new column and copy your formula to the bottom of the sheet. You should see a month number value in each cell. If it still has a date format, change the number format to **General** in the **Home** tab.
27. Select the new **[issue_month]** column that contains your formula, then **Copy [Ctrl+C]** and **Paste Special [Ctrl+Alt+V]**. Choose **Values [V]**. Click **OK**.
28. Save your file.
29. Take a screenshot (label it 2-5C) of your cleaned data file, showing the new date columns.

> Q5. Why do you think it is useful to reformat and extract parts of the dates before you conduct your analysis? What do you think would happen if you didn't?

> Q6. Did you run into any major issues when you attempted to clean the data? How would you resolve those?

End of Lab

Lab 2-4   Generate Summary Statistics in Excel

When you're working with a new or unknown set of data, validating the data is very important. When you make a data request, the IT manager who fills the request should also provide some summary statistics that include the total number of records and mathematical sums to ensure nothing has been lost in the transmission. This lab will help you calculate summary statistics in Excel.

Company summary

LendingClub is a peer-to-peer marketplace where borrowers and investors are matched together. The goal of LendingClub is to reduce the costs associated with these banking transactions and make borrowing less expensive and investment more engaging. LendingClub provides data on loans that have been approved and rejected since 2007, including the assigned interest rate and type of loan. This provides several opportunities for data analysis.

Data
- LendingClub dataset: ApproveStats2014

Technique
- Some experience with Excel is useful for this lab.

Software needed
- Excel
- Screen capture tool (Windows: Snipping Tool; Mac: Cmd + Shift + 4)

In this lab, you will:
- Calculate summary statistics using Excel.

Calculate Summary Statistics in Excel

For basic validation, we'll use Excel. Remember, there is a limitation on the number of records that Excel can handle, so this is best for smaller- to medium-sized files. Excel's toolbar at the bottom of the window provides quick access to a summary of any selected values.

Note: If you've already downloaded **LendingClub** data from 2014, you can skip to step 5.

1. Open your web browser and go to: https://www.lendingclub.com/info/download-data .action.
2. In the **Download Loan Data** section, choose "2014" from the drop-down list, then click **Download**.
3. Locate your downloaded zip files on your computer, and extract the .csv files to a convenient location (e.g., desktop or Documents).
4. Open the **LoanStats3c.csv** file in Excel.
5. Select the **[loan_amnt]** column. At the bottom of the window, you will see the **Average**, **Count**, and **Sum** calculations, shown in LAB Exhibit 2-4A. Compare those to the validation given by LendingClub:

   Funded loans: $3,503,840,175

   Number of approved loans: 235,629

LAB EXHIBIT 2-4A
Summary Statistics Provided by the Excel Toolbar at the Bottom Showing Average, Count, and Sum

Source: Microsoft Excel 2016

Q1. Do your numbers match the numbers provided by **LendingClub**? What explains the discrepancy, if any?

6. Right-click on the **summary** toolbar and choose **Numerical Count** from the list. You should now see four values in the bar.

Q2. Does the Numerical Count provide a more useful/accurate value for validating your data? Why or why not do you think that is the case?

Q3. What other summary values might be useful for validating your data?

7. Take a screenshot (label it 2-4A) showing your expanded summary toolbar with four (or more) values.

End of Lab

Lab 2-5   College Scorecard Extraction and Data Preparation

This lab will help you learn how to extract data from a text file in preparation for analysis in Excel. This lab is in preparation for future labs in chapter 3 that will analyze college scorecard data.

Data summary

The data used are a subset of the College Scorecard dataset that is provided by the U.S. Department of Education. These data provide federal financial aid and earnings information, insights into the performance of schools eligible to receive federal financial aid, and the outcomes of students at those schools. You can learn more about how the data are used and view the raw data yourself at https://collegescorecard.ed.gov/data/. However, for this lab, you should use the text file provided to you.

Data

- CollegeScorecard Datasets: CollegeScorecard_RawData

Technique

- Some experience with Excel is useful for this lab.

Software needed

- Text Editor (Windows: Notepad; Mac: TextEdit)
- Excel
- Screen capture tool (Windows: Snipping Tool; Mac: Cmd + Shift + 4)

In this lab, you will:

- Extract data into a text editor and transform it into structured, ready-to-analyze data in Excel.

Part 1: Identify the Questions

Because this lab is focused on mastering the data, the question has been identified for you. We will begin with a simple question with two variables, SAT average and completion rate for first-time, full-time students at four-year institutions.

Part 2: Master the Data

1. Open the text file CollegeScoreCardRawData.txt.
2. Select all of the data in the text file and copy them.
3. Open a new Excel workbook. With the active cell as A1, paste the text data.
4. Take a screenshot (label it 2-5A).
5. The data defaulted to pasting into only column A. To view each attribute in its own column, you will need to parse the data using the Text to Columns feature in Excel. Navigate to the **Data** tab in Excel's ribbon.
6. Make sure that the all of the data in column A are selected (not just the first row of data), then click the **Text to Columns** button to open up a wizard to guide your data transformation.
7. The wizard provides two options: delimited and fixed width. Delimited means separated, and in Excel (and other applications), it references a character that separates (or delimits) data.

   Q1. By looking through the data in the text file, what do you think the delimiter is?

8. Leaving **delimited** checked (as is the default), click **Next** in the wizard, and select the appropriate delimiter. Make sure to un-check the **default** option, tab.

9. Click **Finish** in the wizard.

10. Take a screenshot (label it 2-5B).

11. To ensure that you captured all of the data through the extraction from the txt file, we need to validate it. Validate the following checksums:
   - You should have 7,704 records (rows).
   - Compare the attribute names (column headers) to the attributes listed in the data dictionary. Are you missing any, or do you have any extras?
   - The average SAT score should be 1,059.07 (this is leaving NULL values as NULL).

   Q2. In the checksums, you validated that the average SAT score for all of the records is 1,059.07. When we work with the data more rigorously, several tests will require us to transform NULL values. If you were to transform the NULL SAT values into 0, what would happen to the average (would it stay the same, decrease, or increase)? How would that change to the average affect the way you would interpret the data? Do you think it's a good idea to replace NULL values with 0s in this case?

12. Now that the data have been validated, you can clean the data. How you clean the data is determined by the question you intend to answer. In this case, we're preparing our data to run a regression test using the two attributes SAT_AVG and C150_4. As you'll learn in chapter 3, a regression test won't run with non-numeric values (i.e., we can't leave the NULL values in, and we can't transform them to blanks). Earlier you discussed the cons of replacing NULL values with 0s.

   To avoid the issues with NULL, blanks, and 0s, we will remove all of the records that contain NULL values in either SAT_AVG or C150_4. Do so.

13. Perform a =COUNT() to verify the number of records that remain after removing all records associated with NULL values in SAT_AVG or C150_4. 1,271 records should remain.

14. Take a screenshot (label it 2-5C).

   Your data is now ready for the test plan. This lab will continue in chapter 3.

Lab 2-6 Comprehensive Case: Dillard's Store Data: How to Create an Entity-Relationship Diagram

Company summary

Dillard's is a department store with approximately 330 stores in 29 states. Its headquarters is in Little Rock, Arkansas. You can learn more about **Dillard's** by looking at finance.yahoo.com (Ticker symbol = DDS) and the Wikipedia site for DDS. You'll quickly note that William T. Dillard II is an accounting grad of the University of Arkansas and the Walton College of Business, which may be why he shared transaction data with us to make available for this lab and labs throughout this text.

Data

The data for this lab and other all **Dillard's** labs are available at http://walton.uark.edu/enterprise/. Your instructor will either give you specific instructions on how to access the data, or there will be information available on Connect. The 2016 **Dillard's** data cover all transactions over the period 1/1/2014 to 10/17/2016.

Software needed

- Microsoft SQL Server Management Studio (available on the Remote Desktop at the University of Arkansas)

In this lab, you will:

- Create an ERD (entity-relationship diagram), which provides some quick information on the data that's provided in the database. In one diagram, you can view all tables to see the entire database, or you can pick just the two you're working with to focus on those attributes.

Part 1: Identify the Questions

Dillard's is trying to figure out when its customers spend more on individual transactions. We ask questions regarding how Dillard's sells its products.

Q1. How would a view of the entire database or certain tables out of that database allow us to get a feel for the data?

Q2. What types of data would you guess that **Dillard's**, a retail store, gathers that might be useful? How could **Dillard's** suppliers use these data to predict future purchases?

Part 2: Master the Data and Part 3: Perform an Analysis of the Data

For this lab, we will create an ERD (entity-relationship diagram) to view the structure of the database.

1. Log on to **Remote Desktop** at the University of Arkansas.
2. Open **Microsoft SQL Server Management Studio** to access the **UA_Dillards_2016** data.
3. Input the **Server Name** in the **Connect to Server** window that you were provided through the Walton.uark.edu/enterprise website.

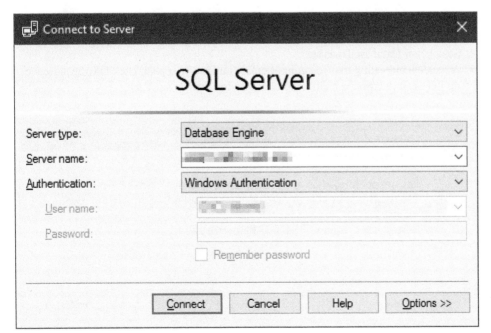

LAB EXHIBIT 2-6A

Source: Microsoft SQL Server Management Studio

4. Leave the default for authentication to Windows Authentication, and **click Connect**.
5. Expand the **Databases** folder in the **Object Explorer** window.

LAB EXHIBIT 2-6B

Source: Microsoft SQL Server
Management Studio

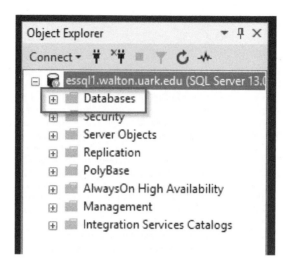

6. Scroll down to the **UA_Dillards_2016** database and expand it.
7. Right-click **Database Diagrams** to reveal the below window.

LAB EXHIBIT 2-6C

Source: Microsoft SQL Server
Management Studio

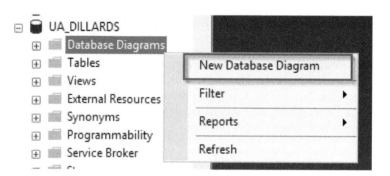

8. Select **New Database Diagram**.
9. A window indicating that you cannot create tables will appear, click **OK**. Because we do not need to create or edit any tables, viewing them is sufficient.

LAB EXHIBIT 2-6D

Source: Microsoft SQL Server
Management Studio

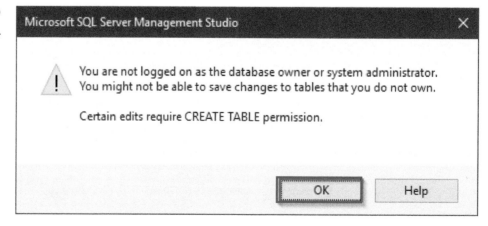

10. Select the tables you would like to view. For this lab, select all of them.
11. Take a screenshot (label it 2-6A).

Part 4: Address and Refine Results

Q3. What is the primary key for the TRANSACT table? What is the primary key for the SKU table?

Q4. How do we connect the SKU database to the TRANSACT table? How do we join tables from two different related tables?

End of Lab

Company summary

Dillard's is a department store with approximately 330 stores in 29 states. Its headquarters is in Little Rock, Arkansas. You can learn more about **Dillard's** by looking at finance.yahoo.com (Ticker symbol = DDS) and the Wikipedia site for DDS. You'll quickly note that William T. Dillard II is an accounting grad of the University of Arkansas and the Walton College of Business, which may be why he shared transaction data with us to make available for this lab and labs throughout this text.

Data

The data for this lab and other all **Dillard's** labs are available at http://walton.uark.edu/enterprise/. Your instructor will either give you specific instructions on how to access the data, or there will be information available on Connect. The 2016 **Dillard's** data cover all transactions over the period 1/1/2014 to 10/17/2016.

Software needed

- Microsoft SQL Server Management Studio (available on the Remote Desktop at the University of Arkansas)

In this lab, you will:

- Learn how to get a snippet of the data to better understand the data fields, what they contain, and what their data structure looks like to inform additional queries and database analysis.

Part 1: Identify the Questions

Data Analytics requires a lot of give and take. Where you learn a bit, modify the search, modify the analysis, and try again. All the while, you are asking yourself questions, trying to make your search efficient and effective. Questions like these:

Q1. How would a view of the entire database or certain tables out of that database allow us to get a feel for the data?

Q2. What types of data would you guess that **Dillard's**, a retail store, gathers that might be useful? How could **Dillard's** suppliers use these data to predict future purchases?

Part 2: Master the Data and Part 3: Perform an Analysis of the Data

1. Log on to **Remote Desktop** at the University of Arkansas.
2. Open **Microsoft SQL Server Management Studio** to access the **UA_Dillards_2016** data.
3. Input the **Server Name** in the **Connect to Server** window that you were provided through the Walton.uark.edu/enterprise website.

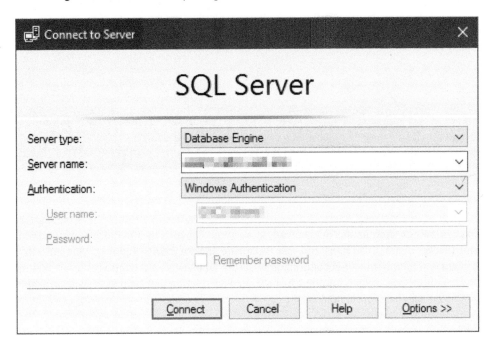

4. Leave the default for authentication to **Windows Authentication** and click **Connect**.
5. Select **New Query** from the menu at the top of the SQL Server application.

6. If the drop-down indicating which database you are intending to query doesn't say "UA_Dillards_2016" (e.g., it frequently defaults to "Master"), select the drop-down window and scroll down to UA_Dillards_2016, then click **Enter**. You could also type UA_Dillards_2016 instead of waiting to scroll to it.

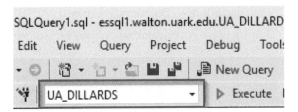

7. Because this dataset is massive, it can take a very long time for the system to return the complete set of data for some of the bigger tables (such as TRANSACT). If you would like to view just the top few rows of a dataset to get the feel for what type of data is in the table, you can do so with a query.

In the SELECT line, you can type TOP # before the columns you would like to see. Any type of filtering, aggregating, and ordering will still work through the rest of the query, but selecting the top few will help the query run faster by returning a subset of the result.

8. To view the top 10 rows in the TRANSACT table, type the following query into the query window:

```
SELECT TOP 10 *
FROM TRANSACT
```

In SQL, SELECT indicates the columns you would like to view. * is a shortcut to indicate that you'd like to view all of the columns. The TOP command limits the amount of rows that are returned.

FROM indicates the tables that contains the data you'd like to view.

9. To see the result of the query, click **Execute**. **F5** also works to run queries as a PC shortcut.

LAB EXHIBIT 2-7D

Source: Microsoft SQL Server Management Studio

10. Take a screenshot of your results (label it 2-7A).
11. When you look at these results, you may wonder what some of the attributes represent. For example, TRAN_TYPE only returns values with P. To view other types of values, you could filter out any record that has a TRAN_TYPE of P.

To filter in SQL, use WHERE. The WHERE line follows FROM:

```
SELECT TOP 10 *
FROM TRANSACT
WHERE TRAN_TYPE [[<>]] `P'
```

The WHERE code has three parts:
- The attribute that you are filtering on (in this case, TRAN_TYPE).
- The way you are filtering—a few to start with are:
  ○ = if you want to see only rows that correspond with a certain value.
  ○ <> if you want to exclude rows that correspond with a certain value.
  ○ > for all values greater than a certain value, < for all values less than a certain value.
- The value that you are filtering based on. In this case, 'P'.

12. Execute the query.

Part 4: Address and Refine Results

Q3. What do you think 'P' and 'R' represent in the TRAN_TYPE table? How might transactions differ if they are represented by 'P' or 'R'?

Q4. What benefit can you gain from selecting only the top few rows of your data, particularly from a large dataset?

End of Lab

Company summary

Dillard's is a department store with approximately 330 stores in 29 states. Its headquarters is in Little Rock, Arkansas. You can learn more about Dillard's by looking at finance.yahoo.com (Ticker symbol = DDS) and the Wikipedia site for DDS. You'll quickly note that William T. Dillard II is an accounting grad of the University of Arkansas and the Walton College of Business, which may be why he shared transaction data with us to make available for this lab and labs throughout this text.

Data

The data for this lab and other all Dillard's labs are available at http://walton.uark.edu/enterprise/. Your instructor will either give you specific instructions on how to access the data, or there will be information available on Connect. The 2016 Dillard's data cover all transactions over the period 1/1/2014 to 10/17/2016.

Software needed

- Microsoft SQL Server Management Studio (available on the Remote Desktop at the University of Arkansas)
- Excel 2016 (available on the Remote Desktop at the University of Arkansas)

In this lab, you will:

- Learn how to access databases, run queries, and perform analyses in Excel.

Part 1: Identify the Questions

Because, as accountants, we are most familiar with Microsoft Excel, we'd like to learn how to access the data and run queries in excel. But the question is still why use Excel?

Q1. What can you do in Excel that is much more difficult to do in other data management programs?

Q2. Because most accountants are familiar with Excel, name three data management functions you can do easier in Excel than any other program. How does that familiarity help you with your analysis?

Part 2: Master the Data and Part 3: Perform an Analysis of the Data

1. Log on to **Remote Desktop** at the University of Arkansas.
2. Open **Microsoft SQL Server Management** Studio to access the **UA_Dillards_2016** data.

Connecting Excel to a SQL Server Database

While executing queries in SQL Server is a great method for viewing data, if you want to eventually load data into Excel for additional analysis or visualization, it is easiest to write the queries directly in Excel. This puts the entire ETL process in one tool, Excel.

3. Open a new Excel workbook.
4. From the **Data** tab, click **New Query** > **From Database** > **From SQL Server Database**.

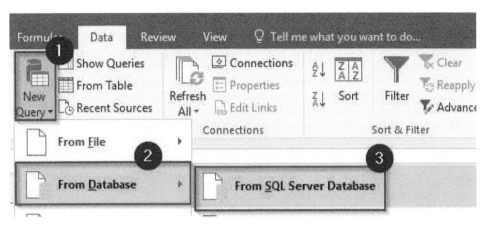

5. In the Microsoft SQL database pop-up window, input the server name that you were provided through the Walton.uark.edu/enterprise website. The database name is UA_Dillards_2016.

6. Click **OK**.
7. On the next window, keep the default to use your current credentials, and then click **Connect**.

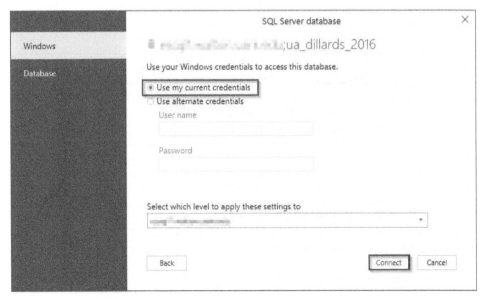

8. Click **OK** in the **Encryption Support** pop-up window.
9. The tables in the **UA_Dillards_2016** database are available for you to select in the **Navigator** window. Click once on **STORE** to preview the data.

LAB EXHIBIT 2-8D

Source: Microsoft SQL Server
Management Studio

10. The data will preview on the right side of the **Navigator** window. Click **Load** to load the data into a table in Excel.

    As long as the dataset that you have loaded is under the Excel row limit of 1,048,576, the entire table will be available for you to work with in Excel. You can analyze the data using Excel's formulas, functions, and statistical tools, as well as create PivotTables and charts.
11. Create a PivotTable for this set of data by selecting all of the data from the Store table and then clicking **PivotTable** on the **Insert** tab of the Excel ribbon.

LAB EXHIBIT 2-8E

Source: Microsoft Excel 2016

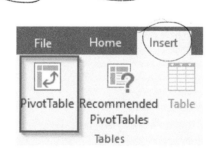

12. We can quickly view a count of how many stores are in each state. Drag and drop STATE into the **ROWS** section of the **PivotTable Fields** window and **STORE** into the **VALUES** section.

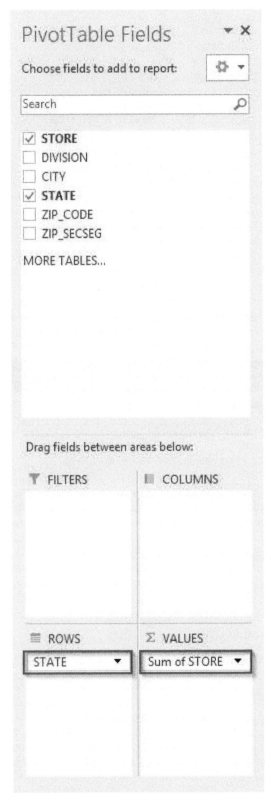

13. It is likely that the PivotTable assumed you wanted to SUM the Store ID, which provides nonsense data. We need to change that aggregate to a COUNT instead.

     Click the drop-down next to Sum of STORE in the **VALUES** section of the **PivotTable Fields** window and select **Value Field Settings**.

14. Select **Count** to change the way the data for number of stores per state are summarized.

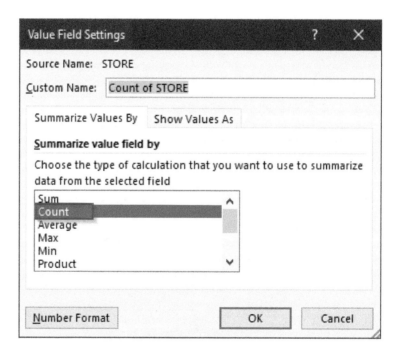

15. Take a screenshot (label it 2-8A) of the PivotTable.

Q3. Reference your PivotTable and find which state has the highest number of **Dillard's** stores. Which states have the fewest? How many stores are there across the country?

Q4. Counting the number of stores per state is one example of how the data that have been loaded from SQL Server into Excel can become useful information through a PivotTable. What are other ways that you could organize the STORE data in a PivotTable to come up with meaningful information?

✗ Writing Queries Directly in Excel

While executing queries in SQL Server is a great method for viewing data, if you want to eventually load data into Excel for analysis or visualization, it is easiest to write the queries directly in Excel. This puts the entire ETL process in one tool, Excel.

1. Open a new Excel workbook.
2. From the **Data** tab, click **New Query** > **From Database** > **From SQL Server Database**.

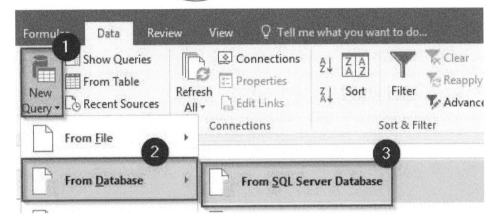

3. In the **Microsoft SQL database** pop-up window, input the server information that you received when accessing the UA_Dillards_2016 data. The Database name is UA_Dillards_2016.

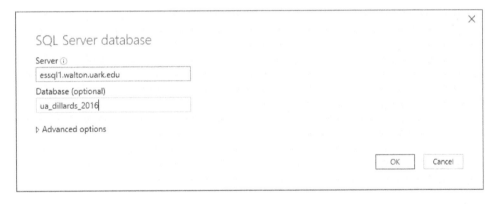

Important Note: If you just worked through the first part of this lab (connecting to data), this step is where the process begins to be different. Instead of clicking **OK**, you will click **SQL statement (optional)**.

SQL Server database

Server ⓘ

Database (optional)

▷ Advanced options

4. For this query, we will pull in enough data to answer a variety of questions about transaction line items in each state. We'll select all of the columns from the TRANSACT table and the STATE column from the STORE table. In order to do that, we'll join the two tables together in our query.

Q5. Joins are made based on their primary key/foreign key relationship. Looking at the ERD or the dataset, which two columns form the relationship between the TRANSACT and STORE tables?

5. Type this query into the **SQL statement** box:

```
SELECT TRANSACT.*, STATE
FROM TRANSACT
INNER JOIN STORE
ON TRANSACT.STORE = STORE.STORE
WHERE TRAN_DATE BETWEEN '20160901' AND '20160915'
```

LAB EXHIBIT 2-8L

Source: Microsoft SQL Server Management Studio

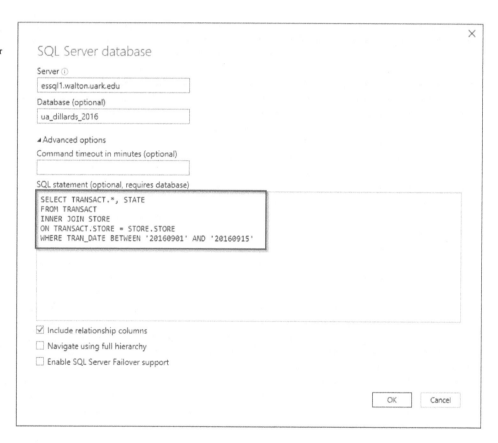

6. Click **OK** to continue.
7. Click **Connect** using your current credentials in the next window.
8. Click **OK** on the **Encryption Support** window.
9. Excel will provide you a preview of your data before loading it. If the query loads successfully (i.e., if you see the preview, instead of an error), click **Close & Load** to load the data into an Excel table.

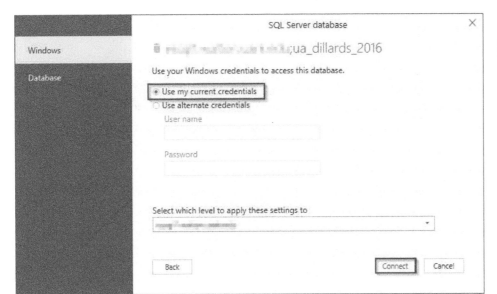

LAB EXHIBIT 2-8M

Source: Microsoft SQL Server Management Studio

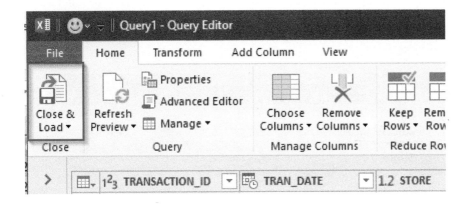

LAB EXHIBIT 2-8N

Source: Microsoft Excel 2016

10. It may take a few minutes to load. Even though the query we ran was only for 15 days of transactions, there are still more than 1 million transactions (or rows) to return.

Part 4: Calculate Summary Statistics

Calculating summary statistics such as mean, median, and mode for quantitative data can be helpful to get a quick feeling for the components of a large dataset.

11. While you can calculate these statistics by hand, you can also have Excel calculate them automatically through the Data Analysis ToolPak. If you haven't added this component into Excel yet, follow this menu path: **File > Options > Add-ins**. From this window, select the **Go. . .** button, and then place a check mark in the box next to **Analysis ToolPak**. Once you click **OK**, you will be able to access the ToolPak from the **Data** tab on the Excel ribbon.

12. We will calculate descriptive statistics for the attributes ORIG_PRICE, SALE_PRICE, TRAN_AMT.

Q6. Looking at the first several rows of data, compare the amounts in ORIG_PRICE, SALE_PRICE, TRAN_AMT. What do you think TRANS_AMT represents?

13. Click the **Data Analysis** button from the **Data** tab on the Excel ribbon and select **Descriptive Statistics.**

LAB EXHIBIT 2-8O

Source: Microsoft Excel 2016

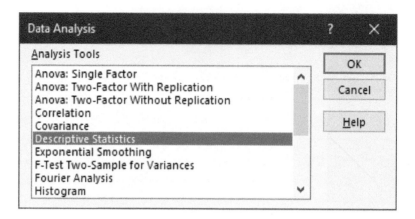

14. For the **Input Range**, select the three columns associated with the three attributes that we are measuring. Leave the default to columns, and place a check-mark in **Labels in First Row**.
15. Place a check mark next to **Summary Statistics**, then press **OK**.

LAB EXHIBIT 2-8P

Source: Microsoft Excel 2016

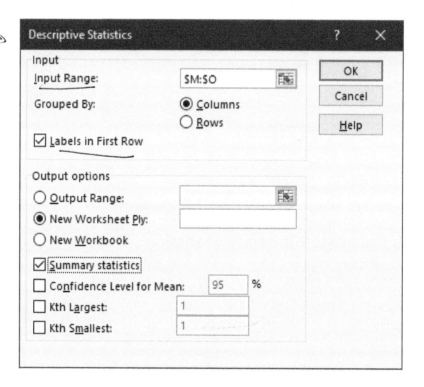

It may take awhile for the statistics to run because you're working with so many rows.

Q7. What are the means for each of the attributes?

Q8. The mean from TRAN_AMT is lower than the means for both ORIG_PRICE and SALE_PRICE, why do you think that is? (*Hint*: It is not an error).

Part 5: Address and Refine Results

Q9. How does doing a query within Excel allow quicker and more efficient access and analysis of the data?

Q10. Is 15 days of data sufficient to capture the statistical relationship among and between different variables? What will Excel do if you have more than 1 million rows? There are statistical programs such as SAS and SPSS that allow for transformation and statistical analysis of bigger datasets.

End of Lab

Lab 2-9 Comprehensive Case: Dillard's Store Data: Joining Tables

Company summary

Dillard's is a department store with approximately 330 stores in 29 states. Its headquarters is in Little Rock, Arkansas. You can learn more about Dillard's by looking at finance.yahoo.com (Ticker symbol = DDS) and the Wikipedia site for DDS. You'll quickly note that William T. Dillard II is an accounting grad of the University of Arkansas and the Walton College of Business, which may be why he shared transaction data with us to make available for this lab and labs throughout this text.

Data

The data for this lab and other all Dillard's labs are available at http://walton.uark.edu/enterprise/. Your instructor will either give you specific instructions on how to access the data, or there will be information available on Connect. The 2016 Dillard's data cover all transactions over the period 1/1/2014 to 10/17/2016.

Technique

- This lab is most easily performed if Labs 2-6 and 2-7 have already been completed.

Software needed

- Microsoft SQL Server Management Studio (available on the Remote Desktop at the University of Arkansas)

In this lab, you will:

- Learn how to do a table join, joining two tables all on your own and running an analysis of the data.

Part 1: Identify the Questions

1. Consult the entity-relationship diagram to view the variables available in the TRANSACT table and the CUSTOMER table. Consult Lab 2-5 to access the ERD or http://walton.uark.edu/enterprise/.

Q1. If we wanted to join the TRANSACT and the CUSTOMER tables, what fields (or variables) would we use to join them?

Q2. Because most accountants are familiar with Excel, name three data management functions you can do easier in Excel than any other program. How does that familiarity help you with your analysis?

Part 2: Master the Data and Part 3: Perform an Analysis of the Data

2. Log on to **Remote Desktop** at the University of Arkansas.
3. Open **Microsoft SQL Server Management Studio** to access the **UA_Dillards_2016** data.
4. Input the **Server Name** in the **Connect to Server** window that you were provided through the Walton.uark.edu/enterprise website.

LAB EXHIBIT 2-9A

Source: Microsoft SQL Server Management Studio

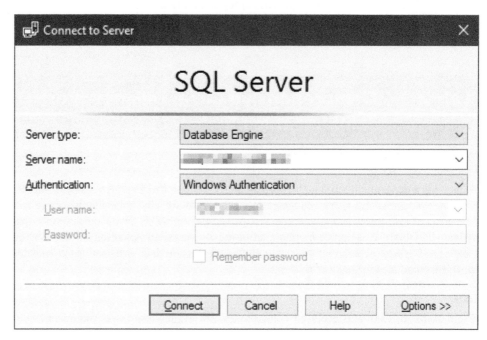

5. Leave the default for authentication to **Windows Authentication**, and click **Connect**.
6. Select **New Query** from the menu at the top of the **SQL Server** application.

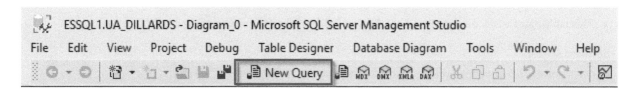

LAB EXHIBIT 2-9B

Source: Microsoft SQL Server Management Studio

7. If the drop-down indicating which database you are intending to query doesn't say "UA_Dillards_2016" (e.g., it frequently defaults to "Master"), select the drop-down window and scroll down to UA_Dillards_2016, then click **Enter**. You could also type UA_Dillards_2016 instead of waiting to scroll to it.

LAB EXHIBIT 2-9C

Source: Microsoft SQL Server Management Studio

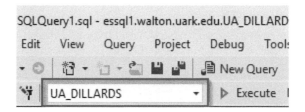

8. Given the description in the text and in Labs 2-6 and 2-7, you have the tools you need to join two tables, TRANSACT and CUSTOMER and run a query on customer state (note this is where the customer lives and not where the store is located). Input a query that will show how many customers have shopped at **Dillard's**, grouped by their respective states. Run the query for the entire dataset; do not filter based on a limited set of days.

9. This query may take a few minutes to run. Once the results have returned, you can check your results by looking at how many customers have shopped at **Dillard's** from Arkansas (AR): 2673089.

   Q3.   How many different states are listed?

   Q4.   Why are there so many more states listed than 50?

   Q5.   What do you assume the Other, XX, blank, and Null states represent? If you were to analyze these data to learn more about the number of customers from different places have shopped at **Dillard's**, what would you do with these data: group them, leave them out, leave them alone? Why?

End of Lab

Chapter 3

Modeling and Evaluation: Going from Defining Business Problems and Data Understanding to Analyzing Data and Answering Questions

A Look at This Chapter

Understanding various models and techniques used for data analytics is an increasingly important skill for accountants. In this chapter, we evaluate several different approaches and models and identify when to use them and how to interpret the results. We also provide specific accounting-related examples of when each of these specific data approaches and models is appropriate to address our particular question.

A Look Back

Chapter 2 provided a description of how data are prepared and scrubbed to be ready to use to answer business questions. We explained how to extract, transform, and load data and then how to validate and normalize the data. In addition, we explained how data standards are used to facilitate the exchange of data between both senders and receivers.

A Look Ahead

Chapter 4 will demonstrate various techniques that can be used to effectively communicate the results of your analyses. Additionally, we discuss how to refine your results and translate your findings into useful information for decision makers.

kurhan/123RF

Liang Zhao Zhang, a San Francisco–based janitor, made more than $275,000 in 2015. The average janitor in the area earns just $26,180 a year. Zhang, a **Bay Area Rapid Transit (BART)** janitor, has a base pay of $57,945 and $162,050 in overtime pay. With benefits, the total was $276,121. While some call his compensation "outrageous and irresponsible," Zhang signed up for every available overtime slot that became available. To be sure, Zhang worked more than 4,000 hours last year and received overtime pay. Can BART predict who might take advantage of overtime pay? Should it set a policy restricting overtime pay? Would it be better for BART to hire more regular, full-time employees instead of offering so much overtime?

Can Data Analytics help with these questions?

Using a profiling data analytics approach detailed in this chapter, BART could generate summary statistics of its workers and their overtime pay to see the extent that overtime is required and taken advantage of.

Using regression and classification approaches to Data Analytics would help to classify which employees are most likely to exceed normal bounds and why. BART, for example, has a policy of offering overtime by seniority. So do the most senior employees sign up first and leave little overtime to others? Will a senior employee get paid more for overtime than more junior-level employees? If so, is that the best policy for the company and its employees?

Source: http://www.cnbc.com/2016/11/04/how-one-bay-area-janitor-made-276000-last-year.html.

OBJECTIVES

After reading this chapter, you should be able to:

LO 3-1   Define Data Analytics approaches

LO 3-2   Explain the profiling approach to Data Analytics

LO 3-3   Describe the data reduction approach to Data Analytics

LO 3-4   Understand the regression approach to Data Analytics

LO 3-5   Understand the classification approach to Data Analytics

LO 3-6   Understand the clustering approach to Data Analytics

<table>
<tr><td>

LO 3-1

Define Data
Analytics
approaches

</td></tr>
</table>

PERFORMING THE TEST PLAN: DEFINING DATA ANALYTICS APPROACHES

Using the IMPACT cycle model, in chapter 1 we listed various approaches that business analysts use to address business questions. In chapter 1, we mentioned the process of identifying the questions, the "I" in the IMPACT cycle model. In chapter 2, we discussed the techniques and processes of mastering the data, the "M" in the IMPACT cycle model. The third step of the IMPACT cycle model, or the "P," is "performing test plan." That is, how are we going to test or analyze the data to answer the question before us? Which Data Analytics approaches or techniques are appropriate to address our business questions?

Before we discuss these approaches, we need to bring you up to speed on some data-specific terms:

- A *target* is an expected attribute or value that we want to evaluate. For example, if we are trying to predict whether a transaction is fraudulent, the target might be a specific "fraud score." If we're trying to predict an interest rate, the target would be "interest rate."
- A *class* is a manually assigned category applied to a record based on an event. For example, if the credit department has rejected a credit line for a customer, the credit department assigns the class "Rejected" to the customer's master record. Likewise, if the internal auditors have confirmed that fraud has occurred, they would assign the class "fraud" to that transaction.

There are numerous models to choose from when evaluating a given set of data. The choice of model depends on the desired outcome of the business question. If you don't have a specific question and are simply exploring the data for potential patterns of interest, you would use an **unsupervised approach**. For example, consider the question: *"Do our vendors form natural groups based on similar attributes?"* In this case, there isn't a specific target because you don't yet know what similarities our vendors have. You may use **clustering** to evaluate the vendor attributes and see which ones are closely related, shown in Exhibit 3-1.

EXHIBIT 3-1

Clustering

Clustering is an unsupervised method that is used to find natural groupings within the data. In this case, we have three natural clusters of vendors.

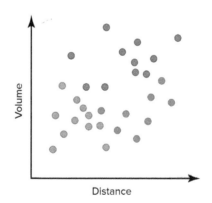

You could also use **co-occurrence grouping** to match vendors by geographic region; **data reduction** to simplify vendors into obvious categories, such as wholesale or retail or based on overall volume of orders; or **profiling** to evaluate vendors with similar on-time delivery behavior, shown in **Exhibit 3-2**. In any of these cases, the data drive the decision, and you evaluate the output to see if it matches our intuition. These exploratory exercises may help to define better questions, but are generally less useful for making decisions.

On the other hand, we may ask questions with specific outcomes, such as: "Will a new vendor ship a large order on time?" When you are performing analysis that uses historical data to predict a future outcome, you will use a **supervised approach**. We use historical data

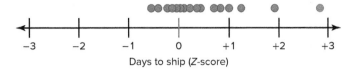

EXHIBIT 3-2 (Profiling) Profiling is an unsupervised method that is used to discover patterns of behavior. In this case, the higher the Z-score (farther away from the mean), the more likely a vendor will have a delayed shipment (green circle). We use profiling to explore the attributes of that vendor that we may want to avoid in the future.

to create the new model. Using a **classification** model, you can predict *whether* a new vendor belongs to one class or another based on the behavior of the others, shown in Exhibit 3-3. You might also use **regression** to predict a *specific value* to answer a question such as, "How many days do we predict it will take a new vendor to ship an order?" Again, the prediction is based on the activity we have observed from other vendors, shown in Exhibit 3-4. **Causal modeling**, **similarity matching**, and **link prediction** are additional supervised approaches

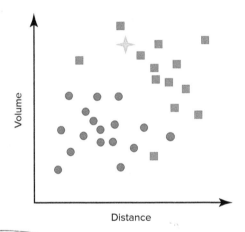

EXHIBIT 3-3 (Classification) Classification is a supervised method that can be used to predict the class of a new observation. In this case, blue circles represent "on-time" vendors. Green squares represent "delayed" vendors. The gold star represents a new vendor with no history.

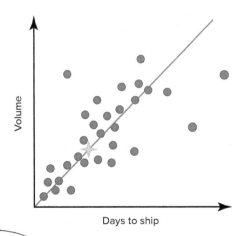

EXHIBIT 3-4 (Regression) Regression is a supervised method used to predict specific values. In this case, the number of days to ship is dependent on the number of items in the order. Therefore, we can use regression to predict the "days to ship" of the gold star based on the volume in the order.

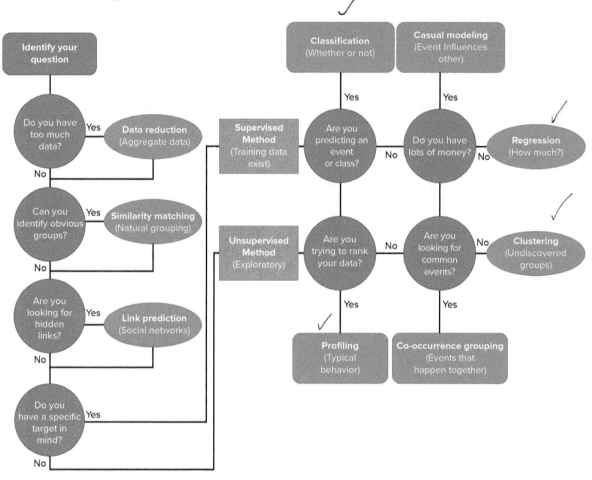

EXHIBIT 3-5 Flowchart to Help Choose an Appropriate Data Model

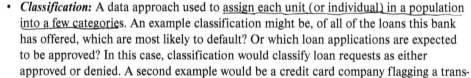

where you attempt to identify causation (which can be expensive), identify a series of characteristics that predict a model, or attempt to identify other relationships, respectively.

Ultimately, the model you use comes down to the questions you are trying to answer. The flowchart in Exhibit 3-5 shows several decisions that will help you select an appropriate model, or data approach. By evaluating your data, the question that needs to be addressed as well as the desired outcomes, an appropriate data approach can be determined. Once you've selected an approach, then your analysis can begin.

We highlighted the data analytics approaches in chapter 1 and provide them again here for reference:

- *Classification:* A data approach used to assign each unit (or individual) in a population into a few categories. An example classification might be, of all of the loans this bank has offered, which are most likely to default? Or which loan applications are expected to be approved? In this case, classification would classify loan requests as either approved or denied. A second example would be a credit card company flagging a transaction as being approved or potentially being fraudulent and denying payment.
- *Regression:* A data approach used to estimate or predict, for each unit, the numerical value of some variable using some type of statistical model. An example of regression analysis might be, given a balance of total accounts receivable held by a firm, what is the appropriate level of allowance for doubtful accounts for bad debts?

- *Similarity matching:* A data approach used to identify similar individuals based on data known about them. The opening vignette in chapter 1 mentioned Alibaba and its attempt to identify seller and customer fraud based on various characteristics known about them to see if they were similar to known fraud cases.
- *Clustering:* A data approach used to divide individuals (like customers) into groups (or clusters) in a useful or meaningful way. In other words, identifying groups of similar data elements and the underlying drivers of those groups. For example, clustering might be used to segment a customer into a small number of groups for additional analysis and marketing activities. In a like way, transactions might also be put into clusters to analyze them.
- *Co-occurrence grouping:* A data approach used to discover associations between individuals based on transactions involving them. Amazon might use this to sell another item to you by knowing what items are "frequently bought together" or "Customers who bought this item also bought . . ." as shown in chapter 1.
- *Profiling:* A data approach used to characterize the "typical" behavior of an individual, group, or population by generating summary statistics about the data (including mean, standard deviations, etc.). By understanding the typical behavior, we'll be able to identify abnormal behavior more easily. When behavior departs from that typical behavior, which we'll call an *anomaly,* then further investigation is warranted. Profiling might be used in accounting to identify fraud or just those transactions that might warrant some additional investigation (e.g., travel expenses that are three standard deviations above the norm).
- *Link prediction:* A data approach used to predict a relationship between two data items. This might be used in social media. For example, if two individuals have mutual friends on social media and both attended the same university, it is likely that they know each other and the site may make a recommendation for them to connect. Chapter 1 provides an example of this used in Facebook. Link prediction in an accounting setting might work to use social media to look for relationships between related parties that are not otherwise disclosed to identify related party transactions.
- *Data reduction:* A data approach used to reduce the amount of information that needs to be considered to focus on the most critical items (i.e., highest cost, highest risk, largest impact, etc.). It does this by taking a large set of data (perhaps the population) and reducing it with a smaller set that has the vast majority of the critical information of the larger set. An example might include the potential to use these techniques in auditing. While auditing has employed various random and stratified sampling over the years, Data Analytics suggests new ways to highlight which transactions do not need the same level of vetting as other transactions.

While these are all important and applicable data approaches, in the rest of the chapter we highlight the five approaches that are used most frequently in accounting and auditing: profiling, data reduction, regression, classification, and clustering data approaches. You'll find that these data approaches are not mutually exclusive and that actual analysis may involve parts of several approaches to arrive at the intended test of the data and result.

✓ **PROGRESS CHECK**

1. Using the flowchart in Exhibit 3-5, identify the appropriate approach for the following questions:
    a. Will a customer purchase item X if given incentive A?
    b. Which item (X, Y, or none) will a customer likely purchase given incentive A?
    c. How many items will the customer purchase?
2. What is the main difference between supervised and unsupervised methods?
3. Evaluate the model shown in Exhibit 3-3. Which class would you predict the new vendor belongs to?

LO 3-2

Explain the profiling approach to Data Analytics

PROFILING

As you recall, profiling involves gaining an understanding of a typical behavior of an individual, group, or population (or sample). Profiling is done primarily using **structured data**—that is, data that are stored in a database or spreadsheet and are readily searchable. Using these data, analysts can use common summary statistics to describe the individual, group, or population, including knowing its mean, standard deviation, sum, etc. Profiling is generally performed on data that are readily available, so the data have already been gathered and are ready for further analysis.

Data profiling can be as simple as calculating summary statistics on transactional data, such as the average number of days to ship a product, the typical amount we pay for a product, or the number of hours an employee is expected to work. On the other hand, profiling can be used to develop complex models to predict potential fraud. For example, you might create a profile for each employee in a company that may include a combination of salary, hours worked, and travel and entertainment purchasing behavior. Sudden deviations from an employee's past behavior may represent risk and warrant follow-up by the internal auditors.

Similar to evaluating behavior, data profiling is typically used to assess data quality and internal controls. For example, data profiling may identify customers with incomplete or erroneous master data or mistyped transactions.

Data profiling typically involves the following steps:

1. *Identify the objects or activity you want to profile.* What data do you want to evaluate? Sales transactions? Customer data? Credit limits? Imagine a manager wants to track sales volume for each store in a retail chain. She might evaluate total sales dollars, asset turnover, use of promotions and discounts, and/or employee incentives.
2. *Determine the types of profiling you want to perform.* What is your goal? Do you want to set a benchmark for minimum activity, such as monthly sales? Have you set a budget that you wish to follow? Are you trying to reduce fraud risk? In the retail store scenario, the manager would likely want to compare each store to the others to identify which ones are underperforming or overperforming.
3. *Set boundaries or thresholds for the activity.* This is a benchmark that may be manually set, such as a budgeted value, or automatically set, such as a statistical mean, quartile, or percentile. The retail chain manager may define underperforming stores as those whose sales activity falls below the 20th percentile of the group and overperforming stores as those whose sales activity is above the 80th percentile. These thresholds are automatically calculated based on the total activity of the stores, so the benchmark is dynamic.
4. *Interpret the results and monitor the activity and/or generate a list of exceptions.* Here is where dashboards come into play. Management can use dashboards to quickly see multiple sets of profiled data and make decisions that would affect behavior. As you evaluate the results, try to understand what a deviation from the defined boundary represents. Is it a risk? Is it fraud? Is it just something to keep an eye on? To evaluate her stores, the retail chain manager may review a summary of the sales indicators and quickly identify under- and overperforming stores. She is likely to be more concerned with underperforming stores as they represent major challenges for the chain. Overperforming stores may provide insight into marketing efforts or customer base.
5. *Follow up on exceptions.* Once a deviation has been identified, management should have a plan to take a course of action to validate, correct, or identify the causes of the abnormal behavior. When the retail chain manager notices a store that is underperforming compared to its peers, she may follow up with the individual store manager to understand his concerns or offer a local promotion to stimulate sales.

As with most analyses, data profiles should be updated periodically to reflect changes in firm activity and identify activity that may be more relevant to decision making.

Example of Profiling in Management Accounting

Advanced Environmental Recycling Technologies (ticker symbol AERT) makes wood-plastic composite for decking that doesn't rot and keeps its form, color, and shape indefinitely (Exhibit 3-6). It has developed a recipe and knows the standards of how much wood, plastic, and coloring goes into each foot of decking. AERT has developed standard costs and constantly calculates the means and standard deviations of the use of wood, plastic, coloring, and labor for each foot of decking. As the company profiles each production batch, it knows that when significant variances from the standard cost occur, those variances need to be investigated further. This is an example of how profiling might be used in management accounting.

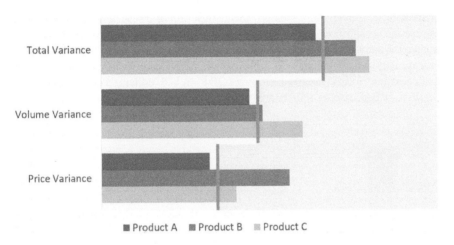

EXHIBIT 3-6 Example of Price and Volume Variance Profiling Note that there are multiple benchmarks. The blue line is the standard behavior; the green area contains favorable variances; the orange area shows unfavorable variances.

Example of Profiling in an Internal Audit

Profiling might also be used by internal auditors to evaluate travel and entertainment (T&E) expenses. In some organizations, total annual T&E expenses are second only to payroll and so represent a major expense for the organization. By profiling the T&E expenses, we can understand the average amount and range of expenditures and then compare and contrast with prior period's mean and range to help identify changing trends and potential risk areas for audit and potentially for tax purposes. This will help indicate areas where there is a lack of controls, changes in procedures, or individuals more willing to spend excessively in potential types of T&E expenses, etc., which might be associated with higher risk.

The use of profiling in internal audits might unearth when employees misuse company funds, like in the case of Tom Coughlin, an executive at Walmart, who misused "company funds to pay for CDs, beer, an all-terrain vehicle, a customized dog kennel, even a computer as his son's graduation gift—all the while describing the purchases as routine business expenses."[1]

---

[1]http://www.washingtonpost.com/wp-dyn/content/article/2005/07/14/AR2005071402055.html (accessed August 2, 2017).

Example of Profiling in Auditing and Continuous Auditing

Profiling is also useful in continuous auditing. If we consider the dollar amount of each transaction, we can develop a Z-score by knowing the mean and standard deviation. Using our statistics knowledge and assuming a normal distribution, any transaction that has a Z-score of 3 or above would represent abnormal transactions that might be associated with higher risk. We can investigate further seeing if those transactions had appropriate approvals and authorization.

An analysis of **Benford's law** could also be used to assess a set of transactions. Benford's law is an observation about the frequency of leading digits in many real-life sets of numerical data. The law states that in many naturally occurring collections of numbers, the significant leading digit is likely to be small. If the distribution of transactions for an account like "sales revenue" is substantially different than Benford's law would predict, then we would investigate the sales revenue account further and see if we can explain why there are differences from Benford's law. Exhibit 3-7 shows an illustration of Benford's law using the first digit of a company's gross domestic product (GDP) in U.S. dollars. We will show additional applications of Benford's law in chapter 6.

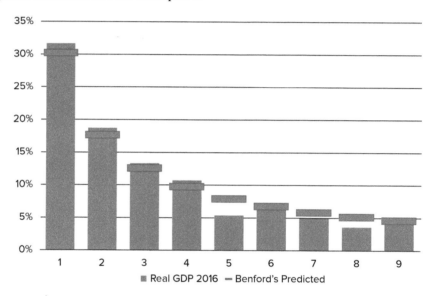

EXHIBIT 3-7 **Benford's Law** Benford's law predicts the distribution of first digits. In this example, the GDP is given (in U.S. dollars) for countries around the world from 2016; note its departure from what we would expect given Benford's law.

Source: data.worldbank.org

✓ PROGRESS CHECK

4. Profiling is also used in law enforcement, such as offender or criminal profiling. Offender profiling is a tool used by law enforcement to identify likely suspects and analyzing data patterns to help predict future offenses by criminals and identify potential victims. Compare and contrast this type of profiling with the profiling data approach used in accounting (mentioned earlier in this section).

5. Identify a reason the sales amount of any single product may or may not follow Benford's law.

DATA REDUCTION

As you recall, the data reduction approach attempts to reduce the amount of detailed information considered to focus on the most critical, interesting, or abnormal items (i.e., highest cost, highest risk, largest impact, etc.). It does this by filtering through a large set of data (perhaps the total population) and reducing it to a smaller set that has the vast majority of the critical information of the larger set. The data reduction approach is done primarily using *structured data*—that is, data that are stored in a database or spreadsheet and are readily searchable.

Data reduction involves the following steps:

1. *Identify the attribute you would like to reduce or focus on.* For example, an employee may commit fraud by creating a fictitious vendor and submitting fake invoices. Rather than evaluate every employee, an auditor may be interested only in employee records that have addresses that match vendor addresses.
2. *Filter the results.* This could be as simple as using filters in Excel, queries with a WHERE phrase. It may also involve a more complicated calculation. For example, employees who create fictitious vendors will often use addresses that are similar, but not exactly the same, as their own address to foil basic SQL queries. Here the auditor should use a tool that allows fuzzy matching, which uses probability to identify likely similar addresses.
3. *Interpret the results.* Once you have eliminated irrelevant data, take a moment to see if the results make sense. Calculate the summary statistics. Have you eliminated any obvious entries? Looking at the list of matching employees, the auditor might tweak the probability in the fuzzy match to be more or less precise to narrow or broaden the number of employees who appear.
4. *Follow up on results.* At this point, you will continue to build a model or use the results as a targeted sample for follow-up. The auditor should review company policy and follow up with each employee who appears in the reduced list as it represents risk.

Example of Data Reduction in Internal and External Auditing

An example might include the potential to use the data reduction approach in auditing. While auditing has employed various random and stratified sampling over the years, Data Analytics suggests new ways to highlight transactions that do not need the same level of vetting or further analysis as other transactions. One example might be to filter the travel and entertainment (T&E) transactions to find specific values, including whole-dollar amounts of T&E expenses. Whole-dollar amounts have a greater likelihood of being made up or fraudulent (as illustrated in Exhibit 3-8).

Another filter might be to consider only those transactions being paid to Square Payments because anyone can create a Square Payments account. If there are vendors that accept payment via Square Payments, there is a higher potential for the existence of a fictitious vendor.

Vendor	Amount
A	$4.35
B	$10.00
C	$17.00
A	$5.32
D	$54.23
B	$32.33
C	$33.00

Vendor	Amount
B	$10.00
C	$17.00
C	$33.00

EXHIBIT 3-8

Data Reduction
Data reduction is used to focus on data of interest—in this case, filtering on whole numbers.

The data reduction approach allows us to focus more time and effort on those vendors and transactions that might require additional analysis to make sure they are legitimate.

An example of the data reduction approach might be to do gap detection, such as looking for a missing check number in a sequence of checks. Finding out why certain check numbers were skipped and not recorded requires additional analysis and consideration.

Another application of the data reduction approach is to filter all the transactions between known related party transactions. Focusing specifically on related party transactions allows the auditor to focus on those transactions that might potentially be sensitive and/or risky.

Another example might be the comparison between the address of vendors and the address of employees to ensure that employees are not siphoning funds to themselves. Such a filter might require the use of a computer-assisted technique, called **fuzzy match**, to match addresses that do not perfectly match 100 percent. Use of fuzzy match looks for correspondences between portions, or segments, of the text of each potential match. Once potential matches between vendors and employees are found, additional analysis must be conducted to figure out if funds have been, or potentially could be, siphoned.

Examples of Data Reduction in Other Accounting Areas

Data reduction approaches are also used in operational audit settings. For example, filtering the data to find cases where there are duplicate invoice payments might be an efficient way to find errors or fraud. Once duplicate invoice payments are found, additional work can be done to identify the reasons this has occurred. It may also be a way to reduce costs when duplicate payments are found and procedures are set in place to mitigate duplicate payments from occurring in the future.

Data reduction approaches may also be useful in a financial statement analysis setting, perhaps performed by financial analysts, pension funds, or individual investors. Among other uses, **XBRL (eXtensible Business Reporting Language)** is used to facilitate the exchange of financial reporting information between the company and the Securities and Exchange Commission (SEC). The SEC then makes it available to all interested parties, including suppliers, competitors, investors, and financial analysts. XBRL requires that the data be tagged according to the XBRL taxonomy. Using these tagged data, financial analysts, loan officers, and investors develop models to access all the relevant financial or nonfinancial data to help interpret the financial data to predict future earnings, forecast solvency or liquidity, and analyze profitability. The use of XBRL and the modeling by financial data takes all the details of the financial statements, footnotes, and other financial and nonfinancial data and summarizes them in models of future earnings, solvency, liquidity, and profitability. We'll explore XBRL further in chapter 8.

 PROGRESS CHECK

> 6. Describe how the data reduction approach is used to consider T&E expenses.
> 7. Explain how XBRL might be used to focus on specific areas of interest by lenders.

<table>
<tr><td>

LO 3-4

Understand the regression approach to Data Analytics

</td></tr>
</table>

REGRESSION

Regressions allow the accountant to develop models to predict expected outcomes. These expected outcomes might be to predict the level of the allowance of doubtful accounts needed for a given accounts receivable balance.

Regression analysis involves the following process:

1. *Identify the variables that might predict an outcome.* The inputs are called independent variables, where the output is a dependent variable.

2. ***Determine the functional form of the relationship.*** Is it a linear relationship where each input plots to another? Are you trying to divide the records into different groups or classes?

3. ***Identify the parameters of the model.*** What are the relative weights of each variable or the thresholds of each branch in a classification?

The following discussion primarily identifies the structure of the model—that is, the relationship between the dependent variable and the plausible independent variables—in this way:

$$\text{Dependent variable} = f(\text{independent variables})$$

The dependent variable might be the amount that should be considered in an allowance for doubtful accounts; the independent variables that might predict the level needed to reserve it may be current aged loans, loan type, customer loan history, and collections success. We develop this further later.

We provide a multitude of examples in this next section.

Examples of the Regression Approach in Managerial Accounting

Accounting firms experience a great amount of employee turnover each year (between 15 and 25 percent each year).[2] Understanding and predicting employee turnover is a particularly important determination for accounting firms. Each year, they must predict how many new employees might be needed to accommodate growth, to supply needed areas of expertise, and to replace employees who have left. Accounting firms might predict employee turnover by predicting the following regression model in this way:

$$\text{Employee turnover} = f(\text{current professional salaries, health of the economy [GDP],}$$
$$\text{salaries offered by other accounting firms or by corporate accounting, etc.})$$

Using such a model, accounting firms could then begin to collect the necessary data to test their model and predict the level of employee turnover.

Examples of the Regression Approach in Auditing

One of the key tasks of auditors of a bank is to consider the amount of the allowance for loan losses or for nonbanks to consider the allowance for doubtful accounts (i.e., those receivables that may never be collected). These allowances are often subject to manipulation to help manage earnings.[3] The Financial Accounting Standards Board (FASB) recently issued Accounting Standards Update 2016-13, which requires that banks provide an estimate of expected credit losses (ECLs) by considering historical collection rates, current information, and reasonable and supportable forecasts, including estimates of prepayments.[4] Using these historical and industry data, auditors may work to test a model to establish a loan loss reserve in this way:

$$\text{Allowance for loan loses amount} = f(\text{current aged loans, loan type,}$$
$$\text{customer loan history, collections success})$$

---

[2]http://www.cpafma.org/articles/inside-public-accounting-releases-2015-national-benchmarking-report/ (accessed November 9, 2016).

[3]A. S. Ahmed, C. Takeda, and S. Thomas, "Bank Loan Loss Provisions: A Reexamination of Capital Management, Earnings Management and Signaling Effects," *Journal of Accounting and Economics* 28, no. 1 (1999), pp. 1–25.

[4]http://www.pwc.com/us/en/cfodirect/publications/in-brief/fasb-new-impairment-guidance-financial-instruments.html (accessed November 9, 2016).

Other Examples of the Regression and Classification Approach in Accounting

For example, in chapter 1, we worked to understand why LendingClub rejected certain loan applications. As we considered all of the possible explanations, we found that there were at least three possible indicators that a loan might be rejected, including the debt-to-income ratios, length of employment, and credit (risk) scores, suggesting a model that:

$$\text{Loan rejection} = f(\text{debt-to-income ratio, length of employment,} \\ \text{credit [risk] score})$$

Another example of the regression and classification approach might be the approval of individual credit card transactions. Assume you go on a trip; in the morning you are in Pittsburgh and by the very next day, you are in Shanghai. Will your credit card transaction in Shanghai automatically be rejected? Credit card companies establish models to predict fraud and decide whether to accept or reject a proposed credit card transaction. A potential model may be the following:

$$\text{Transaction approval} = f(\text{location of current transaction, location of last transaction,} \\ \text{amount of current transaction, prior history of travel of credit card holder, etc.})$$

LO 3-5

Understand the classification approach to Data Analytics.

CLASSIFICATION

The goal of classification is to predict whether an individual we know very little about will belong to one class or another. For example, will a customer have his or her balance written off? The key here is that we are predicting *whether* the write-off will occur or not (in other words, there are two classes: "Write-Off" and "Good").

Classification is a little more involved as we are now dealing with machine learning and complex probabilistic models. Here are the general steps:

1. *Identify the classes you wish to predict.*
2. *Manually classify an existing set of records.*
3. *Select a set of classification models.*
4. *Divide your data into training and testing sets.*
5. *Generate your model.*
6. *Interpret the results and select the "best" model.*

Classification Terminology

First, a bit of terminology to prepare us for our discussion.

Training data are existing data that have been manually evaluated and assigned a class. We know that some customer accounts have been written off, so those accounts are assigned the class "Write-Off." We will train our model to learn what it is that those customers have in common so we can predict whether a new customer will default or not.

Test data are existing data used to evaluate the model. The classification algorithm will try to predict the class of the test data and then compare its prediction to the previously assigned class. This comparison is used to evaluate the accuracy of the model, or the probability that the model will assign the correct class.

Decision trees are used to divide data into smaller groups. **Decision boundaries** mark the split between one class and another.

Exhibit 3-9 provides an illustration of both decision trees and decision boundaries. Decision trees split the data at each branch into two or more groups. In this example, the first branch divides the vendor data by geographic distance and inserts a decision boundary through the middle of the data. Branches 2 and 3 split each of the two new groups by vendor volume. Note that the decision boundaries are different for each grouping.

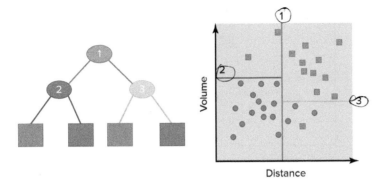

EXHIBIT 3-9
Example of Decision
Trees and Decision
Boundaries

Pruning removes branches from a decision tree to avoid overfitting the model. *Pre-pruning* occurs during the model generation. The model stops creating new branches when the information usefulness of an additional branch is low. *Post-pruning* evaluates the complete model and discards branches after the fact. Exhibit 3-10 provides an illustration of how pruning might work in a decision tree.

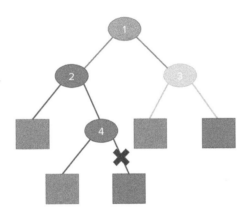

EXHIBIT 3-10
Illustration of Pruning
a Decision Tree

Linear classifiers are useful for ranking items rather than simply predicting class probability. These classifiers are used to identify a decision boundary. Exhibit 3-11 shows an illustration of linear classifiers segregating the two classes. Note the error observation that shows that this linear classifier is not perfect in segregating the two classes.

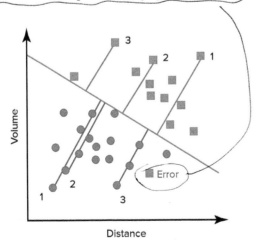

EXHIBIT 3-11
Illustration of Linear
Classifiers

EXHIBIT 3-12

Support Vector Machines

With support vector machines, first find the widest margin (biggest pipe); then find the middle line.

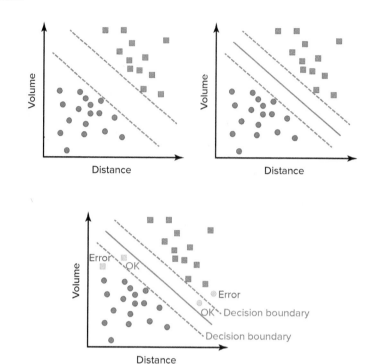

EXHIBIT 3-13

Support Vector Machine Decision Boundaries

SVMs have two decision boundaries at the edges of the pipes.

Linear discriminants use mathematical equations to draw the line that separates the two classes. In the example noted here, the classification is a function of both volume and distance:

$$\text{Class}(x) = \bullet \quad \text{if } 1.0 \times \text{Volume} - 1.5 \times \text{Distance} + 50 > 0$$

$$\text{Class}(x) = \blacksquare \quad \text{if } 1.0 \times \text{Volume} - 1.5 \times \text{Distance} + 50 \le 0$$

Support vector machine is a discriminating classifier that is defined by a separating hyperplane that works first to find the widest margin (or biggest pipe) and then works to find the middle line. Exhibits 3-12 and 3-13 provide an illustration of support vector machines and how they work to find the best decision boundary.

Evaluating Classifiers

When classifiers wrongly classify an observation, they are penalized. The larger the penalty (error), the less accurate the model is at predicting a future value, or classification.

Overfitting

Rarely will datasets be so clean that you have a clear decision boundary. You should always be wary of classifiers that are too accurate. Exhibit 3-14 provides an illustration of overfitting and underfitting. You want a good amount of accuracy without being too perfect. Notice how the error rate declines from 6 to 3 to 0. You want to be able to generalize your results, and complete accuracy creates a complex model with little predictive value. Exhibit 3-15 provides a good illustration of the trade-offs between the complexity of the model and the accuracy of the classification. While you may be able to come up with a very complex model with the training data, chances are it will not improve the accuracy of the test data. There is, in some sense, a sweet spot, where the model is most accurate without being so complex to thus allow classification of both the training as well as the test data.

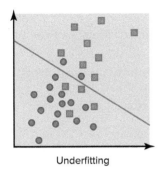
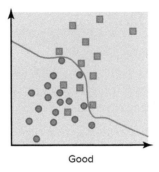
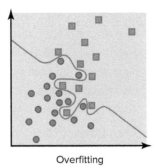

Underfitting   Good   Overfitting

EXHIBIT 3-14
Illustration of
Underfitting and
Overfitting the Data
with a Predictive Model

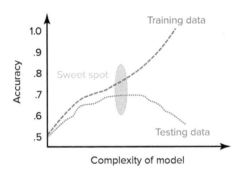

EXHIBIT 3-15
Illustration of the
Trade-Off between
the Complexity of the
Model and the Accuracy
of the Classification

✓ PROGRESS CHECK

8. If we are trying to predict the extent of employee turnover, do you believe the health of the economy, as measured using GDP, will be positively or negatively associated with employee turnover?

9. If we are trying to predict whether a loan will be rejected, would you expect credit score to be positively or negatively associated with loan rejection by a bank such as **LendingClub**?

CLUSTERING

LO 3-6

Understand
the clustering
approach to Data
Analytics

The clustering data approach works to identify groups of similar data elements and the underlying drivers of those groups. More specifically, clustering techniques are used to group data/observations in a few segments so that data within any segment are similar, while data across segments are different.

As an example, **Walmart** may want to understand the types of customers who shop at its stores. Because **Walmart** has good reason to believe there are different market segments of people, it may consider changing the design of the store or the types of products to accommodate the different types of customers, emphasizing the ones that are most profitable to **Walmart**. To learn about the different types of customers, managers may ask whether customers agree with the following statements using a scale of 1–7 (on a Likert scale):

Statement 1: I enjoy shopping.
Statement 2: I try to avoid shopping because it is bad for the budget.
Statement 3: I like to combine my shopping with eating out.

Statement 4: I use coupons when I shop.

Statement 5: I care more about the quality of the products than I do about the price.

Statement 6: I don't care about shopping.

Statement 7: You can save a lot of money by comparing prices between various stores.

Income: The household income of the respondent (in dollars).

Shopping at **Walmart**: How many times a month do you visit **Walmart**?

The answers to these various questions may help cluster the various customers into different clusters and help **Walmart** to cater to its various customer clusters better through superior insights.

Heat maps are another example of cluster analysis, showing a high concentration of customers who purchase a particular product by the region in which they live. This might help us to determine the appropriate region to focus sales resources.

Example of the Clustering Approach in Auditing

The clustering data approach may also be used in an auditing setting. Imagine a group insurance setting where fraudulent claims associated with payment were previously found by internal auditors through happenstance and/or through hotline tips. Based on current internal audit tests, payments are the major concern of the business unit. Specifically, the types of related risks identified are duplicate payments, fictitious names, improper/incorrect information entered into the systems, and suspicious payment amounts.

Clustering is useful for anomaly detection in payments to insurance beneficiaries, suppliers, etc. as shown in Figure 3-16. By identifying transactions with similar characteristics, transactions are grouped together into clusters. Those clusters that consist of few transactions or small populations are then flagged for investigation by the auditors as they represent groups of outliers. Examples of these flagged clusters include transactions include transactions with large payment amounts, a long delay in processing the payment.

The dimensions used in clustering may be simple correlations between variables, such as payment amount and time to pay, or more complex combinations of variables, such as ratios or weighted equations. As they explore the data, auditors develop attributes that the think will be relevant through intuition or data exploration. Figure 3-16 illustrates clustering base on the following attributes:

1. Payment amount: The value of the payment for routine transactions.
2. Days to Pay: The number of days from the original recorded transaction to the payment date.

The data are normalized to reduce the distortion of the data and other outliers are removed. They are then plotted with the number of days to pay on the y axis and the payment amount on the x axis. Of the eight clusters identified, three clusters highlight potential anomalies that may require further investigation as part of an internal or external audit.

- Cluster 6 payments (purple) have a long duration between the processing to payment dates.
- Cluster 7 payments (pink) have high payment amounts.
- Cluster 8 payments (brown) have high payment amounts and a long duration between the processing date and the payment date.

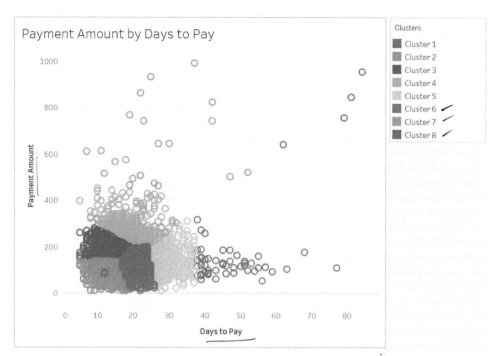

EXHIBIT 3-16
Example of Cluster Analysis of Group Insurance Claim Payments

Source: Thiprungsri S., and M.A. Vasarhelyi, 2011, page 79.

✓ **PROGRESS CHECK**

10. Name three clusters of customers who might shop at **Walmart**.
11. Cluster 1 of the group insurance highlighted claims have a long period from death to payment dates. Why would that cluster be of interest to internal auditors?

Summary

- In this chapter, we addressed the third step of the IMPACT cycle model: the "P" for "performing test plan." That is, how are we going to test or analyze the data to address a problem we are facing?
- Based on our problem and the data available, we provided a flowchart that helps the analyst to choose the most appropriate model, noting the differences when we use a supervised versus an unsupervised approach.
- Specifically, we addressed five data analytics approaches or techniques are most common to address our accounting questions: profiling, data reduction, regression, classification, and clustering. We also provided examples of accounting and auditing problems addressed by these data approaches.
- We introduced the concepts of Benford's law and fuzzy match, which we will use in subsequent chapters.

- We presented some classification terminology—including test and training data, decision trees and boundaries, linear classifiers, and support vector machines—and talked about the perils of under- and overfitting the training data and their consequences in predictions using the test data.

Key Words

Benford's law (*100*) An observation about the frequency of leading digits in many real-life sets of numerical data. The law states that in many naturally occurring collections of numbers, the significant lending digit is likely to be small.

causal modeling (*95*) A data approach similar to regression, but used when the relationship between independent and dependent variables where it is hypothesized that the independent variables cause or are associated with the dependent variable.

classification (*95*) A data approach used to assign each unit in a population into a few categories potentially to help with predictions.

clustering (*94*) A data approach used to divide individuals (like customers) into groups (or clusters) in a useful or meaningful way.

co-occurrence grouping (*94*) A data approach used to discover associations between individuals based on transactions involving them.

data reduction (*94*) A data approach used to reduce the amount of information that needs to be considered to focus on the most critical items (i.e., highest cost, highest risk, largest impact, etc.).

decision boundaries (*104*) Technique used to mark the split between one class and another.

decision tree (*104*) Tool used to divide data into smaller groups.

fuzzy match (*102*) A computer-assisted technique of finding matches that are less than 100 percent perfect by finding correspondencies between portions of the text of each potential match.

link prediction (*95*) A data approach used to predict a relationship between two data items.

profiling (*94*) A data approach used to characterize the "typical" behavior of an individual, group, or population by generating summary statistics about the data (including mean, standard deviations, etc.).

regression (*95*) A data approach used to estimate or predict, for each unit, the numerical value of some variable using some type of statistical model.

similarity matching (*95*) A data approach used to identify similar individuals based on data known about them.

structured data (*98*) Data that are organized and reside in a fixed field with a record or a file. Such data are generally contained in a relational database or spreadsheet and are readily searchable by search algorithms.

supervised approach/method (*94*) Approach used to learn more about the basic relationships between independent and dependent variables that are hypothesized to exist.

support vector machine (*106*) A discriminating classifier that is defined by a separating hyperplane that works first to find the widest margin (or biggest pipe).

training data (*104*) Existing data that have been manually evaluated and assigned a class, which assists in classifying the test data.

test data (*104*) A set of data used to assess the degree and strength of a predicted relationship established by the analysis of training data.

unsupervised approach/method (*94*) Approach used for data exploration looking for potential patterns of interest.

XBRL (*102*) (eXtensible Business Reporting Language) A global standard for exchanging financial reporting information that uses XML.

✓ ANSWERS TO PROGRESS CHECKS

1. a. Link prediction
   b. Classification
   c. Regression

2. In **supervised** learning, there is some idea of the basic relationships either because of theory or because we have learned from our training data. In **unsupervised** learning, we are primarily exploring the data for potential patterns that might exist which may ultimately turn into supervised learning.

3. Exhibit 3-3 suggests that the new observation would likely belong to the "delayed vendors" instead of the "on-time vendors" based on the volume shipped and the distance and where it appears relative to the other observations.

4. In some sense, profiling techniques to find criminals and accounting anomalies are very similar. Profiling to find criminals often looks to the physical characteristics (race, sex, mental state, etc.) to predict whether the person has or is likely to commit a crime (and is illegal to use in some jurisdictions). Accounting looks to other, nonphysical characteristics such as the amounts, totals, and types of expenditures to identify potential anomalies.

5. A dollar store might have everything for exactly $1.00. In that case, the use of Benford's law for any single project or even for every product would not follow Benford's law!

6. Data reduction may be used to filter out ordinary travel and entertainment expenses so an auditor can focus on those that are potentially erroneous or fraudulent.

7. The XBRL tagging allows an analyst or decision maker to focus on one or a category of expenses of most interest to a lender. For example, lenders might be most interested in monitoring the amount of long-term debt, interest payments, and dividends paid to assess if the borrower will be able to repay the loan. Using the capabilities of XBRL, lenders could focus on just those individual accounts for further analysis.

8. We certainly could let the data speak and address this question directly. In general, when the health of the economy is stronger, there are fewer layoffs and fewer people out looking for a job, which means less turnover.

9. Chapter 1 illustrated that **LendingClub** collects the credit score data and the initial analysis there suggested the higher the credit score the less likely to be rejected. Given this evidence, we would predict a negative relationship between credit score and loans that are rejected.

10. Three clusters of customers who might consider **Walmart** could include thrifty shoppers (looking for the lowest price), shoppers looking to shop for all of their household needs (both grocery and non-grocery items) in one place, and those customers who live close to the store (good location).

11. The longer time between the death and payment dates begs one to ask why it has taken so long for payment to occur and if the interest required to be paid is likely large. Because of these issues, there might be a possibility that the claim is fraudulent or at least deserves a more thorough review to explain why there was such a long delay.

▣ connect

Multiple Choice Questions

1. _____ is a set of data used to assess the degree and strength of a predicted relationship.
   a. Training data
   b. Unstructured data
   c. Structured data
   d. Test data

2. Data that are organized and reside in a fixed field with a record or a file. Such data are generally contained in a relational database or spreadsheet and are readily searchable by search algorithms. The term matching this definition is:

   a. Training data.

   b. Unstructured data.

   c. Structured data.

   d. Test data.

3. The observation that the frequency of leading digits in many real-life sets of numerical data is called:

   a. Leading digits hypothesis.

   b. Moore's law.

   c. Benford's law.

   d. Clustering.

4. Which approach to data analytics attempts to predict a relationship between two data items?

   a. Similarity matching

   b. Classification

   c. Link prediction

   d. Co-occurrence grouping

5. In general, the more complex the model, the greater the chance of:

   a. Overfitting the data.

   b. Underfitting the data.

   c. Pruning the data.

   d. The need to reduce the amount of data considered.

6. In general, the simpler the model, the greater the chance of:

   a. Overfitting the data.

   b. Underfitting the data.

   c. Pruning the data.

   d. The need to reduce the amount of data considered.

7. _____ is a discriminating classifier that is defined by a separating hyperplane that works first to find the widest margin (or biggest pipe) and then works to find the middle line.

   a. Linear classifier

   b. Support vector machine

   c. Decision tree

   d. Multiple regression

8. _____ mark (marks) the split between one class and another.

   a. Decision trees

   b. identified questions

   c. Decision boundaries

   d. Linear classifiers

9. Models associated with regression and classification data approaches have all *except* this important part:

   a. Identifying which variables (we'll call these independent variables) might help predict an outcome (we'll call this the dependent variable).

   b. The functional form of the relationship (linear, nonlinear, etc.).

   c. The numeric parameters of the model (detailing the relative weights of each of the variables associated with the prediction).

   d. Test data.

10. Which approach to data analytics attempts to assign each unit in a population into a small set of classes where the unit belongs?
    a. Classification
    b. Regression
    c. Similarity matching
    d. Co-occurrence grouping

Discussion Questions

1. What is the difference between a target and a class?
2. What is the difference between a supervised and an unsupervised approach?
3. What is the difference between training datasets and test (or testing) datasets?
4. Using Exhibit 3-5 as a guide, what are three data approaches associated with the supervised approach?
5. Using Exhibit 3-5 as a guide, what are three data approaches associated with the unsupervised approach?
6. How might the data reduction approach be used in auditing?
7. How might classification be used in approving or denying a potential fraudulent credit card transaction?
8. How is similarity matching different from clustering?
9. How does fuzzy match work? Give an accounting situation where it might be most useful.
10. Compare and contrast the profiling data approach and the development of standard cost for a unit of production at a manufacturing company. Are they substantially the same, or do they have differences?
11. Exhibits 3-1, 3-2, 3-3, and 3-4 suggest that volume and distance are the best predictors of "days to ship" for a wholesale company. Any other variables that would also be useful in predicting the number of "days to ship"?

Problems

1. How could the fuzzy match be used to find undisclosed related party transactions that might need to be disclosed?
2. An auditor is trying to figure out if the inventory at an electronics store chain is obsolete. What characteristics might be used to help establish a model predicting inventory obsolescence?
3. An auditor is trying to figure out if the goodwill its client recognized when it purchased a factory has become impaired. What characteristics might be used to help establish a model predicting goodwill impairment?
4. How might clustering be used to explain customers that owe us money (accounts receivable)?
5. Why would the use of data reduction be useful to highlight related party transactions (e.g., CEO has her own separate company that the main company does business with)?
6. How could an investor use XBRL to do an analysis of the industry's inventory turnover?
7. Name three accounts that would be appropriate and interesting to apply Benford's law in auditing those accounts. Why would an auditor choose those three accounts? When would a departure from Benford's law encourage the auditor to investigate further?

Answers to Multiple Choice Questions

1. D 2. C 3. C 4. C 5. A 6. B 7. B 8. C 9. D 10. A

Appendix: Setting Up a Classification Analysis

To answer the question "Will a new vendor ship a large order on time?" using classification, you should clearly identify your variables, define the scope of your data, and assign classes. This is related to "master the data" in the IMPACT model.

Identify Your Variables

As the question is related to vendors and order shipments, take a moment to think about attributes that might be predictive. Would the total number of order items potentially cause a delay? Would the types of items? How about the overall shipping weight? Does the vendor's physical distance from your warehouse matter? How about the age of vendor relationship or number of vendor employees? What else?

Define the Scope

Because you are looking at vendor shipments, you would need—at the basic level—data related to the original purchase order (order date, number of items), shipping data (shipping date, weight), and vendor master data (location, age, size). This will help you narrow down your data request and make it more likely that you'll get the data you request more quickly. As you're preparing your data, you'll want to join these tables so that each record represents an order. You'll also want to calculate any figures of merit, such as the number of days (Ship date – Order date), volume (total number of items on the order or physical size) or distance (Vendor address – Warehouse address*) (see Table 3-1).

TABLE 3-1
Vendor Shipments

PO#	Total Items: Sum(Qty)	Order Date	Ship Date	Days to Ship: (Ship Date – Order Date)	Vendor	Distance (mi): (V Coordinates – WH Coordinates)*	Weight (lb)
123456	15	7/30/2020	8/2/2020	3	ABC Company	45	160

*Software such as Tableau can calculate distances, but it requires a little more work. See http://www.vizwiz.com/2012/01/tableau-tip-calculating-distance.html to learn how.

Distance Formula

(Use first number 3959 for miles or 6371 for kilometers)

```
3959 * ACOS
(
SIN(RADIANS([Lat])) * SIN(RADIANS([Lat2])) + COS(RADIANS([Lat])) *
COS(RADIANS([Lat2])) * COS(RADIANS([Long2]) – RADIANS([Long]))
)
```

Assign Classes

Take a moment to define your classes. You are trying to predict whether a given order shipment will either be "On-time" or "Delayed" based on the number of days it takes from the order date to the shipping date. What does "on-time" mean? Let's define "on-time" as an order that ships in 5 days or less and a "delayed" order as one that ships later than 5 days. You'll use this rule to add the class as a new attribute to each of your historical records (see Table 3-2).

On-time = (Days to ship ≤ 5)

Delayed = (Days to ship > 5)

PO#	Total Items: Sum (Qty)	Order Date	Ship Date	Days to ship: (Ship Date – Order Date)	Vendor	Distance (mi): (V Coordinates – WH Coordinates)*	Weight (lb)	Class
123456	15	7/30/2020	8/2/2020	3	ABC Company	45	160	On-time
123457	20	7/30/2020	8/5/2020	6	XYZ Company	120	800	Delayed

TABLE 3-2
Shipment Class

CHAPTER 3 LABS

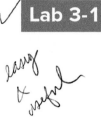

Auditors use data reduction to focus their efforts on testing internal controls and limiting their scope. For example, they may want to look only at transactions for a given year. In this lab, you will learn to use filters in Excel and perform some fuzzy matches on vendor and employee records, a common auditor analysis.

Company summary

These data are for a generic manufacturing company. You have been asked to see if there are any potentially fictitious vendors or employees who may have created fake companies in an effort to commit fraud.

Data

- Fuzzy.xlsx—contains employee and vendor data

Technique

- Some Excel experience is handy here. You will use tables, filters, and the Fuzzy Lookup add-in.

Software needed

- Excel
- Fuzzy Lookup add-in https://www.microsoft.com/en-us/download/details.aspx?id=15011

In this lab, you will:

Part 1: Identify a problem that will require data reduction techniques.

Part 2: Master the data and prepare for analysis.

Part 3: Perform data reduction.

Part 1: Identify the Problem

Fictitious vendors represent risk to a company. One way employees can embezzle funds from a company is to create a fictitious vendor and then submit an invoice for services that were never performed. Where there are poor internal controls, the employee receives the payment and deposits the check.

> Q1.   What data do you think might exist to show that a vendor is related to an employee? Which attributes would you focus on?

> Q2.   How might you attempt to detect these connections between vendors and employees?

> Q3.   If you were the employee committing fraud, what would you try to do with the data to evade detection?

Part 2: Master the Data and Prepare for Analysis

You have requested the employee and vendor master data tables to aid in your analysis. The IT supervisor has sent you an Excel sheet with the following tables and attributes:

Employees

EmployeeID
EmployeeFirstName
EmployeeLastName

EmployeeGender

EmployeeHireDate

EmployeeStreetAddress

EmployeeCity

EmployeeState

EmployeeZip

EmployeePhone

Vendors

VendorID

VendorName

VendorType

VendorSince

VendorContact

VendorBillingAddress

VendorBillingCity

VendorBillingState

VendorBillingZip

VendorBillingPhone

Your first step is to understand the data and prepare it in Excel to perform some matching.

1. Open **Fuzzy.xlsx** in Excel.
2. Quickly browse through the worksheets to ensure that they are complete.
3. Go to the **Employees** tab and click any data element.
4. Select the entire data table (**Ctrl + A**).
5. Go to the **Home** tab, **Styles** section, and click **Format as Table**. Any style will do.
6. In the **Format As Table** box that appears, make sure the **My table has headers** box is checked, and click **OK**.
7. In the **Table Tools > Design** tab, under **Properties**, change the table name from **Table1** to **Employees**.
8. Now go to the **Vendors** tab and click any data element. Repeat steps 4–7 and name the new table **"Vendors"**.
9. Take a screenshot of either table (label it 3-1A).
10. Save your file as **Fuzzy-Tables.xlsx**.

Part 3: Perform Data Reduction

Now you're ready to find those fictitious vendors. There are many different approaches for working with the data to narrow your focus. These can be used with other data sources as well.

Tool: Filtering

Excel Filters allow you to quickly find data with common attributes and help to limit the scope of your analysis. Assume that the auditors have analyzed all vendors prior to 2019 and have resolved any outstanding issues. By analyzing only the vendors from 2019, you avoid unnecessary analysis and reduce the time it will take for the computer to run the analysis.

11. Open **Fuzzy-Tables.xlsx** and click the **Vendors** worksheet.
12. Click the drop-down arrow next to **VendorSince** to show filtering options, shown below.

13. To select only 2019 records, uncheck **Select All** and then check the box next to **2019**.

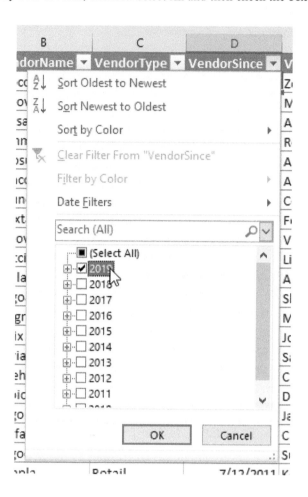

14. Select the table and headers (**Ctrl + A** twice) and copy the values (**Ctrl + C**).
15. Create a new worksheet tab called **"Vendors2019"** and paste the filtered values there.
16. Select your new table and format it as a table called **"Vendors2019"**.
17. Take a screenshot (label it 3-1B).
18. Save your file as **Fuzzy-Tables-2019.xlsx**.

Tool: Fuzzy Match

SQL queries and PivotTables require exact matches between two data points to identify related data. Foreign keys must match primary keys exactly in databases or else a relationship doesn't exist. Names and addresses, as well as other manually entered text values are more prone to errors and manipulation. Think about your questions from Part 1 of this lab. Wouldn't one way to avoid detection be to change something subtle in the address—for example "Street" to "St." or "Center Ave" to "Center"? A human could understand that these are the same thing, but a computer cannot without some help.

Fuzzy Lookup is a plugin for Excel that enables these mostly similar matches and finds things that might otherwise evade detection by a computer system.

19. Download and enable **Fuzzy Lookup for Excel** if you haven't already.
20. Open **Fuzzy-Tables-2019.xlsx** if you haven't already.
21. In the ribbon, click **Fuzzy Lookup > Fuzzy Lookup**. A panel will appear on the right showing the tables you defined in Part 2 of this lab.

22. For the **Left Table**, choose **Vendors2019**, and for the **Right Table**, choose **Employees**.
23. In the **Left Columns** list, click **VendorBillingAddress**, and from the **Right Columns** list, click **EmployeeStreetAddress**.
24. Click the **Join** icon button in between the two lists. A new relationship will appear in the **Match Columns** list.
25. In the **Output Columns** list, uncheck everything except:
    a. VendorName
    b. VendorContact
    c. VendorBillingAddress
    d. VendorBillingZip
    e. EmployeeFirstName
    f. EmployeeLastName
    g. EmployeeStreetAddress
    h. EmployeeZip
    i. FuzzyLookup.Similarity
26. **Number of Matches** should be 1.
27. The **Similarity Threshold** slider represents the percentage similarity. You can slide it left if you want less similar matches or slide it right for more similar. 1.0 is an exact match.

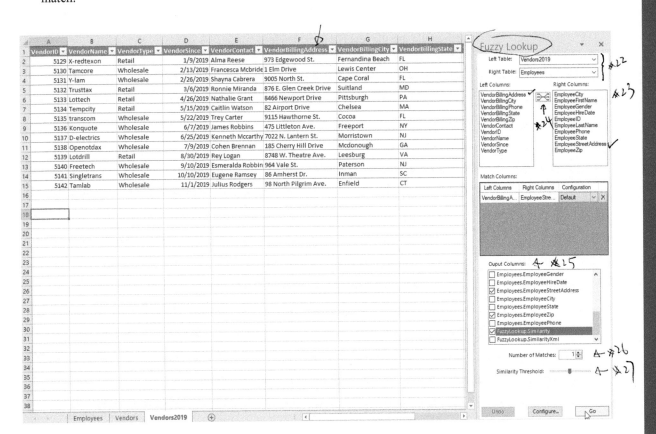

LAB EXHIBIT 3-1B

Source: Microsoft Excel 2016

28. Create a new worksheet tab called **FuzzyMatch**.
29. Click cell **A1**, then click **Go** in the **Fuzzy Lookup** panel. A list will appear with all of the vendors and any potential fuzzy match.

30. Format the output as a table named **FuzzyMatch**, then filter out any records with 0.0000 Similarity.

    Q4.   How many vendors have similar addresses to employees?

    Q5.   What do you notice about the street vendor and employee street addresses?

    Q6.   Are there any false positives (fuzzy matches that aren't really matches)?

31. Take a screenshot (label it 3-1C).

End of Lab

Lab 3-2   Regression in Excel

Company summary

The data used are a subset of the **College Scorecard** dataset that is provided by the U.S. Department of Education. These data provide federal financial aid and earnings information, insights into the performance of schools eligible to receive federal financial aid, and the outcomes of students at those schools. You can learn more about how the data are used and view the raw data yourself at https://collegescorecard.ed.gov/data/. However, for this lab, you should use the text file provided to you.

Data

- CollegeScorecard Datasets: CollegeScorecard_CleanedData from Lab 2-5

Technique

- Some experience with Excel is useful for this lab.

Software needed

- Excel
- Screen capture tool (Windows: Snipping Tool; Mac: Cmd + Shift + 4)

In this lab, you will:

Part 1: Identify the questions.

Part 2: Load the data.

Part 3: Perform a regression analysis in Excel.

Part 1: Identify the Questions

This lab relies upon the steps completed in Lab 2-5 in which the data were prepared.

We will begin with a simple regression with two variables, SAT average and completion rate for first-time, full-time students at four-year institutions.

    Q1.   Would you expect SAT average and completion rate to be correlated? If so, would you expect the correlation to be positive or negative?

    Q2.   When determining relationships between variables, one of the criteria for a potential causal relationship is that the cause must happen before the effect. Regarding SAT average and completion rate, which would you determine to be the potential cause? Which would be the effect?

    Q3.   Identifying the cause and effect as you did in Q2 can help you determine the explanatory and response variables. Which variable, SAT average or completion rate, is the explanatory variable?

Part 2: Master the Data

These steps were performed in Lab 2-5. You can either use the already prepared data in the file Lab 3-3, College Scorecard Data (Cleaned post-Lab 2-5).xlsx, or you can use the file that you saved after completing Lab 2-5.

Part 3: Perform an Analysis of the Data

1. To perform a regression test in Excel, you need to first download the **Data Analysis ToolPak**. To do so, Follow this menu path: **File > Options > Add-ins.** From this window, select the **Go. . .** button, and then place a checkmark in the box next to **Analysis ToolPak**. Once you click **OK**, you will be able to access the **ToolPak** from the **Data** tab on the Excel ribbon.
2. Click the **Data Analysis** button from the **Data** tab on the Excel ribbon and select **Regression**.
3. A window will pop up for you to input the **Y range** and the **X range**.

LAB EXHIBIT 3-2A

Source: Microsoft Excel 2016

4. Select the entire set of data that is associated with the response variable for the Y range, then select the entire set of data that is associated with the explanatory variable for the X range.
5. If you selected the labels in your ranges, place a checkmark in the box next to **Labels**.
6. Click **OK**. This will run the regression test and place the output on a new spreadsheet in your Excel workbook.
7. Take a screenshot of your regression output (label it 3-2A).

End of Lab

[handwritten notes in margin: "Weka!", "No presentation."]

Company summary

LendingClub is a peer-to-peer marketplace where borrowers and investors are matched together. The goal of LendingClub is to reduce the costs associated with these banking transactions and make borrowing less expensive and investment more engaging. LendingClub provides data on loans that have been approved and rejected since 2007, including the assigned interest rate and type of loan. This provides several opportunities for data analysis.

Data

- **LendingClub** datasets: LendingClub-Classification

Software needed

- Excel
- Weka—available at www.cs.waikato.ac.nz/ml/weka
- Screen capture tool (Windows: Snipping Tool; Mac: Cmd + Shift + 4)

In this lab, you will:

- Analyze the data using various classification models.

Part 1: Identify the Questions

Thinking about **LendingClub**'s function as a marketplace for investors and borrowers, what might stakeholders want to know? Has **LendingClub**'s model changed over the years? If we understood what affected an interest rate decision, could we game the system to our advantage? Take a moment and come up with some general questions that could be answered through data analysis.

Q1. Thinking about loan applicants in general, how would you expect them to fall into different groups?

Q2. When evaluating previous loan data, what would you expect your target variable to be?

Q3. What factors do you think would affect whether a loan will be accepted or rejected?

Q4. Identify the data you would need to answer your questions and validate your hypothesis.

Part 2: Master the Data

For this lab, you should download the lending data from **LendingClub** and prepare it for some more advanced analysis in chapter 3. The **LendingClub** data contains two different file types including LoanStats for approved loans and RejectStats for rejected loans. There are significantly more data available for LoanStats. There are 107 different attributes. To save some time, we've identified 19 of the most interesting in Lab Tables 3-3A and 3-3B.

Q5. Given this list of attributes, what concerns do you have with the data's ability to predict answers to the questions you identified before?

Between the two groups of data files, we notice that there are some attributes in common, though not very many (see Lab Table 3-3C).

Attribute	Description
id	Loan identification number
member_id	Membership id
loan_amnt	Requested loan amount
emp_length	Employment length
issue_d	Date of loan issue
loan_status	Fully paid or charged off
pymnt_plan	Payment plan: yes or no
purpose	Loan purpose: e.g., wedding, medical, debt_consolidation, car
zip_code	The first three digits of the applicant's zip code
addr_state	State
dti	Debt-to-income ratio
delinq_2y	Late payments within the past two years
earliest_cr_line	Oldest credit account
inq_last_6mnths	Credit inquiries in the past 6 months
open_acc	Number of open credit accounts
revol_bal	Total balance of all credit accounts
revol_util	Percentage of available credit in use
total_acc	Total number of credit accounts
application_type	Individual or joint application

LAB TABLE 3-3A
LoanStatsXXXX.csv

Attribute	Description
Amount Requested	Requested loan amount
Application Date	Date of loan application
Loan Title	Brief description of loan purpose
Risk_Score	LendingClub's calculated value
Debt-To-Income Ratio	Debt-to-income ratio
Zip Code	The first three digits of the applicant's zip code
State	State
Employment Length	Employment length
Policy Code	Internal number

LAB TABLE 3-3B
RejectStats.csv

Common	RejectStats	ApproveStats
AmountRequested	Amount Requested	loan_amount
Month	=MONTH("Application Date")	=MONTH("issue_d")
Purpose	Loan Title	purpose
DebtToIncome	Debt-to-Income	dti
State	State	addr_state
YearsOfEmployment	Employment (Find/Replace)	emp_length (Find/Replace)
Class	"REJECT"	"APPROVE"

LAB TABLE 3-3C
Common Attributes

Q6. What does the lack of attributes in the RejectData files tell us about the data that **LendingClub** retains on rejected loans?

Q7. How will that affect a classification analysis?

We will need to convert the data into a useful format before we can perform any analysis. We need to generate two sets of data, one for classification and one for regression and clustering.

Cleaning the Data for Classification

Goal: Combine approved and rejected data for a given year, assign a class to each record.

Issues

- Approved and rejected loans contain different data attributes.
- Date data values are recorded in different formats (1/9/2009 vs. Jan-2009).
- Years of employment contain text values and should be numbers.

In Excel

1. Select a year you would like to analyze between 2007 and 2012.
2. Create a new spreadsheet.
3. Type the common attributes from Table 3-3C into the first row.
4. Open the LoanStats and RejectStats for your chosen year.
5. Delete all columns that don't match those listed in Table 3-3C.
6. Use the =MONTH formula to extract the month from the date.
7. Copy the Month column and **Paste Special** > **Values** into the **Date** column.
8. Add a new column for the class and add **REJECT** to the rejected loans and **APPROVE** to the approved loans.
9. Copy and paste the values for your chosen year from each .csv file into your new spreadsheet.
10. Find and replace the employment values using Lab Table 3-3D.

LAB TABLE 3-3D

Original Value	New Value
na	0
< 1 year	0
1 year	1
2 years	2
3 years	3
4 years	4
5 years	5
6 years	6
7 years	7
8 years	8
9 years	9
10+ years	10
, (comma)	(blank)

11. Save your file as **LoanClassificationXXXX.csv**, replacing XXXX with your year. Be sure to choose .csv as the file type.
12. Take a screenshot (label it 3-3A).

Part 3: Perform an Analysis of the Data

We will try multiple classification models and compare their results using Weka.

13. Open **Weka** > **Explorer**.
14. Open **file. . .** > **Locate your LoanClassificationXXXX.csv** file.
15. Click **Visualize All**.
16. Take a screenshot (label it 3-3B).

17. Click **Classify**.
18. Run each of the following classification models:
    a. **Weka > Trees > Random Forest.**
    b. **Weka > Meta > AdaBoostM1.**
    c. **Weka > Functions > Logistic.**
    d. **Weka > Bayes > BayesNet.**

    Q8. Which model has the highest accuracy? How do you know?

Part 4: Address and Refine Results

Q9. How useful is your classification model in predicting which applicants will be approved or rejected? How do you know?

Q10. How would you interpret the results of your analysis in plain English?

End of Lab

Lab 3-4 Comprehensive Case: Dillard's Store Data: Data Abstract (SQL) and Regression (Part I)

Company summary

Dillard's is a department store with approximately 330 stores in 29 states. Its headquarters is in Little Rock, Arkansas. You can learn more about Dillard's by looking at finance.yahoo .com (Ticker symbol = DDS) and the Wikipedia site for DDS. You'll quickly note that William T. Dillard II is an accounting grad of the University of Arkansas and the Walton College of Business, which may be why he shared transaction data with us to make available for this lab and labs throughout this text.

Data

The data for this lab and other all **Dillard's** labs are available at http://walton.uark.edu/ enterprise/. Your instructor will either give you specific instructions on how to access the data, or there will be information available on connect. The 2016 **Dillard's** data cover all transactions over the period 1/1/2014 to 10/17/2016.

Software needed

- Microsoft SQL Server Management Studio (available on the Remote Desktop at the University of Arkansas)
- Excel 2016 (available on the Remote Desktop at the University of Arkansas)

In this lab, you will:

- Conduct analysis on three important questions that help us understand when customers spend more on individual transactions.

Part 1: Identify the Questions

Dillard's is trying to figure out when its customers spend more on individual transactions. We ask questions regarding how **Dillard's** sells its products.

Q1. Customers in which states had the highest transaction balances over the entire sample period?

Q2. Do customers in the state with the highest transaction balances have a significantly higher transaction balance from September 1, 2016, to September 15, 2016, than all other states?

Q3. Are online transaction amounts statistically greater than or lesser than non-online transactions during the time period September 1, 2016, to September 15, 2016?

Part 2: Master the Data

For this lab, you should access the TRANSACT and the STORE tables from the Dillard's 2016 dataset from the University of Arkansas. You may have learned how to do so from past labs, or feel free to ask your instructor for access.

As you recall the entity-relationship diagram looks like the one given in Lab Exhibit 3-4A.

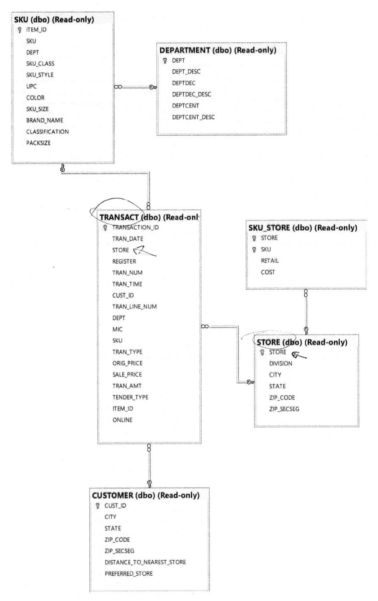

LAB EXHIBIT 3-4A Common Attributes from the STORE and TRANSACT Tables of 2016 Dillard's Data (http://walton.uark.edu/enterprise/dillardshome.php)

Source: http://walton.uark.edu/enterprise/dillardshome.php

Attribute	Description	Values
SKU	Stock Keeping Unit number of the stock item	4757355, 2128748, . . .
Store	Store Number	2, 3, 4, 100
Register	Register Number of the Current Transaction	580, 30, 460, . . .
TranCode (or Trannum)	Transaction Code	09700, 018000
Saledate	Sale date of the Item Stock	2005-01-20, 2005-06-02, . . .
Seq	Sequence Number	298100028, 213500030, . . .
Interid	Internal ID	265005802, 671901998, . . .
Stype	Type of Transaction (Return or Purchase)	P, R
Quantity	Item Quantity of the Transaction	1, 2, 3, 4, . . .
OrgPrice	Original price of the item stock	75.00, 44.00, . . .
SPrice	Sale price of the item stock	26.25, 65.00, . . .
Amt	Total amount of the transaction charge to the customer	26.25, 44.00, . . .
Mic	Master Item Code	862, 689, . . .
City	City where the store is located	St. Louis, Tampa, . . .
State	State where the store is located	FL, MO, AR, . . .
Zip	Zip code	33710, 63126, . . .

1. Run the following SQL query on Microsoft SQL Server Management Studio to address the question regarding which state had the highest transaction balance. (Recall that transaction is defined for each individual item purchased.)

```
SELECT STATE, AVG(TRAN_AMT) AS Average
FROM TRANSACT
INNER JOIN STORE
ON TRANSACT.STORE = STORE.STORE
GROUP BY STATE
```

The output should look like this:

AL 27.992390

AR 41.379066

AZ 27.845655

CA 28.315362

CO 27.297332

FL 28.760791

GA 27.270740

IA 24.879376

ID 29.408952

IL 24.787586

IN 26.066528

KS 27.771021

KY 28.206677

LA 30.282367

MO 25.546692

MS 28.338400

MT 28.941823

NC 25.576096

NE 26.904771

NM 28.826383

NV 30.021116

NY 21.757447

OH 26.432211

OK 29.088865

SC 28.241007

TN 29.178345

TX 29.477805

UT 25.254111

VA 26.500511

WY 26.429770

Part 3: Perform an Analysis of the Data

2. Take a screenshot of your results (label it 3-4A).

Noting that Arkansas (State ='AR') has the highest transaction balance, let's address our second question: "Do customers in the state with the highest transaction balances have a significantly higher transaction balance from September 1, 2016, to September 15, 2016, than all other states?"

3. To address Q2, run the following SQL query to extract the data needed for additional analysis. You can do this analysis in SQL Server or you can do it in Excel:

```
SELECT TRANSACT.*, STORE.STATE
FROM TRANSACT
INNER JOIN STORE
ON TRANSACT.STORE = STORE.STORE
WHERE TRAN_DATE BETWEEN '20160901' AND '20160915'
ORDER BY TRAN_DATE
```

4. If you choose to do the SQL query in Excel, here are the steps:

Create query through Excel 2016

4.1 **Data tab > New Query > From Database > From SQL Server Database**

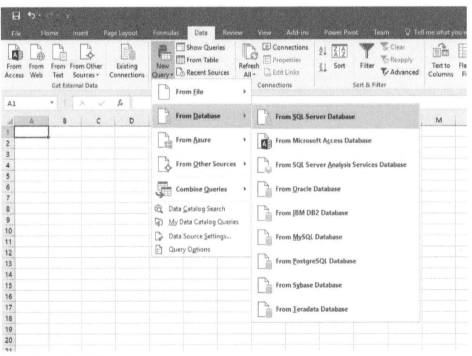

Source: Microsoft Excel 2016

4.2 Enter the **Server** (essql1.walton.uark.edu) and the **Database**
(UA_Dillards_2016) – not case-sensitive

Click **Advanced options** to input the query text:

```
SELECT TRANSACT.*, STORE.STATE
FROM TRANSACT
INNER JOIN STORE
ON TRANSACT.STORE = STORE.STORE
WHERE TRAN_DATE BETWEEN '20160901' AND '20160915'
ORDER BY TRAN_DATE
```

×

SQL Server database

Server ⓘ

| essql1.walton.uark.edu |

Database (optional)

| UA_Dillards_2016 |

▲ Advanced options

Command timeout in minutes (optional)

| |

SQL statement (optional, requires database)

```
select transact.*, store.STATE
from transact
inner join store
on transact.store = store.STORE
where TRAN_DATE BETWEEN '20160901' and '20160915'
order by tran_date
```

☑ Include relationship columns

☐ Navigate using full hierarchy

☐ Enable SQL Server Failover support

| OK | | Cancel |

Source: Microsoft Excel 2016

4.3 Click **OK**.

4.4 If the query did not have typos or errors, a preview of your data will show the
following: If the query runs correctly, you can hit the **Load** button and load it
directly into Excel ready for analysis.

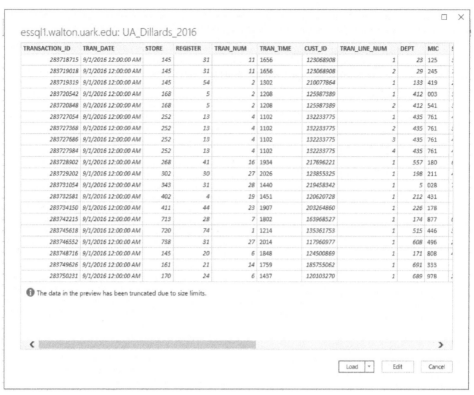

essql1.walton.uark.edu: UA_Dillards_2016

TRANSACTION_ID	TRAN_DATE	STORE	REGISTER	TRAN_NUM	TRAN_TIME	CUST_ID	TRAN_LINE_NUM	DEPT	MIC
283718715	9/1/2016 12:00:00 AM	145	31	11	1656	123068908	1	23	125
283719018	9/1/2016 12:00:00 AM	145	31	11	1656	123068908	2	29	245
283719319	9/1/2016 12:00:00 AM	145	54	2	1302	210077864	1	133	419
283720542	9/1/2016 12:00:00 AM	168	5	2	1208	125987389	1	412	003
283720848	9/1/2016 12:00:00 AM	168	5	2	1208	125987389	2	412	541
283727054	9/1/2016 12:00:00 AM	252	13	4	1102	132233775	1	435	761
283727368	9/1/2016 12:00:00 AM	252	13	4	1102	132233775	2	435	761
283727686	9/1/2016 12:00:00 AM	252	13	4	1102	132233775	3	435	761
283727984	9/1/2016 12:00:00 AM	252	13	4	1102	132233775	4	435	761
283728902	9/1/2016 12:00:00 AM	268	41	16	1934	217696221	1	557	180
283729202	9/1/2016 12:00:00 AM	302	30	27	2026	123855325	1	198	211
283731054	9/1/2016 12:00:00 AM	343	31	28	1440	219458342	1	5	028
283732581	9/1/2016 12:00:00 AM	402	4	19	1451	120620728	1	212	431
283734150	9/1/2016 12:00:00 AM	411	44	23	1907	203264860	1	226	178
283742215	9/1/2016 12:00:00 AM	713	28	7	1802	163968527	1	174	877
283745618	9/1/2016 12:00:00 AM	720	74	1	1214	135361753	1	515	446
283746552	9/1/2016 12:00:00 AM	738	31	27	2014	117960977	1	608	496
283748716	9/1/2016 12:00:00 AM	145	20	6	1848	124500869	1	171	808
283749626	9/1/2016 12:00:00 AM	161	21	14	1759	185755062	1	691	333
283750231	9/1/2016 12:00:00 AM	170	24	6	1437	120103270	1	689	978

ℹ The data in the preview has been truncated due to size limits.

Load ▾ Edit Cancel

Source: Microsoft Excel 2016

(If you have an error, click **Edit** to return to your query and resolve the error.)

Example of error text:

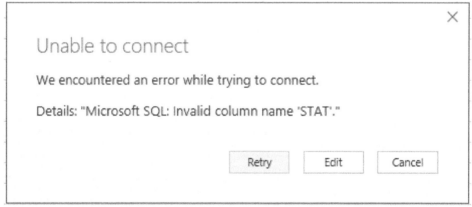

Unable to connect

We encountered an error while trying to connect.

Details: "Microsoft SQL: Invalid column name 'STAT'."

Retry Edit Cancel

Source: Microsoft Excel 2016

(This error indicates that there is a typo in the State column name).

4.5 From the **Data preview** screen, you can click **Load** to immediately load the dataset into your Excel workbook.

Excel
starts
here

5. Once the data are in Excel, you'll need to transform the State data to perform regression analysis on the state of Arkansas to address Q2. To do so, make a new column just right of the existing dataset and label it **Arkansas-dummy in column 1**. Write the formula "(=IF([@STATE]="AR",1,0) in each row. It will assign a value of 1 to transactions at stores in Arkansas and a value of 0 for transactions at stores outside of the Arkansas. Copy this formula all the way down to cover each row.

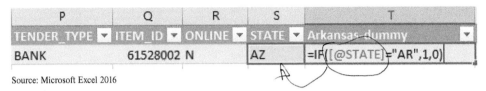

P	Q	R	S	T
TENDER_TYPE	ITEM_ID	ONLINE	STATE	Arkansas-dummy
BANK	61528002 N		AZ	=IF([@STATE]="AR",1,0)

Source: Microsoft Excel 2016

6. Perform a regression analysis by performing the following steps.
   6.1 Click on **Data Analysis** button. Make sure your **Data Analysis Toolpak** is added by doing the following steps:
       6.1.1 Click the **File** tab, click **Options**, and then click the **Add-Ins.**
       6.1.2 In the **Manage** box, select **Excel Add-ins** and then click **Go.**
       6.1.3 In the **Add-Ins** box, check the **Analysis ToolPak** check box, and then click **OK.**
   6.2 Click **Regression** (as shown below).

Source: Microsoft Excel 2016

   6.3 Reference the cells that contain the Tran_AMT in the **Input Y Range** and Arkansas-dummy in the **Input X Range** and then click **OK.**

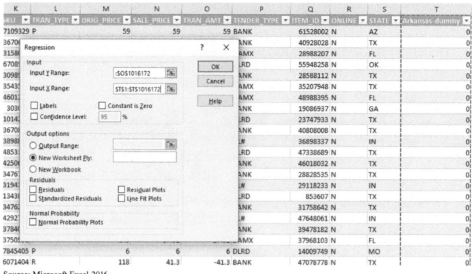

Source: Microsoft Excel 2016

6.4 Your output should look like the screenshot below. The **t Stat** greater than 2.0 suggests that the transaction amount (Tran_Amt) is statistically greater in Arkansas than in all other states.

SUMMARY OUTPUT

Regression Statistics	
Multiple R	0.098397082
R Square	0.009681986
Adjusted R Square	0.009681011
Standard Error	50.34953996
Observations	1016171

ANOVA

	df	SS	MS	F	Significance F
Regression	1	25185276.13	25185276.13	9934.721643	0
Residual	1016169	2576065821	2535.076174		
Total	1016170	2601251097			

	Coefficients	Standard Error	t Stat	P-value	Lower 95%
Intercept	26.24767466	0.052427587	500.6462424	0	26.14491835
Arkansas	17.19296482	0.172493575	99.67307381	0	16.85488323

Source: Microsoft Excel 2016

7. Take a screenshot of your results (label it 3-4B).

We are now ready to address our third question: Are online transaction amounts statistically greater than or lesser than non-online transactions during the time period

September 1, 2016, to September 15, 2016? Because we found that transactions in Arkansas are statistically higher than all other states, we will include that finding in our analysis as well, making this a multivariate regression.

8. To address this question we need to transform the **Online** variable into an online-dummy variable. The **Online** variable carries values of "Y" for online and "N" for Not online. To do our analysis, we will transform this into a dummy variable that allows statistical analysis. Dummy variables carry the value of "1" or "0". We transform it in the following way:

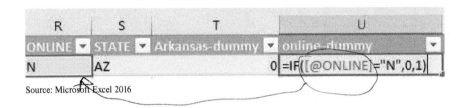

Source: Microsoft Excel 2016

Once this is complete, copy the calculation for all cells in the column.

We're now ready for regression analysis. Reference the cells that contain the **Tran_AMT** in the **Input Y Range** and **Arkansas-dummy** and reference **Online-dummy** in the **Input X Range** and click **OK**.

Regression ? ✕

Input

Input Y Range: O1$O$101617;

Input X Range: $T$2:$U$1016172

☐ Labels ☐ Constant is Zero

☐ Confidence Level: 95 %

Output options

◯ Output Range:

◉ New Worksheet Ply:

◯ New Workbook

Residuals

☐ Residuals ☐ Residual Plots

☐ Standardized Residuals ☐ Line Fit Plots

Normal Probability

☐ Normal Probability Plots

OK

Cancel

Help

Source: Microsoft Excel 2016

The results of the regression analysis suggesting that both Transactions in Arkansas and Transactions done online are associated with greater transaction amounts are below.

SUMMARY OUTPUT

Regression Statistics	
Multiple R	0.12253037
R Square	0.015013692
Adjusted R Square	0.015011753
Standard Error	50.21384501
Observations	1016171

ANOVA

	df	SS	MS	F	Significance F
Regression	2	39054381.84	19527190.92	7744.489884	0
Residual	1016168	2562196715	2521.430231		
Total	1016170	2601251097			

	Coefficients	Standard Error	t Stat	P-value	Lower 95%
Intercept	26.24767466	0.052286292	501.9991594	0	26.14519528
Arkansas-dummy	1.666764244	0.270960466	6.15131894	7.68697E-10	1.135690857
Online-dummy	25.04194061	0.33765037	74.16529889	0	24.38015725

Source: Microsoft Excel 2016

9. Take a screenshot of your results (label it 3-4C).

Part 4: Address and Refine Results

Q4. How would you interpret the results of your analysis of Q1 in plain English? Why do you think the state of Arkansas had the highest transaction volume?

Q5. The analysis of Q2 addressed whether Arkansas had a statistically higher transaction volume than other states. How did the regression tests show or not show a statistical difference? Does this have any implications for the marketing for **Dillard's**? Do you think it is because Arkansas is the home base for **Dillard's**?

Q6. The regression analysis suggests that online sales are associated with greater transactions amounts. Why do you think that is so?

End of Lab

Lab 3-5 Comprehensive Case: Dillard's Store Data: Data Abstract (SQL) and Regression (Part II)

Company summary

Dillard's is a department store with approximately 330 stores in 29 states. Its headquarters is in Little Rock, Arkansas. You can learn more about **Dillard's** by looking at finance.yahoo .com (Ticker symbol = DDS) and the Wikipedia site for DDS. You'll quickly note that

William T. Dillard II is an accounting grad of the University of Arkansas and the Walton College of Business, which may be why he shared transaction data with us to make available for this lab and labs throughout this text.

Data

The data for this lab and other all Dillard's labs are available at http://walton.uark.edu/enterprise/. Your instructor will either give you specific instructions on how to access the data, or there will be information available on connect. The 2016 Dillard's data cover all transactions over the period 1/1/2014 to 10/17/2016.

Software needed

- Microsoft SQL Server Management Studio (available on the Remote Desktop at the University of Arkansas)
- Excel 2016 (available on the Remote Desktop at the University of Arkansas)

In this lab, you will:

- Conduct analysis on one important question that helps us understand when customers spend more on individual transactions.

Part 1: Identify the Questions

Dillard's is trying to figure out when its customers spend more on individual transactions. We ask questions regarding how Dillard's sells its products.

Q1. Did customers who charged their purchases to a Dillard's credit card spend more on each transaction during the time period September 1, 2016, to September 15, 2016?

Part 2: Master the Data

1. See Lab 3-4 to see how to access the dataset and to see the ERD and data dictionary.

Part 3: Perform an Analysis of the Data

2. To get the necessary data to address Q1, you will need to run the same query as Lab 3-4 and get the data into Excel ready for analysis.
3. For those who use the Dillard's credit card, it is noted as "DLRD" in the TENDER_TYPE field. We need to compare those who use the Dillard's credit card to all other transactions. To prepare for this analysis, we need to make a DLRD-dummy variable (labeled as "DLRD-dummy") that carries the value of 1 if a Dillard's credit card was used and a value of 0 otherwise. Please make the transformation in this way and copy down for every row as in Lab Exhibit 3-5A.

P	Q	R	S	T	U	V	W
TENDER_TYPE	ITEM_ID	ONLINE	STATE	Arkansas-dummy	online-dummy	DLRD-dummy	
BANK	61528002 N		AZ	0		0 =IF([@[TENDER_TYPE]]=	
BANK	40928028 N		TX	0		0 "DLRD ",1,0)	
DAMX	28988207 N		FL	0		0	0
DLRD	55948258 N		OK	0		0	1

LAB EXHIBIT 3-5A

Source: Microsoft Excel 2016

Note: Sometimes DLRD may have a space after it because of the way that it is brought into Excel. You can take of this problem using the TRIM() command or changing your DLRD in your IF command to "DLRD" (note the space after the second "D" to make the dummy variable).

4. Once this is complete, we are ready for statistical analysis. Given the results of Lab 3-4 that transaction amount is positively associated with the state of Arkansas and online sales, we will include them in our multivariate analysis. Click the **Data Analysis** button and select **regression** as pictured below.

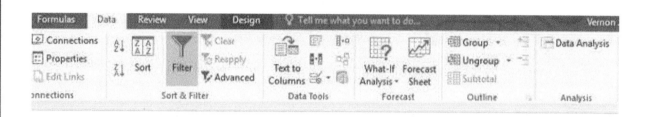

AN_NUM	TRAN_TIME	CUST_ID	TRAN_LINE_NUM	DEPT	MIC	SKU	TRAN_TYPE	ORIG_PRICE	SALE
12	1406	213173853	1	187	150	7109329	P		59
5	1521	180075626	2	128	366	3670657	P		24.99
8	1554	115883018	1	661	421	3158065	P		69.99
8	1657	117226910	1	243	555	6708946	P		32
62	1519	152163680	1	657	766	3098964	P		60
70	1939	190775934	1	674	023	3543581	P		145
				181	153	4601260	R		59
				611	803	303054	P		99.99
				773	287	1014259	R		39.99
				128	366	3670856	P		32
				650	010	3898870	P		79.99
				162	332	4853397	R		79.5
				128	366	4250661	P		38
				545	520	3476714	P		89.5
				679	020	3194336	P		98
14	1651	146716142	1	8	128	1343840	R		18.5

Data Analysis dialog:

Analysis Tools
- Descriptive Statistics
- Exponential Smoothing
- F-Test Two-Sample for Variances
- Fourier Analysis
- Histogram
- Moving Average
- Random Number Generation
- Rank and Percentile
- Regression
- Sampling

OK · Cancel · Help

LAB EXHIBIT 3-5B

Source: Microsoft Excel 2016

5. Click **Regression** and include **Tran_Amt** as the Y variable and **Arkansas-dummy**, **Online-dummy**, and **DLRD-dummy** as the X variables and run the regression.

6. Take a screenshot (label it 3-5A) of your results.

Part 4: Address and Refine Results

Q2. How would you interpret the results of your analysis of Q1 in plain English? Was the relationship statistically significant (Was the *t*-statistic greater than 2)? Why do you think the use of the **Dillard's** card increased the amount spent on each transaction?

Q3. Why did we also include Arkansas state sales and online sales as other explanatory variables (X- or independent variables) in this regression analysis? Are these results still significant after the inclusion of the use of the **Dillard's** credit card?

Q4. Are there any other data from the TRANSACT table that might help us predict the transaction amount?

Q5. If we had any other data to predict transaction amount, what would you use? Brainstorm freely to come up with what could explain these different levels of transaction amounts!

End of Lab

Chapter 4

Visualization: Using Visualizations and Summaries to Share Results with Stakeholders

A Look at This Chapter

This chapter wraps up the introduction to the IMPACT model by explaining how to communicate your results through data visualization and through written reports. Creating a chart takes more skill and practice than simply adding in a bar chart through the Excel chart wizard, and this chapter will help you identify the purpose for your data visualization so that you can choose the best chart for your dataset and your purpose. We will also help you learn how to refine your chart so that it communicates as efficiently and effectively as possible. The chapter concludes by describing how to provide a written report tailored to specific audiences who will be interested in the results of your data analysis project.

A Look Back

In chapter 3, we considered various models and techniques used for data analytics and discussed when to use them and how to interpret the results. We also provide specific accounting-related examples of when each of these specific data approaches and models is appropriate to address our particular question.

A Look Ahead

Because most of the focus of data analytics in accounting is on auditing, chapter 5 considers how both internal and external auditors are using technology in general—and audit analytics specifically—to evaluate firm data and generate support for management assertions. We emphasize audit working papers, audit planning, continuous monitoring, and continuous data assurance.

Before the 2016 presidential election, almost all polls predicted a Hillary Clinton win. But many of those polls assumed that Hillary Clinton would receive the same support and passion from Obama's 2012 supporters, which turned out not to be the case.

Exhibit 4-1 shows the 2016 election results relative to the polling predictions prior to the election. This one graph pretty much encapsulates why Donald Trump won and Hillary Clinton lost. And that is the focus of the chapter: how we capture and communicate information to better understand a good or a bad decision. As noted in the chapter, data are important, and Data Analytics are effective, but they are only as important and effective as we can communicate and make the data understandable.

Source: http://fivethirtyeight.com/features/why-fivethirtyeight-gave-trump-a-better-chance-than-almost-anyone-else/ (accessed August 3, 2017).

©Justin Sullivan/Getty Images

EXHIBIT 4-1

OBJECTIVES

After reading this chapter, you should be able to:

LO 4-1 Determine the purpose of your data visualization

LO 4-2 Choose the best chart for your dataset

LO 4-3 Refine your chart to communicate efficiently and effectively

LO 4-4 Communicate your results in a written report

Data are important, and Data Analytics are effective, but they are only as important and effective as we can communicate and make the data understandable. One of the authors often asks her students what they would do if they were interns and their boss asked them to supply information regarding in which states all of the customers her organization served were located. Would they simply point their boss to the Customers table in the sales database? Would they go a step further and isolate the attributes to the Company Name and the State? Perhaps they could go a step further and run a quick query or PivotTable to perform a count on the number of customers in each different state that the company serves. If they were to give their boss what she actually wanted, however, they should provide a short written summary of the answer to the research question, as well as an organized chart to visualize the results. Data visualization isn't just for people who are "visual" learners. When the results of data analysis are visualized appropriately, the results are made easier and quicker to interpret for everybody. Whether the data you are analyzing are "small" data or "big" data, they still merit synthesis and visualization to help your stakeholders interpret the results with ease and efficiency.

Think back to some of the first data visualizations and categorizations you were exposed to (the food guide pyramid/food plate, the animal kingdom, the periodic table) and, more modernly, how frequently infographics are applied to break down a series of complicated information on social media. These charts and infographics make it easier for people to understand difficult concepts by breaking them down into categories and visual components.

LO 4-1

Determine the purpose of your data visualization

DETERMINE THE PURPOSE OF YOUR DATA VISUALIZATION

As with selecting and refining your analytical model, communicating results is more art than science. Once you are familiar with the tools that are available, your goal should always be to share critical information with stakeholders in a clear, concise manner. This could involve a chart or graph, a callout box, or a few key statistics. Visualizations have become very popular over the past three decades. Managers use dashboards to quickly evaluate key performance indicators (KPIs) and quickly adjust operational tasks; analysts use graphs to plot stock price and financial performance over time to select portfolios that meet expected performance goals.

In any project that will result in a visual representation of data, the first charge is ensuring that the data are reliable and that the content necessitates a visual. In our case, however, ensuring that the data are reliable and useful has already been done through the first three steps of the IMPACT model.

At this stage in the IMPACT model, determining the method for communicating your results requires the answers to two questions:

1. Are you explaining the results of previously done analysis, or are you exploring the data through the visualization? (Is your purpose declarative or exploratory?)
2. What type of data is being visualized (conceptual, qualitative data or data-driven, quantitative data)?

Scott Berinato, senior editor at **Harvard Business Review**, summarizes the possible answers to these questions[1] in a chart shown in Exhibit 4.2. The majority of the work that we will do with the results of data analysis projects will reside in quadrant 2 of Exhibit 4-2, the declarative, data-driven quadrant. We will also do a bit of work in Exhibit 4-2's quadrant 4, the data-driven, exploratory quadrant. There isn't as much qualitative work to be done,

---

[1]S. Berinato, *Good Charts: The HBR Guide to Making Smarter, More Persuasive Data Visualizations* (Boston: Harvard Business Review Press, 2016).

although we will work with categorical qualitative data occasionally. When we do work with qualitative data, it will most frequently be visualized using the tools in quadrant 1, the declarative, conceptual quadrant.

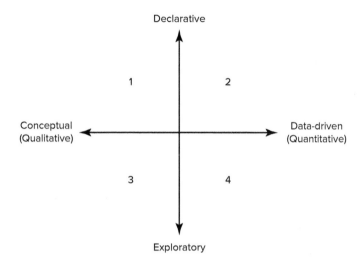

EXHIBIT 4-2
The Four Chart Types

S. Berinato, *Good Charts: The HBR Guide to Making Smarter, More Persuasive Data Visualizations* (Boston: Harvard Business Review Press, 2016).

Once you know the answers to the two key questions and have determined which quadrant you're working in, you can determine the best tool for the job. Is a written report with a simple chart sufficient? If so, Word or Excel will suffice. Will an interactive dashboard and repeatable report be required? If so, Tableau may be a better tool. Later in the chapter, we will discuss these two tools in more depth, along with when they should be used.

Quadrants 1 and 3 versus Quadrants 2 and 4: Qualitative versus Quantitative

Qualitative data are categorical data. All you can do with these data is count them and group them, and in some cases, you can rank them. Qualitative data can be further defined in two ways, nominal data and ordinal data. **Nominal data** are the simplest form of data. Examples of nominal data are hair color, gender, and ethnic groups. If you have a set of data on people with different hair color, you can count the number of individuals who fit into the same hair color category, but you cannot rank it (brown hair isn't better than red hair), nor can you take an average or do any other further calculations beyond counting (you can't take an average of "blonde"). Increasing in complexity, but still categorized as qualitative data, are ordinal data. **Ordinal data** can also be counted and categorized like nominal data but can go a step further—the categories can also be ranked. Examples of ordinal data include gold, silver, and bronze medals, 1–5 rating scales on teacher evaluations, and letter grades. If you have a set of data of students and the letter grades they have earned in a given course, you can count the number of instances of A, B, C, and so on, and you can categorize them, just like with nominal data. You can also sort the data meaningfully—an A is better than a B, which is better than a C, and so on. But that's as far as you can take your calculations—as long as the grades remain as letters (and aren't transformed into the corresponding numerical grade for each individual), you cannot calculate an average, standard deviation, or any other more complex calculation.

Beyond counting and possibly sorting (if you have ordinal data), the primary statistic used with quantitative data is **proportion**. The proportion is calculated by counting the number of items in a particular category, then dividing that number by the total number of observations. For example, if I had a dataset of 150 people and had each individual's corresponding hair color with 25 people in my dataset having red hair, I could calculate the proportion of red-haired people in my dataset by dividing 25 (the number of people with red hair) by 150 (the total number of observations in my dataset). The proportion of red-haired people, then, would be 16.7 percent.

Qualitative data (both nominal and ordinal) can also be referred to as "conceptual" data because such data are text-driven and represent concepts instead of numbers.

Quantitative data are more complex than qualitative data because not only can they be counted and grouped just like qualitative data, but the differences between each data point are meaningful—when you subtract 4 from 5, the difference is a numerical measure that can be compared to subtracting 3 from 5. Quantitative data are made up of observations that are numerical and can be counted and ranked, just like ordinal qualitative data, but that can also be averaged. A standard deviation can be calculated, and datasets can be easily compared when standardized (if applicable). Chapter 3 mentions the concept of the **normal distribution** in the context of profiling in continuous auditing. The normal distribution is a phenomenon that many naturally occurring datasets in our world follow, such as SAT scores and heights and weights of newborn babies. For a distribution of data to be considered normal, the data should have equal median, mean, and mode, with half of the observations falling below the mean and the other half falling above the mean. If you are comparing two datasets that follow the normal distribution, even if the two datasets have very different means, you can still compare them by **standardizing** the distributions with Z-scores. By using a formula, you can transform every normal distribution into a special case of the normal distribution called the **standard normal distribution**, which has 0 for its mean (and thus, for its mode and median, as well) and 1 for its standard deviation. The benefit of standardizing your data when comparing is no longer comparing wildly different numbers and trying to eyeball how one observation differs from the other—if you standardize both datasets, you can place both distributions on the same chart and more swiftly come to your insights.

Similar to qualitative data, quantitative data can be categorized into two different types: interval and ratio. However, there is some dispute among the analytics community on whether the difference between the two datasets is meaningful, and for the sake of the analytics and calculations you will be performing, the difference is not pertinent. Ratio data are considered the most sophisticated type of data, and the simplest way to express the difference between interval and ratio data is that **ratio data** have a meaningful 0 and interval data do not. In other words, for ratio data, when a dataset approaches 0, 0 means "the absence of." Consider money as ratio data—we can have 5 dollars, 72 dollars, or 8,967 dollars, but as soon as we reach 0, we have "the absence of" 0.

The other scale for quantitative data is interval data, which are not as sophisticated as ratio data. **Interval data** do not have a meaningful 0; in other words, in interval data, 0 does not mean "the absence of" but is simply another number. An example of interval data is the Fahrenheit scale of temperature measurement, where 90 degrees is hotter than 70 degrees, which is hotter than 0 degrees, but 0 degrees does not represent "the absence of" temperature—it's just another number on the scale.

Quantitative data can be further categorized as either discrete or continuous data. **Discrete data** are data that are represented by whole numbers. An example of discrete data is points in a basketball game—you can earn 2 points, 3 points, or 157 points, but you cannot earn 3.5 points. On the other hand, **continuous data** are data that can take on any value within a range. An example of continuous data is height: you can be 4.7 feet, 5 feet, or 6.27345 feet. The difference between discrete and continuous data can be blurry sometimes because you can express a discrete variable as continuous—for example, the number of children a person can have is discrete (a woman can't have 2.7 children, but she could have 2 or 3), but if you are researching the average number of children that women aged 25–40 have in the United States, the average would be a continuous variable. Whether your data are discrete or continuous can also help you determine the type of chart you create because continuous data lend themselves more to a line chart than do discrete data.

Quadrants 1 and 2 versus Quadrants 3 and 4: Declarative versus Exploratory

In the context of the labs and tools we're providing through this textbook, the majority of your data visualizations created in step C of the IMPACT model will be created with a declarative purpose. **Declarative visualizations** are the product of wanting to "declare" or present your findings to an audience. The data analysis projects begin with a question, proceed through analysis, and end with communicating those findings. This means that while the visualization may prompt conversation and debate, the information provided in the charts should be solid. Even if your analysis in the previous steps of the IMPACT model had been exploratory, by the time you have arrived to communicate your results, you are declaring what you have found.

On the other hand, you will sometimes use data visualizations to satisfy an **exploratory visualization** purpose. When this is done, the lines between steps **P** (perform test plan), **A** (address and refine results), and **C** (communicate results) are not as clearly divided. Exploratory data visualization will align with performing the test plan within visualization software—for example, Tableau—and gaining insights while you are interacting with the data. Often the presenting of exploratory data will be done in an interactive setting, and the answers to the questions from step **I** (identify the questions) won't have already been answered before working with the data in the visualization software.

Exhibit 4-3 is similar to the first four chart types presented to you in Exhibit 4-2, but Exhibit 4-3 has more detail to help you determine what to do once you've answered the first two questions. Remember that the quadrant represents two main questions:

1. Are you explaining the results of the previously done analysis, or are you exploring the data through the visualization? (Is your purpose declarative or exploratory?)
2. What type of data is being visualized (conceptual qualitative data or data-driven quantitative data)?

Once you have determined the answers to the first two questions, you are ready to begin determining which type of visualization will be the most appropriate for your purpose and dataset.

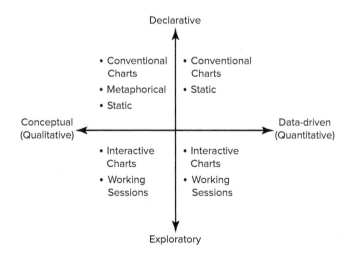

EXHIBIT 4-3
The Four Chart Types Quadrant with Detail

S. Berinato, *Good Charts: The HBR Guide to Making Smarter, More Persuasive Data Visualizations* (Boston: Harvard Business Review Press, 2016).

PROGRESS CHECK

1. What are two ways that complicated concepts were explained to you via categorization and data visualization as you were growing up?
2. Using the Internet or other resources (other textbooks, a newspaper, or a magazine), identify an example of a data visualization for each possible quadrant.
3. Identify which type of data scale the following variables are measured on (qualitative nominal, qualitative ordinal, or quantitative):
   a. Instructor evaluations in which students select excellent, good, average, or poor.
   b. Weekly closing price of gold throughout a year.
   c. Names of companies listed on the Dow Jones Industrial Average.
   d. Fahrenheit scale for measuring temperature.

CHOOSING THE RIGHT CHART

LO 4-2

Choose the best chart for your dataset

Once you have determined the type of data you're working with and the purpose of your data visualization, the next questions have to do with the design of the visualization—color, font, graphics—and most importantly, type of chart/graph. The visual should speak for itself as much as necessary, without needing too much explanation for what's being represented. Aim for simplicity over bells and whistles that "look cool," but end up being distracting.

Charts Appropriate for Qualitative Data

Because qualitative and quantitative data have such different levels of complexity and sophistication, there are some charts that are not appropriate for qualitative data that do work for quantitative data.

When it comes to visually representing qualitative data, the charts most frequently considered for depicting qualitative data are:

- Bar charts.
- Pie charts.
- Stacked bar chart.

The pie chart is probably the most famous (some would say infamous) data visualization for qualitative data. It shows the parts of the whole; in other words, it represents the proportion of each category as it corresponds to the whole dataset.

Similarly, a bar chart also shows the proportions of each category as compared to each of the others.

In most cases, a bar chart is more easily interpreted than a pie chart because our eyes are more skilled at comparing the height of columns (or the lengths of horizontal bars, depending on the orientation of your chart) than they are at comparing sizes of pie, especially if the proportions are relatively similar.

Consider the two different charts from the Sláinte dataset in Exhibit 4-4. Each compares the proportion of each beer type sold by the brewery.

The magnitude of the difference between the Imperial Stout and the IPA is almost impossible to see in the pie chart. This difference is easier to digest in the bar chart.

Of course, we could improve the pie chart by adding in the percentages associated with each proportion, but it is much quicker for us to see the difference in proportions by glancing at the order and length of the bars in a bar chart (Exhibit 4-5).

EXHIBIT 4-4
Pie Charts and Column Chart Show Different Ways to Visualize Proportions

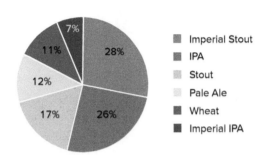

EXHIBIT 4-5

The same set of data could also be represented in a stacked bar chart or a 100 percent stacked bar chart (Exhibit 4-6). This chart is not a default option in Excel, but it does work in another data visualization tool that we introduce later in this chapter, Tableau. The first figure in Exhibit 4-6 is a stacked bar chart, which shows the proportion of each type of beer sold expressed in the number of beers sold for each product, while the latter shows the proportion expressed in terms of percentage of the whole in a 100 percent stacked bar chart.

While bar charts and pie charts are among the most common charts used for qualitative data, there are several other charts that function well for showing proportions:

- *Tree maps and heat maps:* These are similar types of visualizations, and they both use size and color to show proportional size of values. While tree maps show proportions using physical space, heat maps use color to highlight the scale of the values. However, both are heavily visual, so they are imperfect for situations where precision of the numbers or proportions represented is necessary.
- *Symbol maps:* Symbol maps are geographic maps, so they should be used when expressing qualitative data proportions across geographic areas such as states or countries.
- *Word clouds:* If you are working with text data instead of categorical data, you can represent them in a word cloud. Word clouds are formed by counting the frequency of each word mentioned in a dataset; the higher the frequency (proportion) of a given word, the larger and bolder the font will be for that word in the word cloud. Consider analyzing the results of an open-ended response question on a survey; a word cloud would be a great way to quickly spot the most commonly used words to tell if there is a positive or negative feeling toward what's being surveyed. There are also settings that you can put into place when creating the word cloud to leave out the most commonly used English words—such as *the, an,* and *a*—in order to not skew the data. Exhibit 4-7 is an example of a word cloud for the text of chapter 2 from this textbook.

EXHIBIT 4-6

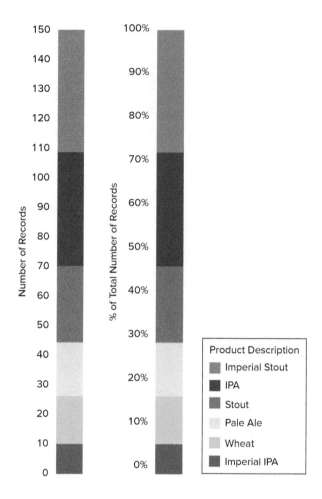

EXHIBIT 4-7
Word Cloud Example
from chapter 2 Text

Charts Appropriate for Quantitative Data

The data visualization and chart possibilities for charting quantitative data are similar to how quantitative data have the same characteristics of qualitative data (you can group and count it), but they have even more sophistication. You can use pie charts (with the same varying level of success) and bar charts with quantitative data, but you can also use a lot more.

There are many different methods for visualizing quantitative data. With the exception of the word cloud, all of the methods mentioned in the previous section for qualitative data can work for depicting quantitative data, but the following charts can depict more complex data:

- *Line charts:* Show similar information to what a bar chart shows, but line charts are good for showing data changes or trend lines over time. Line charts are useful for continuous data, while bar charts are often used for discrete data. For that reason, line charts are not recommended for qualitative data, which by nature of being categorical, can never be continuous.
- *Box and whisker plots:* Useful for when quartiles, median, and outliers are required for analysis and insights.
- *Scatter plots:* Useful for identifying the correlation between two variables or for identifying a trend line or line of best fit.
- *Filled geographic maps:* As opposed to symbol maps, a filled geographic map is used to illustrate data ranges for quantitative data across different geographic areas such as states or countries.

A summary of the chart types just described appears in Exhibit 4-8. Each chart option works equally well for exploratory and declarative data visualizations. The chart types are categorized based on when they will be best used (e.g., when comparing qualitative variables, a bar chart is an optimal choice), but this figure shouldn't be used to stifle creativity—bar charts can also be used to show comparisons among quantitative variables, just as many of the charts in the listed categories can work well with other datatypes and purposes than their primary categorization below.

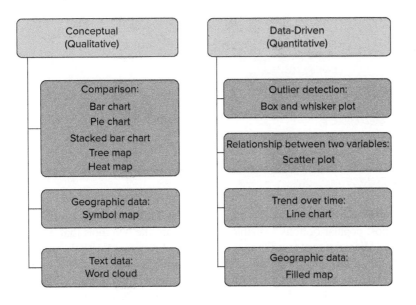

EXHIBIT 4-8
Summary of chart types. RT

As with selecting and refining your analytical model, communicating results is more art than science. Once you are familiar with the tools that are available, your goal should always be to share critical information with stakeholders in a clear, concise manner. While visualizations can be incredibly impactful, they can become a distraction if you're not careful. For example, bar charts can be manipulated to show a bias and, while novel, 3D graphs are incredibly deceptive because they may distort the scale even if the numbers are fine.

Tools to Help When Picking a Visual

There are many tools available for data visualization and exploratory data analysis. Gartner annually assesses a collection of these tools and creates the "magic quadrant" for business intelligence, depicted in Exhibit 4-9. The magic quadrant can provide insight into which tools you should consider using.

EXHIBIT 4-9

Gartner Magic Quadrant for Business Intelligence and Analytics Platforms

Source: R. L. Sallam, C. Howson, C. J. Idoine, T. W. Oestreich, J. L. Richardson, and J. Tapadinhas, "Magic Quadrant for Business Intelligence and Analytics Platforms," Gartner RAS Core Research Notes, Gartner, Stamford, CT (2017).

Based on Gartner's quadrant, it is easy to see that Tableau and Microsoft are two of the best and most popular options available, and these are the two tools that we will focus on as well. The Microsoft tool that Gartner analyzed and compared with the other products is not just Excel, it includes the entire Microsoft BI suite, of which Excel is only a part. We will focus on Excel as the main driver of the Microsoft toolkit in this text. Tableau is ranked slightly higher than Microsoft on its ability to execute, while Microsoft is ranked slightly higher than Tableau in completeness of vision. This distinction makes sense because Tableau is a newer product and has placed the majority of its focus on data visualization, while Microsoft Excel has a much more robust platform for data analysis. Excel's biggest advantage over Tableau (and over any other data visualization software in the market) is its ubiquity. Excel has been on the market longer than any of its competitors, and it is rare to find a business or university that doesn't have a version of Excel on every computer. *If your data analysis project is more declarative than exploratory, it is more likely that you will perform your data visualization to communicate results in Excel,* simply because it is likely that you performed steps 2 through 4 in Excel, and it is convenient to create your charts in the same tool that you performed your analysis.

Tableau earns high praise for being intuitive and easy to use, which makes it ideal for exploratory data analysis. You may even find that you would prefer to immediately load your data from Excel or Access (or wherever your data are stored) into Tableau during the second step of the IMPACT model and work on your analysis inside the tool, instead of waiting for step 5 to just communicate your results through Tableau. If your question isn't fully defined or specific, exploring your dataset in Tableau and changing your visualization type to discover different insights is as much a part of performing data analysis as crafting your communication. One of the biggest disadvantages to Tableau is its cost, but fortunately, Tableau is a tremendous supporter of education, and as a student, you can download a free academic license to use Tableau on your PC or Mac. The link to download your free license of Tableau is: https://www.tableau.com/academic/students. Once you have downloaded your license, we recommend opening the Superstore sample workbook provided. You will find it at the bottom of the start screen under "Sample workbooks" (Exhibit 4-10).

Once you open the workbook, you will see a variety of tabs at the bottom of the workbook that you can page through and see different ways that the same dataset can be analyzed and visualized. When you perform exploratory analysis in Tableau, or even if you have already performed

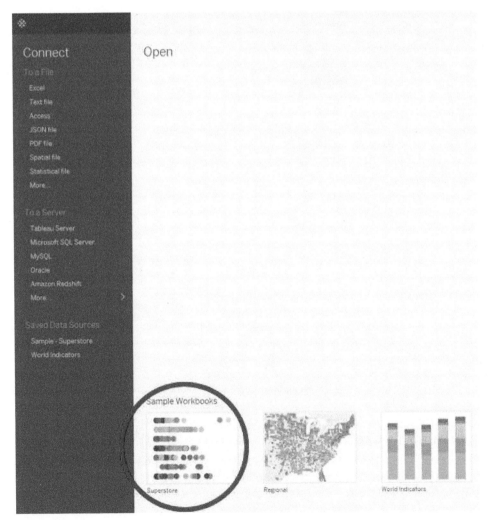

EXHIBIT 4-10

your analysis and you have uploaded the dataset into Tableau to communicate insights, we recommend trying several different types of charts to see which one makes your insights stand out the most effectively. In the top right corner of the Tableau workbook, you will see the Show Me window, which provides different options for visualizing your dataset (Exhibit 4-11).

EXHIBIT 4-11

In the Show Me tab, only the visualizations that will work for your particular dataset will appear in full color.

Learning to Create a Good Chart by (Bad) Example

Other than getting practice by looking at good visualizations and modifying the way you visualize your dataset in Tableau to see how different insights are showcased, one of the best ways to learn how to create a good visualization is to look at some problematic visualizations.

In this chart, the *Daily Mail,* a UK-based newspaper, tries to emphasize an upgrade in the estimated growth of British economy. The estimate from the Office of National Statistics indicated that Q4 growth would be 0.7 percent instead of 0.6 percent (a relatively small increase of about 15 percent). Yet the visualization makes it appear as if this is a 200 percent increase because of the scale the newspaper chose. The other obvious issue is that some time has passed between the estimates, and we don't see that disclosed here (Exhibit 4-12).

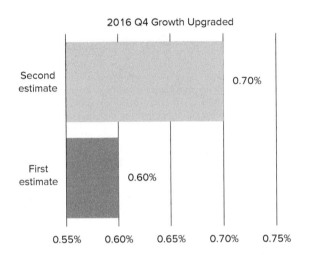

EXHIBIT 4-12
This bar chart distorts the data comparison by using an inappropriate scale.

If we reworked the data points to show the correct scale (starting at 0 instead of 0.55) and the change over time (plotting the data along the horizontal axis), we'd see something like Exhibit 4-13. If we wanted to emphasize growth, we might choose a chart like Exhibit 4-14. Notice that both new graphs show an increase that is less dramatic and confusing.

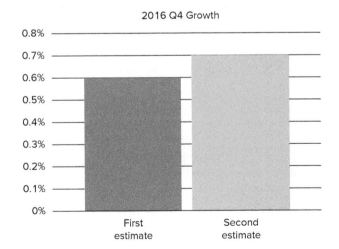

EXHIBIT 4-13
This bar chart uses an appropraite scale for a less biased comparison.

See Exhibit 4-15. Is a pie chart really the best way to present these data?

EXHIBIT 4-14

An alternative stacked bar chart showing growth.

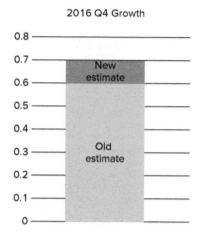

EXHIBIT 4-15

This pie chart is difficult to interpret.

Source: http://viz.wtf/ post/155727224217/the- authors-explain-furthermore- we-present-the.

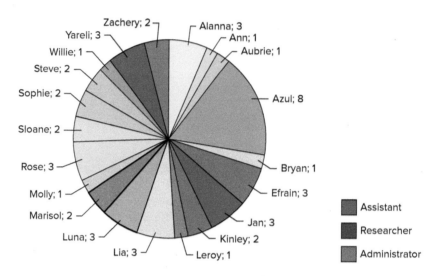

If you want to emphasize users, consider a rank-ordered bar chart like Exhibit 4-16. To emphasize the category, a comparison like that in Exhibit 4-17 may be helpful. Or to show proportion, maybe a stacked bar (Exhibit 4-18). In any case, there are much better ways to clearly communicate.

EXHIBIT 4-16

This rank-ordered bar chart is more clear.

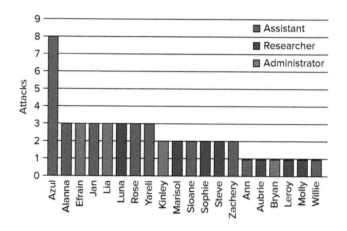

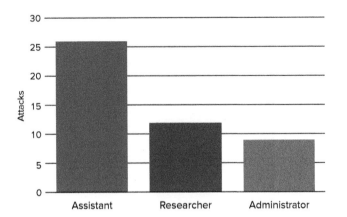

EXHIBIT 4-17
This bar chart emphasizes attacks by job function.

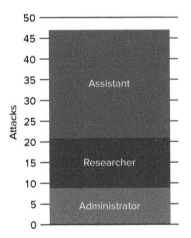

EXHIBIT 4-18
This stacked bar chart emphasizes proportion of attacks by job function.

<svg><circle/><path d="checkmark"/></svg> **PROGRESS CHECK**

4. The following two charts represent the exact same data—the quantity of beer sold on each day in the Sláinte Sales Subset dataset. Which chart is more appropriate for working with dates, the column chart or the line chart? Which do you prefer? Why?

a.

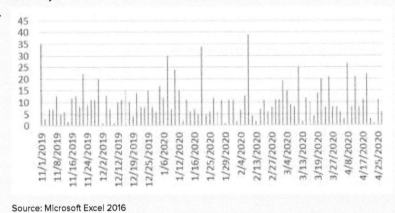

Source: Microsoft Excel 2016

b.

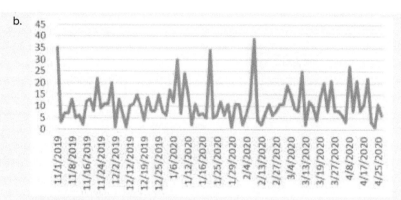

Source: Microsoft Excel 2016

5. The same dataset was consolidated into quarters. This chart was made with the chart wizard feature in Excel, which made the creation of it easy, but something went wrong. Can you identify what went wrong with this chart?

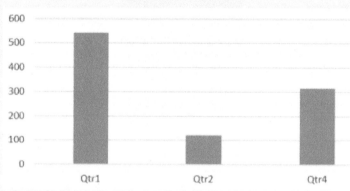

Source: Microsoft Excel 2016

6. The following four charts represent the exact same data quantity of each beer sold. Which do you prefer, the line chart or the column chart? Whichever you chose, line or column, which of the pair do you think is the easiest to digest?

a.

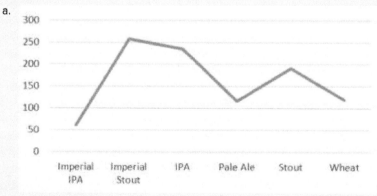

Source: Microsoft Excel 2016

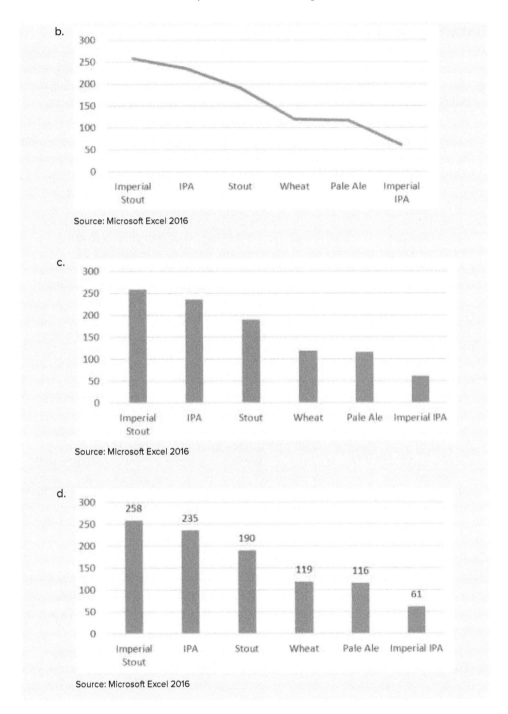

b.

Source: Microsoft Excel 2016

c.

Source: Microsoft Excel 2016

d.

Source: Microsoft Excel 2016

FURTHER REFINING YOUR CHART TO COMMUNICATE BETTER

After identifying the purpose of your visualization and which type of visual will be most effective in communicating your results, you will need to further refine your chart to pick the right data scale, color, and format.

LO 4-3
——————
Refine your chart to communicate efficiently and effectively

Data Scale and Increments

As tools such as Excel and Tableau become more intuitive and more powerful, considering your data scale and increments is less of a concern because both tools will generally come up with scales and increments that make sense for your dataset. With that being said, there are still four main questions to consider when creating your data scale and increments:

1. How much data do you need to share in the visual to avoid being misleading, yet also avoid being distracting? (For example, do you need to display the past four years, or will the past two quarters suffice? When you consider leaving out some data, is it to show only the insights that are meaningful, or is it an attempt to skew the data or to hide poor performance? Be careful to not hide data that are meaningful just because they don't align with your expectations.

2. If your data contain outliers, should they be displayed, or will they distort your scale to the extent that you can leave them out? If the purpose of your chart is to call attention to the outliers, then they need to remain (and you need to ensure that they are not errors, but this should have been done in step 2 of the IMPACT model when you mastered the data). If the purpose of your chart is to display the middle pack of the data, the outliers may not be relevant to the insights, and they could be left out.

3. Other than determining how much data you need to share, what scale should you place those data on? Typically, charts should begin with a baseline of 0, but if 0 is meaningless to your dataset, you could find a different baseline that makes sense. Be careful to not overexaggerate the height or the baseline so that your trendline or bar chart is over- or underemphasized; your trend line should take up two-thirds of the chart. Once you decide on a data scale, the increments for your data scale should be "natural" such as 1s, 2s, 5s, 100s, etc. (e.g., not 3s or 0.02s).

4. Do you need to provide context or reference points to make the scale meaningful? For example, if you were provided with a stock price of $100, would you immediately be able to tell if that is a high number or a low number? Not necessarily; without context of the company's stock price over time, the company's industry and its competitors' stock prices, or some other piece of context, certain numbers are not altogether useful.

Color

Similar to how Excel and Tableau have become stronger tools at picking appropriate data scales and increments, both Excel and Tableau will have default color themes when you begin creating your data visualizations. You may choose to customize the theme. However, if you do, here are a few points to consider:

- When should you use multiple colors? Using multiple colors to differentiate types of data is effective. Using a different color to highlight a focal point is also effective. However, don't use multiple colors to represent the same type of data. Be careful to not use color to make the chart look pretty—the point of the visualization is to showcase insights from your data, not to make art.

- We are trained to understand the differences among red, yellow, and green, with red meaning something negative that we would want to "stop" and green being something positive that we would want to "continue," just like with traffic lights. For that reason, use red and green only for those reasons. Using red to show something positive or green to show something negative is counterintuitive and will make your chart harder to understand. You may also want to consider a color-blind audience. If you are concerned that someone reading your visuals may be color blind, avoid a red/green scale and consider using orange/blue. Tableau has begun defaulting to orange/blue color scales instead of red/green for this reason.

- Once your chart has been created, convert it to grayscale to ensure that the contrast still exists—this is both to ensure your color-blind audience can interpret your visuals and also to ensure that the contrast, in general, is stark enough with the color pallet you have chosen.

⊘ PROGRESS CHECK

7. Often, external consultants will use a firm's color scheme for a data visualization or will use a firm's logo for points on a scatter plot. While this might be a great approach to support a corporate culture, it is often not the most effective way to create a chart. Why would these methods harm a chart's effectiveness?

COMMUNICATION: MORE THAN VISUALS— USING WORDS TO PROVIDE INSIGHTS

> **LO 4-4**
>
> Communicate your results in a written report

As a student, the majority of the writing you do is for your professors. You likely write e-mails to your professors, which should carry a respectful tone, or essays for your Comp 1 or literature professors, where you may have been encouraged to use descriptive language and an elevated tone; you might even have had the opportunity to write a business brief or report for your business professors. All the while, though, you were still aware that you were writing for a professor. When you enter the professional world, your writing will need to take on a different tone. If you are accustomed to writing with an academic tone, transitioning to writing for your colleagues in a business setting requires some practice. As Justin Zobel says in *Writing for Computer Science,* "good style for science is ultimately, nothing more than writing that is easy to understand. [It should be] clear, unambiguous, correct, interesting, and direct."[2] As an author team, we have tremendous respect for literature and the different styles of writing to be found, but for communicating your results of a data analysis project, you need to write directly to your audience, with only the necessary points included, and as little descriptive style as possible. The point is, get to the point.

Content and Organization

Each step of the IMPACT model should be communicated in your write-up, as noted here:

I: Explain what was being researched. Even if your audience is the people who requested the research, you should still restate the purpose of the project. Include any relevant history as well. If your project is part of a larger program or if it's a continued effort to explain an issue or help a decision come to fruition, then include the background.

M: Depending on your audience, you may not cover too much of what your process was in the "master the data" step of the IMPACT model, but an overview of the data source and which pieces of data are included in the analysis should be present. If your audience is technical and interested, you may go into detail on your ETL process, but it is more likely that you will leave out that piece.

P and A: Similar to how you write about mastering the data, you may not need to include a thorough description of your test plan or your process for refining your results depending on what your audience is interested in and what they need to know, but including an overview of the type of analysis performed and any limitations that you encountered will be important to include.

[2]Justin Zobel, *Writing for Computer Science (Singapore: Springer-Verlag, 1997)*

C: If you are including a data visualization with your write-up, you need to explain how to use the visual. If there are certain aspects that you expect to stand out from the analysis and the accompanying visual, you should describe what those components are—the visual should speak for itself, but the write-up can provide confirmation that the important pieces are gleaned.

T: Discuss what's next in your analysis. Will the visual or the report result in a weekly or quarterly report? What trends or outliers should be paid attention to over time?

Audience and Tone

Carefully considering your audience is critical to ensuring your communication is effective. If you have three messages to write—one letting your mom know that you are coming home this weekend and you'll need to do laundry, one to your professor letting her know that you will miss class on Friday, and one to your best friend asking if he wants to join you for Chipotle— efficiency would suggest that you type it all into one e-mail and click send. That would defi- nitely be the quickest way to get out the message. But is it a good idea? Certainly not. Your mom does not need to know that you're not going to class on Friday, and you probably don't want your professor to show up at Chipotle to have lunch with you and your friend. Instead of sending the same message to all three people, you tailor the delivery—that is, you consider the audience. You include all of the information that they need to know and nothing else.

You should do the same thing when crafting your communication regarding your data analysis. If you have several different people to communicate results to, you may consider crafting several different versions: one that contains all of the extraction, transformation, and loading (ETL) details for the programmers and database administrators, one that is light on ETL but heavy on interpretation of the visual and results for your managers, and so on. Consider the knowledge and skill of your audience—don't talk down to them, but don't overwhelm a nontechnical crowd with technical jargon. Explain the basics when you should, and don't when you shouldn't.

Revising

Just as you addressed and refined your results in the fourth step of the IMPACT model, you should refine your writing. Until you get plenty of practice (and even once you consider yourself an expert), you should ask other people to read through your writing to make sure that you are communicating clearly. Justin Zobel suggests that revising your writing requires you to "be egoless—ready to dislike anything you have previously written. . . . If someone dislikes something you have written, remember that it is the readers you need to please, not yourself."[3] Always placing your audience as the focus of your writing will help you maintain an appropriate tone, provide the right content, and avoid too much detail.

 PROGRESS CHECK

Progress Checks 5 and 6 display different charts depicting the quantity of beer sold on each day in the Sláinte Sales Subset dataset. If you had created those visuals, starting with the data request form and the ETL process all the way through data analysis, how would you tailor the written report for the following two roles?

8. For the CEO of the brewery who is interested in how well the different products are performing.

9. For the programmers who will be in charge of creating a report that contains the same information that needs to be sent to the CEO on a monthly basis.

[3]Ibid.

Summary

- This chapter focused on the fifth step of the IMPACT model, or the "C," to discuss how to communicate the results of your data analysis projects. Communication can be done through a variety of data visualizations and written reports, depending on your audience and the data you are exhibiting.
- In order to select the right chart, you must first determine the purpose of your data visualization. This can be done by answering two key questions:
  - Are you explaining the results of a previously done analysis, or are you exploring the data through the visualization? (Is your purpose declarative or exploratory?)
  - What type of data is being visualized (conceptual qualitative data or data-driven quantitative data)?
- The differences between each type of data (declarative and exploratory, qualitative and quantitative) are explained, as well as how each datatype impacts both the tool you're likely to use (generally either Excel or Tableau) and the chart you should create.
- After selecting the right chart based on your purpose and datatype, your chart will need to be further refined. Selecting the appropriate data scale, scale increments, and color for your visualization is explained through the answers to the following questions:
  - How much data do you need to share in the visual to avoid being misleading, yet also avoid being distracting?
  - If your data contain outliers, should they be displayed, or will they distort your scale to the extent that you can leave them out?
  - Other than how much data you need to share, what scale should you place those data on?
  - Do you need to provide context or reference points to make the scale meaningful?
  - When should you use multiple colors?
- Finally, this chapter discusses how to provide a written report to describe your data analysis project. Each step of the IMPACT model should be communicated in your write-up, and the report should be tailored to the specific audience to whom it is being delivered.

Key Words

continuous data (*142*)   One way to categorize quantitative data, as opposed to discrete data. Continuous data can take on any value within a range. An example of continuous data is height.

declarative visualizations (*143*)   Made when the aim of your project is to "declare" or present your findings to an audience. Charts that are declarative are typically made after the data analysis has been completed and are meant to exhibit what was found in the analysis steps.

discrete data (*142*)   One way to categorize quantitative data, as opposed to continuous data. Discrete data are represented by whole numbers. An example of discrete data is points in a basketball game.

exploratory visualizations (*143*)   Made when the lines between steps **P** (perform test plan), **A** (address and refine results), and **C** (communicate results) are not as clearly divided as they are in a declarative visualization project. Often when you are exploring the data with visualizations, you are performing the test plan directly in visualization software such as Tableau instead of creating the chart after the analysis has been done.

interval data (*142*)   The third most sophisticated type of data on the scale of nominal, ordinal, interval, and ratio; a type of quantitative data. Interval data can be counted and grouped like qualitative data, and the differences between each data point are meaningful. However, interval data do not have a meaningful 0. In interval data, 0 does not mean "the absence of" but is simply another number. An example of interval data is the Fahrenheit scale of temperature measurement.

nominal data (*141*)   The least sophisticated type of data on the scale of nominal, ordinal, interval, and ratio; a type of qualitative data. The only thing you can do with nominal data is count, group, and take a proportion. Examples of nominal data are hair color, gender, and ethnic groups.

normal distribution (*142*)   A type of distribution in which the median, mean, and mode are all equal, so half of all the observations fall below the mean and the other half fall above the mean. This phenomenon is naturally occurring in many datasets in our world, such as SAT scores and heights and weights of newborn babies. When datasets follow a normal distribution, they can be standardized and compared for easier analysis.

ordinal data (*141*)   The second most sophisticated type of data on the scale of nominal, ordinal, interval, and ratio; a type of qualitative data. Ordinal can be counted and categorized like nominal data and the categories can also be ranked. Examples of ordinal data include gold, silver, and bronze medals.

proportion (*141*)   The primary statistic used with quantitative data. Proportion is calculated by counting the number of items in a particular category, then dividing that number by the total number of observations.

qualitative data (*141*)   Categorical data. All you can do with these data are count and group, and in some cases, you can rank the data. Qualitative data can be further defined in two ways: nominal data and ordinal data. There are not as many options for charting qualitative data because they are not as sophisticated as quantitative data.

quantitative data (*142*)   More complex than qualitative data. Quantitative data can be further defined in two ways: interval and ratio. In all quantitative data, the intervals between data points are meaningful, allowing the data to be not just counted, grouped, and ranked, but also to have more complex operations performed on them such as mean, median, and standard deviation.

ratio data (*142*)   The most sophisticated type of data on the scale of nominal, ordinal, interval, and ratio; a type of quantitative data. They can be counted and grouped just like qualitative data, and the differences between each data point are meaningful like with interval data. Additionally, ratio data have a meaningful 0. In other words, once a dataset approaches 0, 0 means "the absence of." An example of ratio data is currency.

standard normal distribution (*142*)   A special case of the normal distribution used for standardizing data. The standard normal distribution has 0 for its mean (and thus, for its mode and median, as well), and 1 for its standard deviation.

standardization (*142*)   The method used for comparing two datasets that follow the normal distribution. By using a formula, every normal distribution can be transformed into the standard normal distribution. If you standardize both datasets, you can place both distributions on the same chart and more swiftly come to your insights.

 # ANSWERS TO PROGRESS CHECKS

1. Certainly, answers will vary given our own individual experiences. But we can note that complex topics can be explained and understood by linking them to categorizations or pictures.

2. Answers will vary.

3. a. Qualitative ordinal

   b. Quantitative (ratio data)

   c. Qualitative nominal

   d. Quantitative (interval data)

4. While this question does ask for your preference, it is likely that you prefer image b because time series data are continuous and can be well represented with a line chart instead of bars.

5. Notice that the quarters are out of order (1, 2, then 4); this looks like quarter 3 has been skipped, but quarter 4 is actually the last quarter of 2019 instead of the last quarter of 2020, while quarters 1 and 2 are in 2020. Excel defaulted to simply ordering the quarters numerically instead of recognizing the order of the years in the underlying data. You want to be careful to avoid this sort of issue by paying careful attention to the charts, ordering, and scales that are automatically created through Excel (and other tools) wizards.

6. Answers will vary. Possible answers include: Quantity of beer sold is a discrete value, so it is likely better modeled with a bar chart than a line chart. Between the two line charts, the second one is easier to interpret because it is in order of highest sales to lowest. Between the two bar charts, it depends on what is important to convey to your audience—are the numbers critical? If so, the second chart is better. Is it most important to simply show which beers are performing better than others? If so, the first chart is better. There is no reason to provide more data than necessary because they will just clutter up the visual.

7. Color in a chart should be used purposefully; it is possible that a firm's color scheme may be counterproductive to interpreting the chart. The icons as points in a scatter plot might be distracting, which could make it take longer for a reader to gain insights from the chart.

8. Answers will vary. Possible answers include: Explain to the CEO how to read the visual, call out the important insights in the chart, tell the range of data that is included (is it one quarter, one year, all time?).

9. Answers will vary. Possible answers include: Explain the ETL process, exactly what data are extracted to create the visual, which tool the data were loaded into, and how the data were analyzed. Explain the mechanics of the visual. The particular insights of this visual are not pertinent to the programmer because the insights will potentially change over time. The mechanics of creating the report are most important.

▣ connect

Multiple Choice Questions

1. Gold, silver, and bronze medals would be examples of:
   a. Nominal data.
   b. Ordinal data.
   c. Structured data.
   d. Test data.

2. In the late 1960s, Ed Altman developed a model to predict if a company was at severe risk of going bankrupt. He called his statistic Altman's Z-score, now a widely used score in finance. Based on the name of the statistic, which statistical distribution would you guess this came from?
   a. Normal distribution
   b. Poisson distribution
   c. Standardized normal distribution
   d. Uniform distribution

3. Justin Zobel suggests that revising your writing requires you to "be egoless—ready to dislike anything you have previously written," suggesting that it is _____ you need to please:
   a. Yourself
   b. The reader
   c. The customer
   d. Your boss

4. Which of the following is *not* a typical example of nominal data?
   a. Gender
   b. SAT scores
   c. Hair color
   d. Ethnic group

5. The Fahrenheit scale of temperature measurement would best be described as an example of:

   a. Interval data.

   b. Discrete data.

   c. Nominal data.

   d. Continuous data.

6. _____ data would be considered the least sophisticated type of data.

   a. Ratio

   b. Interval

   c. Ordinal

   d. Nominal

7. _____ data would be considered the most sophisticated type of data.

   a. Ratio

   b. Interval

   c. Ordinal

   d. Nominal

8. Line charts are not recommended for what type of data?

   a. Normalized data

   b. Qualitative data

   c. Continuous data

   d. Trend lines

9. Exhibit 4-8 gives chart suggestions for what data you'd like to portray. Those options include all of the following *except*:

   a. Relationship.

   b. Comparison.

   c. Distribution.

   d. Normalization.

10. What is the most appropriate chart when showing a relationship between two variables (according to Exhibit 4-8)?

   a. Scatter chart

   b. Bar chart

   c. Pie graph

   d. Histogram

Discussion Questions

1. Explain Exhibit 4-2 and why these four dimensions are helpful in describing information to be communicated? Exhibit 4-2 lists conceptual and data-driven as being on two ends of the continuum. Does that make sense, or can you think of a better way to organize and differentiate the different chart types?

2. According to Exhibit 4-8, which is the best chart for showing a distribution of a single variable, like height? How about hair color? Major in college?

3. Box and whisker plots (or box plots) are particularly adept at showing extreme observations and outliers. In what situations would it be important to communicate these data to a reader? Any particular accounts on the balance sheet or income statement?

4. Based on the data from datavizcatalogue.com, a line graph is best at showing comparisons, relationships, compositions, or distributions? Name the best two.

5. Based on the data from datavizcatalogue.com, what are some major flaws of using word clouds to communicate the frequency of words in a document?

6. Based on the data from datavizcatalogue.com, how does a box and whisker plot show if the data are symmetrical?

7. What would be the best chart to use to illustrate earnings per share for one company over the past five years?

8. The text mentions, "*If your data analysis project is more declarative than exploratory, it is more likely that you will perform your data visualization to communicate results in Excel.*" In your opinion, why is this true?

9. According to the text and your own experience, why is Tableau ideal for exploratory data analysis?

Problems

1. Why was the graphic associated with the opening vignette regarding the 2016 presidential election an effective way to communicate the voter outcome for 50 states? What else could have been used to communicate this, and would it have been more or less effective in your opinion?

2. Evaluate the use of multiple colors in the graphic associated with the opening vignette regarding the 2016 presidential election. Would you consider its use effective or ineffective? Why? Can you think of a better way to communicate the extent to which pollsters incorrectly predicted the outcome in many of the states and in the country overall?

3. According to Exhibit 4-8, which is the best chart for comparisons of earnings per share over many periods? How about for only a few periods?

4. According to Exhibit 4-8, which is the best chart for static composition of a data item of the Accounts Receivable balance at the end of the year? Which is best for showing a change in composition of Accounts Receivable over two or more periods?

5. The Big 4 accounting firms (Deloitte, EY, KPMG, and PwC) dominate the audit and tax market in the United States. What chart would you use to show which accounting firm dominates in each state in terms of audit revenues? Any there other interesting ways you could use to find opportunities within the audit market?

6. Datavizcatalogue.com lists seven types of maps in its listing of charts. Which one would you use to assess geographic customer concentration by number? How could you show if some customers buy more than other customers on such a map? Would you use the same chart or a different one?

7. In your opinion, is the primary reason that analysts use inappropriate scales for their charts primarily due to an error related to naiveté (or ineffective training), or are the inappropriate scales used so the analyst can sway the audience one way or the other?

Answers to Multiple Choice Questions

1. B
2. C
3. B
4. B
5. A
6. D
7. A
8. B
9. D
10. A

Lab 4-1 Use PivotCharts to Visualize Declarative Data

This lab relies upon the steps completed in Lab 2-2 concerning the Sláinte brewery and the PivotTable report you prepared showing the total number of each item sold each month between January and April 2020.

When working with a data analysis project that is declarative in nature, the analysis will likely be done in Excel, and the data visualization will be done after the analysis has been completed as a means to communicate results.

Company summary

Sláinte is a fictional brewery that has recently gone through big change. Sláinte sells six different products. The brewery has only recently expanded its business to distributing from one state to distributing to nine states, and now the business has begun stabilizing after the expansion. With that stability comes a need for better analysis. One of Sláinte's first priorities is to identify its areas of success, as well as areas of potential improvement.

Data

- Sláinte dataset

Technique

- Some experience with spreadsheets and PivotTables is useful for this lab.

Software needed

- Excel
- Screen capture tool (Windows: Snipping Tool; Mac: Cmd + Shift + 4)

Parts 1–4 of the IMPACT Model

These steps were performed in Lab 2-2. You can either use the already prepared data in the file **Lab 4-1 Slainte_Pivot.xlsx**, or you can use the file that you saved after completing Lab 4-1, which should have been saved to your computer as **Slainte_Pivot.xlsx**.

Part 5: Communicate Your Findings

We demonstrate two alternate ways of communicating findings. Please work through both alternatives.

Alternative 1: Create a PivotChart

1. Ensuring that the active cell in your workbook is somewhere in the PivotTable, navigate to the **Analyze** tab in the ribbon.
2. If you are working with a PC, you should see a button for **PivotChart**. If you are working with a Mac, you can insert a regular chart from the **Insert** tab on the ribbon. Some of the functionality of this lab will be limited on a Mac, so you may opt to use a virtual PC lab environment to complete this lab.
3. Once you click into **PivotChart**, a window for **Insert Chart** appears, along with a list of options for how you can visualize your PivotTable. It defaults to column chart. Another good option is the bar chart, which displays your data in horizontal bars instead of columns. Create either a bar chart or a column chart by selecting the chart you prefer and clicking **OK**.
4. Take a screenshot that shows the PivotTable and the PivotChart (label it 4-1A).

5. The advantage of working with PivotCharts over regular charts is that you can slice and filter your data in the PivotTable and the PivotChart at the same time. If you are presenting your findings to a live audience and you anticipate questions about specific months or specific products, using Excel's slicer tool is a great way to filter your data in a way that is interactive and transparent. On the **Analyze** tab on the ribbon, you can select **Insert Slicer**.
6. In the window that pops up, select **Product Description**. This will create an interactive filter so that you can drill down into different product descriptions as they perform over the months.
7. Create a second slicer for **Sales_Order_Date (Month)**.
8. Take a screenshot that includes your PivotChart, PivotTable, and both slicers (label it 4-1B).

Q1. Spend a few minutes filtering the data with the slicers. Name three important insights that were easy to identify through this visualization.

Q2. What does the data visualization and the interactivity of the slicer provide your audience that the original PivotTable does not?

Alternative 2: Visualize the PivotTable with Conditional Formatting and Sparklines

Conditional formatting and sparklines are quick ways to visualize and compare data and trends when a full-fledged chart isn't necessary.

9. To quickly visualize how each product's total quantity sold over time compares across all six of Sláinte's projects, we can apply conditional formatting to the **Grand Total** column. Select the data in the **Grand Total** column of your PivotTable, and navigate to the **Home** tab on the ribbon.

Sum of Sales_Order_Quantity_Sold	Column Labels				
Row Labels	April	February	January	March	Grand Total
Imperial IPA	17		23	2	42
Imperial Stout	36	27	61	42	166
IPA	34	35	36	66	171
Pale Ale	18	4	27	32	81
Stout	16	33	65	4	118
Wheat		11	21	54	86
Grand Total	121	110	233	200	664

LAB EXHIBIT 4-1A

Source: Microsoft Excel 2016

10. From the **Home** tab, select the **Conditional Formatting** button, and a menu with the different types of formatting available will appear.
11. Select **Data Bars** and pick the first option for blue gradient fill bars.
12. This conditional formatting is helpful because it allows us to compare grand totals of each product. However, if we would like to see how each product's month-over-month sales compare to one another, we can display mini line charts next to each row with a sparkline. To do so, select all of the "meat" of your PivotTable—that is, don't select any of the product labels (such as Imperial IPA), month labels, or grand totals.
13. Navigate to the **Insert** tab on the ribbon, and select **Line** in the **Sparklines** category.
14. A window will appear specifying the data range you just selected and awaiting input for the **Location Range**. We'd like to see the trend lines to the immediate right of our PivotTable, so you can select the cells in the first empty column after your Grand Totals.

Sum of Sales_Order_Quantity_Sold	Column Labels ⊤				
Row Labels ▾	April	February	January	March	Grand Total
Imperial IPA	17		23	2	42
Imperial Stout	36	27	61	42	166
IPA	34	35	36	66	171
Pale Ale	18	4	27	32	81
Stout	16	33	65	4	118
Wheat		11	21	54	86
Grand Total	121	110	233	200	664

Sum of Sales_Order_Quantity_Sold	Column Labels ⊤					
Row Labels ▾	April	February	January	March	Grand Total	
Imperial IPA	17		23	2	42	
Imperial Stout	36	27	61	42	166	
IPA	34	35	36	66	171	
Pale Ale	18	4	27	32	81	
Stout	16	33	65	4	118	
Wheat		11	21	54	86	
Grand Total	121	110	233	200	664	

15. Click **OK**, and your sparklines will be created.
16. You will notice that there are gaps in the lines, though. If you'd rather see a continuous line to represent zero values for the blank cells, you can change this option. Ensure that one of the cells with the sparkline in it is active, and navigate to the **Sparkline Tools** tab on the ribbon.
17. Click the bottom half of the **Edit Data** button to make a menu appear.
18. From the menu, select **Hidden & Empty Cells. . .**
19. Select the option to **show empty cells as zero**, and click **OK**.
20. Take a screenshot to show the conditional formatting and the sparklines (label it 4-1C).

Q3. When do you think a sparkline and/or conditional formatting would be preferable over creating a PivotChart?

Q4. What other visualizations would be useful to interpret these data? If you were to create a report to be run monthly, what are two visualizations that should be included?

Q5. Provide a written report discussing the data analysis project and the insights that should be gained from this visualization.

End of Lab

Lab 4-2 Use Tableau to Perform Exploratory Analysis and Create Dashboards

When working with a data analysis project that is exploratory in nature, the analysis can be done in Tableau. You will likely enter the data analysis project with an overarching question in mind, but as you answer that question, your exploratory analysis will lead to ongoing questions. The data visualization will help explore the data, as well as ultimately be used as a means to communicate results.

Company summary

Sláinte is a fictional brewery that has recently gone through big change. Sláinte sells six different products. The brewery has only recently expanded its business to distributing from one state to distributing to nine states, and now the business has begun stabilizing after the expansion. With that stability comes a need for better analysis. One of Sláinte's first priorities is to identify its areas of success, as well as areas of potential improvement.

Data

- Sláinte dataset

Software needed

- Tableau. Visit with your instructor for instructions or follow this link to download Tableau, https://www.tableau.com/academic/students, and click **Get Tableau for Free** to register for a free student license. Your student license will last one year.
- Screen capture tool (Windows: Snipping Tool; Mac: Cmd + Shift + 4)

In this lab, you will:

Part 1: Identify appropriate questions.

Part 2: Complete the ETL process to load the data in Tableau for analysis.

Part 3: Analyze the data you receive with data visualization.

Part 4: Communicate the data you receive with a digital dashboard.

Part 1: Identify the Questions

If you completed Lab 2-1 or 2-2, you became familiar with the Sláinte dataset and identified questions regarding Sláinte.

In particular, we worked with this scenario: Sláinte has brought you in to help determine potential areas for sales growth in the next year. Additionally, the company has noticed that its margins aren't as high as it had budgeted and would like you to help identify some areas where it could improve its pricing, marketing, or strategy. Specifically, Sláinte would like to know how many of each product was sold.

We'll start with the same question—identifying the amount of each product sold, overall. The Sláinte data include the following tables and fields, presented in a UML diagram:

Q1. Using the UML diagram, identify which table(s) and attributes you will need to answer your initial question regarding amount of products sold.

Part 2: Master the Data

To complete the ETL process, we will need to extract the data from Access and transform and load it into Tableau.

1. Open Tableau.
2. Select **Access** from the **Connect** to a file options.

3. Browse to the **Slainte_Subset.accdb** file and click **Open**. This will extract the data.

4. The **Data Source** tab will open, with three tables for you to select from. We can begin by just exploring the Sales data. Double-click on the **Sales_Subset** table to load it into Tableau.

5. The data should load into Tableau without any problems. However, it is always a good idea to check the datatypes that each attribute loaded in as. Notice the **Abc** above **Sales Order ID**, and the **calendar** icon above **Sales Order Date**. These indicate that **Sales Order ID** data imported as text, while the **Sales Order Date** imported as calendar data. The number signs above **Sales Order Quantity** and **Product Sale Price** indicate that those attributes were imported as numerical data. This is all set up exactly as we'd like, so there's no need to transform the data.

Abc	📅	Abc	Abc	Abc	#	#
Sales_Subset	Sales_Subset	Sales_Subset	Sales_Subset	Sales_Subset	Sales_Subset	Sales_Subset
Sales Order ID	Sales Order Date	Sales Employee ID	Customer ID	Product Code	Sales Order Quant...	Product Sale Price

Q2. If the Sales Order Date datatype had imported as number, how might that cause a problem with our analysis if we wanted to dig into the data by month, for example?

Q3. Why did your Sales Order ID attribute import as text, when it looks like each field has numerical data in it? Would there be any benefit in Sales Order ID being stored as a number? Why will it not present a problem in our analysis to maintain these data as text?

Part 3: Perform Exploratory Analysis

Click into **Sheet 1** in the bottom left of the Tableau tool to begin working with the data. The Tableau screen can be compared to the way Excel's PivotTable Fields list is laid out. The attributes from the **Sales_Subset** table are categorized into **dimensions** and **measures**.

- **Dimensions** are descriptive attributes—these are the fields that we typically slice or group our data by in a PivotTable.
- **Measures** are numerical—these are the fields that you would typically drag into the VALUES area in the PivotTable to calculate a count, sum, or average of your data.

6. To view the number of products sold, begin by double-clicking on the measure **Sales Order Quantity Sold**.

Notice that Tableau doesn't default to showing you one number, but instead displays one bar of a bar chart. This is a clear indication of how Tableau treats data differently than Excel. Excel defaults to numerical data, while Tableau defaults to visualization.

7. To group the total amount of products sold by the products themselves, double-click on the dimension **Product Code**.
8. Take a screenshot (label it 4-2A).

The visualization you just created summarizes the answer to our initial question (how many of each product has sold), but this visual can be improved.

Q4.   Identify two ways to improve this visual to make it more easily understandable?

9. Sort the bars: Across the top of the Tableau screen are a variety of icons. Toward the middle of that menu are two icons for sorting data. Click the icon to sort your data descending.

10. Add labels to the bars: To the left of your data viz, there is the **Marks** window. It has a variety of ways that you can enhance the way you're viewing the data. Click **Labels**, then place a check mark in the box next to **Show mark labels**.

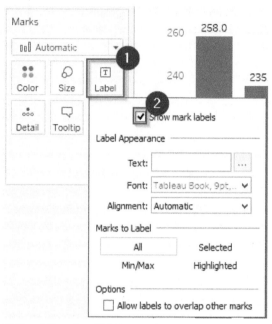

11. Instead of showing **Product Code**, show the **Product Description**; this will require you to join in another table. Click back into the **Data Source** tab in the bottom left.
12. Double-click on the **FGI_Product** table to load the product data into Tableau. You will see the **FGI_Product** data populate, as well as a Venn diagram joining the two datasets. Click on the Venn diagram to ensure the data are joined properly. You want to ensure that the primary key of **FGI_Product** is matched with the corresponding foreign key in the **Sales_Subset** data (the same way the two tables are joined in the UML diagram).

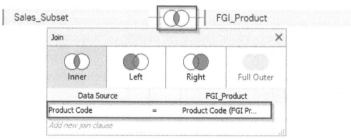

13. Return to **Sheet 1** to work with the new data.
14. Double-click on the dimension **Product Description** to add this detail to your data visualization.
15. Now that you have added the description to the visualization, you can remove the **Product Code** dimension. Remove **Product Code** from the data visualization by dragging and dropping the **Product Code** pill out of the **Columns** shelf. After removing the **Product Code** pill, you will need to sort your data again by using the same sort **descending** icon that you clicked in step 9.

16. Take a screenshot (label it 4-2B).

17. Sometimes when you're performing exploratory data analysis, you'll want to save the visualization you just made, while also giving yourself the opportunity to drill down into the data. We'll name this sheet after the analysis you just did, then duplicate the data to work with it further. Right-click **Sheet 1** and select **Rename Sheet**. Type **Total Products Sold** as the sheet's name.

18. Right-click the sheet tab that you just renamed and select **Duplicate Sheet**.

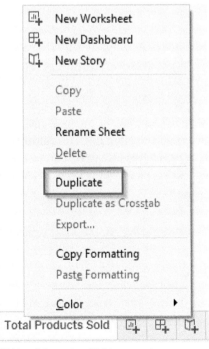

19. Let's dig into how these products have performed year over year. Drag and drop the dimension **Sales Order Date** to the **Columns** shelf, and place it to the left of **Product Description**.

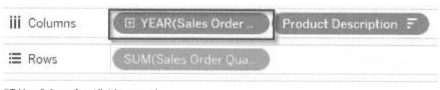

Notice that the pill doesn't just say the name of the attribute, but it says **YEAR** and it has a button to expand the pill.

20. Take a screenshot (label it 4-2C).

If you expand the **Sales Order Date** function once, it will split the data among quarters. If you expand again, it will further drill down into months.

21. Rename this sheet **Total Products Sold by Year**.
22. Navigate to the **Data Source** tab and add in the **Customer** table.

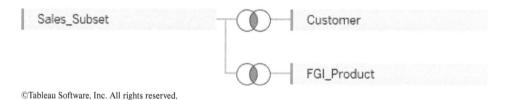

23. Ensure that the join is built on the appropriate primary key/foreign key relationship between **Sales_Subset** and **Customer** according to the UML diagram.
24. For each of the previous tables that we loaded into Tableau, **Sales_Subset** and **FGI_Product**, we didn't need to transform the data. This time, we will want to work with geographic data. Looking at the datatypes for each attribute that loaded in, you can see that Customer City and Customer Zip have **globe** icons for their datatypes, indicating that Tableau was able to intuit that these attributes are geographic. But the **Customer St** attribute has an **Abc** next to it, indicating that Tableau loaded it as only text (not geographic data). Click on the globe above **Customer St** to change its datatype.

25. Select **Geographic Role**, and then select **State/Province**.

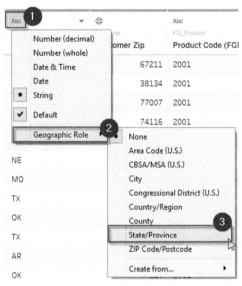

26. Create a new sheet (do not duplicate any of the previous sheets) by clicking the first icon to the right of the **Total Products Sold by Year** tab.

27. This time, we will create a report that shows total products sold by state. Double-click the measure **Customer St**. Tableau automatically populates a map with a dot in each state that's listed in the **Customer** table.
28. Double-click on the measure **Sales Order Quantity Sold**. The dots have changed to vary in size, which is proportional to the amount of sales in each state.
29. We can make the results easier to interpret by changing the visualization type. If the **Show Me** window isn't showing in the upper right corner, click **Show Me**, then select the **Filled Map**.

30. Rename this sheet **Total Products Sold by State**.
31. Take a screenshot (label it 4-2D).

Part 4: Communicate Results

Now that you have created three simple, but meaningful data visualizations, you can create a dashboard to communicate the results. Tableau makes it easy to place all of these visualizations on one interactive pane.

32. Select the icon for **New Dashboard**, which is to the right of the **New Worksheet** icon.

33. In the **Dashboard** view, instead of seeing the various dimensions and measures to drag and drop, you see the three sheets that you have created. You can drag and drop them into the area that says **Drop Sheets Here**, and you can arrange them any way you wish. Replicate this arrangement:

Total Products Sold by State

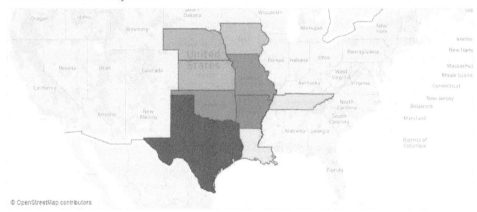

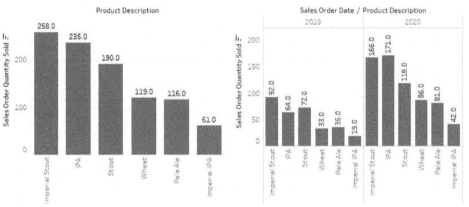

34. You can also use each sheet as a filter. Click the **Total Products Sold** section of your dashboard. There are three small icons in the top right of the sheet when the sheet is active. Clicking the middle one (which looks like a funnel) will allow you to use the bars as filters for the entire dashboard. Click to do so.

35. Follow the same process to make the states work as filters for the dashboard by clicking **Use as Filter** in the **Total Products Sold by State** sheet.

Now, you can click any of the bars in the **Total Products Sold** chart or any of the states in the **Total Products Sold by State**, and the data in each of the three sheets will shift to focus on just those products and/or states.

36. Filter by either a state or a product, and take a screenshot (label it 4-2E).

Q5. After creating these sheets and the dashboard, what additional data would you recommend that Sláinte analyze? What is another data visualization that would be helpful for Sláinte's decision making?

End of Lab

Lab 4-3 Comprehensive Case: Dillard's Store Data: Create Geographic Data Visualizations in Tableau

Company summary

Dillard's is a department store with approximately 330 stores in 29 states. Its headquarters is in Little Rock, Arkansas. You can learn more about **Dillard's** by looking at finance.yahoo .com (Ticker symbol = DDS) and the Wikipedia site for DDS. You'll quickly note that William T. Dillard II is an accounting grad of the University of Arkansas and the Walton College of Business, which may be why he shared transaction data with us to make available for this lab and labs throughout this text.

Data

The data for this lab and other all **Dillard's** labs are available at http://walton.uark.edu/ enterprise/. Your instructor will either give you specific instructions on how to access the data, or there will be information available on Connect. The 2016 **Dillard's** data cover all transactions over the period 1/1/2014 to 10/17/2016.

Software needed

- Microsoft SQL Server Management Studio and Microsoft Excel (available on the Remote Desktop at the University of Arkansas)
- Tableau (available on the Remote Desktop at the University of Arkansas)

In this lab, you will:

- Learn how to prepare data visualization in Tableau.

Part 1: Identify the Questions

Question 2 of Lab 3-4 was as follows: Do customers in the state with the highest transaction balances have a significantly higher transaction balance during the period September 1, 2016, to September 15, 2016, than all other states?

In this lab, we will work to visualize these transaction data in a way that helps users grasp the information needed to make decisions.

Q1. How would this information, average transaction balance by state, help a manager make decisions?

Q2. How would you think managers would like to visualize transaction balance by state? What would be the most (and less) effective ways to visualize these transactions?

Part 2: Master the Data

Load the data into Tableau.

1. Open a new Tableau workbook and connect to Microsoft SQL Server.

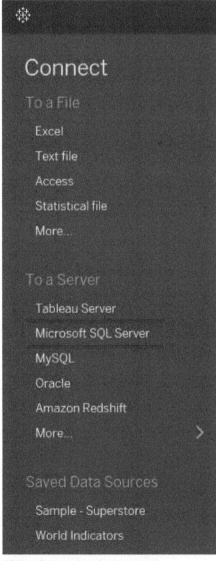

2. Input the **Server** and **Database** information that you received from the Walton.uark.edu/ enterprise page for the Dillard's data, and then click **Sign In**.

Source: Microsoft SQL Server Management Studio

3. Wait for the connection to process, and then you have two options: If you are certain that you will only want to visualize one specific set of query results, you can input a query from the Connections page. Alternatively, you can connect to entire tables if you want the option to drill down into the data and answer more than one question.

Inputting a Custom Query into the Tableau Connections Page

4. Double-click **New Custom SQL**.

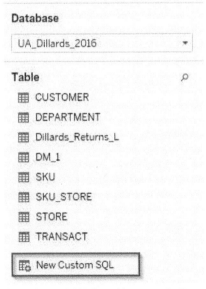

Source: Microsoft SQL Server Management Studio

5. Input your SQL query into the **Edit Custom SQL** window, and then click **OK**.

```
SELECT state, avg(tran_amt) AS Average
FROM transact
INNER JOIN store
ON transact.store = store.store
GROUP BY state
```

6. It may take a couple minutes for the results to populate. Once they do, we'll preview the data.

The data should load without a problem, but because Tableau is automatically interpreting the data, it is a good idea to look through the data to ensure that we don't need to transform them in any way. In Tableau, you should always check which datatype has been assigned to each attribute. The datatype is denoted by a little icon that is an **Abc** for a string of text, a **number sign** for numerical data, a **calendar** for dates, or a **globe** for geographic data.

The two attributes of state are denoted with an **Abc** and a **number sign**:

7. Of particular concern is the way the state data were imported. The **Abc** above the state column indicates that they were imported into Tableau as plain text instead of as a geographic attribute.

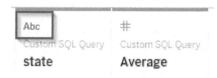

8. For us to view these data more meaningfully, we'll want to change the type of data that state is designated as. Click the **Abc**, then **Geographic Role**, and select **State/Province**.

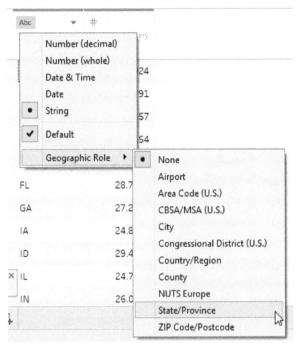

9. Once Tableau has processed the change, click **Sheet 1** on the bottom of the Tableau window to begin working with the data.

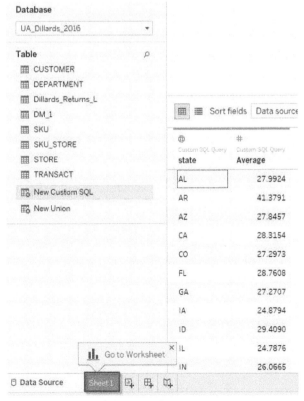

10. Double-click on **state** in **Dimensions**.

You will see that Tableau immediately populates a map with a blue dot in each state that has a **Dillard**'s store.

11. To make these data even more meaningful, we'll add average to this view. Double-click **Average** in **Measures**.

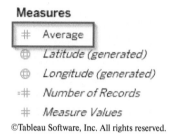

12. Tableau might have defaulted to a symbol map. The difference in averages is easier to interpret with a filled map. Click **Show Me** in the top right corner of Tableau if your **Show Me** window isn't already available, then click **Filled Map**.

End of this process

Joining Tables into the Tableau Connections Page

This option will produce the same visualization that the steps above just created, but it will also provide more flexibility for digging into the data because more data will be loaded into Tableau.

13. Drag the **Transact** table to the **Drag tables here** portion of the Tableau window.
14. Drag the **Store** table to the **Drag tables here** portion of the Tableau window.
15. Tableau will likely default to joining the tables on the appropriate attributes, but double-check that it did by clicking the visual representation of the join (it looks like a Venn diagram).

TRANSACT+ (ua_dillards_2016)

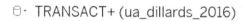

16. The join should indicate that it is an inner join based on the transact.store and store .store attributes. If it says something different, modify the join.

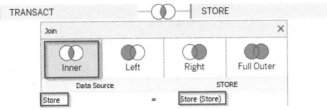

17. Check that the attributes pulled in as the appropriate datatypes. For example, **City** and **Zip Code** pulled in as geographic datatypes, but state did not. Click the **Abc** above the **State** attribute to change the datatype.

#	▾	Abc	⊕	Abc	⊕	Abc
STORE		STORE	STORE	STORE	STORE	STORE
Store (Store)	⫤	Division	City	State	Zip Code	Zip Secseg

18. Click **Geographic Role**, then **State/Province**.

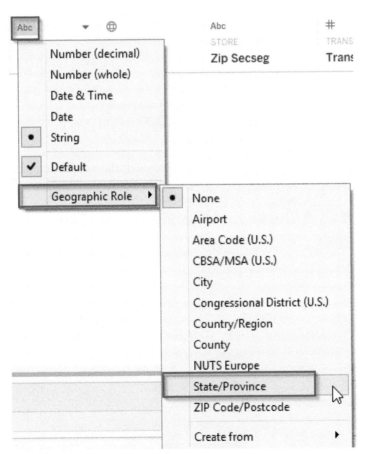

19. Click **Sheet 1** in the bottom left corner of the Tableau screen to begin working with the data.

20. Double-click **State** from **Dimensions**.

Tableau immediately populates a map with a blue dot in each state that has a **Dillard's** store.

21. To make these data even more meaningful, we'll add average transaction amount to this view. Start by double-clicking on **Tran Amt** from the **Measures**.

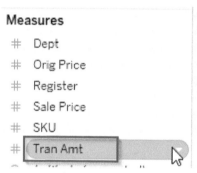

22. It may take a couple minutes for Tableau to populate the data, but the size of the blue dots will adjust to show how the amounts vary across states. The default value for this measure is SUM, though, so we need to edit it to be average.

23. Hover over **SUM(Tran Amt)** in the **Marks** window to make available an arrow for a drop-down window.

24. Click the drop-down, then click **Measure (Sum)** to change the measure to **Average**.

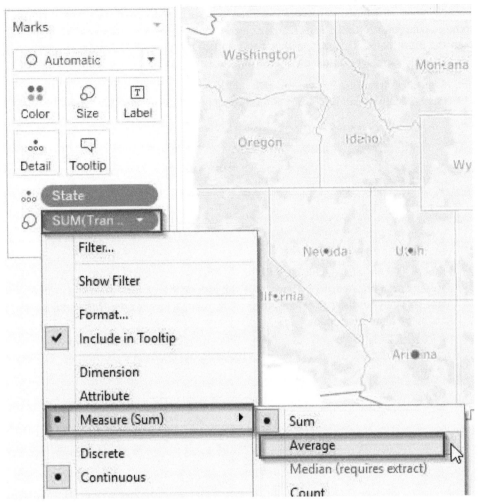

25. Tableau might have defaulted to a symbol map. The difference in averages is easier to interpret with a filled map. Click **Show Me** in the top right corner of Tableau if your **Show Me** window isn't already available, then click **Filled Map**.

26. Take a screenshot of your results (label it 4-3A).

End of this process

Part 3: Perform an Analysis of the Data

Visualizing data often makes it easier to see the answers to your questions, which then leads to more questions. In this case, Arkansas clearly has a higher average transaction amount than the other states. This may lead you to want to drill down into the data to see if the performance is the same across all of the stores in Arkansas, or if there is a stand-out store.

27. If you click **Arkansas**, Tableau will give you the option to filter out all of the other states so that you can drill down into this data point. Click **Keep Only**.

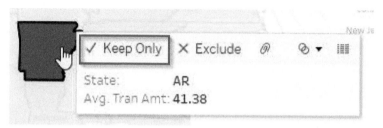

28. From the dimensions, double-click **City**.
29. Tableau doesn't recognize city lines, so it will change from a filled map to a symbol map. This may be easier to read as a bar chart, though, so click the **Horizontal Bars** icon in the **Show Me** window.

Q3. Which city has the highest average transaction amount? (It can be easier to answer this question if you sort the data. Clicking the "sort" button will re-order the bars so that the city with the highest average transaction amount will be the first bar listed.)

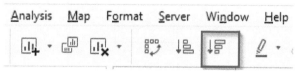

Q4. How would you think managers would like to see transaction balance by state?

Q5. What are further questions that would be meaningful to drill down into with this same dataset, given what you have seen so far?

To dig deeper into the data, we can drill down into which types of items are being sold the most in Maumelle. To do so, we need to join in two more tables. Joining in the SKU table will provide description of the items being sold, and joining in the DEPARTMENT table will provide categorical information for each individual item.

30. Click **Data Source** in the bottom left corner of the Tableau application.

31. Join in the **SKU** and **DEPARTMENT** tables.

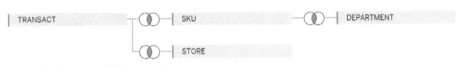

⊖· TRANSACT+ (ua_dillards_2016)

32. Return to your Tableau sheet with the horizontal bar chart, and click **Keep Only** for **Maumelle**.

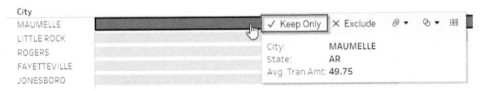

The **DEPARTMENT** and **SKU** data are hierarchical, with an item belonging to a department, which groups into a **deptdec (decade)** through a **deptcent (century)**.

33. Begin by viewing the Maumelle store data by the highest level of the hierarchy, the department century. The description attribute will be the most useful to interpret, so double-click on the **Deptcent Desc** attribute from the **DEPARTMENT** dimensions.

34. To drill down further into the data, add the department decade data to the chart. Double-click on **Deptdec Desc** to add another level of detail.

35. You can also add drill-down capabilities by creating the hierarchy in Tableau. Drag and drop **Deptdec Desc** on top of **Deptcent Cent** in the Dimensions window:

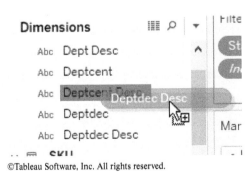

36. Click **OK** on the window to create the hierarchy.

37. Notice that the **Deptcent Desc** pill in the **Rows** shelf changed to include a minus sign—this indicates that the hierarchy has been expanded. Click the minus sign to collapse the hierarchy.

38. Take a screenshot of your results (label it 4-3B).

Part 4: Address and Refine Results

With this much data loaded into Tableau, there is a tremendous amount of analysis and visualization that you can do.

Q6. Based on what you have seen of the average transaction amounts for different departments and products in the Maumelle store, what would you recommend to the Maumelle store manager who is trying to maximize profits? Advertise certain products more? Advertise certain products less? Open an additional store nearby? Close this store, etc.?

Lab 4-4 Comprehensive Case: Dillard's Store Data: Visualizing Regression in Tableau

Company summary

Dillard's is a department store with approximately 330 stores in 29 states. Its headquarters is in Little Rock, Arkansas. You can learn more about **Dillard's** by looking at finance.yahoo .com (Ticker symbol = DDS) and the Wikipedia site for DDS. You'll quickly note that William T. Dillard II is an accounting grad of the University of Arkansas and the Walton College of Business, which may be why he shared transaction data with us to make available for this lab and labs throughout this text.

Data

The data for this lab and other all **Dillard's** labs are available at http://walton.uark.edu/ enterprise/. Your instructor will either give you specific instructions on how to access the data, or there will be information available on Connect. The 2016 **Dillard's** data cover all transactions over the period 1/1/2014 to 10/17/2016.

Specifically, you will need the Excel file that you created and saved in Lab 3-2, **Lab 3-2Dummy.xlsx**. Completing Labs 3-2 and 3-5 and saving the associated Excel file are prerequisites for this lab.

Software needed

- Microsoft SQL Server Management Studio and Microsoft Excel (available on the Remote Desktop at the University of Arkansas)
- Tableau

In this lab, you will:

- Learn how to get visualize regressions in Tableau.

Part 1: Identify the Questions

In chapter 3, you ran a variety of regression and other analyses addressing the following questions:

- Do customers in the state with the highest transaction balances have a significantly higher transaction balance during September 2016 than all other states?
- Are online transaction amounts statistically greater than or lesser than non-online transactions during the period September 1, 2016, to September 15, 2016?
- Do customers who charge their purchases to a Dillard's credit card spend more on each transaction during the time period September 1, 2016, to September 15, 2016?

In this lab, we will work to visualize these data in a way that helps users grasp the information needed to make decisions.

Part 2: Master the Data

To complete the ETL process, we will need to extract the data from the Excel spreadsheet that you saved in the chapter 3 comprehensive labs and transform and load it into Tableau.

1. Open a new Tableau workbook and connect to Microsoft Excel.

2. Browse to the Excel output you created with the dummy variables from Lab 3-2 to Tableau and click **Open**. This will extract the data.
3. When running a regression in Tableau, you will want to place your explanatory variables on the columns and your dependent variables on the rows. To do so, drag and drop the **Arkansas-dummy** measure to the **Columns** shelf and the **Tran Amt Measure** to the **Rows** shelf.

4. Tableau defaults to aggregating the measures, but we are interested in each individual observation. To disaggregate the variables, navigate to the **Analysis** tab and click **Aggregate Measures** to disaggregate the values.

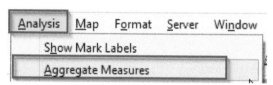

5. It may take some time for the data to disaggregate. Once they do, navigate back to the **Analysis** tab and click **Lines**, and then select **Show All Trend Lines**.

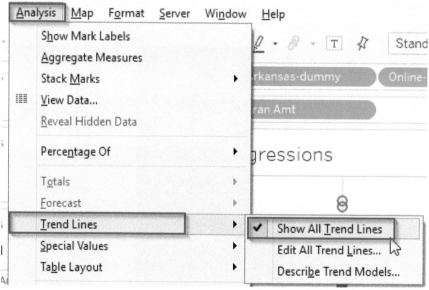

Part 3: Perform an Analysis of the Data

6. Hover over the **trend line** to see the regression formula and the *p*-value.
7. Each variable can be meaningful in explaining the total spent on each transaction (or Tran Amt), but when working with data visualization, it can be even more meaningful to compare models. Compare models by adding the **Online-dummy** and **DLRD-dummy** variables (where DLRD represents the use of a **Dillard's** credit card

in the transaction) to the columns. Note these are univariate analyses in that they compare only Arkansas, online, and the use of a **Dillard's** credit card one-by-one and not altogether.

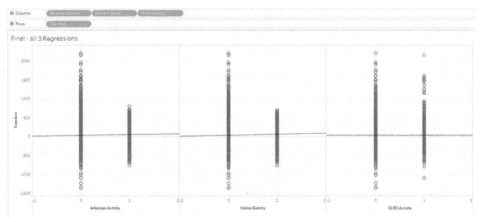

Part 4: Address and Refine Results

Q1.   Which of these three variables has a noticeable trend as compared to the others, suggesting greater explanatory power?

Q2.   Which of these three variables best explains the average transaction amount? (*Hint:* Consider the *r*-squared in each or the *p*-values among the three models.)

Q3.   The coefficient on the DLRD-dummy is negative here. What does that suggest? Is that consistent with the results of Lab 3-2?

Q4.   In the trend line looking at the Arkansas-dummy, what is the base level of Transaction Amount (the *y*-intercept) before considering the Arkansas-dummy?

Q5.   Let's suppose we could capture the net worth of each **Dillard's** customer. Would you expect that to have higher explanatory variable than either of the transaction took place in Arkansas, was an online purchase, or was paid for using a **Dillard's** credit card? Why or why not?

Chapter 5

The Modern Audit and Continuous Auditing

A Look at This Chapter

Most of the focus of Data Analytics in accounting is focused on auditing. This is partly due to the demand for high-quality data and the need for enhancing trust in the assurance process. In this chapter, we look at how both internal and external auditors are using technology in general, and audit analytics specifically, to evaluate firm data and generate support for management assertions. We also introduce how Data Analytics helps facilitate continuous auditing.

A Look Back

Chapter 4 completed our discussion of the IMPACT model by explaining how to communicate your results through data visualization and through written reports. We discussed how to choose the best chart for your dataset and your purpose. We also helped you learn how to refine your chart so that it communicates as efficiently and effectively as possible. The chapter wrapped up by describing how to provide a written report tailored to specific audiences who will be interested in the results of your data analysis project.

A Look Ahead

In chapter 6, you will learn how to use audit software to perform substantive audit tests, including when and how to select samples and how to confirm account balances. Specifically, we discuss the use of different types of descriptive, diagnostic, predictive, and prescriptive analytics as they are used to generate computer-assisted auditing techniques.

The large public accounting firms offer a variety of analytical tools to their customers. Take **PwC**'s Halo, for example, shown in Exhibit 5-1. This tool allows auditors to interrogate a client's data and identify patterns and relationships within the data in a user-friendly dashboard. By mapping the data, auditors and managers can identify inefficiencies in business processes, discover areas of risk exposure, and correct data quality issues by drilling down into the individual users, dates and times, and amounts of the entries. Tools like Halo allow auditors to develop their audit plan by narrowing their focus and audit scope to unusual and infrequent issues that represent high audit risk.

©Shutterstock/Nonwarit

EXHIBIT 5-1

Source: http://halo.pwc.com

OBJECTIVES

After reading this chapter, you should be able to:

LO 5-1   Understand modern auditing techniques
LO 5-2   Evaluate an audit plan
LO 5-3   Understand the nature, extent, and timing of audit tests
LO 5-4   Select appropriate audit tasks and approaches
LO 5-5   Evaluate audit alarms as part of continuous auditing
LO 5-6   Understand working paper platforms

LO 5-1

Understand
modern auditing
techniques

THE MODERN AUDIT

You'll recall from your auditing course that assurance services are crucial to building and maintaining trust within the capital markets. In response to increasing regulation in the United States, the European Union, and other jurisdictions, both internal and external auditors have been tasked with providing enhanced assurance while also attempting to reduce (or at least maintain) the audit fees. This has spurred demand for more audit automation along with an increased reliance on auditors to use their judgment and decision-making skills to effectively interpret and support their audit findings with managers, shareholders, and other stakeholders.

Auditors have been applying simple Data Analytics for decades in evaluating risk within companies. Think about how an evaluation of inventory turnover can spur a discussion on inventory obsolescence or how working capital ratios are used to identify significant issues with a firm's liquidity. From an internal audit perspective, evaluating cost variances can help identify operational inefficiencies or unfavorable contracts with suppliers.

The audit concepts of professional skepticism and reasonable assurance are as much a part of the modern audit as in the past. There has been a shift, however, of simply providing reasonable assurance on the processes to the additional assurance of the robots that are performing a lot of the menial audit work. Where, before, an auditor may have looked at samples and gathered evidence to make inferences to the population, now that same auditor must understand the controls and parameters that have been programmed into the robot. In other words, as these automated bots do more of the routine analytics, auditors will be free to exercise more judgment to interpret the alarms and data while refocusing their effort on testing the parameters used by the robots.

Auditors use Data Analytics to improve audit quality by more accurately assessing risk and selecting better substantive procedures and tests of controls. While the exercises the auditors conduct are fairly routine, the models can be complex and require auditor judgment and interpretation. For example, if an auditor receives 1,000 notifications of a control violation during the day, does that mean there is a control weakness or that the settings on the automated control are too precise? Are all those notifications actual control violations that require immediate attention, or are most of them false positives—transactions that are flagged as exceptions but are normal and acceptable?

The auditors' role is to make sure that the appropriate analytics are used and that the output of those analytics—whether a dashboard, notifications of exceptions, or accuracy of predictive models—correspond to management's expectations and assertions.

The Increasing Importance of the Internal Audit

If you look at the assurance market, there are many trends that are affecting the profession. First, the major applications of Data Analytics in auditing are not solely focused on the financial statements as evaluated by public accounting firms. Rather, these tend to focus on data quality, internal controls, and the complex information systems that support the business process—areas typically reserved for the internal audit department at a firm. Second, the risk and advisory practices of the public accounting firms are experiencing greater growth, in large part due to firms' outsourcing or co-sourcing of the internal audit function. Third, external auditors are permitted to rely on the work of internal auditors to provide support for their opinion of financial statements.

For these reasons, most of the innovations in Data Analytics have originated in internal audit departments, where there is constant pressure to enhance business value while minimizing costs. In the recent past, many companies' experience with Data Analytics in the internal audit department have come from internal auditors who have investigated Data Analytics on their own. These individuals then find a champion with management and are encouraged to continue their work. Under the guidance of the chief audit executive (CAE) or another manager, these individuals build teams to develop and implement analytical techniques to aid the following audits:

1. Process efficiency and effectiveness.
2. Governance, risk, and compliance, including internal controls effectiveness.
3. Information technology and information systems audits.
4. Forensic audits in the case of fraud.
5. Support for the financial statement audit.

Internal auditors are also more likely to have working knowledge of the various enterprise resource planning systems that are in use at their companies. They are familiar with how the general journals from a product like JD Edwards actually reconcile to the general ledger in SAP. Because implementation of these systems varies across organizations (and even within organizations), internal auditors can understand how analytics are not simply a one-size-fits-all type of strategy.

 PROGRESS CHECK

1. How do auditors use Data Analytics in their audit testing?
2. Make the case for why an internal audit is increasingly important in the modern audit. Why is it also important for external auditors and the scope of their work?

Auditing Data

> **LO 5-2**
> ───────────
> Evaluate an audit plan

While organizations have become more data-centric as they have adopted ERP systems over the past few decades, these systems can vary greatly among organizations. Some companies will take a **homogeneous systems approach** by ensuring that all of its divisions and subsidiaries use a uniform installation of SAP. This approach allows management to consolidate the information from various locations and roll them up into the financial statements. Other companies that grow through acquisition, take a **heterogeneous systems approach**, where they attempt to integrate the existing systems of companies that they acquire and use a series of translators to convert the output of those systems (such as PeopleSoft, JD Edwards, and others) into usable financial information. **Systems translator software** attempts to map the various tables and fields from these varied ERP systems and create a **data warehouse**, where all of the data can be analyzed centrally, as shown in Exhibit 5-2.

One of the primary obstacles auditors face is access to appropriate data. As noted in chapter 2, auditors typically request **flat files** or extracts from an IT manager. In some cases, these files may be incomplete, unrelated, limited in scope, or delayed when they are not considered a priority by IT managers. Ideally, auditors will have read-only access to the data warehouse that pulls in not only transaction data, such as purchases and sales, but also the related master data, such as employees and vendors. Thus, they can analyze multiple relationships and explore other patterns in a more meaningful way. In either case, the auditors will work with duplicated data, rather than querying the **production or live systems** directly.

The AICPA's **audit data standards (ADSs)** define common tables and fields that are needed by auditors to perform common audit tasks. They make recommendations to ERP vendors to standardize the output of common data that auditors are likely to use. The goal of the standards is to reduce efforts of the auditors with loading and transforming the data so they can work with the analytics more quickly and have support for more real-time or continuous analytics through access to data warehouses. These standards are voluntary, and actual implementation is currently limited, but they provide a good basis for data needed to audit specific company functions.

EXHIBIT 5-2
Homogeneous Systems, Heterogeneous Systems, and Software Translators

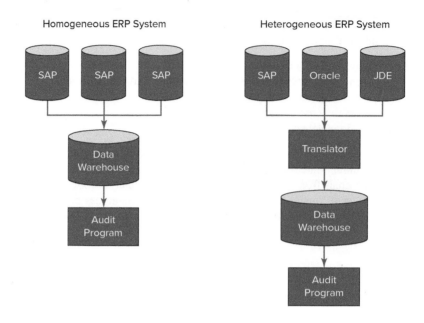

The current set of audit data standards defines the following standards:

- The *Base Standard* defines the format for files and fields as well as some master data for users and business units.
- The *General Ledger Standard* adds the chart of accounts, source listings, trial balance, and GL (journal entry) detail.
- The *Order to Cash Subledger Standard* focuses on sales orders, accounts receivable, shipments, invoices, cash receipts and adjustments to accounts, shown in Exhibit 5-3.

EXHIBIT 5-3
Audit Data Standards
The audit data standards define common elements needed to audit the order-to-cash or sales process.

Source: https://www.aicpa
.org/InterestAreas/FRC/
AssuranceAdvisoryServices/
DownloadableDocuments/
AuditDataStandards/
AuditDataStandards.O2C.
July2015.pdf

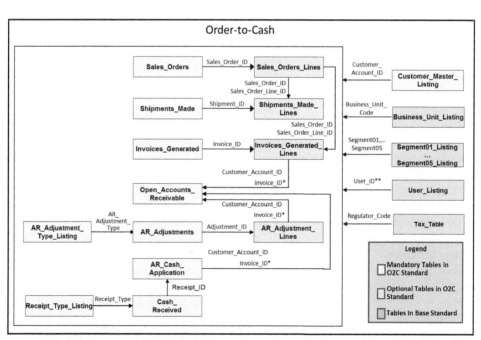

* If receivable balances are tracked by customer only (not by invoice), then Customer_Account_ID is used as a key to join tables to the Open_Accounts_Receivable table instead of both Customer_Account_ID and Invoice_ID

** The User_Listing table can be joined to three fields, all of which contain a user ID – Entered_by, Approved_By, Last_Modified_By

- The *Procure to Pay Subledger Standard* identifies data needed for purchase orders, goods received, invoices, payments, and adjustments to accounts.
- The *Inventory Subledger Standard* defines product master data, location data, inventory on hand data, and inventory movement.

With standard data elements in place, not only will auditors streamline their access to data, but they also will be able to build analytical tools that they can share with others within their company or professional organizations. This can foster greater collaboration among auditors and increased use of Data Analytics across organizations. These data elements will be useful when performing substantive testing in chapter 6.

 PROGRESS CHECK

3. What are the advantages of the use of homogeneous systems? Would a merger target be more attractive if it used a similar financial reporting system as the potential parent company?

4. How does the use of audit data standards facilitate data transfer between auditors and companies? How does it save time for both parties?

AUTOMATING THE AUDIT PLAN

So far, we've discussed many of the tools available to auditors as well as the changing audit environment. The main impact of automation and Data Analytics on the audit profession comes through optimization of the audit plan. When beginning an engagement—whether to audit the financial statements, certify the enterprise resource planning system, or make a recommendation to improve a business process—auditors generally follow a standardized audit plan. The benefit of a standardized audit plan is that newer members of the audit team can jump into an audit and contribute. They also identify the priorities of the audit.

An audit plan consists of the one or more of the following elements:

- A *methodology* that directs that audit work.
- The *scope of the audit,* defining the time period, level of materiality, and expected time for the audit.
- *Potential risk* within the area being audited.
- *Procedures and specific tasks* that the audit team will execute to collect and analyze evidence. These typically include tests of controls and substantive tests of transaction details.
- *Formal evaluation* by the auditor and supervisors.

Because audit plans are formalized and standardized, they lend themselves to the use of Data Analytics and, consequently, automation. For example,

- The methodology may be framed by specific standards, such as the Public Company Accounting Oversight Board's (PCAOB) auditing standards, the Committee of Sponsoring Organizations's (COSO) Enterprise Risk Management framework, or the Information Systems Audit and Control Association's (ISACA) Control Objectives for Information and Related Technologies (COBIT) framework. Data Analytics may be used to analyze the standards and determine which requirements apply to the organization being audited.
- The scope of the audit defines parameters that will be used to filter the records or transactions being evaluated.
- Simple to complex Data Analytics can be applied to a client's data during the planning stage of the audit to identify which areas the auditor should focus on. This may include outlier detection or other substantive tests of suspicious or risky transactions.

LO 5-3

Understand the nature, extent, and timing of audit tests

LO 5-4

Select appropriate audit tasks and approaches

- Audit procedures themselves typically identify data, locations, and attributes that the auditors will evaluate. These are the variables that will provide the input for many of the substantive analytical procedures discussed in chapter 6.
- The evaluation of audit data may be distilled into a risk score. This may be a function of the volume of exceptional records or level of exposure for the functional area. If the judgment and decision making is easily defined, a rule-based analytic could automatically assign a score for the auditor to review. For more complex judgment, the increasing prevalence of artificial intelligence and machine learning discussed in chapter 3 may be of assistance. After all, if we have enough observations of the scores auditors assign to specific cases and outcomes, we can create models that will provide accurate enough classification for these tasks.

Typical internal audit organizations that have adopted Data Analytics to enhance their audit have done so when an individual on the team has begun tinkering with Data Analytics. They convince their managers that there is value in using the data to direct the audit and get a champion in the process. Once they show the value proposition of Data Analytics, they are given more resources to build the program and adapt the existing audit program to include more data-centric evaluation where appropriate.

Because of the potential disruption to the organization, it is more likely that an auditor will adapt an existing audit plan than develop a new system from scratch. Automating the audit plan and incorporating data analytics involve the following steps, which are similar to the IMPACT model:

1. *Identify* the questions or requirements in the existing audit plan.
2. *Master* the data by identifying attributes and elements that are automatable.
3. *Perform* the test plan, in this case by developing analytics (in the form of rules or models) for those attributes identified in step 2.
4. *Address* and refine results. List expected exceptions to these analytics and expected remedial action by the auditor, if any.
5. *Communicate* insight by testing the rules and comparing the output of the analytics to manual audit procedures.
6. *Track* outcomes by following up on alarms and refining the models as needed.

Let's assume that an internal auditor has been tasked with implementing data analytics to automate the evaluation of a segregation of duties control within SAP. The auditor evaluates the audit plan and identifies a procedure for testing this control. The audit plan identifies which tables and fields contain relevant data, such as an authorization matrix, and the specific roles or permissions that would be incompatible. The auditor would use that information to build a model that would search for users with incompatible roles and notify the auditors.

CONTINOUS AUDITING TECHNIQUES

LO 5-5

Evaluate audit alarms as part of continuous auditing

Data Analytics and audit automation allow auditors to continuously monitor and audit the systems and processes within their companies. Whereas a traditional audit may have the internal auditors perform a routine audit plan once every 12 to 36 months or so, the continuous audit evaluates data in a form that matches the pulse of the business. For example, purchase orders can be monitored for unauthorized activity in real time, while month-end adjusting entries would be evaluated once a month. When exceptions occur—for example, a purchase order is created with a customer whose address matches an employee's—the auditors are alerted immediately and given the option to respond right away to resolve the issue.

Continuous auditing is a process that provides real-time assurance over business processes and systems. It involves the application of rules or analytics that perform a *continuous monitoring* function that constantly evaluates internal controls and transactions. It also generates *continuous reporting* on the status of the system so that an auditor can know at any given time whether the system is operating within the parameters set by management or not.

Implementing continuous auditing procedures is similar to automating an audit plan with the additional step of scheduling the automated procedures to match the timing and frequency of the data being evaluated and notifying the auditor when exceptions occur.

Alarms and Exceptions

Whenever an automated or continuous auditing rule is violated, an *exception* occurs. The record is flagged and systems generate an *exception report* that typically identifies the record and the date of the exception.

Alarms are essentially a classification problem. A data value is sent through a simple decision tree based on a series of rules and classified as a positive event (alarm) or a negative event (no alarm). Remember we talked about accuracy of models in chapter 3: These alarms will not always be correct.

Once the notification of the alarm or exception arrives, auditors follow a set of procedures to resolve the issue. First, they must determine whether the alarm represents a *true positive,* a transaction that is problematic, such as an error or fraud, or a *false positive,* where a normal transaction is classified as problematic. When too many alarms are false positive, auditors face *information overload,* where there are too many incorrect alarms that distract them from adequately evaluating the system. Because auditors are mostly concerned with true positives, they should attempt to train or refine the models to minimize the potential *flood of alarm*s that occurs when too many alarms are false positives. This is summarized in Table 5-1.

	Normal Event	Abnormal Event
Alarm	*False positive*	*True positive*
No Alarm	True negative	False negative

TABLE 5.1
Four Types of Alarms That an Auditor Must Evaluate

WORKING PAPERS AND AUDIT WORKFLOW

LO 5-6
Understand working paper platforms

As audit procedures become increasingly technical, documentation continues to be essential as a way for auditors to increase their reliance on automated controls and procedures. The idea of a black-box audit is no longer sufficient; rather, auditors must have a better understanding of the tools they use and the output of those tools. This is where working papers come into play.

Working papers are essential to audit planning, performance, and evaluation. They provide the documentation for the procedures the auditors follow, evidence they collect, and communication with the audit client. As they relate to Data Analytics, working papers should contain the following items:

- Work programs used to document the audit procedures to collect, manipulate, model, and evaluate data.
- IT-related documentation, including flowchart and process maps that provide system understanding.

- Database maps (such as UML diagrams) and data dictionaries that define the location and types of data auditors will analyze.
- Documentation about existing automated controls, including parameters and variables used for analysis.
- Evidence, including data extracts, transformed data, and model output, that provides support for the functioning controls and management assertions.

Policies and procedures that help provide consistent quality work are essential to maintaining a complete and consistent audit. The audit firm or chief audit executive is responsible for providing guidance and standardization so that different auditors and audit teams produce clear results. These standardizations include consistent use of symbols or tick marks and a uniform mechanism for cross-referencing output to source documents or data.

Electronic Working Papers and Remote Audit Work

As audit teams embrace a variety of information and communication technologies to enable collaboration from different locations, audit firms have done so, as well. Increasingly, internal and external audit teams consist of more specialized onsite auditors who interact with a team of experts and data scientists remotely at locations around the world. Many of the routine tasks are offloaded to the remote or seasonal workers, freeing up onsite auditors to use more professional judgment and expertise during the engagement. This results in cost savings for the firm through increased efficiency at the firm level.

The glue that holds the audit team together is the electronic workpaper platform as well as other collaboration tools, such as Microsoft Teams or Slack. The electronic workpaper platforms, such as TeamMate or Xero, automate the workflow of evidence collection, evaluation, and opinion generation on the part of the audit teams. The large accounting firms have proprietary systems that accomplish a similar purpose. For example, PwC uses three systems to automate its audit process. Aura is used to direct the audit by identifying which evidence to collect and analyze, Halo performs Data Analytics on the collected evidence, and Connect provides the workflow process that allows managers and partners to review and sign off on the work. Most of these platforms are hosted in the cloud, so members of the audit team can participate in the various functions from any location. Smaller audit shops can build ad hoc workpaper repositories using OneDrive with Office 365, though there are fewer controls over the documents.

✓ PROGRESS CHECK

5. Continuous audit uses alarms to identify exceptions that might indicate an audit issue and require additional investigation. If there are too many alarms and exceptions based on the parameters of the continuous audit system, will continuous auditing actually help or hurt the overall audit effectiveness?

6. PwC uses three systems to automate its audit process. Aura is used to direct the audit by identifying which evidence to collect and analyze, Halo performs Data Analytics on the collected evidence, and Connect provides the workflow process that allows managers and partners to review and sign off on the work. How does that line up with the steps of the IMPACT model we've discussed throughout the text?

Summary

As auditing has evolved over the past few decades, Data Analytics has driven many of the changes. The ability to increase coverage of the audit using data has made it less likely that key elements are missed. Data Analytics has improved auditors' ability to assess risk, inform their opinions, and improve assurance over the processes and controls in their organizations.

Key Words

audit data standards (ADSs) (*193*) The audit data standards define common tables and fields that are needed by auditors to perform common audit tasks. The AICPA developed these standards.

data warehouse (*193*) A data warehouse is a repository of data accumulated from internal and external data sources, including financial data, to help management decision making.

flat file (*193*) A flat file is a single table of data with user-defined attributes that is stored separately from any application.

homogeneous systems approach (*193*) Homogeneous systems represent one single installation or instance of a system. It would be considered the opposite of a heterogeneous system.

heterogeneous systems approach (*193*) Heterogeneous systems represent multiple installations or instances of a system. It would be considered the opposite of a homogeneous system.

production or live systems (*193*) Production (or live systems) are those active systems that collect and report and are directly affected by current transactions.

systems translator software (*193*) Systems translator software maps the various tables and fields from varied ERP systems into a consistent format.

⊘ ANSWERS TO PROGRESS CHECKS

1. Auditors use Data Analytics to improve audit quality by more accurately assessing risk and selecting better substantive procedures and tests of controls.

2. There are many reasons for this trend, with perhaps the most important being that external auditors are permitted to rely on the work of internal auditors to provide support for their opinion of financial statements.

3. A homogeneous system allows effortless transmission of accounting and auditing data across company units and international borders. It also allows company executives (including the chief executive officer, chief financial officer, and chief information officer), accounting staff, and the internal audit team to intimately know two systems.

4. The use of audit data standards allows an efficient data transfer of data in a format that auditors can use in their audit testing programs. It can also save the company time and effort in providing its transaction data in a usable fashion to auditors.

5. If there are too many alarms and exceptions, particularly with false negatives and false positives, continuous auditing becomes more of a burden than a blessing. Work must be done to ensure more true positives and negatives to be valuable to the auditor.

6. PwC's Aura system would help identify the questions and master the data, the first two steps of the IMPACT model. PwC's Halo system would help perform the test plan and address and refine results, the middle two steps of the IMPACT model. Finally, PwC's Connect system would help communicate insights and track outcomes, the final two steps of the IMPACT model.

Multiple Choice Questions

1. Under the guidance of the chief audit executive (CAE) or another manager, these individuals build teams to develop and implement analytical techniques to aid all of the following audits *except*:

   a. Process efficiency and effectiveness.

   b. Governance, risk, and compliance, including internal controls effectiveness.

   c. Tax compliance.

   d. Support for the financial statement audit.

2. Which audit data standards ledger defines product master data, location data, inventory on hand data, and inventory movement?

   a. Order to Cash Subledger

   b. Procure to Pay Subledger

   c. Inventory Subledger

   d. Base Subledger

3. Which audit data standards ledger identifies data needed for purchase orders, goods received, invoices, payments, and adjustments to accounts?

   a. Order to Cash Subledger

   b. Procure to Pay Subledger

   c. Inventory Subledger

   d. Base Subledger

4. A company has two divisions, one in the United States and the other in China. One uses Oracle and the other uses SAP for its basic accounting system. What would we call this?

   a. Homogeneous systems

   b. Heterogeneous systems

   c. Dual data warehouse systems

   d. Dual lingo accounting systems

5. Which of the following defines the time period, the level of materiality, and the expected time for an audit?

   a. Audit scope

   b. Potential risk

   c. Methodology

   d. Procedures and specific tasks

6. All of the following may serve as standards for the audit methodology *except*:

   a. PCAOB's auditing standards

   b. COSO's ERM framework

   c. ISACA's COBIT framework

   d. FASB's accounting standards

7. When there is an alarm in a continuous audit, but it is associated with a normal event, we would call that a:

   a. False negative.

   b. True negative.

   c. True positive.

   d. False positive.

8. When there is no alarm in a continuous audit, but there is an abnormal event, we would call that a:

   a. False negative.

   b. True negative.

   c. True positive.

   d. False positive.

9. If purchase orders are monitored for unauthorized activity in real time while month-end adjusting entries are evaluated once a month, those transactions monitored in real time would be an example of a:

   a. Traditional audit.

   b. Periodic test of internal controls.

   c. Continuous audit.

   d. Continuous monitoring.

10. Who is most likely to have a working knowledge of the various ERP systems that are in use in the company?

    a. Chief executive officer

    b. External auditor

    c. Internal auditor

    d. IT staff

Discussion Questions

1. Why has most innovation in Data Analytics originated more in an internal audit than an external audit? Or if not, why not?

2. Is it possible for a firm to have general journals from a product like JD Edwards actually reconcile to the general ledger in SAP? Why or why not?

3. Is it possible for multinational firms to have many different financial reporting systems and ERP packages all in use at the same time?

4. How does the systems translator software work? How does it store the merged data into a data warehouse?

5. Why is it better to extract data from a data warehouse than a production or live system directly?

6. Would an auditor view heterogeneous systems as an audit risk? Why or why not?

7. Why would audit firms prefer to use proprietary workpapers rather than just storing working papers on the cloud?

Problems

1. What are the advantages of the use of homogeneous systems? Would a merger target be more attractive if it used a similar financial reporting system as the potential parent company?

2. Consider Exhibit 5-3. Looking at the audit data standards order-to-cash process, what function is there for the AR_Adjustments transaction table—that is, adjustments to the Accounts Receivable? Why is this an audit data standard, and why is it important for an auditor to see?

3. Who developed the audit data standards? In your opinion, why is it the right group to develop and maintain them rather than, say, the Big 4 firms or a small practitioner?

4. Simple to complex Data Analytics can be applied to a client's data during the planning stage of the audit to identify which areas the auditor should focus on. Which types of techniques or tests might be used in this stage?

5. What approach should a company make if its continuous audit system has too many alarms that are false positives? How would that approach change if there are too many missed abnormal events (such as false negatives)?

6. Implementing continuous auditing procedures is similar to automating an audit plan with the additional step of scheduling the automated procedures to match the timing and frequency of the data being evaluated and the notification to the auditor when exceptions occur. In your opinion, will the traditional audit be replaced by continuous auditing?

Answers to Multiple Choice Questions

1. C
2. C
3. B
4. B
5. A
6. D
7. D
8. A
9. C
10. C

Auditors collect evidence in electronic workpapers that include a permanent file with information about policies and procedures and a temporary file with evidence related to the current audit. These files could be stored locally on a laptop, but the increased use of remote communication makes collaboration through the cloud more necessary. There are a number of commercial workpaper applications, but we can simulate some of those features with consumer cloud platforms, like Microsoft OneDrive.

Company summary

You have rotated into the internal audit department at a mid-sized manufacturing company. Your team is still using company e-mail to send evidence back and forth, usually in the form of documents and spreadsheets. There is a lot of duplication of these files, and no one is quite sure which version is the latest. You see an opportunity to streamline this process using OneDrive.

Technique

- Gather documents, explore document history and revisions

Software needed

- A modern web browser

In this lab, you will:

    Part 1: Create a shared folder.

    Part 2: Upload files.

    Part 3: Review revisions.

Part 1: Create a Shared Folder

Note: These instructions are specific to the free consumer version of Microsoft OneDrive. The approach is similar for competing products, such as Box, Dropbox, Google Drive, or other commercial products.

1. Go to OneDrive.com.
2. Click **Sign in** in the top right corner.
3. Sign in with your Microsoft account. (If your organization subscribes to Office 365, use your school or work account here.)
4. On the main OneDrive screen, click **New > Folder**.
5. Name your folder **DA Audit Working Papers**.
6. Open your new folder and click **Share** from the bar at the top of the screen.
7. Add the e-mail address of one of your classmates or your instructor, as directed. Choose **Allow editing** from the drop-down box next to the addresses, then click **Share**.
8. Take a screenshot (label it 5-1A).

    Q1.   What advantage is there to sharing files in one location rather than e-mailing copies back and forth?

Part 2: Upload Files

Now that you have folders, you can upload some documents that will be useful for labs in this chapter and the next.

9. From Connect, download the **Audit Analytics Lab Files 1**, as directed by your instructor.
10. Unzip the file you downloaded to your computer. You should see two folders: **Master Audit File** and **Current Audit File**.

11. Return to your OneDrive **DA Audit Working Papers** folder, and upload the two folders:
    a. Click **Upload > Folders** in OneDrive and navigate to the folder where you unzipped the lab files.
    b. Or drag and drop the two folders from your desktop to the OneDrive window in your browser.
12. You should see two new folders in your OneDrive. Because you added them to a shared folder, the people you shared the folder with can now see these as well.
13. Take a screenshot (label it 5-1B).

> Q2. Explore the two folders you just uploaded. What kinds of documents and files do you see?
>
> Q3. How do you think these files can be used for data analysis?

End of Lab

Lab 5-2   Review Changes to Working Papers (OneDrive)

See Lab 5-1 for background information on this lab. The goal of a shared folder is that other members of the audit team can contribute and edit the documents. Commercial software provides an approval workflow and additional internal controls over the documents to reduce manipulation of audit evidence, for example. For consumer cloud platforms, one control appears in the versioning of documents. As revisions are made, old copies of the documents are kept so that they can be reverted to, if needed.

In this lab, you will:

Part 1: Upload revised documents.

Part 2: Review document revision history.

Part 1: Upload Revised Documents

Let's start by making changes to files in your **DA Working Papers**.

1. From Connect, download **Audit Analytics Lab Files 2**, as directed by your instructor.
2. Unzip the file you downloaded to your computer. You should see two files: **Audit Plan** and **Employee File**.
3. Return to your OneDrive **DA Audit Working Papers** folder, and upload the **Audit Plan** into your **Master Audit File** and the **User_Listing** into your **Current Audit File**. You will be prompted to **Replace** or **Keep Both** files. Click **Replace** for each.
4. Take a screenshot (label it 5-2A).

Part 2: Review Document Revision History

Now let's look at the history of the document.

5. Right-click on one of the newly uploaded files, and choose **Version history** from the menu that appears. The document will open with a version pane appearing on the left.
6. Click the older version of the file from the **Older Versions** list.
7. Take a screenshot (label it 5-2B).
8. Move between the old version of the file and the current version by clicking the time stamp in the panel on the left.

> Q1. What has changed between these two versions?

End of Lab

Lab 5-3   Identify Audit Data Requirements

As the new member of the internal audit team, you have introduced your team to the shared folder and are in the process of modernizing the internal audit at your firm. The chief audit executive is interested in using Data Analytics to make the audit more efficient. Your internal audit manager agrees and has tasked you with reviewing the audit plan. She has provided three "audit action sheets" with procedures that they have been using for the past three years to evaluate the procure-to-pay (purchasing) process and is interested in your thoughts for modernizing them.

Technique

- Review the audit plan, look for procedures involving data, and identify the locations of the data.

Software needed

- A modern web browser

In this lab, you will:

> Part 1: Look for audit procedures that evaluate data.
> Part 2: Identify the location of the data.

Part 1: Look for Audit Procedures That Evaluate Data

1. Open your **DA Audit Working Papers** folder on OneDrive.
2. Look inside the **Master Audit File** for the document titled **Audit Action Sheets** and open it to edit it.
3. Use the **Yellow highlighter** to identify any master or transaction tables, such as "Vendors" or "Purchase Orders."
4. Use the **Green highlighter** to identify any fields or attributes, such as "Name" or "Date."
5. Use the **Blue highlighter** to identify any specific values or rules, such as "TRUE," "January 1st," "Greater than . . ."
6. Create a new spreadsheet called **Audit Automation Summary** in your **Master Audit File** and summarize your highlighted data elements from the three audit action sheets. Use the following headers:

AAS#	Table	Attributes	Values/Rules	Step(s)	Notes

7. Take a screenshot (label it 5-3A).

> Q1. Read the first audit action sheet. What other data elements that are not listed in the procedures do you think would be useful in analyzing this account?

Part 2: Identify the Location of the Data

Now that you have analyzed the action sheets, look through the systems documentation to see where those elements exist.

8. In the **Master Audit File**, open the **UML System Diagram** and **Data Dictionary** files.
9. Using the data elements you identified in your **Audit Automation Summary** file, locate the actual names of tables and attributes and acceptable data values. Add them in three new columns in your summary:

Database Table	Database Attribute	Acceptable Values

10. Take a screenshot (label it 5-3B).

    Q2. Which attributes were difficult to locate or in unexpected places in the database?

11. Save and close your file.

End of Lab

Lab 5-4   Prepare Audit Plan

With the data elements identified, you can formalize your internal audit plan. In the past, your internal audit department performed each of the three action sheets once every 24 months. You have shared how increasing the frequency of some of the tests would provide a better control for the process and allow the auditor to respond quickly to the exceptions. Your internal audit manager has asked you to propose a new schedule for the three audit action sheets.

Technique

- Review the audit plan, identify procedures that must be completed manually, and identify those that can be automated and scheduled.
- Also determine when the procedures should occur.

Software needed

- A modern web browser

In this lab, you will:

- Evaluate the timing and scheduling of audit procedures.

1. Open your **Audit Automation Summary** spreadsheet in OneDrive.
2. Add two new columns:

Auto/Manual	Frequency

3. For each element and rule, determine whether it requires manual review or can be performed automatically and alter auditors when exceptions occur. Add either "Auto" or "Manual" to that column.
4. Finally, determine how frequently the data should be evaluated. Indicate "Daily," "Weekly," "Monthly," "Annually," or "During Audit." Think about when the data are being generated. For example, transactions occur every day, but new employees are added every few months.
5. Take a screenshot (label it 5-4A).
6. Save and close your file.

End of Lab

Chapter 6
Audit Data Analytics

A Look at This Chapter

In this chapter, we focus on substantive testing within the audit setting. We highlight discussion of the audit plan, discuss when population testing is appropriate, and attempt to understand simple audit analyses. We also discuss the use of clustering to detect outliers and the use of Benford's analysis.

A Look Back

In chapter 5, we introduced Data Analytics in auditing by considering how both internal and external auditors are using technology in general, and audit analytics specifically, to evaluate firm data and generate support for management assertions. We emphasized audit planning, audit data standards, continuous auditing, and audit working papers.

A Look Ahead

Chapter 7 explains how to apply Data Analytics to measure performance. By measuring past performance and comparing it to targeted goals, we are able to assess how well a company is working toward a goal. Also, we can determine required adjustments to how decisions are made or how business processes are run, if any.

©Anatolii Babii/Alamy

Internal auditors at **Hewlett-Packard Co. (HP)** understand how data analytics can improve processes and controls. Management identified abnormal behavior with manual journal entries, and the internal audit department responded by working with various governance and compliance teams to develop dashboards that would allow them to monitor accounting activity. The dashboard made it easier for management and the auditors to follow trends, identify spikes in activity, and drill down to identify the individuals posting entries. Leveraging accounting data allows the internal audit function to focus on the risks facing **HP** and act on data in real time by implementing better controls. Audit data analytics provides an enhanced level of control that is missing from a traditional periodic audit.

OBJECTIVES

After reading this chapter, you should be able to:

LO 6-1   Understand different types of analysis for auditing and when to use them

LO 6-2   Understand basic descriptive audit analyses

LO 6-3   Understand more complex statistical analyses, including Benford's law

LO 6-4   Understand advanced predictive and prescriptive analytics

WHEN TO USE AUDIT DATA ANALYTICS

As discussed in chapter 5, Data Analytics can be applied to the auditing function to increase coverage of the audit, while reducing the time the auditor dedicates to the audit tasks. Think about the nature, extent, and timing of audit procedures. Nature represents *why* we perform audit procedures. In other words, nature helps determine the objectives of the audit and the outputs generated by the business processes. Extent indicates *how much* we can test. The prevalence of data has expanded the extent of audit testing. Finally, timing tells us *how often* the procedure should be run. All three of these elements help us identify when to apply Data Analytics to the audit process.

Auditors should evaluate current capabilities within their department and identify the goal of Data Analytics. Does it add value? Does it enhance the process? Does it help the auditor be more efficient and effective? Applying Data Analytics, in theory, should add value. In reality, it is easy to overpromise on the expected benefits of Data Analytics and underdeliver with the results. Without clear objectives and expected outcomes, audit departments will fail with their use of Data Analytics. Here we refer once again to the IMPACT model.

Identify the Problem

What is the audit department trying to achieve using data analytics? Do you need to analyze the segregation of duties to test whether internal controls are operating effectively? Are you looking for operational inefficiencies, such as duplicate payments of invoices? Are you trying to identify phantom employees or vendors? Are you trying to collect evidence that you are complying with specific regulations? Are you trying to test account balances to tie them to the financial statements?

These activities support the functional areas of compliance, fraud detection and investigation, operational performance, and internal controls for internal audit departments as well as the financial reporting and risk assessment functions of external audit.

Master the Data

In theory, auditors should have read-only access to enterprise data through a nonproduction data warehouse. In practice, they make multiple requests for flat files or data extractions from the IT manager that they then analyze with a software tool, such as Excel or Tableau. Most audit data are provided in structured or tabular form, such as a spreadsheet file.

Regardless of the source or type, the audit data standards provide a general overview of the basic data that auditors will evaluate. For example, consider the Sales_Orders table from the standards shown in Table 6-1. An auditor interested in user activity would want to focus on the Sales_Order_ID, Sales_Order_Date, Entered_By, Entered_Date, Entered_Time, Approved_By, Approved_Date, Approved_Time, and Sales_Order_Amount_Local attributes. These may give insight into transactions on unusual dates, such as weekends, or unusually high volume by specific users.

There are also many pieces of data that have traditionally evaded scrutiny, including handwritten logs, manuals and handbooks, and other paper or text-heavy documentation. Essentially, manual tasks including observation and inspection are generally areas where Data Analytics may not apply. While there have been significant advancements in artificial intelligence, there is still a need for auditors to exercise their judgment, and data cannot always supersede the auditor's reading of human behavior or a sense that something may not be quite right even when the data say it is. At least not yet.

Field Name	Description
Sales_Order_ID	Unique identifier for each sales order. This ID may need to be created by concatenating fields (e.g., document number, document type, and year) to uniquely identify each sales order.
Sales_Order_Document_ID	Identification number or code on the sales order.
Sales_Order_Date	The date of the sales order, regardless of the date the order is entered.
Sales_Order_Fiscal_Year	Fiscal year in which the Sales_Order_Date occurs: YYYY for delimited, CCYYMMDD fiscal year-end (ISO 8601) for XBRL-GL.
Sales_Order_Period	Fiscal period in which the Sales_Order_Date occurs. Examples include W1–W53 for weekly periods, M1–M12 for monthly periods, and Q1–Q4 for quarterly periods.
Business_Unit_Code	Used to identify the business unit, region, branch, and so on at the level that financial statements are being audited. Must match a Business_Unit_Code in the Business_Unit_Listing file.
Customer_Account_ID	Identifier of the customer from whom payment is expected or to whom unused credits have been applied. Must match a Customer_Account_ID in the Customer_Master_Listing_YYYYMMDD file.
Entered_By	User_ID (from User_Listing file) for person who created the record.
Entered_Date	Date the order was entered into the system. This is sometimes referred to as the creation date. This should be a system-generated date (rather than user-entered date), when possible. This date does not necessarily correspond with the date of the transaction itself.
Entered_Time	The time this transaction was entered into the system. ISO 8601 representing time in 24-hour time (hhmm) (e.g., 1:00 p.m. = 1300).
Approved_By	User ID (from User_Listing file) for person who approved customer master additions or changes.
Approved_Date	Date the entry was approved.
Approved_Time	The time the entry was approved. ISO 8601 representing time in 24-hour time (hhmm) (e.g., 1:00 p.m. = 1300).
Last_Modified_By	User_ID (from User_Listing file) for the last person modifying this entry.
Last_Modified_Date	The date the entry was last modified.
Last_Modified_Time	The time the entry was last modified. ISO 8601 representing time in 24-hour time (hhmm) (e.g., 1:00 p.m. = 1300).
Sales_Order_Amount_Local	Sales monetary amount recorded in the local currency.
Sales_Order_Local_Currency	The currency for local reporting requirements. See ISO 4217 coding.
Segment01	Reserved segment field that can be used for profit center, division, fund, program, branch, project, and so on.
Segment02	See above.
Segment03	See above.
Segment04	See above.
Segment05	See above.

TABLE 6-1

Elements in the Sales_Order Table from the Audit Data Standards

(Adapted from https://www.aicpa.org/content/dam/aicpa/interestareas/frc/assuranceadvisoryservices/downloadabledocuments/auditdatastandards/auditdatastandards.o2c.july2015.pdf, accessed January 1, 2018)

Data may also be found in unlikely places. An auditor may be tasked with determining whether the steps of a process are being followed. Traditional evaluation would involve the auditor observing or interviewing the employee performing the work. Now that most processes are handled through online systems, an auditor can perform Data Analytics on the time stamps of the tasks and determine the sequence of approvals in a workflow along with the amount of time spent on each task. This form of process mining enables insight into areas where greater efficiency can be applied. Likewise, data stored in paper documents, such as invoices received from vendors, can be scanned and converted to tabular data using specialized software. These new pieces of data can be joined to other transactional data to enable new, thoughtful analytics.

There is an increasing opportunity to work with unstructured Big Data to provide additional insight into the economic events being evaluated by the auditors, such as surveillance video or text from e-mail, but those are still outside the scope of current Data Analytics that an auditor would develop.

Perform the Test Plan

While there are many different tests or models that auditors can incorporate into their audit procedures, Data Analytics procedures in auditing traditionally are found in **computer-assisted audit techniques (CAATs)**. CAATs are automated scripts that can be used to validate data, test controls, and enable substantive testing of transaction details or account balances and generate supporting evidence for the audit. They are especially useful for re-performing calculations, identifying high-risk samples, and performing other analytical reviews to identify unusual patterns of behavior or unusual items.

Most CAATs are designed to summarize and describe the data being evaluated based on a predetermined expected outcome. For example, an auditor evaluating an incentive plan that gives employees bonuses for opening new accounts would evaluate the number of new accounts by employee and the amount of bonus paid to see if they were aligned. The auditor could look for a count of new accounts by account type, count the number of customers, evaluate the opening date, and sort the data by employee to show the top-performing employees. These **descriptive analytics** summarize activity or master data elements based on certain attributes. The auditor may select a *sample* of the accounts to verify that they were opened and the documentation exists.

Once an auditor has a basic understanding of the data, he or she can then perform **diagnostic analytics**, which look for correlations or patterns of interest in the data. For example, the auditor may look for commonalities between the customers' demographic data and the employees' data to see if employees are creating new accounts for fake customers to inflate their performance numbers. They may also focus on customers who have common attributes like location or account age. Outliers may warrant further investigation by the auditor as they represent increased risk and/or exposure.

An auditor then performs **predictive analytics**, where he or she attempts to find hidden patterns or variables that are linked to abnormal behavior. The auditor uses the variables to build models that can be used to predict a likely value or classification. In our example, the predictive model might flag an employee or customer with similar characteristics to other high-risk employees or customers whenever a new account is opened.

Finally, the auditor may generate **prescriptive analytics** that identify a course of action for him or her to take based on the actions taken in similar situations in the past. These analytics can assist future auditors who encounter similar behavior. Using artificial intelligence and machine learning, these analytics become decision support tools for auditors who may lack experience to find potential audit issues. For example, when a new account is created for a customer who has been inactive for more than 12 months, a prescriptive analytic would allow an auditor to ask questions about the transaction to learn whether this new account is potentially fake, whether the employee is likely to create other fake accounts, and whether the account and/or employee should be suspended or not. The auditor would take the output, apply judgment, and proceed with what he or she felt was the appropriate action.

Most auditors will perform descriptive and diagnostic analytics as part of their audit plan. On rare occasions, they may experiment with predictive and prescriptive analytics directly. More likely, they may identify opportunities for the latter analytics and work with data scientists to build those for future use.

Some examples of CAATs and audit procedures related to the descriptive, diagnostic, predictive, and prescriptive analytics can be found in Table 6-2.

Analytic Type	Example CAATs	Example Audit Procedure	
Descriptive—summarizes activity or masters data based on certain attributes	*Age analysis*—groups balances by date *Sorting*—identifies largest or smallest values *Summary statistics*—mean, median, min, max, count, sum *Sampling*—random and monetary unit	Analysis of new accounts opened and employee bonuses by employee and location.	**TABLE 6-2** **Examples of Audit Data Analytics**
Diagnostic—detects correlations and patterns of interest	*Z-score*—outlier detection *Benford's law*—identifies transactions or users with non-typical activity based on the distribution of first digits *Drill-down*—explores the details behind the values *Exact and* **fuzzy matching**—joins tables and identifies plausible relationships *Sequence check*—detects gaps in records and duplicates entries *Stratification*—groups data by categories *Clustering*—groups records by non-obvious similarities	Analysis of new accounts reveals that Jane Doe has an unusual number of new accounts opened for customers who have been inactive for more than 12 months.	
Predictive—identifies common attributes or patterns that may be used to identify similar activity	*Regression*—predicts specific dependent values based on independent variable inputs *Classification*—predicts a category for a record *Probability*—uses a rank score to evaluate the strength of classification *Sentiment analysis*—evaluates text for positive or negative sentiment to predict positive or negative outcomes	Analysis of new accounts opened for customers who have been inactive for more than 12 months collects data that are common to new account opening, such as account type, demographics, and employee incentives.	
Prescriptive—recommends action based on previously observed actions	*What-if analysis*—decision support systems *Applied statistics*—predicts a specific outcome or class *Artificial intelligence*—uses observations of past actions to predict future actions for similar events	Analysis determines procedures to follow when new accounts are opened for inactive customers, such as requiring approval.	

While many of these analyses can be performed using Excel, most CAATs are built on generalized audit software (GAS), such as IDEA, ACL, or TeamMate Analytics. The GAS software has two main advantages over traditional spreadsheet software. First, it enables analysis of very large datasets. Second, it automates several common analytical routines, so an auditor can click a few buttons to get to the results rather than writing a complex set of formulas. GAS is also scriptable and enables auditors to record or program common analyses that may be reused on future engagements.

Address and Refine Results

The models selected by the auditors will generate various results. A sample selection may give auditors a list of high-risk transactions to evaluate. A segregation of duties analysis may spit out a list of users with too much access. In every case, the auditors should develop procedures in the audit plan for handling these lists, exceptions, and anomalies. The process may be to evaluate documentation related to the sample, review employees engaging in risky activity, or simply notify the audit committee of irregular behavior.

Communicate Insights

Many analytics can be adapted to create an audit dashboard, particularly if the firm has adopted continuous auditing. The primary output of CAATs is evidence used to validate assertions about the processes and data. This evidence should be included in the audit workpapers.

Track Outcomes

The detection and resolution of audit exceptions may be a valuable measure of the efficiency and effectiveness of the internal audit function itself. Additional analytics may track the number of exceptions over time and the time taken to report and resolve the issues. For the CAATs involved, a periodic validation process should occur to ensure that they continue to function as expected.

 PROGRESS CHECK

1. Using Table 6-2 as a guide, compare and contrast descriptive and diagnostic analytics. How might these be used in an audit?
2. In a continuous audit, how would a dashboard help to communicate audit findings and spur a response?

LO 6-2

Understand basic descriptive audit analyses

DESCRIPTIVE ANALYTICS

Now that you've been given an overview of the types of CAATs and analytics that are commonly used in an audit, we'll dive a little deeper into how these analytics work and what they generate. Remember that descriptive analytics are useful for sorting and summarizing data to create a baseline for more advanced analytics. These analytics enable auditors to set a baseline or point of reference for their evaluation. For example, if an auditor can identify the median value of a series of transactions, he or she can make a judgment as to how much higher the larger transactions are and whether they represent outliers or exceptions.

In this and the next few sections, we'll present some examples of procedures that auditors commonly use to evaluate enterprise data. In these examples, we show the basic process for Excel, including formulas, and IDEA. Note that in the Excel formulas, we identify data elements in [brackets]. To use these formulas, replace the bracketed [data element] with a value or range of values as appropriate. For example, [Aging date] would be replaced with C3 if the data are in column C, row 3.

Age Analysis

Aging of accounts receivable and accounts payable help determine the likelihood that a balance will be paid. This substantive test of account balances evaluates the date of an order and groups it into buckets based on how old it is, typically in 0–30, 31–60, 61–90, and >90 days, or similar. See Table 6-3 for an example. Extremely old accounts that haven't been resolved or written off should be flagged for follow-up by the auditor. It could mean that (1) the data are bad, (2) a process is broken, (3) there's a reason someone is holding that account open, or (4) it was simply never resolved.

	0-30	31-60	61-90	>90
Total	154,322	74,539	42,220	16,900

TABLE 6-3
Aging of Accounts Receivable

There are many ways to calculate aging in Excel, including using pivot tables. If you have a simple list of accounts and balances, you can calculate a simple age of accounts in Excel using the following procedure.

Data

- Customer/vendor name
- Unpaid order number
- Order date
- Amount

In Excel

1. Open your worksheet.
2. Add a cell with the **aging date**.
3. Add a calculated column for the **days outstanding**: =[Aging date]-[Order date].
4. Add four new calculated columns for the buckets:
   a. **0-30 days:** =IF([Aging date]-[Order date]<=30,[Amount],0).
   b. **31-60 days:** =IF(AND([Aging date]-[Order date]<=60, [Aging date]-[Order date]>30),[Amount],0).
   c. **61-90 days:** =IF(AND([Aging date]-[Order date]<=90, [Aging date]-[Order date]>60),[Amount],0).
   d. **>90 days:** =IF([Aging date]-[Order date]>90),[Amount],0).
5. Copy the formulas for all records.
6. Add a **total** to the bottom of each bucket: =SUM([bucket column]).

In IDEA

1. Open your worksheet.
2. Go to **Analysis > Categorize > Aging**.

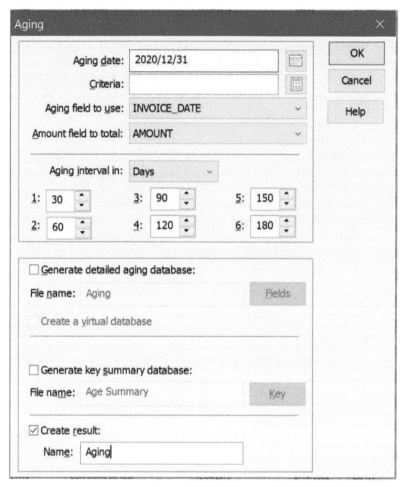

Source: CaseWare IDEA

3. Select **aging date**, field containing **transaction date**, and **amount** for the field to total amount.
4. Click **OK**.

Sorting

Sometimes, simply viewing the largest or smallest values can provide meaningful insight. Sorting in ascending order shows the smallest number values first. Sorting in descending order shows the largest values first.

Data

• Any numerical, date, or text data of interest

In Excel

1. Open your worksheet.
2. Select the data you wish to sort.
3. Go to **Home > Format as Table**.
4. Click the **drop-down arrow** next to the header or the column you want to sort.
5. Click **Sort A to Z** for ascending order **or Sort Z to A** for descending order.

In IDEA

1. Open your data table.
2. Go to **Data > Order > Sort**.
3. Choose your fields and direction, **Ascending** or **Descending**.
4. Click **OK**.

Summary Statistics

Summary statistics provide insight into the relative size of a number compared with the population. The mean indicates the average value, while the median produces the middle value, where all the transactions lined up in a row. The min shows the smallest value, while the max shows the largest. Finally, a count tells how many records exist, where the sum adds up the values to find a total. Once summary statistics are calculated, you have a reference point for an individual record. Is the amount above or below average? What percentage of the total does a group of transactions make up?

Data

- Any numerical data, such as a dollar amount or quantity

In Excel

1. Open your workbook.
2. Add the following calculated values:
   - Mean: =AVERAGE([range]).
   - Median: =MEDIAN([range]).
   - Minimum: =MIN([range]).
   - Maximum: =MAX([range]).
   - Count: =COUNT([range]).
   - Sum: =SUM([range]).
3. Alternatively, format your data as a table and show the total row at the bottom:
   a. Select your data.
   b. Go to **Home > Styles > Format as Table**.
   c. Select a table style and click **OK**.
   d. Go to **Table Tools > Design > Table Style Options** and click the **Total Row** box.
   e. Click the **drop-down arrow** next to the column total value that appears, and choose an appropriate statistic.

In IDEA

1. Open your worksheet.
2. In the **Properties** pane on the right, click **Field Statistics**.
3. Allow IDEA to calculate all uncalculated fields, if prompted.
4. In the output screen, you can click any blue number to locate those transactions.

Sampling

Sampling is useful when you have manual audit procedures, such as testing transaction details or evaluating source documents. The idea is that if the sample is an appropriate size, the features of the sample can be confidently generalized to the population. So, if the sample has no errors (misstatement), then the population is unlikely to have errors as well. Of course, sampling has its limitations. The confidence level is not a guarantee that you won't miss something critical like fraud. But it does limit the scope of the work the auditor must perform.

There are three determinants for sample size: confidence level, tolerable misstatement, and estimated misstatement.

Data

- Any list of transactions or master data

In Excel

1. Enable **Analysis ToolPak**:
   a. Go to **File > Options > Add-ins > Excel Add-ins > Go**.
   b. Check the box next to **Analysis ToolPak**, and click **OK**.
2. Go to **Data > Analysis > Data Analysis**.
3. Click **Sampling**, then **OK**.
   a. Select your **input range**, usually the transaction number.
   b. Choose **Random**, and input the number of samples.
   c. Click **OK**.
4. A new worksheet will appear with a list of your randomly selected transactions.

In IDEA

1. Open your worksheet.
2. Go to **Analysis > Sample > Random**.
   a. Input **number of records** to select for your sample size.
   b. Change other values as needed.
   c. Click **OK**.
3. A new worksheet will be created with your random sample.

Monetary unit sampling (MUS) allows auditors to evaluate account balances. MUS is more likely to pull accounts with large balances (higher risk and exposure) because it focuses on dollars, not account numbers.

Data

- The book value of the financial accounts you're evaluating
- The sample size

In Excel

1. Find the sampling interval. Divide the book value by sample size.
   a. $1,000,000/132 = \mathbf{7,575}$ <- Sampling interval
2. Sort the financial accounts in some type of sequence, and calculate a cumulative balance.
   a. Alphabetically by name.
   b. Numerically by number.
   c. By date.
3. Pick a random number between 1 and your sampling interval.
   a. This will be the starting value. For example, **1,243**.
4. Go down the list of cumulative balances until you pass your random number.
   a. For example, test the first account that passes **1,243**.
5. Continue down the list of cumulative balances until you pass the next sampling interval.
   a. For example, test the second account that passes $1,243 + 7,575 = \mathbf{8,818}$.
6. Repeat step 5 until you run out of accounts.
   a. $8,818 + 7,575 = \mathbf{16,393}$; $16,393 + 7,575 = \mathbf{23,968} \ldots$

In IDEA

1. Open your data table.
2. Go to **Analysis > Sample > Monetary Unit > Plan**.
   a. Choose your **monetary value field**.
   b. Set your **confidence level, tolerable error**, and **expected error**.
   c. Click **Estimate** to calculate your sample size.
   d. Adjust other values as needed, then click **Accept**.
   e. Click **OK**.
3. A new worksheet will appear with your sample transactions.

 PROGRESS CHECK

3. What type of descriptive analytics would you use to find negative numbers that were entered in error?
4. How does monetary unit sampling help you isolate the items of greatest potential significance to an auditor in evaluating materiality?

DIAGNOSTIC ANALYTICS AND BENFORD'S LAW

> **LO 6-3**
>
> Understand more complex statistical analyses, including Benford's law

Diagnostic analytics provide more details into not just the records, but also records or groups of records that have some standout features. They may be significantly larger than other values, may not match a pattern within the population, or may be a little too similar to other records for an auditor's liking. Here we'll identify some common diagnostic analytics and how to use them.

Z-Score

A standard score or Z-score is a concept from statistics that assigns a value to a number based on how many standard deviations it stands from the mean, shown in Exhibit 6-1. By setting the mean to 0, you can see how far a point of interest is above or below it. For example, a point with a Z-score of 2.5 is two-and-a-half standard deviations above the mean. Because most values that come from a large population tend to be normally distributed (frequently skewed toward smaller values in the case of financial transactions), nearly all (98 percent) of the values should be within plus-or-minus three standard deviations. If a value has a Z-score of 3.9, it is very likely an outlier that warrants scrutiny.

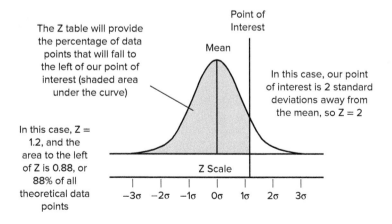

EXHIBIT 6-1

Z-Scores

The Z-score shows the relative position of a point of interest to the population.

http://www.dmaictools.com/wp-content/uploads/2012/02/z-definition.jpg

In Excel

1. Calculate the average: =AVERAGE([range]).
2. Calculate the standard deviation: =STDEVPA([range]).
3. Add a new column called "Z-score" next to your number range.
4. Calculate the Z-score: =STANDARDIZE([value],[mean],[standard deviation])
   a. Alternatively: =([value]-[mean])/[standard deviation].
5. Sort your values by Z-score in descending order.

In IDEA

- Z-score calculation is not a default feature of IDEA.

Benford's Law

Benford's law states that when you have a large set of naturally occurring numbers, the leading significant digit will likely be small. The economic intuition behind it is that people are more likely to make $10, $100, or $1,000 purchases than $90, $900, or $9,000 purchases. This law has been shown in many settings, such as the amount of electricity bills, street addresses, and GDP figures from around the world (as shown in Exhibit 6-2).

EXHIBIT 6-2

Benford's Law
Benford's law predicts the distribution of first digits.

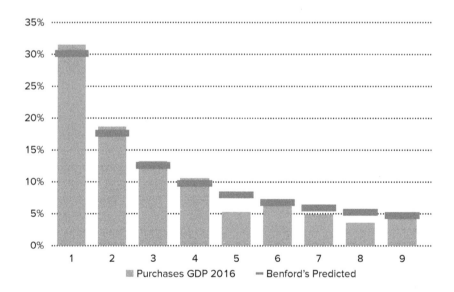

In auditing, we can use Benford's law to identify transactions or users with nontypical activity based on the distribution of the first digit of the number. For example, assume that purchases over $500 require manager approval. A cunning employee might try to make large purchases that are just under the approval limit to avoid suspicion. She will even be clever and make the numbers look random: $495, $463, $488, etc. What she doesn't realize is that the frequency of the leading digit 4 is going to be much higher than it should be, shown in Exhibit 6-3. Benford's law can also detect random computer-generated numbers because those will have equally distributed first digits.

We show an illustration of how to evaluate data and their frequency with respect to Benford's law in both Excel and IDEA.

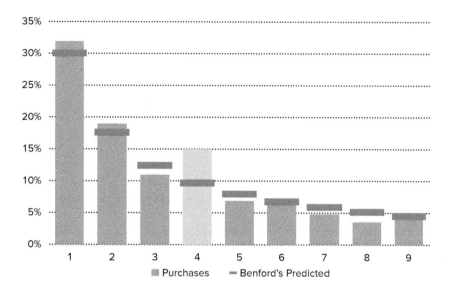

EXHIBIT 6-3
Using Benford's Law
Structured purchases
may look normal,
but they alter the
distribution under
Benford's law.

Data

• Large set of numerical data, such as monetary amounts or quantities

In Excel

1. Open your spreadsheet.
2. Add a new column **and extract the leading digit**: =LEFT([Amount],1).
3. Create a **frequency distribution**:
   a. Create a list on your sheet using values from as shown in Table 6-4 below.

Digit	Actual Count	Actual %	Expected %
1	=COUNTIF([Range],[Digit])	(=[Actual Count]/SUM[Actual Count])	30.1%
2	. . .	. . .	17.6%
3	. . .	. . .	12.5%
4	. . .	. . .	9.6%
5	. . .	. . .	7.9%
6	. . .	. . .	6.7%
7	. . .	. . .	5.8%
8	. . .	. . .	5.1%
9	. . .	. . .	4.6%
	=SUM([Actual Count])	=SUM([Actual %])	=SUM([Expected %])

TABLE 6-4
Illustration of Benford's Law

4. Create a **combo chart** to plot your actual and expected percentages:
   a. Highlight the **Actual %** and **Expected %** columns.
   b. Go to **Insert > Charts > Recommended Charts**.
   c. Click the **All Charts** tab.
   d. Choose **Combo** from the list on the left.
   e. Click **Custom Combination**.

    f. For the **Actual %**, choose **Clustered Column**.

    g. For the **Expected %**, choose **Scatter**.

    h. Click **OK**.

    i. Adjust and format your chart as needed.

In IDEA

1. Open your worksheet.
2. Go to **Analysis > Explore > Benford's Law**.
   a. Choose the **numerical field** to analyze.
   b. Only check **First digit**. Uncheck everything else.
   c. Click **OK**.
3. A graph will appear with the Benford's expected amount and the actual frequency of the dataset.
4. Click any digits that are significantly above the bounds and choose **Extract Records**.

Bonus: Use the average expected Benford's law value to identify specific employees with abnormally large transactions. In this case, a user with lots of transactions should have an average expected Benford's law percentage of 11.1 percent or above. Employees whose average purchases are closer to 8 or 5 percent have a lot of 7, 8, and 9 values that are skewing their average.

In Excel

1. Open your spreadsheet with financial data that contain an employee name and transaction amount.
2. Add a new column and extract the **leading digit**:
   =NUMBERVALUE(LEFT([Amount],1))
3. Add the **expected Benford's law percentages** to your sheet similar to Table 6.5 below:

TABLE 6-5
Expected Benford's
Law Percentages

Digit	Benford Expected %
1	30.1%
2	17.6%
3	12.5%
4	9.6%
5	7.9%
6	6.7%
7	5.8%
8	5.1%
9	4.6%

4. Add a new column next to your data to **look up the expected Benford's law percentage** for your value: =INDEX([Benford Expected %], MATCH([Value],[Digit],0)).
5. Create a PivotTable to see the **average % by user**:
   a. Select your data.
   b. Go to **Insert > Tables > PivotTable**.
   c. Click **OK** to add the **PivotTable** to a new sheet.

    d. Drag **[Employee Name]** to Rows.

    e. Drag **[Benford Expected]** to Values.

    f. Click **Sum of [Benford Expected]** and choose **Value Field Settings**.

    g. Change the summarize value field by to **Average**, and click **OK**.

    h. Select the **[Average of Benford Expected]** column in your PivotTable, and sort it in ascending order: Go to **Data > Sort & Filter > Sort Smallest to Largest**.

In IDEA

- This is not possible by built-in tool.

Drill Down

The most modern Data Analytics software allows auditors to drill down into specific values by simply double-clicking a value. This lets you see the underlying transactions that gave you the summary amount. For example, you might click the total sales amount in an income statement to see the sales general ledger summarizing the daily totals. Click a daily amount to see the individual transactions from that day.

Exact and Fuzzy Matching

Matching in CAAT is used to link records, join tables, and find potential issues. Auditors use *exact matching* to join database tables with a foreign key from one table to the primary key of another. In cases where the data are inconsistent or contain user-generated information, such as addresses, exact matches may not be sufficient. For example, "234 Second Avenue" and "234 Second Ave" are not the same value. To join tables on these values auditors will use a *fuzzy match* based on the similarity of the values. The auditor defines a threshold, such as 50 percent, and if the values share enough common characters, they will be matched. The threshold can be higher to reduce the number of potential matches or lower to increase the likelihood of a match.

    Note that not all matches are the same. Using queries and other database management tools, auditors may want only certain records, such as those that match or those that don't match. These matches require the use of certain join types. **Inner Join** will show only the records from both tables that match and exclude everything that doesn't match. **Left Join** will show all records from the first table and only records from the second table that match. **Right Join** will show all records from the second table and records from the first table that match. **Outer Join** will show all records, including nonmatching ones. Fuzzy matching finds matches that may be less than 100 percent matching by finding correspondences between portions of the text or other entries.

Data needed

- Two tables/sheets with a common attribute, such as a primary key/foreign key, name, or address

In Excel

1. Search the Internet for **Fuzzy Lookup Add-In for Excel**, then download and install it to your computer.
2. Open your spreadsheet with two sheets you'd like to join using a fuzzy match. For example, employees and vendors.
3. Go to **Fuzzy Lookup > Fuzzy Lookup** (Go to **File > Options > Add-ins > COM Add-ins > Go**. . . and check **Fuzzy Lookup Add-in For Excel** if you don't see the bar).

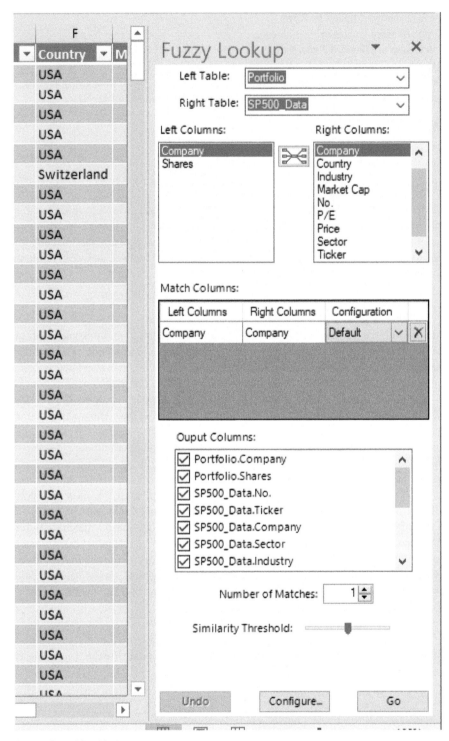

Source: Microsoft Excel 2016

    a. Select the sheet you want for the **Left Table** and a sheet that has similar values for the **Right Table**.

    b. Choose the columns that you expect to find matching values in the **Left** and **Right Columns** pane. *Note:* For addresses, choose Address AND Zip Code for more likely matches.

    c. Select your **output columns**, if needed.

    d. Adjust the **similarity threshold**, if needed.

    e. Open a new **worksheet**.

    f. Click **Go**.

4. Evaluate the similarity.

In IDEA

1. Fuzzy matching isn't available by default in IDEA.

Sequence Check

Another substantive procedure is the sequence check. This is used to validate data integrity and test the completeness assertion, making sure that all relevant transactions are accounted for. Simply put, sequence checks are useful for finding gaps, such as a missing check in the cash disbursements journal, or duplicate transactions, such as duplicate payments to vendors. This is a fairly simple procedure that can be deployed quickly and easily with great success.

In Excel

$$=\text{IF}([\text{second value}]-[\text{first value}]=1,\text{""},\text{"Missing"})$$

    OR

$$= \text{SMALL}(\text{IF}(\text{ISNA}(\text{MATCH}(\text{ROW}([\text{range}]),$$
$$[\text{range}],0)),\text{ROW}([\text{range}])),\text{ROW}([\text{First value in range}))$$

Stratification and Clustering

There are several approaches to grouping transactions or individuals. In most cases, the items can be grouped by similar characteristics or strata. With stratification, the auditor identifies specific groups, such as geographic location or functional area, that can be used to simplify their analysis. When similarities are less obvious, such as personal preference or expressed behavior, clustering may be used to infer these groupings. Both stratification and clustering are generally used for data exploration, rather than substantive testing. The identification of these groupings, whether obvious or not, help narrow the scope of the audit and focus on risk. Clustering is discussed in depth in chapter 3.

 PROGRESS CHECK

5. A sequence check will help us to see if there is a duplicate payment to vendors. Why is that important for the auditor to find?

6. Let's say a company has nine divisions, and each division has a different check number based on its division—so one starts with "1," another with "2," etc. Would Benford's law work in this situation?

CREATING ADVANCED PREDICTIVE AND PRESCRIPTIVE ANALYTICS

Predictive and prescriptive analytics provide less deterministic output than the previous analytics. This is because we're moving away from deterministic values to more probabilistic models, judging things like *likelihood* and *possibility*. Here we'll briefly discuss some application of these different concepts, but we refer you back to chapter 3 for background information.

Regression

Regression allows an auditor to predict a specific dependent value based on independent variable inputs. In other words, what would we expect behavior to be given some inputs and does that match reality? In auditing, we could evaluate overtime booked for workers against productivity or the value of inventory shrinkage given environmental factors.

Classification

Classification in auditing is going to be mainly focused on risk assessment. The predicted classes may be *low risk* or *high risk,* where an individual transaction is classified in either group. In the case of known fraud, auditors would classify those cases or transactions as *fraud/not fraud* and develop a classification model that could predict whether similar transactions might also be potentially fraudulent.

There is a longstanding classification method used to predict whether a company is expected to go bankrupt or not. Altman's Z is a calculated score that helps predict bankruptcy and might be useful for auditors to evaluate a company's ability to continue as a going concern.

When using classification models, it is important to remember that large training sets are needed to generate relatively accurate models. Initially, this requires significant manual classification by the auditors or business process owner so that the model can be useful for the audit.

Probability

When talking about classification, the strength of the class can be important to the auditor, especially when trying to limit the scope (e.g., evaluate only the 10 riskiest transactions). Classifiers that use a rank score can identify the strength of classification by measuring the distance from the mean. That rank order focuses the auditor's efforts on the items of potentially greatest significance.

Sentiment Analysis

Evaluate text (e.g., 10-K or annual report) for positive or negative sentiment to predict positive or negative outcomes or to look for potential bias on management's part. There is more discussion on sentiment analysis in chapter 8.

Applied Statistics

Additional mixed distributions and nontraditional statistics may also provide insight to the auditor. For example, an audit of inventory may reveal errors in the amount recorded in the system. The difference between the error amounts and the actual amounts may provide some valuable insight into how significant or material the problem may be. Auditors can plot the frequency distribution of errors and use Z-scores to hone in the cause of the most significant or outlier errors.

Artificial Intelligence

As the audit team generates more data and takes specific action, the action itself can be modeled in a way that allows an algorithm to predict expected behavior. Artificial intelligence is designed around the idea that computers can learn about action or behavior from the past and predict the course of action for the future. Assume that an experienced auditor questions management about the estimate of allowance for doubtful accounts. The human auditor evaluates a number of inputs, such as the estimate calculation, market factors, and the possibility of income smoothing by management. Given these inputs, the auditor decides to challenge management's estimate. If the auditor consistently takes this action and it is recorded by the computer, the computer learns from this action and makes a recommendation when a new inexperienced auditor faces a similar situation.

Decision support systems that accountants have relied upon for years (e.g., TurboTax) are based on a formal set of rules and then updated based on what the user decides given several choices. Artificial intelligence can be used as a helpful assistant to auditors and may potentially be called upon to make judgment decisions itself.

Additional Analyses

The list of Data Analytics presented in this chapter is not exhaustive by any means. There are many other approaches to identifying interesting patterns and anomalies in enterprise data. Many ingenious auditors have developed automated scripts that can simplify several of the audit tasks presented here. Excel add-ins like TeamMate Analytics provide many different techniques that apply specifically to the audit of fixed assets, inventory, sales and purchase transactions, etc. Auditors will combine these tools with other techniques, such as periodically testing the effectiveness of automated tools by adding erroneous or fraudulent transactions, to enhance their audit process.

 PROGRESS CHECK

7. Why would a bankruptcy prediction be considered classification? And why would it be useful to auditors?
8. If sentiment analysis is used on a product advertisement, would you guess the overall sentiment would be positive or negative?

Summary

This chapter discusses a number of analytical techniques that auditors use to gather insight about controls and transaction data. These include descriptive analytics that are used to summarize and gain insight into the data, diagnostic analytics that identify patterns in the data that may not be immediately obvious, predictive analytics that look for common attributes of problematic data to help identify similar events in the future, and prescriptive analytics that provide decision support to auditors as they work to resolve issues with the processes and controls.

Key Words

computer-assisted audit techniques (CAATs) (*212*)   Computer-assisted audit techniques (CAATs) are automated scripts that can be used to validate data, test controls, and enable substantive testing of transaction details or account balances and generate supporting evidence for the audit.

descriptive analytics (*212*)   Descriptive analytics summarize activity or master data elements based on certain attributes.

diagnostic analytics (*212*)   Diagnostic analytics looks for correlations or patterns of interest in the data.

fuzzy matching (*213*)   Fuzzy matching finds matches that may be less than 100 percent matching by finding correspondences between portions of the text or other entries.

monetary unit sampling (MUS) (*218*)   Monetary unit sampling allows auditors to evaluate account balances. MUS is more likely to pull accounts with large balances (higher risk and exposure) because it focuses on dollars, not account numbers.

predictive analytics (*212*)   Predictive analytics attempt to find hidden patterns or variables that are linked to abnormal behavior.

prescriptive analytics (*212*)   Prescriptive analytics use machine learning and artificial intelligence for auditors as decision support to assist future auditors in finding potential issues in the audit.

 ## ANSWERS TO PROGRESS CHECKS

1. Descriptive activity summarizes activity by computing basic descriptive statistics like means, medians, minimums, maximums, and standard deviations. Diagnostic analytics compares variables or data items to each other and tries to find co-occurrence or correlation to find patterns of interest.

2. Use of a dashboard to highlight and communicate findings will help identify alarms for issues that are occurring on a real-time basis. This will allow issues to be addressed immediately.

3. By computing minimum values or by sorting, you can find the lowest reported value and, thus, potential negative numbers that might have been entered erroneously into the system and require further investigation.

4. Monetary unit sampling is more likely to pull accounts with large balances (higher risk and exposure) because it focuses on the amount of the transaction rather than giving each transaction an equal chance. The larger dollar value of the transaction, the more likely it is to affect materiality thresholds.

5. Duplicate payments to vendors suggest that there is a gap in the internal controls around payments. After the first payment was made, why did the accounting system allow a second payment? Were both transactions authorized? Who signed the checks or authorized payments? How can we prevent this from happening in the future?

6. Benford's law works best on naturally occurring numbers. If the company dictates the first number of its check sequence, Benford's law will not work the same way and thus would not be effective in finding potential issues with the check numbers.

7. Bankruptcy prediction predicts two conditions for a company: bankrupt or not bankrupt. Thus, it would be considered a classification activity. Auditors are required to assess a client's ability to continue as a going concern and the bankruptcy prediction helps with that.

8. Most product advertisements are very positive in nature and would have positive sentiment.

Multiple Choice Questions

1. Which items would be currently out of scope for Data Analytics?
   a. Direct observation of processes
   b. Evaluation of time stamps to evaluate workflow
   c. Evaluation of phantom vendors
   d. Duplicate payment of invoices

2. What would be the sampling interval if we are using a manual approach to monetary unit sampling for a book value of $2,000,000 and a sample size of 200?
   a. 10,000
   b. 1,000
   c. 100,000
   d. Cannot be determined

3. Monetary unit sampling is more likely to:
   a. Sample accounts with smaller balances.
   b. Sample accounts with less risk.
   c. Sample accounts with larger balances.
   d. Sample accounts with more risk.

4. The determinants for sample size include all of the following *except*:
   a. Confidence level.
   b. Tolerable misstatement.
   c. Potential risk of account.
   d. Estimated misstatement.

5. CAATs are automated scripts that can be used to validate data, test controls, and enable substantive testing of transaction details or account balances and generate supporting evidence for the audit. What does CAAT stand for?
   a. Computer-aided audit techniques
   b. Computer-assisted audit techniques
   c. Computerized audit and accounting techniques
   d. Computerized audit aids and tests

6. Which type of audit analytics might be used to find hidden patterns or variables linked to abnormal behavior?
   a. Prescriptive analytics
   b. Predictive analytics
   c. Diagnostic analytics
   d. Descriptive analytics

7. What describes finding correspondences between at least two types of text or entries that may not match perfectly?
   a. Incomplete linkages
   b. Algorithmic matching
   c. Fuzzy matching
   d. Incomplete matching

8. Which testing approach would be used to predict whether certain cases should be evaluated as having fraud or no fraud?

   a. Classification

   b. Probability

   c. Sentiment analysis

   d. Artificial intelligence

9. Which testing approach would be useful in assessing the value of inventory shrinkage given multiple environmental factors?

   a. Probability

   b. Sentiment analysis

   c. Regression

   d. Applied statistics

10. What type of analysis would help auditors find missing checks?

   a. Sequence check

   b. Benford's law analysis

   c. Fuzzy matching

   d. Decision support systems

Discussion Questions

1. How do nature, extent, and timing of audit procedures help us identify when to apply Data Analytics to the audit process?

2. When do you believe that Data Analytics will add value to the audit process? How can it most help?

3. Using Table 6-2 as a guide, compare and contrast predictive and prescriptive analytics. How might these be used in an audit? Or a continuous audit?

4. An example of prescriptive analytics is when an action is recommended based on previously observed actions. For example, an analysis might help determine procedures to follow when new accounts are opened for inactive customers, such as requiring supervisor approval. How might this help address a potential audit issue?

5. One type of descriptive analytics is simply sorting data. Why is seeing extreme values helpful (minimums, maximums, counts, etc.) in evaluating accuracy and completeness and in potentially finding errors and fraud and the like?

Problems

1. One type of descriptive analytics is age analysis. Why are auditors particularly interested in the aging of accounts receivable and accounts payable? How does this analysis help evaluate management judgment on collectability of receivables and potential payment of payables? Would a dashboard item reflecting this aging be useful in a continuous audit?

2. One of the benefits of Data Analytics is the ability to see and test the full population. In that case, why is sampling (even monetary sampling) still used, and how is it useful?

3. What does a Z-score greater than three (or minus three) suggest? How is that useful in finding extreme values? What type of analysis should we do when we find extreme or outlier values?

4. What are some patterns that could be found using diagnostic analysis? Between which types of variables?

5. In a certain company, one accountant records most of the adjusting journal entries at the end of the month. What type of analysis could be used to identify that this happens and the cumulative size of the transactions that the one accountant records? Is this a problem or if not, when would it be?

6. Which distributions would you recommend be tested using Benford's law? What would a Benford's law evaluation of sales transaction amounts potentially show? What would a test of vendor numbers or employee numbers show? Anything different from a test of invoice or check numbers? Any cases where Benford's law wouldn't work?

7. How could artificial intelligence be used to help with the evaluation of the estimate for the allowance for doubtful accounts? Could past allowances be tested for their predictive ability that might be able to help set allowances in the current period?

8. How do you think sentiment analysis of the 10-K might assess the level of bias (positive or negative) of the annual reports? If management is too positive about the results of the company, can that be viewed as being neutral or impartial?

Answers to Multiple Choice Questions

1. A
2. A
3. C
4. C
5. B
6. B
7. C
8. A
9. C
10. A

You're starting to make a name for yourself in the internal audit department. Your manager liked your analysis of the audit plan and now would like you to see what other ways data analytics could be applied beyond the existing audit action sheets.

As you've been reading about risk and fraud, you learned that one common risk is that employees may be tempted to create fictitious suppliers that they use to embezzle money. The premise is simple enough. An employee with access to create master data adds a supplier record for a spouse. She then submits an invoice for "cleaning services" that were never performed and is promptly paid, assuming there isn't good follow-up from the accounts payable department. The employee is smart enough to know that an exact address would raise red flags, so she alters it slightly to avoid detection. Other suspicious addresses may include PO Box addresses because they can obscure the identity of a fictitious supplier.

You know that one way to detect this issue is to look for fuzzy matches, and you're eager to show your manager what you know. Refer to Lab 3-2 for another example. This lab assumes you have completed Lab 5-1.

Techniques

- Data preparation
- Filtering
- Fuzzy matching

Software needed

- Excel

In this lab, you will:

Part 1: Identify the questions.
Part 2: Master the employee and vendor data.
Part 3: Perform the analysis.
Part 4: Address the results.

Part 1: Identify the Questions

Q1.   Given what you know about vendor addresses, what types of addresses would be the most suspicious?

Q2.   How could a vendor be added to an enterprise system with a suspicious address?

Part 2: Master the Employee and Vendor Data

In Excel

1. Open OneDrive and navigate to your **Current Audit File** folder.
2. Create a new **Excel workbook** and call it **User-Supplier Match**.
3. Rename the **Sheet1** to **Users** and add a new sheet called **Suppliers**.
4. Return to your OneDrive tab and open the **User_Listing** and **Supplier_Listing** files.
5. Copy the data from the **User_Listing** file to the **Users** sheet in your new spreadsheet.
6. Copy the data from the **Supplier_Listing** file to the **Suppliers** sheet in your new spreadsheet.
7. From your **User-Supplier Match** spreadsheet, click **Open in Excel** to load it in the desktop version of Excel.
8. Take a screenshot (label it 6-1A).

In IDEA

1. Download the **P2P IDEA Audit Data** from Connect, as directed.
2. Unzip the file on your computer.

3. Open IDEA and go to **Home > Projects > Select**.
4. Click the **External Projects** tab, then navigate to your downloaded **P2P IDEA Audit Data** project folder.
5. Click **OK**.
6. Take a screenshot (label it 6-1B).

Part 3: Perform the Analysis

In Excel

There are a couple ways to look for suspicious addresses. You could look for specific values or use tools to help you link records.

1. Begin by narrowing down addresses with the word "box." This should include "PO Box," "P.O. Box," and "Box."
   a. Select the data in the Supplier sheet, and format it as a table of your choosing (**Home > Styles > Format as Table**).
   b. Click the drop-down arrow next to the **Supplier_Physical_Street_Address1** field to show the sort and filter menu.
   c. Choose **Text Filters > Contains. . .**
   d. Enter **box** and click **OK**.
2. Take a screenshot (label it 6-1C).

In IDEA

1. Open your **Supplier_Listing** table.
2. Go to **Data > Search > Search**.
   a. Text to find: **box**
   b. Fields to look in: **Supplier_Physical_Street_Address1**
   c. Click **OK**.
3. Take a screenshot (label it 6-1D).

   Q3.   How many PO Box addresses appear?

   Q4.   Why should you follow up on PO Box addresses?

Now let's look for fuzzy matches.

In Excel

1. Click the drop-down arrow next to the Address field, and choose **Clear Filter From "Supplier_Physical_Street_Address1"**.
2. Perform a fuzzy match on the **Supplier_Physical_Street_Address1,** and **Supplier_Physical_ZipPostalCode** from the **Suppliers** sheet and the **User_Physical_Street_Address1** and **User_Physical_Street_ZipPostalCode** from the **Users** sheet. Refer to the example in chapter 6 or Lab 3-2 for specific step-by-step instructions.
3. Take a screenshot (label it 6-1E).

In IDEA

IDEA doesn't support fuzzy matching directly, but this works with a few steps by merging the supplier and user tables, and then looking for fuzzy duplicate records. The resulting table will show duplicate records that will match despite not being exact.

1. Open the **Supplier_Listing** table.
2. Click **Data > Append**.
   a. Field name: **Type**
   b. Field type: **Virtual Character**
   c Length: **20**

d. Parameter: **"Supplier"**

e. Click **OK**.

3. Open the **User_Listing** table.

4. Click **Data > Append**.

a. Field name: **Type**

b. Field type: **Virtual Character**

c. Length: **20**

d. Parameter: **"Employee"**

e. Click **OK**.

5. Go to **Analysis > Relate > Append**.

a. Double-click **Supplier_Listing**.

b. Click **OK**.

6. Go to **Data > Append**.

a. Field name: **Combo_Address**

b. Field type: **Virtual Character**

c. Length: **100**

d. Parameter: **= Supplier_Physical_Street_Address1 + User_Physical_Street_Address1**

e. Click **OK**.

7. In your new **Append Databases** table, click **Analysis > Explore > Duplicate Key > Fuzzy**.

a. Output: **Fuzzy matches**

b. Similarity degree (%): **Adjust as needed**

c. Key: **Combo_Address**

d. Click **OK**.

8. Take a screenshot (label it 6-1F).

Q5. How many fuzzy matches appeared?

Q6. Which of the matches are suspicious?

Q7. Which of the matches are normal?

Part 4: Address the Results

Q8. Are there any limitations to the way you just evaluated addresses?

Q9. What other data values would indicate that there may be fictitious suppliers in the system?

End of Lab

Lab 6-2   Perform Substantive Tests of Account Balances

Account balances do not exist in databases. Rather, they are the combination of data elements that are added together to come up with a total through queries and formulas. The balance for accounts payable, for example is the combination of invoices received, cash disbursements, and debit memos.

As an internal auditor, you have been tasked with validating the balance in accounts receivable. Your audit manager has given you a list of receivables for comparison. Additionally, company policy states that accounts receivables should be collected within 60 days of the sale. To test this policy, you have been asked to perform an aging of outstanding accounts.

Techniques

- Use Excel tools to calculate account balances
- Use Excel tools to group accounts by age

Software

- Access

In this lab, you will:

Part 1: Identify the questions
Part 2: Master the purchase order and payment data
Part 3: Perform the analysis

Part 1: Identify the questions

Q1.   What data do you need to calculate the account balances?

Q2.   What is the formula needed to compute the balance in accounts payable?

Q3.   How would you compute and group the age of each receivable?

Part 2: Master the Data

1. To address the question of the data needed, we will compute the accounts receivable for each customer. That is, as of 9/30/2019 how many customers have yet to pay the amount they owe?

2. Open the File **SlainteAging-Sept.xlsx**.

3. Create a PivotTable using the Sales_Order data. Ensure that the PivotTable will use the Internal Data Model so that you can retrieve fields from both of the tables in the spreadsheet by placing a check mark next to **Add this data to the Data Model** in the Create PivotTable window.

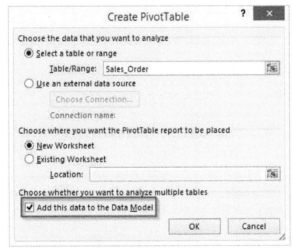

Source: Microsoft Excel 2016.

4. In the PivotTable Fields window, click **All** to view both tables in the workbook.

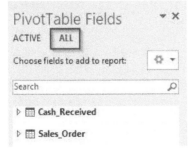

Source: Microsoft Excel 2016.

5. Create a PivotTable that shows the Sales_Order_Total and the Receipt_Total for each Sales_Order_ID.

Source: Microsoft Excel 2016.

6. The data will look odd at first, and you will be prompted to create relationships. You can allow Excel to auto-detect the relationships, and it will identify the relationship between the Primary and Foreign Keys that exist between the two tables.

Q4.   What are the primary and foreign keys that relate the two tables in this workbook?

7. After creating the relationships, the top few records of your PivotTable output should look like the following:

Row Labels ▼	Sum of Sales_Order_Total	Sum of Receipt_Amount
20001	319.43	319.43
20002	2425.5	2425.5
20003	848.58	848.58
20004	2024.02	2024.02
20005	4217.51	4217.51
20006	2309.93	2309.93

Source: Microsoft Excel 2016.

8. Copy the data in the PivotTable to a **new spreadsheet** to convert the PivotTable data to a range. Doing so will allow us to be able to identify which of the invoices have yet to be paid in full yet. You can ensure that you're copying only the range by selecting and copying **all of the data** in the PivotTable, **except** for the last row containing the Grand Total.

9. Add a **column** to your new range, and calculate the **difference** between the Sales_Order_Total and the Receipt_Amount.

10. Add a **filter** to the **Difference** column, and filter out all values that appear as **0's**. This will allow you to view all of the invoices that haven't been paid in full yet.

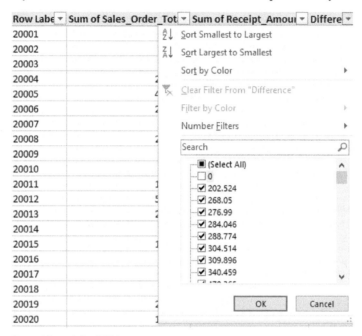

Source: Microsoft Excel 2016.

11. This data can be made more interesting by identifying how late the payments are. Return to the **Cash_Received** spreadsheet in your workbook.

12. Add a new **column** to the Cash_Received table called **Sales_Order_Date**. This will allow you to easily compare the date of the original Sales Order to the date of the payment.

13. Use a False VLookup formula to look up the date that corresponds with the Sales_Order_ID that each cash receipt corresponds to.

Source: Microsoft Excel 2016.

14. Now that you have the Sales_Order_Date easily accessible, you can create another column to calculate the difference between the dates. Create a new **column** labeled **Age**, and subtract the **Sales_Order_Date** from the **Cash_Receipt_Date**.

15. Your next step is to create a True VLookup formula to assign each cash receipt to an aging bucket. Create an **aging table** with the following information somewhere on your spreadsheet:

0	0-30
30	31-60
60	61-90
90	>90

16. Add another new **column** to the Cash_Received table labeled **Bucket**, and create a True VLookup formula to identify the bucket for each invoice.

H	I	J	K	l
bucke ▾				
=VLOOKUP([@Age],buckets,2,TRUE)				
0-30				
0-30				
0-30				
0-30				
0-30				
0-30		0	0-30	
0-30		30	31-60	
0-30		60	61-90	
0-30		90	>90	
0 30				

Source: Microsoft Excel 2016.

17. We can quickly create a summary of how many invoices fall into each bucket using Excel's COUNTIF function. In the column to the right of your aging table, create a **column** labeled **Count**.

18. In the cell to the right of your 0–30 bucket, type the COUNTIF function. COUNTIF requires two arguments, **range** and **criteria**. The range in this case is the Buckets column. The criteria is 0–30. COUNTIF will count every instance of 0–30 in the buckets column.

H	I	J	K	L	M	N	O
bucke ▾				Count			
0-30		0	0-30	=COUNTIF(Cash_Received[buckets],K2)			
0-30		30	31-60	285			
0-30		60	61-90	33			
0-30		90	>90	0			
0-30							
0 30							

Source: Microsoft Excel 2016.

19. Repeat the steps for the remaining three buckets. The top two records in the Count column should return the following data:

		Count
0	0-30	350
30	31-60	285

Source: Microsoft Excel 2016.

20. Return to your **PivotTable**, and refresh the data so that you can pull in your new fields for further analysis. You can refresh your data by clicking the **Refresh** button in the **Analyze** tab from the ribbon.

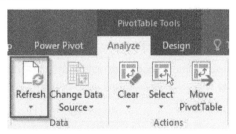

Source: Microsoft Excel 2016.

21. You should now be able to add the **Buckets** field to the PivotTable. Do so.

Source: Microsoft Excel 2016.

22. Collapse the fields so that you do not see the detail of each invoice within the buckets, but only the totals. The top two records of the PivotTable will appear as the following:

Row Labels ▼	Sum of Receipt_Amount
⊞ >90	8428.414
⊞ 0-30	333198.629

Source: Microsoft Excel 2016.

23. Save your file.

Q5. Of the not yet collected balances in each of the four buckets, which bucket is least likely to be collected? Which bucket is most likely to be collected? How would this help us come up with an allowance for doubtful accounts?

24. Now, let's assume that three more months have passed. Open up the spreadsheet **SlainteAging-Dec.xlsx**.

Q6. Based on what you have viewed with the September data, what do you expect to find as far as outstanding balances now that the year has finished at the end of December?

25. Repeat the same steps as you did above in the new dataset.
    a. Create a PivotTable that shows the Sales_Order_Total and Receipt_Amount for each Sales_Order_ID.
       i. Remember to use the Internal Data Model and to build relationships so that the data in your PivotTable is accurate.
    b. Create a range from your PivotTable data and calculate the difference between the Sales_Order_Total and the Receipt_Amount. Filter the Difference column to show only the invoices that haven't been paid in full yet.
    c. Return to the Cash_Received table and create the additional columns so that you can identify the aging bucket for each invoice.
    d. Create a PivotTable to identify which invoices fall into each bucket.

26. Save your file as Lab6-2December.xslx, ensuring that the PivotTable with buckets is included in your final spreadsheet.

End of Lab

Lab 6-3   Finding Duplicate Payments

Companies will occasionally make duplicate payments to suppliers. This is partly due to a lack of internal controls and partly due to an error that has been made. Duplicate payments also have the potential to be fraudulent.

Technique
- Search for duplicates

Software needed
- Excel or IDEA

In this lab, you will:
    Part 1: Identify the questions.
    Part 2: Master the purchase order and payment data.
    Part 3: Perform the analysis.

Part 1: Identify the Questions

Q1.   Before computerization or Data Analytics, how would companies find that they had made duplicate payments?

Part 2: Master the Data

Q2.   What data items do you need to be able to find duplicate payments? Would the date of the duplicate payments usually be the same or different?

Part 3: Perform the Analysis

In Excel

1. Open OneDrive and go to the **Current Audit Data** folder.
2. Open the **Payments_Made** spreadsheet.
3. Click **Open in Excel** to load it in the desktop version of Excel.
4. Select the **Invoice_Reference** column and choose **Home > Styles > Conditional Formatting > Highlight Cell Rules > Duplicate Values. . .** and click **OK**.

5. Select all of the data, choose **Home > Styles > Format as Table**, and pick a light, non-banded theme.
6. Click the drop-down next to **Invoice_Reference**, choose **Filter by color. . .**, and select the highlight color used in step 4.
7. Take a screenshot (label it 6-3A).
8. Remove the filter on **Invoice_Reference** and repeat steps 4–6 on the **Payment_Amount** column.

In IDEA

1. Open the **P2P IDEA Audit Data** project in IDEA.
2. Open the **Payments_Made** table.
3. Go to **Analysis > Explore > Duplicate Key > Detection**.
   a. Click **Output duplicate records**.
   b. Key: **Invoice_Reference**.
   c. Click **OK**.
4. Take a screenshot (label it 6-3B).

5. Repeat steps 2–3 on the **Payment_Amount** column.

   Q3. How many duplicate records did you locate?

   Q4. What course of action would you recommend?

End of Lab

Lab 6-4   Comprehensive Case: Dillard's Store Data: Hypothesis Testing (Part I)

Company summary

Dillard's is a department store with approximately 330 stores in 29 states. Its headquarters is in Little Rock, Arkansas. You can learn more about Dillard's by looking at finance.yahoo.com (Ticker symbol = DDS) and the Wikipedia site for DDS. You'll quickly note that William T. Dillard II is an accounting grad of the University of Arkansas and the Walton College of Business, which may be why he shared transaction data with us to make available for this lab and labs throughout this text.

Data

The data for this lab and other all Dillard's labs are available at http://walton.uark.edu/enterprise/. Your instructor will either give you specific instructions on how to access the data, or there will be information available on connect. The 2016 Dillard's data covers all transactions over the period 1/1/2014 to 10/17/2016.

Software needed

- Microsoft SQL Server Management Studio (available on the Remote Destkop at the University of Arkansas)
- Excel 2016 (available on the Remote Destkop at the University of Arkansas)
- PowerPivot add-in for Excel (available on the Remote Destkop at the University of Arkansas). If you do not see the PowerPivot tab on the Excel ribbon, you will need to enable the add-in.

In this lab, you will:

- Test a hypothesis in Excel. Specifically, we will see if the returns in January are greater than the rest of the year.

Part 1: Identify the Questions

January sales are associated with Christmas. Most retail establishments have fairly generous return policies in case a gift received was the wrong size or just not the desired item. Do retail companies have the same generous policies throughout the year, and do customers apply them throughout the year?

Therefore, our specific question that we hope to test is whether there a significant difference in the amount of returns in January compared to the rest of the year.

Part 2: Master the Data

1. Extract data from SQL Server into Excel using Excel's **Get & Transform** functionality using the following query:

```
Select Tran_Date, Tran_Type, SUM(Tran_Amt) AS Amount
From Transact
Group By Tran_Date, Tran_Type
Order By Tran_Date
```

This query will load all of the transactional history for both sales and refunds, grouped by day, as well as transactional type. The way the data are organized, all of the dollar amounts for sales and for refunds are in the same attribute, Tran_Amt, and the transaction type (i.e., Sale or Return) is differentiated with the attribute Tran_Type. In order to create a measure based on sales and refunds as separate values, we need to split the Tran_Amt data into two columns, one dedicated to sales, and one for the refund amounts. To do so, we will use the Query Editor to transform the data by "pivoting" the Tran_Type column.

2. From the **Query Editor** tool, select the **Tran_Type** column and click **Pivot Column** from the **Transform** tab.

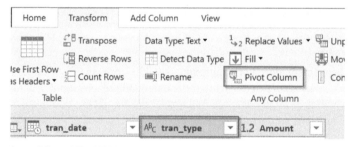

Source: Microsoft Excel 2016.

3. Change the **Values Column** drop-down to **Amount** in the **Pivot Column** window, then click **OK**.

Source: Microsoft Excel 2016.

4. Now that the data have been transformed, you can load them into Excel. Click **Close & Load** from the **Home** tab. It will take a moment for all of the data (1,014 rows) to load into Excel.

5. Create a PivotTable by clicking PivotTable from the **Insert** tab on the Excel ribbon.
6. Even though you have loaded the data into Excel, you have not added it to Excel's Internal Data Model. To do so, place a check mark in the box next to **Add this data to the Data Model** in the **Create PivotTable** window.

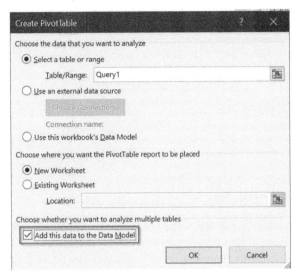

Source: Microsoft Excel 2016.

7. To create a measure for **Refunds over Purchases**, select **Measures > New Measure. . .** from the **PowerPivot** tab in the Excel ribbon.

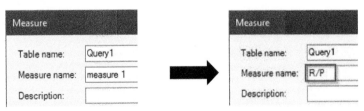

Source: Microsoft Excel 2016.

8. The new measure's name defaults to **Measure 1**, which isn't very descriptive. Because we'll be measuring average Transaction amount, we'll change the name to R/P. Type **R/P** over the default text.

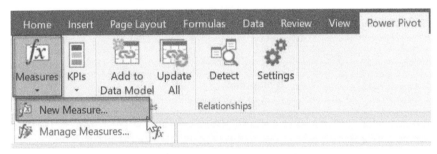

Source: Microsoft Excel 2016.

9. The formula will auto-populate as you type; begin typing SUM, then fill in the remainder of the measure to divide the purchasing transactions by the refund transactions: =sum(Query1[R])/SUM(Query1[P]).
10. At the bottom of the **Measure** window is an option to select a category. The Category has no bearing on how the measure or the KPI will work. For this measure, we'll leave it on the default of General. Click **OK** to create the measure.

Source: Microsoft Excel 2016.

11. Now that the measure is created, it has been added to the **PivotTable Fields** window. Create a PivotTable to view only the January dates (place **Tran_Date(Month)** in the filter) and days along the rows. Use the new measure you created, **R/P**, as the value.

Source: Microsoft Excel 2016.

Parsing out month and day will require placing **Tran_Date** in the rows column first, then removing the **Year** and **Quarter** attributes that automatically populate. Drag and Drop **Tran_Date(month)** to the filter, and keep the **Tran_Date** attribute in the rows.

This PivotTable will provide the data we need for one part of our hypothesis test—the values from all January dates in the database. Now we need to separate the values from all non-January dates in the database. We'll do this by copying the PivotTable you just created, and modifying the filter.

12. Select the entire PivotTable (including the Filter cells), and copy the selection.

	A	B
1	tran_date (Month)	Jan
2		
3	Row Labels	sum of R/P
4		
5		
6		
7		

Source: Microsoft Excel 2016.

13. Place your cursor in cell **D1,** and paste the PivotTable there.
14. Now you can modify the filter. Place a check mark in the box next to **Select Multiple Items,** then scroll to the top of the filter options to select **All.** Finally, scroll down to take the check mark out of the box next to **January.** This will provide the data for all transactions, except for the items that are from January.
15. Take a screenshot of your results (label it 6-4A).
16. To clarify the difference between the two PivotTables, you can rename the labels that say sum of R/P in each table. Place your cursor inside the cell with the **sum of R/P** label, and type in **January** and **Rest of the Year** in its place:

	A	B	C	D	E
1	tran_date (Month)	Jan		tran_date (Month)	(Multiple Items)
2					
3	Row Labels	January		Row Labels	Rest of the Year
4					

Source: Microsoft Excel 2016.

Part 3: Perform an Analysis of the Data

To run a hypothesis test in Excel, you need to first enable the **Data Analysis ToolPak** add-in. To do so, follow this menu path: **File > Options > Add-ins.** From this window, select the **Go. . .** button, and then place a check mark in the box next to **Analysis ToolPak.** Once you click **OK** you will be able to access the ToolPak from the **Data** tab on the Excel ribbon.

17. Click the **Data Analysis** button from the Excel ribbon and select **t-Test: Two-Sample Assuming Unequal Variances.** This will allow us to run a hypothesis test to see if there are significant differences between the January transactions and the rest of the year.
18. In the **t-Test** window, you will need to input your variable ranges. For **Variable 1 Range,** select all of the values that correspond with the January PivotTable (just the values—you do not need to select the corresponding dates).

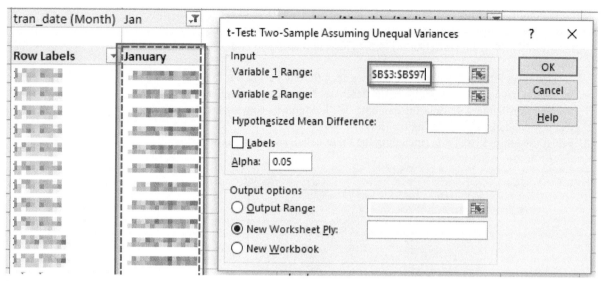

Source: Microsoft Excel 2016.

19. Follow the same pattern for Variable 2 by selecting all of the data that correspond with the second PivotTable's values.

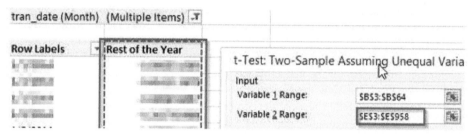

Source: Microsoft Excel 2016.

20. Place a check mark in the box next to **Labels** to ensure that the labels for the data (**January** and **Rest of the Year**) show up in the resulting output, and click **OK**.

t-Test: Two-Sample Assuming Unequal Variances

Input
Variable 1 Range: $B$3:$B$64
Variable 2 Range: $E$3:$E$958
Hypothesized Mean Difference:
☑ Labels
Alpha: 0.05

Output options
○ Output Range:
◉ New Worksheet Ply:
○ New Workbook

OK
Cancel
Help

Source: Microsoft Excel 2016.

Part 4: Address and Refine the Results

Q1. Using the *p*-values (or the *t*-statistic and critical values), are the returns as a percentage of sales in January greater, less than, or the same as the returns as a percentage of sales for the rest of the year?

Q2. What can we conclude about returns?

Q3. Do you think most Christmas sales are returned in January, or do they also occur in early January? How would you modify your tests to take this into account?

Part 5: Communicate Insights and Track Outcomes

In chapter 7, we'll learn more about dashboards and ways to communicate these results to management.

Q4. Do you think knowing the level of returns is important to management?

Q5. Assuming management want returns information, do you think they need this information on a daily, weekly, or monthly basis? Due to information overload, they can't track everything on a daily basis, but some information is important to disclose frequently.

End of Lab

Lab 6-5   Comprehensive Case: Dillard's Store Data: Hypothesis Testing (Part II—Data Visualization)

Company summary

Dillard's is a department store with approximately 330 stores in 29 states. Its headquarters is in Little Rock, Arkansas. You can learn more about Dillard's by looking at finance.yahoo.com (Ticker symbol = DDS) and the Wikipedia site for DDS. You'll quickly note that William T. Dillard II is an accounting grad of the University of Arkansas and the Walton College of Business, which may be why he shared transaction data with us to make available for this lab and labs throughout this text.

Data

The data for this lab and other all Dillard's labs are available at http://walton.uark.edu/enterprise/. Your instructor will either give you specific instructions on how to access the data, or there will be information available on connect. The 2016 Dillard's data covers all transactions over the period 1/1/2014 to 10/17/2016.

Software needed

- Microsoft SQL Server Management Studio (available on the Remote Destkop at the University of Arkansas)
- Excel 2016 (available on the Remote Destkop at the University of Arkansas)
- Tableau (available on the Remote Destkop at the University of Arkansas)

In this lab, you will:

- Develop a dashboard to display returns percentages across months and across states.

Prerequisite

- **Lab 6-4.** This lab requires some of the skills covered in Lab 6-4 for steps 1–4. If you haven't completed Lab 6-4, then you can still read through the steps in that lab to see the screenshots of the ETL process in Excel.
- **Lab 4-2.** Some Tableau skills from Lab 4-2 are also expected. If you haven't completed Lab 4-2, you can still read through the steps in that lab to learn the basics of how to build a map and a dashboard in Tableau.

Part 1: Identify the Questions

After performing a hypothesis test to determine that there is a significant difference between January's returns percentage and the rest of the months in a given year, you would like to dig further into the data to visualize that difference across months, and also across stores and in comparison to sales data.

Part 2: Master the Data

1. Loading the data into Tableau from the original SQL Server database first requires some transformation in Excel. Extract and load the transactional and store data into Excel's Query Editor using the following query:

```
Select Tran_Date, Tran_Type, State, Store.Store, SUM(Tran_amt) AS Amount
From Transact
Inner Join Store
On Transact.Store = Store.Store
Group By Tran_Date, Tran_Type, State, Store.Store
Order by Tran_Date
```

2. Pivot the **Tran_Type** column on the **Tran_Amt** values in the **Query Editor** window.
3. Close and load the data into Excel.
4. Once the data have loaded (297,705 rows), save the spreadsheet as Lab 6-6.xlsx.
5. Open Tableau, and connect to an Excel Data source. Browse and open the file you just saved. Now that the data are loaded into their final destination for analysis, Tableau, you have one more step to prepare the data. You need to create the Returns Percentage measure, just like it had to be created in Lab 6-4 in Excel.
6. On **Sheet 1**, create a **Calculated Field**. Right-click in the **Measures**, and select **New Calculated Field**.

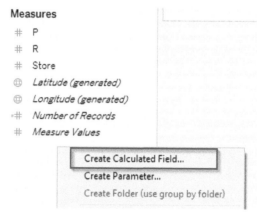

Source: Microsoft Excel 2016.

7. Name your new field **R/P**, and create the calculation SUM([R])/SUM([P]), then click **OK**.

Source: Microsoft Excel 2016.

Part 3: Perform the Analysis

8. We will create three data visualizations to display on a returns dashboard. First, we will create a map displaying the sales dollars per state.
9. Drag and drop the **state** dimension into the middle of the Tableau drawing to start your map.
10. Double-click the **P** measure to display customer purchases. Tableau will default to a symbol map, so change this to a filled map using the **Show Me** window.
11. Name the sheet **Sales by State** and take a screenshot (label it 6-5A).
12. Right-click your new **Sales by State** sheet, and click **Duplicate** to start a new sheet with this map as a base.
13. In the new sheet, drag the **P** measure out of the **Marks** window, and replace it with the calculated measure that you created, **R/P**.
14. Name the sheet **Returns Percentage by State** and take a screenshot (label it 6-5B).
15. Open a new sheet. Drag **Tran_Date** to the rows. It will default to **Years**, but you can expand the pill twice to see **Quarters**, then **Months**. Remove the **Years** and **Quarters** pills so that only the **Months** remains.
16. Double-click **R/P** so that it appears in the **Marks**.
17. In the **Show Me** tab, replace the tabular data that Tableau defaults to with a highlight table. This may have caused Tableau to change your **Months** pill from the **Rows** to the **Columns**. You can just drag the **Months** pill back down to **Rows**.
18. Create a new dashboard. Arrange the three visualizations in whichever way you find most visually pleasing and easiest to read and take a screenshot (label it 6-5C).
19. Using the small filter button in the top right of the **Returns Percentage by State** visual on the dashboard, designate that visual as a filter for the entire dashboard. Now, you can click any of the states on that map to focus on that state in the sales map, as well as to see how the **Returns Percentages** differ monthly for that particular state.
20. Take a screenshot (label it 6-5D).

Part 4: Address and Refine the Results

Q1. What does getting the detail data (or drilled-down data) allow you to test and see? Which of these detail data would be most useful for management?

Q2. Why would it be useful to get return data by product code or product category? Would that cause the company to change its return policy for certain items?

Q3. What other data visualizations would be meaningful to drill down into these data?

End of Lab

Chapter 7

Generating Key Performance Indicators

A Look at This Chapter

This chapter explains how to apply Data Analytics to measure performance. By measuring past performance and comparing it to targeted goals, we are able to assess how well a company is working toward a goal. Also, we can determine required adjustments to how decisions are made or how business processes are run, if any.

A Look Back

In chapter 6, we focused on substantive testing within the audit setting. We highlighted discussion of the audit plan, and account balances were checked. We also highlighted the use of statistical analysis to find errors or fraud in the audit setting. We also discussed the use of clustering to detect outliers and the use of Benford's analysis.

A Look Ahead

In chapter 8, we will focus on how to access and analyze financial statement data. The data are accessed via XBRL in a quick and efficient manner. We also discuss how ratios are used to analyze financial performance, and how sparklines help users visualize trends in the data. Finally, we discuss the use of text mining to analyze the sentiment in financial reporting data.

For years, **Kenya Red Cross** had attempted to refine its strategy and align its daily activities with its overall strategic goals. It had annual strategic planning meetings with external consultants that always resulted in the consultants presenting a new strategy to the organization that the **Red Cross** didn't have a particularly strong buy-in to, and the **Red Cross** never felt confident in what was developed or what it would mean for its future. When **Kenya Red Cross** went through a Data Analytics–backed Balanced Scorecard planning process for the first time, though, it immediately felt like its organization's mission and vision was involved in the strategic planning and that "strategy" was no longer so vague. The Balanced Scorecard approach helped the **Kenya Red Cross** align its goals into measurable metrics. The organization prided itself on being "first in and last out" but hadn't actively measured its success in that goal, nor had the organization fully analyzed how being the first in and last out of disaster scenarios affected other goals and areas of its organization. Using Data Analytics to refine its strategy and assign measurable performance metrics to its goals, **Kenya Red Cross** felt confident that its everyday activities were linked to measurable goals that would help the organization reach its goals and maintain a strong positive reputation and impact through its service. Exhibit 7-1 gives an illustration of the Balanced Scorecard at the **Kenyan Red Cross**.

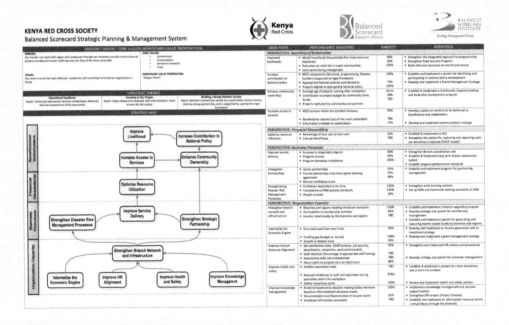

EXHIBIT 7-1 The Kenya Red Cross Balanced Scorecard

Source: Reprinted with permission from Balanced Scorecard Institute, a Strategy Management Group company. Copyright 2008–2017.

OBJECTIVES

After reading this chapter, you should be able to:

LO 7-1   Evaluate management requirements and identify useful KPIs from a list

LO 7-2   Evaluate underlying data quality used for KPI

LO 7-3   Create a dashboard using KPIs

In the past six chapters, you learned how to apply the IMPACT model to data analysis projects in general and, specifically, to internal and external auditing and financial statement analysis. The same accounting information used in internal and external auditing and financial statement analysis can also be used to determine how closely an organization is meeting its strategic objectives. In order to better determine the gaps in actual company performance and targeted strategic objectives, data should be condensed into easily digestible and useful digital dashboards, providing precisely the information needed to help make operational decisions that support a company's strategic direction.

This chapter brings us to how to apply Data Analytics to measuring performance. More specifically, we measure past performance and compare it to targeted goals to assess how well a company is working toward a goal. In addition, we can determine required adjustments to how decisions are made or how business processes are run, if any.

Because data are increasingly available and affordable for companies to access and store, and because the growth in technology has created robust and affordable business intelligence tools, data and information are becoming the key components for decision making, replacing gut response. Specifically, various measures and metrics are defined, compiled from the data, and used for decision making. **Performance metrics** are, rather simply, any number used to measure performance at a company. The amount of inventory on hand is a metric, and that metric gains meaning when compared to a baseline (e.g., how much inventory was on hand yesterday?). A specific type of performance metric is **key performance indicators (KPIs)**. Just like any performance metric, a KPI should help managers keep track of performance and strategic objectives, but the KPIs are performance metrics that stand out as the most important—that is, "key" metrics that influence decision making and strategy. Nearly every organization can use data to create the same performance metrics (although, of course, with different results), but it is dependent upon each organization's particular strategy which performance metrics that organization would deem to be a KPI.

As you will recall from chapter 4, the most effective way to communicate the results of any data analysis project is through data visualization. A project in which you are determining the right KPIs and communicating them to the appropriate stakeholders is no different. One of the most common ways to communicate a variety of KPIs is through a digital dashboard. A **digital dashboard** is an interactive report showing the most important metrics to help users understand how a company or an organization is performing. There are many public digital dashboards available; for example, the Walton College of Business at the University of Arkansas has an interactive dashboard to showcase enrollment, where students are from, where students study abroad, student retention and graduation rates, and where alumni work after graduation (https://walton.uark.edu/osie/reports/data-dashboard.php). The public dashboard detailing student diversity at the Walton College can be used by prospective students to learn more about the university and by the university itself to assess how it is doing in meeting goals. If the university has a goal of increasing gender balance in enrollment, for example, then monitoring the "Diverse Walton" metrics, pictured in Exhibit 7-2, can help the university understand how it is doing at reaching that goal.

Digital dashboards provide interesting information, but their value is maximized when the metrics provided on the dashboard are used to affect decision making and action. One iteration of a digital dashboard is the Balanced Scorecard. The **Balanced Scorecard** was created by Robert S. Kaplan and David P. Porter in 1996 to help companies turn their strategic goals into action by identifying the most important metrics to measure, as well as identifying target goals to compare metrics against.

The Balanced Scorecard is comprised of four components: financial (or stewardship), customer (or stakeholder), internal process, and organizational capacity (or learning and growth). As depicted in Exhibit 7-3, the measures in each category affect other categories, and all four should be directly related to the strategic objectives of an organization.

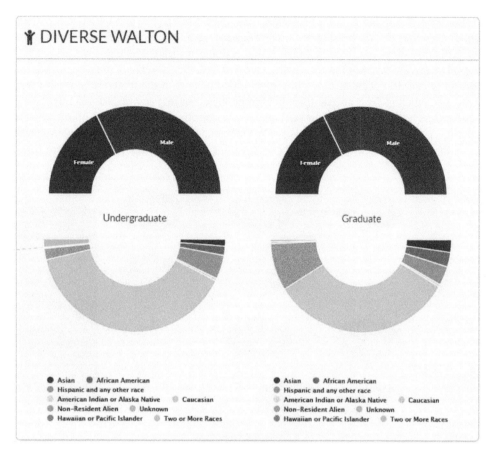

EXHIBIT 7-2
Walton College Digital
Dashboard—Diverse
Walton

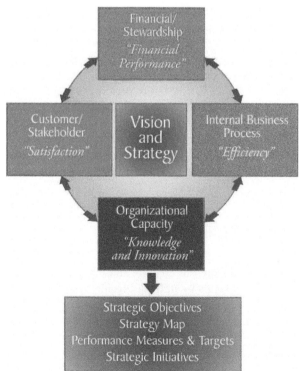

EXHIBIT 7-3
**Components of the
Balanced Scorecard**

Reprinted with permission
from Balanced Scorecard
Institute, a Strategy
Management Group Company.
Copyright 2008-2017.

For each of the four components, objectives, measures, targets, and initiatives are identified. *Objectives* should be aligned with strategic goals of the organization, *measures* are the KPIs that show how well the organization is doing at meeting its objective, and *targets* should be achievable goals toward which to move the metric. *Initiatives* should be the actions that an organization can take to move its specified metrics in the direction of their stated target goal. Exhibit 7-4 is an example of different objectives that an organization might identify for each component. You can see how certain objectives relate to other objectives—for example, if the organization increases process efficiency (in the internal process component row), that should help with the objective of lowering cost in the financial component row.

EXHIBIT 7-4

An Example of a Balanced Scorecard

Reprinted with permission from Balanced Scorecard Institute, a Strategy Management Group Company. Copyright 2008-2017.

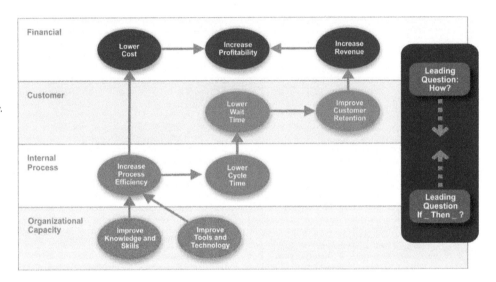

Understanding how the four components interact to answer different types of questions and meet different strategic goals is critical when it comes to identifying the right measures to include in the dashboard, as well as using those measures to help with decision making. Creating a Balanced Scorecard or any type of digital dashboard to present KPIs for decision making follows the IMPACT model.

Bernard Marr identified 75 KPIs to measure performance in the different components that he considers the most important for decision makers to know, and these 75 KPIs are compiled in Exhibit 7-5. In a Balanced Scorecard, each component should focus on 3 or 4 KPIs. Including all 75 of these metrics in a given dashboard would be overwhelming and difficult to manage, but depending on the strategy of the company and the initiatives that are chosen as focal points, any of the KPIs in Exhibit 7-5 may be optimal for measuring (and ultimately improving) performance.

IDENTIFY THE QUESTIONS

LO 7-1

Evaluate management requirements and identify useful KPIs from a list

The Balanced Scorecard is based around a company's strategy. A well-defined mission, vision, and set of values are integral in creating and maintaining a successful culture. In many cases, when tradition appears to stifle an organization, the two concepts of culture and tradition must be separated. An established sense of purpose and a robust tradition of service can serve as a catalyst to facilitate successful organizational changes. A proper strategy for growth considers what a firm does well and how it achieves it. With a proper strategy, an organization is less likely to be hamstrung by a "this is how we've always done it" mentality.

Financial Performance KPIs	1. Net Profit
	2. Net Profit Margin
	3. Gross Profit Margin
	4. Operating Profit Margin
	5. EBITDA
	6. Revenue Growth Rate
	7. Total Shareholder Return (TSR)
	8. Economic Value Added (EVA)
	9. Return on Investment (ROI)
	10. Return on Capital Employed (ROCE)
	11. Return on Assets (ROA)
	12. Return on Equity (ROE)
	13. Debt-to-Equity (D/E) Ratio
	14. Cash Conversion Cycle (CCC)
	15. Working Capital Ratio
	16. Operating Expense Ratio (OER)
	17. CAPEX to Sales Ratio
	18. Price-to-Earnings Ratio (P/E Ratio)
Customer KPIs	19. Net Promoter Score (NPS)
	20. Customer Retention Rate
	21. Customer Satisfaction Index
	22. Customer Profitability Score
	23. Customer Lifetime Value
	24. Customer Turnover Rate
	25. Customer Engagement
	26. Customer Complaints
Marketing KPIs	27. Market Growth Rate
	28. Market Share
	29. Brand Equity
	30. Cost per Lead
	31. Conversion Rate
	32. Search Engine Rankings (by keyword) and Click-Through Rate
	33. Page Views and Bounce Rate
	34. Customer Online Engagement Level
	35. Online Share of Voice (OSOV)
	36. Social Networking Footprint
	37. Klout Score
Operational KPIs	38. Six Sigma Level
	39. Capacity Utilization Rate (CUR)
	40. Process Waste Level
	41. Order Fulfilment Cycle Time
	42. Delivery in Full, on Time (DIFOT) Rate
	43. Inventory Shrinkage Rate (ISR)
	44. Project Schedule Variance (PSV)
	45. Project Cost Variance (PCV)
	46. Earned Value (EV) Metric
	47. Innovation Pipeline Strength (IPS)

EXHIBIT 7-5

Suggested KPIs That Every Manager Needs to Know[1]

(Continued)

[1]https://www.linkedin.com/pulse/20130905053105-64875646-the-75-kpis-every-manager-needs-to-know.

EXHIBIT 7-5
(*Continued*)

	48. Return on Innovation Investment (ROI2)
	49. Time to Market
	50. First-Pass Yield (FPY)
	51. Rework Level
	52. Quality Index
	53. Overall Equipment Effectiveness (OEE)
	54. Process or Machine Downtime Level
	55. First Contact Resolution (FCR)
Employee Performance KPIs	56. Human Capital Value Added (HCVA)
	57. Revenue per Employee
	58. Employee Satisfaction Index
	59. Employee Engagement Level
	60. Staff Advocacy Score
	61. Employee Churn Rate
	62. Average Employee Tenure
	63. Absenteeism Bradford Factor
	64. 360-Degree Feedback Score
	65. Salary Competitiveness Ratio (SCR)
	66. Time to Hire
	67. Training Return on Investment
Environmental and Social Sustainability KPIs	68. Carbon Footprint
	69. Water Footprint
	70. Energy Consumption
	71. Saving Levels Due to Conservation and Improvement Efforts
	72. Supply Chain Miles
	73. Waste Reduction Rate
	74. Waste Recycling Rate
	75. Product Recycling Rate

If a strategy is already developed, or after the strategy has been fully defined, it needs to be broken down into goals that can be measured. Identifying the pieces of the strategy that can be measured is critical. Without tracking performance and measuring results, the strategy is only symbolic. The adage "what gets measured, gets done" shows the motivation behind aligning strategy statements with KPIs—people are more inclined to focus their work and their projects on initiatives that are being paid attention to and measured. Of course, simply measuring something doesn't imply that anything will be done to improve the measure—the attainable initiative attached to a metric indicating how it can be improved is a key piece to ensuring that people will work to improve the measure.

(✓) **PROGRESS CHECK**

1. To illustrate what KPIs emphasize in "what gets measured, gets done," **Walmart** has a goal of a "zero waste future."[2] How does reporting **Walmart's** waste recycling rate help the organization figure out if it is getting closer to its goal? Do you believe it helps the organization accomplish its goals?

2. How can management identify useful KPIs? How could Data Analytics help with that?

[2]http://corporate.walmart.com/2016grr/enhancing-sustainability/moving-toward-a-zero-waste-future (accessed August 2017).

MASTER THE DATA AND PERFORM THE TEST PLAN

LO 7-2

Evaluate underlying data quality used for KPI

Once the measures have been determined, the data that are necessary to showcase those measures need to be identified. You were first introduced to how to identify and obtain necessary data in chapter 2 through the ETL (extract, transform, and load) process. In addition to working through the same data request process that is detailed in chapter 2, there are two other questions to consider when obtaining data and evaluating their quality:

1. How often do the data get updated in the system? This will help you be aware of how up-to-date your metrics are so that you interpret the changes over time appropriately.
2. Additionally, how often do you need to see updated data? If the data in the system are updated on a near-real-time basis, it may not be necessary for you to have new updates pushed to your scorecard as frequently. For example, if your team will assess their progress only in a once-a-week meeting, there is no need to have a constantly updating scorecard.

While the data for calculating KPIs are likely stored in the company's ERP or accounting information system, the digital dashboard containing the KPIs for data analysis should be created in a data visualization tool, such as Excel or Tableau. Loading the data into these tools should be done with precision and should be validated to ensure the data imported were complete and accurate.

Designing data visualizations and selecting the right way to express data (as whole numbers, percentages, or absolute values, etc.) was discussed in chapter 4. Specifically for digital dashboards, the format of your dashboard can follow the pattern of a Balanced Scorecard with a strategy map, or it can take on a different format. Exhibit 7-6 shows a template for building out the objectives, measures, targets, and initiatives into a Balanced Scorecard format.

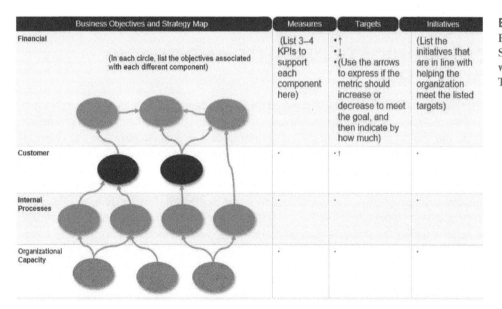

EXHIBIT 7-6

Balanced Scorecard Strategy Map Template with Measures, Targets, and Initiatives

If not following the strategy map template, the most important KPIs should be placed in the top left corner, as our eyes are most naturally drawn to that part of any page that we are reading.

LO 7-3

Create a dashboard using KPIs

ADDRESS AND REFINE RESULTS

Once the dashboard is in use, an active communication plan should be implemented to ensure that the dashboard's metrics are meeting the needs of the business and the users. If there are multiple audiences who use dashboards, then either different dashboards should be created, or the dashboard should provide different views and ways to filter the information so users can customize their experience and see exactly the metrics they need for decision making and monitoring. Because dashboards tend to be monitored on a daily (or even more frequent) basis, then communication with all of the users is imperative to ensure that the identified metrics are appropriate and useful.

Some questions that would be helpful in determining how the dashboard could be refined are the following:

1. Which metric are you using most frequently to help you make decisions?
2. Are you downloading the data to do any additional analysis after working with the dashboard, and if so, can the dashboard be improved to save those extra steps?
3. Are there any metrics that you do not use? If so, why aren't they helpful?
4. Are there any metrics that should be available on the dashboard to help you with decision making?

Checking in with the users will help to address any potential issues of missing or unnecessary data and refine the dashboard so that it is meeting the needs of the organization and the users appropriately.

COMMUNICATE INSIGHTS AND TRACK OUTCOMES

After the results have been refined and each user of the dashboard is receiving the right information for decision making, the dashboard should enter regular use across the organization. Recall that the purpose of creating a digital dashboard is to communicate how the organization is performing so decision makers can improve their judgment and decisions and so workers can understand where to place their priority in their day-to-day jobs and projects. Ensuring that all of the appropriate stakeholders continue to be involved in using the dashboard and continually improving it is key to the success of the dashboard. The creation of a Balanced Scorecard or any type of digital dashboard is iterative—just as the entire IMPACT cycle should be iterative throughout any data analysis project—so it will be imperative to continually check in with the users of the dashboard to learn how to continually improve it and its usefulness.

Summary

- In order to better determine the gaps in actual company performance and targeted strategic objectives, data should be condensed into easily digestible and useful digital dashboards providing precisely the information needed to help make operational decisions that support a company's strategic direction.
- Because data are increasingly available and affordable for companies to access and store, and because the growth in technology has created robust and affordable business intelligence tools, data and information are becoming the key components for decision making, replacing gut response.
- Performance metrics are defined, compiled from the data, and used for decision making. A specific type of performance metrics, key performance indicators—or "key" metrics that influence decision making and strategy—is the most important.
- One of the most common ways to communicate a variety of KPIs is through a digital dashboard. A digital dashboard is an interactive report showing the most important metrics to help users understand how a company or an organization is performing. Their value is maximized when the metrics provided on the dashboard are used to affect decision making and action.
- One iteration of a digital dashboard is the Balanced Scorecard, which is used to help companies turn their strategic goals into action by identifying the most important metrics to measure, as well as identifying target goals to compare metrics against. The Balanced Scorecard is comprised of four components: financial (or stewardship), customer (or stakeholder), internal process, and organizational capacity (or learning and growth).
- For each of the four components, objectives, measures, targets, and initiatives are identified. Objectives should be aligned with strategic goals of the organization, measures are the KPIs that show how well the organization is doing at meeting its objective, and targets should be achievable goals toward which to move the metric. Initiatives should be the actions that an organization can take to move its specified metrics in the direction of its stated target goal.
- Regardless of whether you are creating a Balanced Scorecard or another type of digital dashboard to showcase performance metrics and KPIs, the IMPACT model should be used to complete the project.

Key Words

Balanced Scorecard (*252*)   A particular type of digital dashboard that is made up of strategic objectives, as well as KPIs, target measures, and initiatives, to help the organization reach its target measures in line with strategic goals.

digital dashboard (*252*)   An interactive report showing the most important metrics to help users understand how a company or an organization is performing. Often created using Excel or Tableau.

key performance indicator (KPI) (*252*)   A particular type of performance metric that an organization deems the most important and influential on decision making.

performance metric (*252*)   Any calculation measuring how an organization is performing, particularly when that measure is compared to a baseline.

 ## ANSWERS TO PROGRESS CHECKS

1. If waste reduction is an important goal for **Walmart**, having a KPI and, potentially, a digital dashboard that reports how well the organization is doing will likely be useful in helping it accomplish its goal. Using a digital dashboard helps an organization to see if, indeed, it is making progress.

2. The KPIs that are the most helpful are those that are consistent with the company strategy and measure how well the company is doing in meeting its goals. Data Analytics will help gather and report the necessary data to report on the KPIs. The Data Analytics IMPACT model introduced in chapter 1—from identifying the question to tracking outcomes—will be helpful in getting the necessary data.

3. The frequency of updating KPIs is always a good question. One determinant will be how often the data get updated in the system, and the second determinant is how often the data will be considered by those looking at the data. Whichever of those two determinants takes longer is probably correct frequency for updating KPIs.

4. Because our eyes are most naturally drawn to that part of any page that we are reading, the most important KPIs should be placed in the top left corner.

5. By identifying the KPIs that are most important to corporate strategy and finding the necessary data to support them and then reporting on them in a digital dashboard, decision makers will have the necessary information to make effective decisions and track outcomes.

6. As noted in the opening vignette, using Data Analytics to refine its strategy and assign measurable performance metrics to its goals, **Kenya Red Cross** felt confident that its everyday activities were linked to measurable goals that would help the organization reach its goals and maintain a strong positive reputation and impact through its service.

![Mc Graw Hill Education] **connect**

Multiple Choice Questions

1. What would you consider to be Financial Performance KPIs?
   a. Total Shareholder Return
   b. Customer Profitability Score
   c. Market Growth Rate
   d. Klout Score

2. What would you consider to be an Operational KPI?
   a. Inventory Shrinkage Rate
   b. Brand Equity
   c. CAPEX to Sales Ratio
   d. Revenue per Employee

3. What does *KPI* stand for?
   a. Key performance index
   b. Key performance indicator
   c. Key paired index
   d. Key paired indicator

4. The most important KPIs should be placed in the _____ corner of the page even if we are not following a strategy map template.
   a. Bottom right
   b. Bottom left
   c. Top left
   d. Top right

5. According to the text, which of these are *not* helpful in refining a dashboard?

   a. Which metric are you using most frequently to help you make decisions?

   b. Are you downloading the data to do any additional analysis after working with the dashboard, and if so, can the dashboard be improved to save those extra steps?

   c. Are there any metrics that you do not use? If so, why aren't they helpful?

   d. Which data are the easiest to access or least costly to collect?

6. On a Balanced Scorecard, which is *not* included as a component?

   a. Financial Performance

   b. Customer/Stakeholder

   c. Internal Process

   d. Employee Capacity

7. On a Balanced Scorecard, which is *not* included as a component?

   a. Financial Performance

   b. Customer/Stakeholder

   c. Order Process

   d. Organizational Capacity

8. What is defined as an interactive report showing the most important metrics to help users understand how a company or an organization is performing?

   a. KPI

   b. Performance metric

   c. Digital dashboard

   d. Balanced Scorecard

9. What is defined as any calculation measuring how an organization is performing, particularly when that measure is compared to a baseline?

   a. KPI

   b. Performance metric

   c. Digital dashboard

   d. Balanced Scorecard

10. What would you consider to be Marketing KPIs?

    a. Conversion Rate

    b. Six Sigma Level

    c. Employee Churn Rate

    d. Customer Engagement

Discussion Questions

1. We know that a Balanced Scorecard is comprised of four components: financial (or stewardship), customer (or stakeholder), internal process, and organizational capacity (or learning and growth). What would you include in a dashboard for the financial and customer components?

2. We know that a Balanced Scorecard is comprised of four components: financial (or stewardship), customer (or stakeholder), internal process, and organizational capacity (or learning and growth). What would you include in a dashboard for the internal process and organizational capacity components? How do digital dashboards make KPIs easier to track?

3. **Amazon**, in the author's opinion, has cared less about profitability in the short run but has cared about gaining market share. Arguably **Amazon** gains market share by

taking care of the customer. Given the "Suggested 75 KPIs That Every Manager Needs to Know" from Exhibit 7-5, what would be a natural KPI for the customer aspect for **Amazon**? How do digital dashboards make KPIs easier to track?

4. For an accounting firm like **PwC**, how would the Balanced Scorecard help balance the desire to be profitable for its partners with keeping the focus on its customers?

5. For a company like **Walmart**, how would the Balanced Scorecard help balance the desire to be profitable for its shareholders with continuing to develop organizational capacity to compete with **Amazon** (and other online retailers)?

6. Why is Customer Retention Rate a great KPI for understanding your **Tesla** customers?

7. If the data underlying your digital dashboard are updated in real time, why would you want to update your digital dashboard in real time? Are there situations when you would not want to update your digital dashboard in real time? Why or why not?

8. In which of the four components of a Balanced Scorecard would you put the **Walton College**'s diversity initiative? Why do you think this is important for a public institution of higher learning?

Problems

1. From Exhibit 7-5, choose 5 Financial Performance KPIs to answer the following three questions. This URL (https://www.linkedin.com/pulse/20130905053105-64875646-the-75-kpis-every-manager-needs-to-know) provides links with background information for each individual KPI that may be helpful in understanding the individual KPIs and answering the questions.

   a. Identify the equation/relationship/data needed to calculate the KPI. If you need data, how frequently would the data need to be incorporated to be most useful?

   b. Describe a simple visualization that would help a manager track the KPI.

   c. Identify a benchmark for the KPI from the Internet. Choose an industry and find the average, if possible. This is for context only.

2. From Exhibit 7-5, choose 10 Employee Performance KPIs to answer the following three questions. This URL (https://www.linkedin.com/pulse/20130905053105-64875646-the-75-kpis-every-manager-needs-to-know) provides links with background information for each individual KPI that may be helpful in understanding the individual KPIs and answering the questions.

   a. Identify the equation/relationship/data needed to calculate the KPI. How frequently would it need to be incorporated to be most useful?

   b. Describe a simple visualization that would help a manager track the KPI.

   c. Identify a benchmark for the KPI from the Internet. Choose an industry and find the average, if possible. This is for context only.

3. From Exhibit 7-5, choose 10 Marketing KPIs to answer the following three questions. This URL (https://www.linkedin.com/pulse/20130905053105-64875646-the-75-kpis-every-manager-needs-to-know) provides links with background information for each individual KPI that may be helpful in understanding the individual KPIs and answering the questions.

   a. Identify the equation/relationship/data needed to calculate the KPI. How frequently would it need to be incorporated to be most useful?

   b. Describe a simple visualization that would help a manager track the KPI.

   c. Identify a benchmark for the KPI from the Internet. Choose an industry and find the average, if possible. This is for context only.

4. How does Data Analytics help facilitate the use of the Balanced Scorecard and tracking KPIs? Does it make the data more timely? Are you able to access more information easier or faster, or what capabilities does it give?

5. If ROA is considered a key KPI for a company, what would be an appropriate benchmark? The industry's ROA? The average ROA for the company for the past five years? The competitors' ROA?

    a. How will you know if the company is making progress?

    b. How might Data Analytics help with this?

    c. How often would you need a measure of ROA? Monthly? Quarterly? Annually?

6. If Time to Market is considered a key KPI for a company, what would be an appropriate benchmark? The industry's Time to Market? The average Time to Market for the company for the past five years? The competitors' Time to Market?

    a. How will you know if the company is making progress?

    b. How might Data Analytics help with this?

    c. How often would you need a measure of Time to Market? Monthly? Quarterly? Annually?

7. Why is Order Fulfillment Cycle Time an appropriate KPI for a company like **Wayfair** (which sells furniture online)? How long does **Wayfair** think customers will be ready to wait if **Amazon** Prime promises items delivered to its customers in two business days? Might this be an important basis for competition?

Answers to Multiple Choice Questions

1. A
2. A
3. B
4. C
5. D
6. D
7. C
8. C
9. B
10. A

Lab 7-1 Evaluate Management Requirement and Identify Useful KPIs from a List

Key performance indicators help managers keep track of performance and strategic objectives.

Bernard Marr came up with a list of 75 KPIs that he believes every manager needs to know.[3]

In this lab, you will:

- Learn about many of the key performance indicators.
- Evaluate which KPIs best work for Tesla.
- Consider the data needed and the desired frequency to provide each of these KPIs.

> Q1. Imagine you work for Tesla. Choose 20 KPIs that you believe are most important to Tesla's management (include 5 from each category).

The 75 KPIs Every Manager Needs to Know (Bernard Marr)

To measure financial performance:	
	1. Net Profit
	2. Net Profit Margin
	3. Gross Profit Margin
	4. Operating Profit Margin
	5. EBITDA
	6. Revenue Growth Rate
	7. Total Shareholder Return (TSR)
	8. Economic Value Added (EVA)
	9. Return on Investment (ROI)
	10. Return on Capital Employed (ROCE)
	11. Return on Assets (ROA)
	12. Return on Equity (ROE)
	13. Debt-to-Equity (D/E) Ratio
	14. Cash Conversion Cycle (CCC)
	15. Working Capital Ratio
	16. Operating Expense Ratio (OER)
	17. CAPEX to Sales Ratio
	18. Price-to-Earnings Ratio (P/E Ratio)
To understand your customers:	
	19. Net Promoter Score (NPS)
	20. Customer Retention Rate
	21. Customer Satisfaction Index
	22. Customer Profitability Score
	23. Customer Lifetime Value
	24. Customer Turnover Rate
	25. Customer Engagement
	26. Customer Complaints

[3]https://www.linkedin.com/pulse/20130905053105-64875646-the-75-kpis-every-manager-needs-to-know/ (accessed 10/13/2017).

To gauge your market and marketing efforts:	27. Market Growth Rate
	28. Market Share
	29. Brand Equity
	30. Cost per Lead
	31. Conversion Rate
	32. Search Engine Rankings (by keyword) and Click-Through Rate
	33. Page Views and Bounce Rate
	34. Customer Online Engagement Level
	35. Online Share of Voice (OSOV)
	36. Social Networking Footprint
	37. Klout Score
To measure your operational performance:	38. Six Sigma Level
	39. Capacity Utilisation Rate (CUR)
	40. Process Waste Level
	41. Order Fulfilment Cycle Time
	42. Delivery in Full, on Time (DIFOT) Rate
	43. Inventory Shrinkage Rate (ISR)
	44. Project Schedule Variance (PSV)
	45. Project Cost Variance (PCV)
	46. Earned Value (EV) Metric
	47. Innovation Pipeline Strength (IPS)
	48. Return on Innovation Investment (ROI2)
	49. Time to Market
	50. First-Pass Yield (FPY)
	51. Rework Level
	52. Quality Index
	53. Overall Equipment Effectiveness (OEE)
	54. Process or Machine Downtime Level
	55. First Contact Resolution (FCR)
To understand your employees and their performance:	56. Human Capital Value Added (HCVA)
	57. Revenue per Employee
	58. Employee Satisfaction Index
	59. Employee Engagement Level
	60. Staff Advocacy Score
	61. Employee Churn Rate
	62. Average Employee Tenure
	63. Absenteeism Bradford Factor
	64. 360-Degree Feedback Score
	65. Salary Competitiveness Ratio (SCR)
	66. Time to Hire
	67. Training Return on Investment
To measure your environmental and social sustainability performance:	68. Carbon Footprint
	69. Water Footprint
	70. Energy Consumption
	71. Saving Levels Due to Conservation and Improvement Efforts
	72. Supply Chain Miles
	73. Waste Reduction Rate
	74. Waste Recycling Rate
	75. Product Recycling Rate

Part 1: Identify the Questions

For each of these 20 KPIs:

Q2. Identify the specific equation/relationship/data needed to calculate the KPI. If you need frequent data, how frequent?

Q3. Describe a simple visualization or dashboard that would help a manager track the KPI. Is it red, yellow, and green indicators, or do you have something else in mind that would be better?

Part 2: Master the Data

Q4. Identify a benchmark for five of these KPIs for **Tesla**. How would you set it? Would you base it on averages for **Tesla** or on performance from the prior week, month or year? For the car industry or a different industry?

End of Lab

Lab 7-2   Create a Balanced Scorecard Dashboard in Tableau

Superstore has brought you in to help it develop some metrics to evaluate performance across different dimensions of its business, including finance, customers, process, and employee growth.

Company summary

Superstore is a large seller of retail and wholesale office supplies, furniture, and technology. It operates in the United States and has divided its sales regions into North, South, East, and West. Each region has a regional sales representative who interacts with the customers to take orders and deal with returns.

Data

Sales order data are available from 2013 to 2016, including demographic data about the customers, as well as main categories and subcategories of products.

Technique

- In this lab, you will use Tableau to generate a dashboard to evaluate four key performance indicators.

Software needed

- Tableau

In this lab, you will:

- Generate some key performance indicators.
- Evaluate the data.
- Perform analyses and generate visualizations.

Part 1: Identify the Questions

Your understanding of key performance indicators has given you some insight into how management at Superstore might measure and evaluate performance across different aspects of the business. They depend on your expertise to do just that.

Assuming you'll have access to sales order and returns data, as well as the sales representatives involved, think about different ways you could measure performance.

Q1. What KPIs would you consider using to evaluate sales financial performance?

Q2. What KPIs would you consider using to evaluate customer relationships?

Q3. What KPIs would you consider using to evaluate process efficiency?

Q4. What KPIs would you consider using to evaluate employee growth?

Q5. For each KPI, identify a benchmark value or KPI goal that you think management might use.

Part 2: Generate a Request for Data

The following data are available:

Orders	Returns	People
Row ID	Order ID	Person
Order ID		Region
Order Date		
Ship Date		
Ship Mode		
Customer ID		
Customer Name		
Segment		
Country City		
State		
Postal Code		
Region Product ID		
Category		
Subcategory		
Product Name		
Sales		
Quantity		
Discount		
Profit		

LAB EXHIBIT 7-2A

Q6. Using the available fields, identify some calculations or relationships that would support your KPIs from Q1 to Q4.

Q7. Are there any KPIs you selected that don't have supporting data fields?

Part 3: Perform an Analysis of the Data

Now you'll use Tableau to generate some analytics that will provide visualizations for management to quickly evaluate some of the KPIs. To simplify the process, here are four KPIs that management has identified as high priorities:

Finance: Which product categories provide the highest amount of profit? The goal is 13 percent return on sales. Use *Profit ratio = Total profit/Total sales.*

Process: How long does it take to ship our product to each state on average? Management would like to see four days or less. Use *Delivery time in days = Ship date – Order date.*

Customers: Which regions have the highest return rates? Management says only 10 percent of sales orders should be returned normally. *Return rate = Number of returned/Number of orders.*

Employees: Who are our top-performing employees by sales each month? *Rank the total number of sales by employee.*

Now it's your turn to build a Balanced Scorecard dashboard in Tableau for each of these metrics. First, you'll create four individual worksheets; then you'll combine them into a dashboard for quick review.

Note: To compare actual performance to management's goals, you'll need to set some parameters and create some additional calculated fields.

1. Open Tableau, and create a new Tableau book.
2. Click **Data > New Data Source > Excel**.
3. Navigate to **Documents > My Tableau Repository > Datasources > XX.X > en_US-US > Sample – Superstore.xls** or choose **Sample – Superstore** from the saved data sources on the open data screen.
4. Click **Open**.
5. In **Data Source**, drag **Orders** and **People** to the top pane to inner join them. Then drag **Returns** to the whitespace and create a left join.
6. Create your parameters for management goals. To create parameters, in the left pane, click the down-arrow next to **Dimensions** and choose **Create Parameter. . .**
    a. **Name:** KPI Target–Return on Sales
        i. **Datatype:** Float
        ii. **Current value:** 0.13 <- *This is management's 13 percent return on sales goal.*
        iii. **Display format:** Percentage, 0 decimals
        iv. **Allowable values:** Range
        v. **Minimum:** 0.01
        vi. **Maximum:** 1
        vii. **Step size:** 0.01
    b. **Name:** KPI Target–Delivery Days
        i. **Datatype:** Float
        ii. **Current value:** 4 <- *This is management's four-day shipping goal.*
        iii. **Display format:** Automatic
        iv. **Allowable values:** Range
        v. **Minimum:** 1
        vi. **Maximum:** 10
        vii. **Step size:** 0.5
    c. **Name:** Return Rate
        i. **Datatype:** Float
        ii. **Current value:** 0.1 <- *This is management's 10 percent order return rate goal.*
        iii. **Display format:** Percentage, 0 decimals
        iv. **Allowable values:** Range
        v. **Minimum:** 0
        vi. **Maximum:** 1
        vii. **Step size:** 0.05

    d. **Name**: Top Salespeople
        i. **Datatype**: Integer
        ii. **Current value**: 1 <- *This shows the number of top employees management wants to recognize.*
        iii. **Display format**: Number (standard)
        iv. **Allowable values**: Range
        v. **Minimum**: 0
        vi. **Maximum**: 3
        vii. **Step size**: 1

7. Create the four worksheets. *For simplicity, full instructions are provided for the first sheet. For subsequent sheets, drag the attributes to the appropriate places.*
    a. Create a new worksheet called **Finance**.
        i. Create calculated fields—click the down-arrow next to Dimensions in the left pane and choose **Create Calculated Field**. Enter the name of the new field, then type the expression in the box below.
            1. **Profit Ratio**: SUM([Profit])/SUM([Sales]).
            2. **Actual vs Target – Return on Sales**: [Profit Ratio] > [KPI Target – Return on Sales].
        ii. Drag the following attribute to the Columns pane: **Profit Ratio** -> becomes AGG(Profit Ratio).
        iii. Drag the following attributes to the Rows pane: **Category**, **Sub-Category**.
        iv. Drag the following attribute to the Filters pane: **Product Name**. Double-click the value and select **Custom Value List** in the window that appears. Then click **OK**.
        v. Drag the following attribute to the Marks pane: **Actual vs Target – Return on Sales** becomes AGG (Actual vs Target – Return on Sales). Click the icon next to it and select **Color** from the list.
        vi. Click the **Analytics** tab in the left pane. In the **Custom** section, drag **Reference Line** onto the Finance table. In the window that appears, choose the following options:
            1. **Entire Table**
            2. **Value**: KPI Target – Return on Sales
        vii. Click **OK** and save your project.
        viii. Take a screenshot (label it 7-2A).

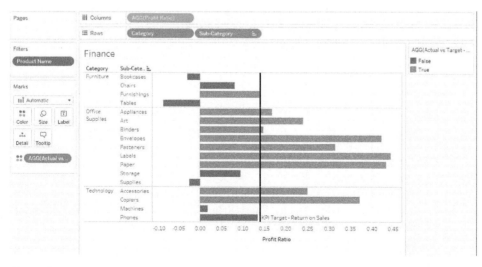

b. Create a new worksheet called **Process**.
  i. **Create calculated fields**:
     1. **Delivery Time Days**: ROUND(FLOAT(DATEDIFF('day', [Order Date], [Ship Date])),2)
     2. **Actual vs Target – Delivery**: AVG([Delivery Time Days]) < [KPI Target – Delivery Days]
  ii. **Columns: Longitude (generated)**
  iii. **Rows: Latitude (generated)**
  iv. **Type: Filled Map**
  v. Marks:
     1. **Delivery Time Days** > Average > Color
     2. **Country** > Detail
     3. **State** > Detail
  vi. Double-click **AVG(Delivery Time Days)** color scale:
     1. Red-Green Diverging
     2. Reversed
     3. Advanced: Center: 4
  vii. Take a screenshot (label it 7-2B).

c. Create a new worksheet called **Customer**.
  i. Create calculated fields:
     1. **Return Rate**: COUNT([Returned])/COUNT([Order ID])
     2. **Actual vs Target – Return Rate**: **[Return Rate]** < **[Parameters][Return Rate]**
  ii. **Columns: YEAR(Order Date)**
  iii. **Rows: AGG(Return Rate)**
  iv. **Type: Line**
  v. **Marks**:
     1. **AGG(Actual vs Target – Return Rate)** > **Color**
     2. **Region** > **Label**
  vi. Take a screenshot (label it 7-2C).

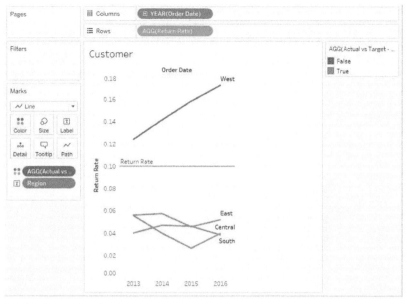

d. Create a new worksheet called **Growth**.
   i. Create calculated fields:
      1. **Rank**: Index( )
      2. **Actual vs Target – Seller**: [Rank] <= [Top Salespeople]
   ii. **Columns**: **SUM(Sales)**
   iii. **Rows**: **Person**
   iv. **Type**: **Bar**
   v. **Marks**:
      1. **Actual vs Target – Seller > Color**
      2. **SUM(Sales) > Label**
   vi. **Pages**: **MONTH(Order Date)** <- *This will allow you to select a month to see the top-performing seller for a given month.*
   vii Take a screenshot (label it 7-2D).

8. Finally, create a new dashboard called **Balanced Scorecard**.
   a. Drag **Finance, Customer, Process**, and **Growth** to main body of your dashboard.
   b. To enable management to adjust its goals (and corresponding reference lines), add the parameters to the dashboard along the top. Click **Show/Hide Cards** > **Parameters**, and add the parameters to the dashboard, then drag them along the top.

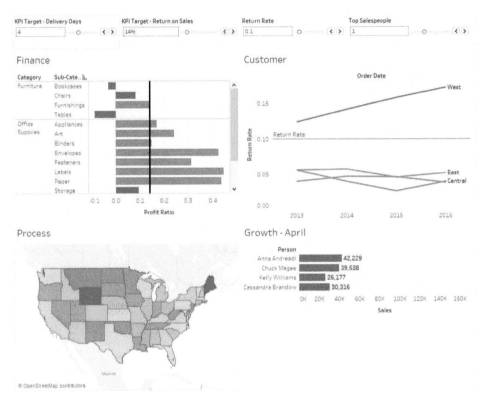

Part 4: Address and Refine Results

Now that you've created the dashboard, take a moment to interpret the results.

Q8.   Which product categories have fallen below the profit goal of 13 percent?

Q9.   Which states are taking significantly more than four days to ship to?

Q10. Which region(s) has (have) experienced a higher than 10 percent return rate from customers?

Q11. Which sales representative is leading the rest for the most recent month?

End of Lab

Lab 7-3 Comprehensive Case: Dillard's Store Data: Creating KPIs in Excel (Part I)

Company summary

Dillard's is a department store with approximately 330 stores in 29 states. Its headquarters is in Little Rock, Arkansas. You can learn more about Dillard's by looking at finance.yahoo .com (Ticker symbol = DDS) and the Wikipedia site for DDS. You'll quickly note that William T. Dillard II is an accounting grad of the University of Arkansas and the Walton College of Business, which may be why he shared transaction data with us to make available for this lab and labs throughout this text.

Data

If you completed comprehensive Labs 3-4 and Labs 3-5, you can use the same Excel file that you created and saved in Lab 3-5.

If you did not complete those labs, you will need to extract those data and load them into Excel using the following query. If you need to review how to extract data from SQL Server and load them into Excel, see Part 3 of Comprehensive Labs 3-4. Steps 4.1–4.5 are the same steps necessary to load the data into Excel.

```
Select Transact.*, Store.STATE
From Transact
Inner Join Store
On Transact.Store = Store.STORE
Where TRAN_DATE BETWEEN '20160901' and '20160915'
Order By Tran_Date
```

Software needed

- Microsoft SQL Server Management Studio (available on the Remote Desktop at the University of Arkansas)
- Excel 2016 (available on the Remote Desktop at the University of Arkansas)
- Power Pivot Excel add-in. To create a date table, we'll extract and load the data through Power Pivot instead of through the Get & Transform tab. If you don't see Power Pivot as a tab in the Excel ribbon, you will need to activate the add-in.

In this lab, you will:

- Learn to build a KPI. In this case, we are trying to assess whether we are improving sales over the same date a year earlier.
- Specifically, create a baseline measure in Excel and set a target value. These two measures will be used to create a KPI to compare sales data across two different periods.

a. From the **File** tab on the ribbon, open **Options**.

Source: Microsoft Excel 2016.

b. Select **Add-ins** from the left side of the **Excel Options** window.

Source: Microsoft Excel 2016.

c. From the drop-down window at the bottom of the **Add-ins** screen, select **COM add-ins**, then click **Go. . .**

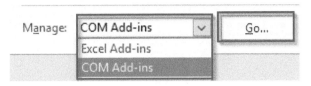

Source: Microsoft Excel 2016.

d. Place a check mark in the box next to **Microsoft Power Pivot for Excel**, then click **OK**.

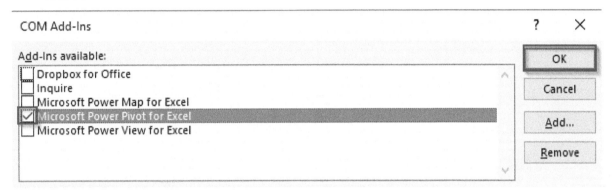

Source: Microsoft Excel 2016.

Part 1: Identify the Questions

Our question for this lab is whether sales from September 1 to September 15, 2016, are different (better, worse, approximately the same) than the average sales from the same time period in 2015.

Q1. Why would comparing current year sales to prior year sales be useful?

Part 2: Mastering the Data and Performing the Analysis

While you loaded the data into the spreadsheet originally with a query from an external data source, that didn't automatically load it into Excel's Internal Data Model. Excel has a way to super-charge its conditional formatting by creating KPIs in Power Pivot. Power Pivot is a plug-in to Excel 2013 and 2010 and compares pre-prepared as an add-in to Excel 2016. Because you'll be using Excel in Walton College's virtual lab, you'll have access to Excel 2016. To create KPIs in Excel, the data must be added to the Internal Data Model.

- Identify a base performance metric, and create a **measure**. Measures can be implicit or explicit.
  - Implicit measures are measures created in a PivotTable—anytime you drag and drop a field into the values section of the PivotTable, it becomes an implicit measure. Implicit measures are restricted to the value field settings' standard aggregations (SUM, COUNT, MIN, MAX, DISTINCTCOUNT, or AVG). These implicit measures cannot be used to create KPIs.
  - Explicit measures can be created in the Power Pivot Data Model window or in the Excel main window Form the Measure dialog box in the Power Pivot tab on the Excel ribbon.
- Identify a **target value** to compare the measure to the baseline.
- Create a **KPI** to signal performance of the measure in comparison to the baseline.

1. From the **Insert** tab on the ribbon, click **PivotTable**.

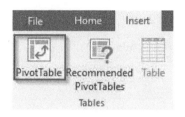

Source: Microsoft Excel 2016.

2. In the **Create PivotTable** window, make sure to place a check mark in the box next to **Add this data to the Data Model**. Then click **OK**.

Source: Microsoft Excel 2016.

3. Once the PivotTable has been created (this may take a few moments as the data are loaded into the data model), you can create a measure and a KPI. Navigate to the **Power Pivot** tab in the ribbon.
   Click **Measures**, then select **New Measure. . .**

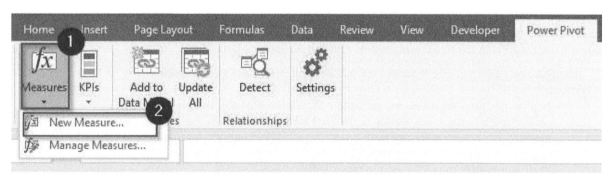

Source: Microsoft Excel 2016.

4. The new measure's name defaults to **Measure 1**, which isn't very descriptive. Because we'll be measuring average Transaction amount, we'll change the name to **AVG(Tran_Amt)**. Type AVG(Tran_Amt) over the default text.

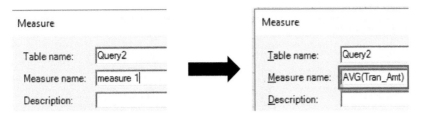

Source: Microsoft Excel 2016.

5. The formula will auto-populate as you type. Begin typing average, and then begin typing the field Tran_Amt to fill in the formula.

Source: Microsoft Excel 2016.

6. The category has no bearing on how the measure or the KPI will work. For this measure, we'll leave it on the default of **General**. Click **OK** to create the measure.

Source: Microsoft Excel 2016.

7. If you scroll down on the **PivotTable Fields** window, you will see that the explicit measure has been added to the bottom of the field list.

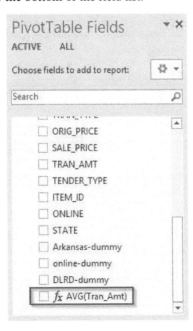

Source: Microsoft Excel 2016.

8. Now we will create the KPI. In the Power Pivot tab of the ribbon, click **KPIs** and select **New KPI. . .**

Source: Microsoft Excel 2016.

9. Because you have only one measure added to this spreadsheet for now, the base field defaults to your newly created measure. If you had more than one measure, you would use the drop-down to select the measure you wanted to use for your base field. The target value can be defined by another measure or by an absolute value. For this first KPI, we'll define it by an Absolute Value. Let's assume that **Dillard's** has a goal of averaging at least $28 per Transaction.

   Input **28** as the **Absolute value** for the target value.

   Leave the default for the **status thresholds**.

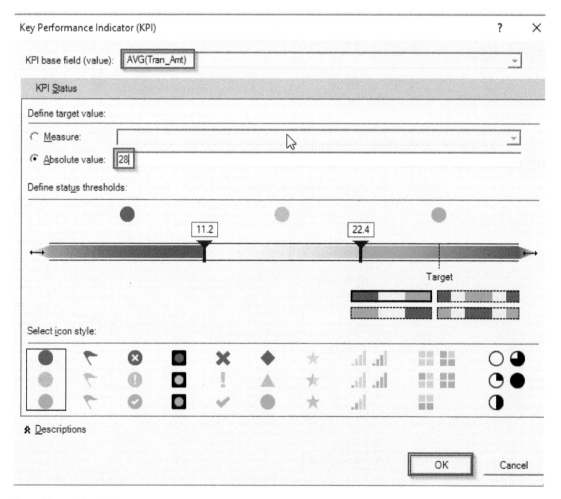

Source: Microsoft Excel 2016.

Q2. Why might you want to edit the status thresholds? Does 22.4 seem low for the upper limit?

10. Now that you have your KPI created, you can see each of them in the PivotTable Fields list.

Occasionally, if the KPI status was automatically added to your PivotTable, the stoplight signals show as −1, 0, and 1. If you remove the status field from the field list and put it back in, this will correct the issue and the stoplight icons will show.

If you expand the KPI fields, you see three options:

- The Value (2016 Sales) will show the actual sale totals associated with the year 2016 (or sliced by month or day, depending on the other values you drill into in the PivotTable).
- The Goal will show 2015 sales totals—this is the measure that you are using to compare 2016 sales against. The Goal is for the sales to be at least 2 percent higher than the previous year's sales.
- The Status will show stoplight icons indicating red, yellow, or green circles based on the thresholds you selected when setting the KPI.

11. Create a PivotTable that shows the KPI status for average Transaction by each of the 15 days in your data range.
12. Take a screenshot (label 7-3A).

Q3. How did **Dillard's** perform in September 2016 compared to September 2015? Do you think the target is set too high or too low? Which day(s) performed the worst, compared to the same date(s) in the previous period? Why do you think that is?

End of Lab

Lab 7-4 Comprehensive Case: Dillard's Store Data: Creating KPIs in Excel (Part II)

Company summary

Dillard's is a department store with approximately 330 stores in 29 states. Its headquarters is in Little Rock, Arkansas. You can learn more about **Dillard's** by looking at finance.yahoo.com (Ticker symbol = DDS) and the Wikipedia site for DDS. You'll quickly note that William T. Dillard II is an accounting grad of the University of Arkansas and the Walton College of Business, which may be why he shared transaction data with us to make available for this lab and labs throughout this text.

Data

The data for this lab and other all **Dillard's** labs are available at http://walton.uark.edu/enterprise/. Your instructor will either give you specific instructions on how to access the data, or there will be information available on connect. The 2016 **Dillard's** data cover all transactions over the period 1/1/2014 to 10/17/2016.

Software needed

- Microsoft SQL Server Management Studio (available on the Remote Desktop at the University of Arkansas)
- Excel 2016 (available on the Remote Desktop at the University of Arkansas)

In this lab, you will:

- Compare total sales across all Dillard's stores year over year, month over month, and day over day and develop it as a KPI.

Part 1: Identify the Questions

Compare 2014, 2015, and 2016 sales data in parallel periods.

Part 2: Master the Data

1. Before we can create measures and KPIs to analyze the data, we need to extract the data from SQL Server and load them into Excel. To do so, click **New Query** from the **Data** tab, and follow the path to select **From Database** and **From SQL Server Database**.

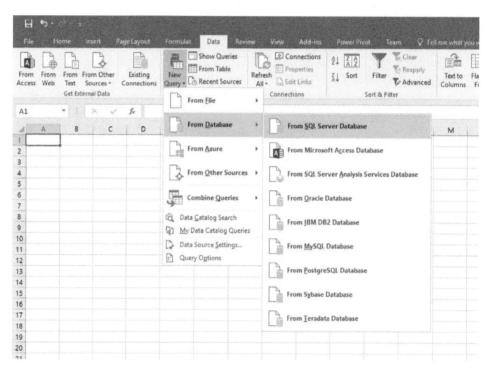

Source: Microsoft Excel 2016.

2. Enter the **Server** name and the **Database** name as provided to you through the walton.uark.edu/enterprise site, and then click **Advanced options** to input the query text:

   Select year(Tran_Date) as year, month(Tran_Date) as month, day(Tran_Date) as day, sum(Tran_Amt) as amount

   From TRANSACT

   Where TRAN_TYPE = 'P'

   Group By year(Tran_Date), month(Tran_Date), day(Tran_Date)

   Order By year(Tran_Date), month(Tran_Date), day(Tran_Date)

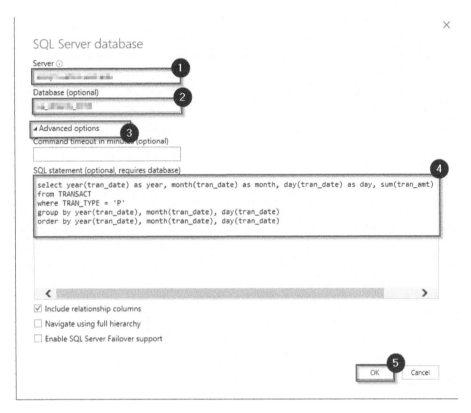

Source: Microsoft Excel 2016.

3. Click **OK**.
4. A preview of your data will load. Instead of immediately loading these data into Excel, you need to transform them in the **Query Editor**. Click **Edit**.

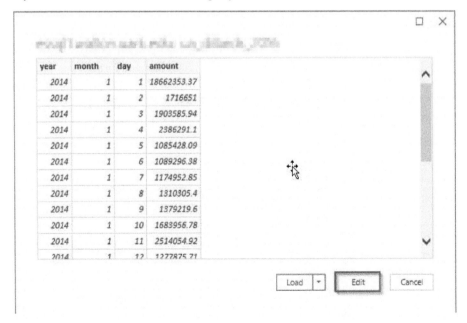

Source: Microsoft Excel 2016.

The data have been fully extracted from SQL Server into Excel's Internal Data Model, but they need to be transformed so that we can more easily compare daily sales amounts year over year. Instead of seeing a separate record for each day, beginning with January 1, 2014, and ending with October 17, 2016, we would prefer to see only 365 records—one record for each day in a calendar year, but with separate columns for each year (2014, 2015, and 2016), each with the transaction amount associated with that year's month and day.

5. Select the **year** column.
6. Select **Pivot Column** from the **Transform** tab on the **Query Editor** ribbon.

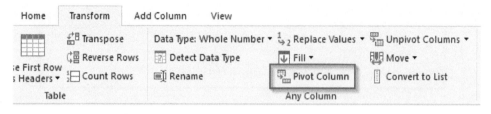

Source: Microsoft Excel 2016.

7. Select **Amount** from the drop-down for the **Values** column and click **OK**.

Source: Microsoft Excel 2016.

8. Now that the data have been transformed, we're ready to load them into Excel. From the **Home** button on the **Query Editor**'s ribbon, click **Close and Load**.
9. Excel has a way to super-charge its conditional formatting by creating KPIs in Power Pivot. In the **Create PivotTable** window, make sure to place a check mark in the box next to **Add this data to the Data Model**. Then click **OK**.

Source: Microsoft Excel 2016.

Once the PivotTable has been created (this may take a few moments as the data are loaded into the data model), you can create a measure and a KPI. KPIs require three decisions:

- Identify a base performance metric, and create a measure. Measures can be implicit or explicit.
    - Implicit measures are measures created in a PivotTable—anytime you drag and drop a field into the values section of the PivotTable, it becomes an implicit measure. Implicit measures are restricted to the value field settings' standard aggregations (SUM, COUNT, MIN, MAX, DISTINCTCOUNT, or AVG). These implicit measures cannot be used to create KPIs.
    - Explicit measures can be created in the Power Pivot Data Model window or in the Excel main window from the Measure dialog box in the Power Pivot tab on the Excel ribbon.
- Identify a target value to compare the measure to.
- Create a KPI to signal performance of the measure in comparison to the baseline, and determine the range of values that indicate poor performance, good performance, and great performance.

We will need to create three measures, the sums of each of the year's sales Transactions.

10. Navigate to the **Power Pivot** tab in the ribbon. Click **Measures**, then Select **New Measure. . .**

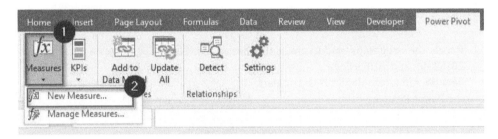

Source: Microsoft Excel 2016.

11. The new measure's name defaults to **Measure 1**, which isn't very descriptive. Because we'll be measuring average transaction amount, we'll change the first KPI's name to **2014 Sales**. Type 2014 Sales over the default text.

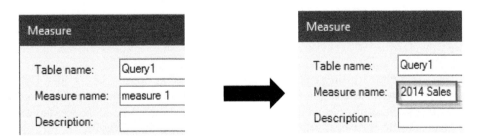

Source: Microsoft Excel 2016.

12. The formula will auto-populate as you type, begin typing SUM, then fill in the parentheses with the column name **2014**.
13. At the bottom of the Measure window is an option to select a category. The Category has no bearing on how the measure or the KPI will work. For this measure, we'll leave it on the default of **General**. Click **OK** to create the measure.

Measure

Table name: Query1

Measure name: measure 1

Description:

Formula: f_x | Check formula

```
=SUM([2014])
=SUM(ColumnName)
```

Formatting Options

Category:

```
General
Number
Currency
Date
TRUE/FALSE
```

OK | Cancel

Source: Microsoft Excel 2016.

14. Repeat the same steps used to create the measure for 2014 sales to create measures for 2015 sales and 2016 sales.

15. Now we will create the KPIs to compare 2015 sales to 2014, and 2016 sales to 2015. In the Power Pivot tab of the ribbon, click **KPIs** and select **New KPI. . .**

Source: Microsoft Excel 2016

16. The first KPI we will create is comparing 2016 sales to the previous year's sales. Use the drop-down to select 2016 Sales for your base field. The target value can be defined by another measure or by an absolute value. We have already defined the measure to compare 2016 sales to, so select 2015 Sales for the target value Measure.

We will define excellent performance as a 2 percent improvement over last year's sales, so move the upper range of the target slider to 102%. Poor performance will be defined as a 2 percent decline from last year's sales. Move the lower range of the target slider to 98%.

Q1. Do you think +/− 2 percent is the right benchmark to set? Would you propose a different percentage change to track here?

Once all of your settings are correct, click OK to create the KPI.

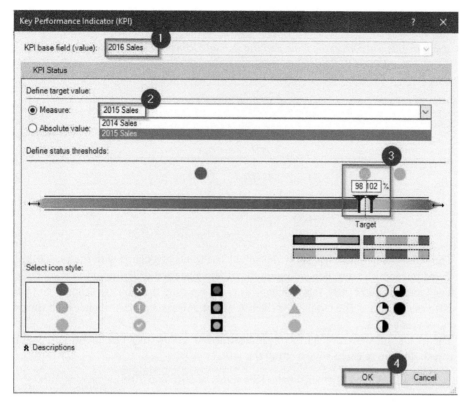

Source: Microsoft Excel 2016.

17. Create the KPI comparing 2015 sales to 2014 sales using the same thresholds for measuring performance.

18. Now that you have your two KPIs created, you can see each of them in the PivotTable Fields list.

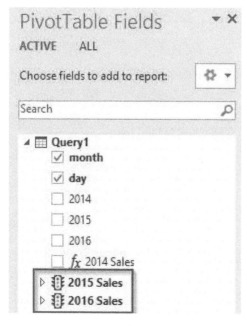

Source: Microsoft Excel 2016.

Occasionally, if the KPI status is automatically added to your PivotTable, the stoplight signals show as −1, 0, and 1. If you remove the status field from the fields list and put it back in, this will correct the issue and the stoplight icons will show.

If you expand the KPI fields, you see three options:

- The Value (2016 Sales) will show the actual sale totals associated with the year 2016 (or sliced by month or day, depending on the other values you drill into in the PivotTable).
- The Goal will show 2015 sales totals—this is the measure that you are using to compare 2016 sales against. The Goal is for the sales to be at least 2 percent higher than the previous year's sales.
- The Status will show stoplight icons indicating red, yellow, or green circles based on the thresholds you selected when setting the KPI.

19. Create a PivotTable that shows the KPI status of 2015 and 2016 sales by month.

To do so, drag and drop **Months** into the **Rows** and Status for both KPIs into the **Values**.

If you just place a check mark in the box next to the month field, you will notice that the PivotTable defaults to reading Month values as numerical data instead of calendar data, so it places it as a value and sums the month numbers. You just need to drag and drop it outside of Values and into Rows.

20. Take a Screenshot (label it 7-4A).
21. To provide some drill-down capabilities, add the **Day** field to the **Rows** (beneath **Month**).

> Q2. Do you notice a pattern with how frequently the "bad" (red icon) days appear in 2016 in relation to 2015?
>
> Q3. What do you think is the potential problem with comparing days (e.g., comparing September 1, 2016 to September 1, 2015)? How could this be improved?

End of Lab

Lab 7-5   Comprehensive Case: Dillard's Store Data: Creating KPIs in Excel (Part III)

Company summary

Dillard's is a department store with approximately 330 stores in 29 states. Its headquarters is in Little Rock, Arkansas. You can learn more about **Dillard's** by looking at finance.yahoo.com (Ticker symbol = DDS) and the Wikipedia site for DDS. You'll quickly note that William T. Dillard II is an accounting grad of the University of Arkansas and the Walton College of Business, which may be why he shared transaction data with us to make available for this lab and labs throughout this text.

Data

The data for this lab and other all **Dillard's** labs are available at http://walton.uark.edu/enterprise/. Your instructor will either give you specific instructions on how to access the data, or there will be information available on connect. The 2016 **Dillard's** data cover all transactions over the period 1/1/2014 to 10/17/2016.

Software needed

- Microsoft SQL Server Management Studio (available on the Remote Desktop at the University of Arkansas)
- Excel 2016 (available on the Remote Desktop at the University of Arkansas)
- Power Pivot Excel add-in. To create a date table, we'll extract and load the data through Power Pivot instead of through the Get & Transform tab. If you don't see Power Pivot as a tab in the Excel ribbon, you will need to activate the add-in.

a. From the **File** tab on the ribbon, open **Options**.

Source: Microsoft Excel 2016.

b. Select **Add-ins** from the left side of the **Excel Options** window.

Source: Microsoft Excel 2016.

c. From the drop-down window at the bottom of the **Add-ins** screen, select **COM add-ins**, then click **Go. . .**

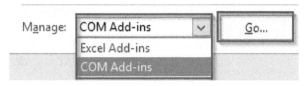

Source: Microsoft Excel 2016.

d. Place a check mark in the box next to **Microsoft Power Pivot for Excel**, then click **OK**.

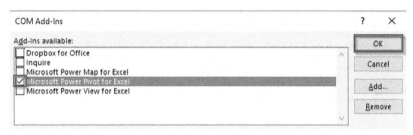

Source: Microsoft Excel 2016.

Part 1: Identify the Questions

How do we line up sales periods to be in parallel periods, by day of week in one period with day of week with previous period?

Part 2: Master the Data

1. To extract and load the data into Power Pivot, click **Manage** on the **Power Pivot** tab in the Excel ribbon.

Source: Microsoft Excel 2016.

2. In the **Power Pivot for Excel** window, click **Get External Data** from the **Home** tab, then navigate through **From Database** and **From SQL Server**.

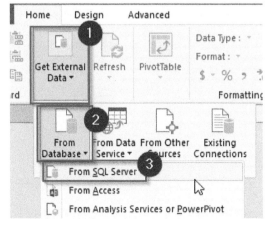

Source: Microsoft Excel 2016.

3. The **Table Import Wizard** window will open. Input the SQL Server name and the Database name that you received from Walton.uark.edu/enterprise, then click **Next**.

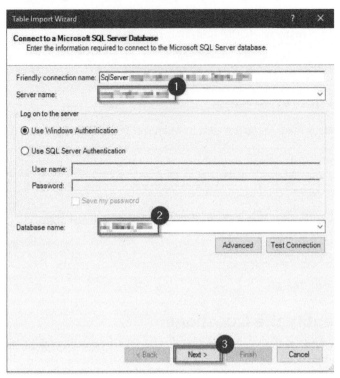

Source: Microsoft Excel 2016.

4. We will import the data with a query, so select the radio button next to Write a query that will specify the data to import.

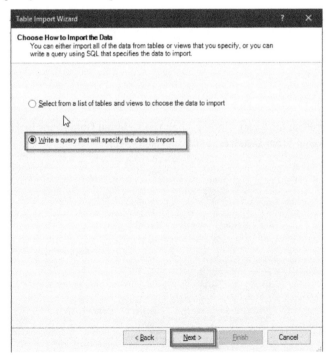

Source: Microsoft Excel 2016.

5. We need to bring in only two attributes. In Lab 7-2, we had to parse out the different date parts in order to group our data by month and year, instead of just by day. In this lab, we will use Excel's Power Pivot tool to create a **Date** table. The tool will be able to parse out the date parts for us, instead of us having to do so with our query. This will also allow us to view more interesting date parts, such as the day of the week (not just the date).

Input the following query into the **Table Import Wizard** window to extract the total amount of Transactions for each day in the database:

> Select Tran_Date, SUM(Tran_Amt) AS Sales
> From Transact
> Group By Tran_Date

After entering the SQL text, click Validate to ensure the query will run, and then click Finish.

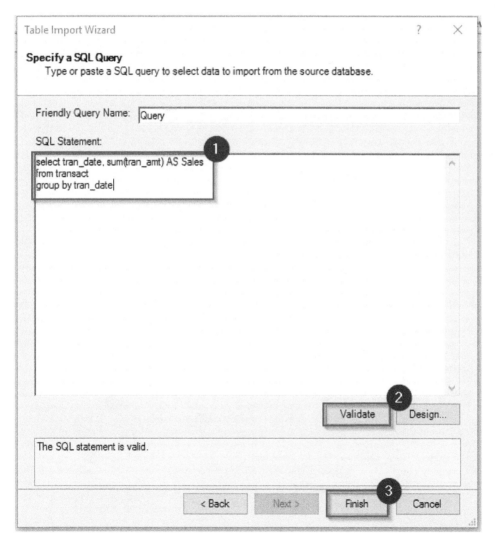

Source: Microsoft Excel 2016.

The table will import. This may take a few moments.

6. Once the data are loaded, you can close the **Table Import Wizard** window. Click **Close**.

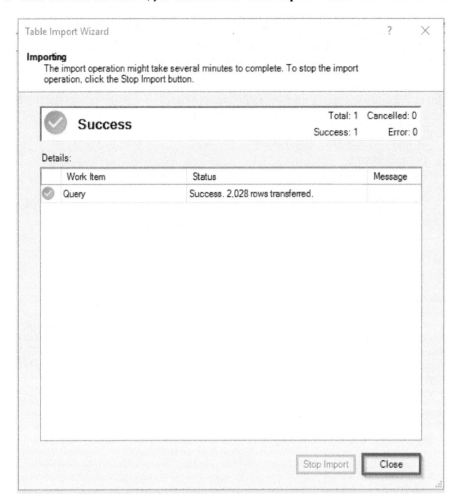

Source: Microsoft Excel 2016.

7. After closing the **Table Import Wizard**, you will see your data loaded into Power Pivot. This does not mean the data have been loaded into Excel yet, so you can transform the data within the Power Pivot tool first. Creating the date table takes three steps: Select the **Tran_Date** column, click **Date** Table from the **Design** tab on the ribbon, then click **New**.

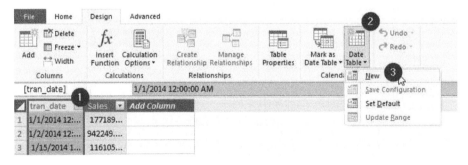

Source: Microsoft Excel 2016.

You have created a **Date** table. Now it's time to load the transformed data into Excel.

8. Return to the **Home** tab on the **Power Pivot** ribbon, and select **PivotTable**.

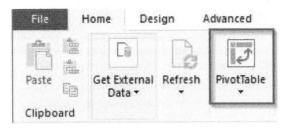

Source: Microsoft Excel 2016.

9. Select **OK** to create the PivotTable in a New Worksheet.

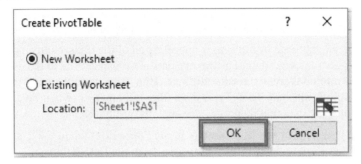

Source: Microsoft Excel 2016.

The PivotTable Fields list contains two tables, **Calendar** and **Query**. The **Calendar** table contains the **Date Hierarchy** for drilling down, but it also contains attributes beneath the **More Fields** title. These contain the same attributes in the hierarchy, as well as different ways of viewing the data, such as **Day of Week**. The **Query** table contains the data that you extracted with your SQL query. The valuable field from the query table is **Sales**, which you will use as a value (or an implicit measure).

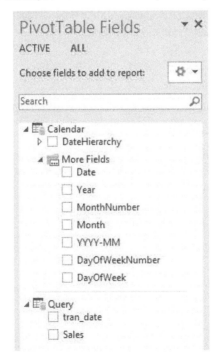

Source: Microsoft Excel 2016.

Part 3: Perform an Analysis of the Data

10. Create a PivotTable to compare sales performance on different weekdays of each month, year over year. To do so, drag and drop year (from the **Calendar > More fields** drop-down) into **Columns**, **Month** and **DayofWeek** into **Rows**, and **Sales** into **Values**). The Sales data will be transformed into a measure, Sum of Sales, automatically.

11. Take a screenshot (label it 7-5A).

Q1. Something should seem a bit off with your numbers. There are some big disparities month over month for some weekdays. Look back over our query and the ER Diagram (and if you completed Lab 7-2, compare the query you executed in this lab to the query from that lab). What did we leave out of this query? How could it cause us to make poor decisions?

Part 4: Analyze and Refine the Results

The query can be improved by not simply importing all of the transaction amount data, but by bringing in only the sales data. The way the data are organized, all of the dollar amounts for sales and for refunds are in the same attribute, Tran_Amt, and the transaction type is differentiated with the attribute Tran_Type. If we filter out any record that holds return data, we can load only the data that hold sales transactions into Excel.

12. To edit our original query, click **Manage** in the **Power Pivot** tab in the Excel ribbon.

13. In the **Power Pivot** tool, click **Table Properties** from the **Design** tab.

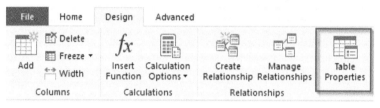

Source: Microsoft Excel 2016.

14. Add in a WHERE clause to the query, validate the new query, and save it.

```
Select Tran_Date, SUM(Tran_Amt) AS Sales
From Transact
Where Tran_Type = 'p'
Group By Tran_Date
```

Source: Microsoft Excel 2016.

15. The data will be automatically refreshed in the **Power Pivot** tool and in the Excel worksheet with the PivotTable. Close the **Power Pivot** tool.

Part 5: Communicate Results

The refreshed data in the PivotTable is better for making decisions with, but it still isn't easy to read at a glance. Adding some data visualization or conditional formatting can make these data more meaningful and easier to interpret.

Q2. What would be the best way to visualize these data to ease decision making and insight?

End of Lab

Lab 7-6 Comprehensive Case: Dillard's Store Data: Creating KPIs in Excel (Part IV—Putting It All Together)

Company summary

Dillard's is a department store with approximately 330 stores in 29 states. Its headquarters is in Little Rock, Arkansas. You can learn more about Dillard's by looking at finance.yahoo .com (Ticker symbol = DDS) and the Wikipedia site for DDS. You'll quickly note that William T. Dillard II is an accounting grad of the University of Arkansas and the Walton College of Business, which may be why he shared Transaction data with us to make available for this lab and labs throughout this text.

Data

The data for this lab and other all Dillard's labs are available at http://walton.uark.edu/ enterprise/. Your instructor will either give you specific instructions on how to access the data, or there will be information available on connect. The 2016 Dillard's data cover all transactions over the period 1/1/2014 to 10/17/2016.

Software needed

- Microsoft SQL Server Management Studio (available on the Remote Desktop at the University of Arkansas)
- Excel 2016 (available on the Remote Desktop at the University of Arkansas)
- Power Pivot Excel add-in. To create a date table, we'll extract and load the data through Power Pivot instead of through the Get & Transform tab. If you don't see Power Pivot as a tab in the Excel ribbon, you will need to activate the add-in.

In this lab, you will:

- Develop a dashboard to display a variety of KPIs that you can drill into for state and store details.

Prerequisite

- **Labs 7-4 and 7-5.** If you haven't completed these labs, then you can still read through the steps in Labs 7-4 and 7-5 to see the screenshots of the ETL process in Excel (Lab 7-5) and the KPI creation process (Lab 7-4) to be ready for this lab.

Part 1: Identify the Questions

In Lab 7-4, you created KPIs for comparing 2015 sales to 2014 sales, but the date was parsed out from the original Tran_Date attribute. In Lab 7-5, you created a date table so that the date fields were more descriptive in the Excel report, but you didn't create any KPIs. In this lab, we will combine those two skills to create a descriptive report with KPIs. We will also expand the reports capabilities by extracting and loading state and store data in addition to date and transaction data.

Part 2: Master the Data

1. Loading the data into Tableau from the original SQL Server database requires some transformation in Excel's Power Pivot tool. Extract and load Dillard's transactional and store data into Power Pivot using the following query:

```
Select Tran_Date, State, Store.Store, SUM(Tran_Amt) AS Amount
From Transact
Inner Join Store
On Transact.Store = Store.Store
Where Tran_Type = 'p'
Group By Tran_Date, State, Store.Store
Order By Tran_Date
```

2. It will take a few minutes for these data to load. Once they do (297,702 rows), close the **Table Import Wizard** window. Locate the **Tran_Date** attribute and use it to create a **Date Table** (*Hint:* Look in the **Design** tab.)
3. Now that you have two tables in your data model, return to the **Home** tab to create a **PivotTable** in Excel, and close the **Power Pivot** tool.
4. In the **Power Pivot** tab in the Excel ribbon, create a new measure for Sum(amount). You can call this measure **Current Year**. This measure will be used as a base measure to compare to previous year's sales data.
5. Open the window to create a new measure to calculate the previous year's sales. To create this measure, you will use Microsoft's Data Analysis Expressions language (DAX), which is a formula language for creating custom calculations and measures. The function you will use is the =CALCULATE function, which allows you to not only create a calculation, but also filter it.

    Enter the following expression in the **formula box**:

```
=CALCULATE([Sum of Amount],SAMEPERIODLASTYEAR('Calendar'[Date]))
```

    You can name this measure **Last Year**.
6. Create a new KPI, setting Current Year as the Base Measure and Last Year as the Target Measure. Change the Status Thresholds to the following:
    ○ Anything below 98 percent of last year's sales (the target) should be red.
    ○ Anything between 98 percent and 102 percent of the target should be yellow.
    ○ Anything above 102 percent of the target should be green.
7. This KPI will function only with the Date Hierarchy (not with the date parts). Create a PivotTable with the **Date Hierarchy** on the rows and the KPI Status as the values (if the KPI status is showing −1, 0, and 1 instead of the stoplight icons, remove the KPI status from the value fields and then place it back in).

    Create another KPI, this time to compare any month with the month that precedes it (so instead of comparing September 2016 to September 2015, you will compare September 2016 to August 2016).
8. Even though the calculation for current month is technically the same as the calculation for current year (Sum(Amount)), we have to create a new measure to use as the

KPI's base. Each base measure can only have one KPI assigned to it. Create a new measure called **Current Month** to calculate sales (this will be the exact same as how you created **Current Year** in step 4, but with a different Measure Name).

9. Create a new measure to use as the monthly target measure. The DAX expression for calculating last month's sales is:

=CALCULATE([Sum of Amount],PREVIOUSMONTH('Calendar'[Date]))

You can name this measure **Previous Month**.

10. Create a new KPI comparing current sales (your base measure) to previous month as your target measure. Create the same status thresholds as the KPI comparing years (<98%, 98%–102%, >102%).

11. Add this KPI status to your PivotTable.

12. Take a screenshot (label it 7-6A).

Part 3: Address and Refine the Results

This report may be useful at a very high level, but for state-level and store-level analysis, the level is too high. Next, we will add in two slicers to help filter the data based on state and store.

13. From the **PivotTable Analyze** tab in the Excel ribbon, click **Slicer** to insert an interactive filter.

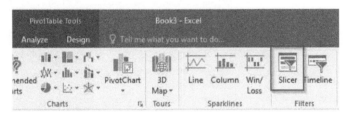

Source: Microsoft Excel 2016.

14. Place a check mark in the boxes next to **State** and **Store** to create the slicers.

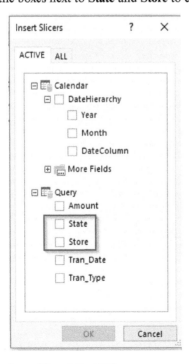

Source: Microsoft Excel 2016.

15. Notice what happens as you select different states: Not only do the data change to reflect the KPI status for the state that you selected, but the stores that are associated with that state shift to the top of the store slicer, making it easier to drill down.

16. Take a screenshot (label it 7-6B).

We can ease drill-down capabilities even more by creating a hierarchy between state and store.

17. Open the **Power Pivot** tool by clicking **Manage** from the **Power Pivot** tab in the Excel ribbon.

18. From the **Power Pivot Home** tab, switch to **Diagram View**.

Source: Microsoft Excel 2016.

19. Select both the **State** and the **Store** attributes from the **Query** table, then right-click one of the attributes to create a hierarchy.

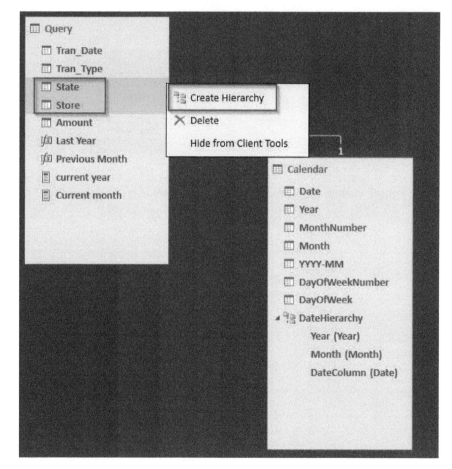

Source: Microsoft Excel 2016.

20. You can change the name of the **Hierarchy** to **Store** and **State Hierarchy**.

21. Close the **Power Pivot** tool. The PivotTable will have refreshed automatically.

22. You will see that the hierarchy has been added to your PivotTable Fields list. Drag and drop the hierarchy to the Rows (above the Date hierarchy).

23. Take a screenshot (label it 7-6C).

Source: Microsoft Excel 2016.

Now you can drill down from **State** to **Store** directly in the PivotTable, or you can filter it via the slicer.

Q1. How does the ability to drill down into the state and store data give management critical information and help them to identify issues that are occurring or opportunities that might be available?

Q2. What would you get sales changes of certain products (SKUs) or product categories from one month to the next? Having this type of information will help you do what to help plan future promotions or future purchases?

End of Lab

Chapter 8
Financial Statement Analytics

A Look at This Chapter

In this chapter, we focus on how to access and analyze financial statement data. We highlight the use of XBRL to quickly and efficiently gain computer access to financial statement data. Next, we discuss how ratios are used to analyze financial performance. We also discuss the use of sparklines to help users visualize trends in the data. Finally, we discuss the use of text mining to analyze the sentiment in financial reporting data.

A Look Back

Chapter 7 focused on generating and evaluating key performance metrics that are used primarily in managerial accounting. By measuring past performance and comparing it to targeted goals, we are able to assess how well a company is working toward a goal. Also, we can determine required adjustments to how decisions are made or how business processes are run, if any.

Sometimes the future is now. The StockSnips app uses sentiment analysis, machine learning, and artificial intelligence to aggregate and analyze news related to publicly traded companies on **Nasdaq** and the **New York Stock Exchange** to "gain stock insights and track a company's financial and business operations." The use of Data Analytics helps classify the news to help predict revenue, earnings, and cash flows and uses those data to help predict stock price performance that is most relevant to predicting company performance. What will Data Analytics do next?

©S Narayan/Dinodia Photo/agefotostock

EXHIBIT 8-1

OBJECTIVES

After reading this chapter, you should be able to:

LO 8-1   Describe how XBRL tags financial reporting data

LO 8-2   Understand how different types of ratio analysis can be facilitated by XBRL

LO 8-3   Explain how to create and read visualizations of financial statement data

LO 8-4   Describe the value of text mining and sentiment analysis of financial reporting

XBRL

LO 8-1

Describe how
XBRL tags financial
reporting data

XBRL is a global standard for Internet communication among businesses. XBRL stands for eXtensible Business Reporting Language and is a type of XML (extensible markup language) used for organizing and defining financial elements. By each company providing tags for each piece of its financial data, XBRL data can be computer readable and immediately available for each type of financial statement user, be they financial analysts, investors, or lenders, for their own specific use.

As of June 2011, the Securities and Exchange Commission requires all public company filers to file financial statements prepared in accordance with U.S. GAAP (generally accepted accounting principles), including smaller reporting companies, and all foreign private issuers to tag their financial statements in accordance with XBRL. This includes tagging the five basic financial statements:

- Balance sheet
- Income statement
- Statement of comprehensive income
- Statement of cash flows
- Statement of stockholders' equity

In addition, detailed tagging of the numbers included in the footnotes by use of XBRL tags is also required. This means that numbers in the footnotes (e.g., facts, figures, years, and percentages) are also tagged, as well as the text disclosure of the major footnotes.

XBRL uses a taxonomy to help define and describe each key data element (like cash or accounts payable). The **XBRL taxonomy** also defines the relationships between each element—such as cash being a component of current assets and current assets being a component of total assets or accounts payable being a component of current liabilities and current liabilities, in turn, being a component of total liabilities.

The 2017 U.S. GAAP Financial Reporting Taxonomy is found at this website: https://xbrl.us/xbrl-taxonomy/2017-us-gaap/. It defines more than 19,000 elements. Using such a taxonomy, each unique financial data item is tagged to an element within the taxonomy.

For example, the XBRL tag for cash is labeled "Cash" and is defined as follows:

> Amount of currency on hand as well as demand deposits with banks or financial institutions. Includes other kinds of accounts that have the general characteristics of demand deposits. Excludes cash and cash equivalents within disposal group and discontinued operation.[1]

The XBRL tag for cash and cash equivalents footnote disclosure is labeled as "CashAndCashEquivalentsDisclosureTextBlock" and is defined as follows:

> The entire disclosure for cash and cash equivalent footnotes, which may include the types of deposits and money market instruments, applicable carrying amounts, restricted amounts and compensating balance arrangements. Cash and equivalents include: (1) currency on hand (2) demand deposits with banks or financial institutions (3) other kinds of accounts that have the general characteristics of demand deposits (4) short-term, highly liquid investments that are both readily convertible to known amounts of cash and so near their maturity that they present insignificant risk of changes in value because of changes in interest rates. Generally, only investments maturing within three months from the date of acquisition qualify.[2]

---

[1]https://xbrl.us/xbrl-taxonomy/2017-us-gaap/
[2]https://xbrl.us/xbrl-taxonomy/2017-us-gaap/

The use of tags allows data to be quickly transmitted and received, and the tags serve as an input for financial analysts valuing a company, an auditor finding areas where an error might occur, or regulators seeing if firms are in compliance with various regulations and laws (like the SEC or IRS).

Extensible Reporting in XBRL and Standardized Metrics

The next thing to note is that the X in XBRL stands for "extensible," which means firms can make their own tags if they feel their financial data item does not fit within the existing framework. Between having some 19,000 financial elements to choose from and the ability of firms to make their own tags, sometimes the comparability of quite similar financial data items have unique tags, making direct comparisons between companies difficult if not impossible. Sometimes outside data vendors create **standardized metrics** to make the company reported XBRL data more comparable. For example, Calcbench, a data vendor that eases financial analysis for XBRL uses, makes standardized metrics, noting:

> IBM labels revenue as "Total revenue" and uses the tag "Revenues", whereas Apple, labels their revenue as "Net sales" and uses the tag "SalesRevenueNet". This is a relatively simple case, because both companies used tags from the FASB taxonomy.

> Users are typically not interested in the subtle differences of how companies tag or label information. In the previous example, most users would want Apple and IBM's revenue, regardless of how it was tagged. To that end, we create standardized metrics.[3]

Different data vendors such as XBRLAnalyst and Calcbench both provide a trace function that allows you to trace the standardized metric back to the original source to see which XBRL tags are referenced or used to make up the standardized metric.[4]

Exhibit 8-2 shows what a report using standardized metrics looks like for Boeing's balance sheet. Note the standardized tags used for Boeing could be used for any of the SEC filers to gather their balance sheet and other financial statements.

XBRL, XBRL-GL, and Real-Time Financial Reporting

Instead of waiting weeks or months to get the financial statements, some suggest real-time financial reporting. That is, the moment a transaction is recorded in the accounting books, it can be put into the financial statements and sent to any interested user. Many financial reporting systems within enterprise systems such as Oracle and SAP have a general ledger that is consistent with XBRL, called **XBRL-GL** (XBRL-General Ledger). That means once the numbers are input into a financial system, they are already tagged and able to be transmitted in real time to interested users.

Of course, there is a multitude of reasons this information is not transmitted in real time. For example, the accounting information has not yet been audited, and it may contain errors. Other information such as goodwill or long-term debt will likely not change on a minute-by-minute basis, so there would be no use for it on a real-time basis. But as systems advance and continuous, real-time auditing becomes more prevalent, and with our understanding of how and exactly what type of real-time information might be used, there may be a chance of providing real-time accounting information in the relative short term by use of XBRL-GL.

---

[3]https://knowledge.calcbench.com/hc/en-us/articles/230017408-What-is-a-standardized-metric (accessed August 2017).
[4]https://knowledge.calcbench.com/hc/en-us/articles/230017408-What-is-a-standardized-metric.

Exhibit 8-2

Balance Sheet from XBRL Data

Note the XBRL tag names in the far left column.

Source: https://www .calcbench.com/xbrl_to_excel

Ticker	BA	Boeing Co	
Year	2015	2014	2013
Period	Y	Y	Y
Calcbench Normalized Point			
Assets			
Current Assets			
Cash	$11,302,000,000	$11,733,000,000	$9,088,000,000
AccountsReceivable	$8,713,000,000	$7,729,000,000	$6,546,000,000
Inventory	$47,257,000,000	$46,756,000,000	$42,912,000,000
PrepaidExpense	#N/A	#N/A	#N/A
CurrentAssets	$68,234,000,000	$67,767,000,000	$65,074,000,000
PPE	$12,076,000,000	$11,007,000,000	$10,224,000,000
Goodwill	$5,126,000,000	$5,119,000,000	$5,043,000,000
LongTermInvestments	$1,284,000,000	$1,154,000,000	$1,204,000,000
Assets	$94,408,000,000	$92,921,000,000	$92,663,000,000
Liabilities And Equity			
AccountsPayable	$10,800,000,000	$10,667,000,000	$9,498,000,000
AccruedLiabilities	$14,014,000,000	$13,462,000,000	$14,131,000,000
ShortTermDebt	$1,234,000,000	$929,000,000	$1,563,000,000
DeferredRevenue	$24,364,000,000	$23,175,000,000	$20,027,000,000
CurrentLiabilities	$50,412,000,000	$48,233,000,000	$51,486,000,000
NonCurrentLiabilities			
LongTermDebt	$8,730,000,000	$8,141,000,000	$8,072,000,000
NonCurrentTaxLiability	$2,392,000,000	#N/A	#N/A
PensionAndOtherPostretirementDe	$17,783,000,000	$17,182,000,000	$10,474,000,000
Liabilities	$88,011,000,000	$84,131,000,000	$77,666,000,000
Equity			
RetainedEarnings	$38,756,000,000	$36,180,000,000	$32,964,000,000
TreasuryStockValue	$29,568,000,000	$23,298,000,000	$17,671,000,000
StockHoldersEquity	$6,397,000,000	$8,790,000,000	$14,997,000,000

✓ **PROGRESS CHECK**

1. How does XBRL facilitate Data Analytics by analysts?
2. How might standardized XBRL metrics be useful in comparing the financial statements of **General Motors, Alphabet,** and **Alibaba**?
3. Assuming XBRL-GL is able to disseminate real-time financial reports, which real-time financial elements (account names) might be most useful to decision makers? And which information might not be useful?

RATIO ANALYSIS

Financial statement analysis is used by investors, analysts, auditors, and other interested stakeholders to review and evaluate a company's financial statements and financial performance. Such analysis allows the stakeholder to gain an understanding of the financial health of the company to allow more insightful and, hopefully, more effective decision making. A major component of financial statement analysis is the use of ratio analysis. **Ratio analysis** is a tool used to evaluate relationships among different financial statement items to help understand a company's financial and operating performance.

LO 8-2

Understand how different types of ratio analysis can be facilitated by XBRL

Financial ratio analysis is a key tool used by accounting, auditing, and finance professionals to assess the financial health of a business organization, to assess the reasonableness of reported financial results, and to predict future performance. Analytical procedures, including ratio analysis, are recognized as an essential component of both planning an audit and carrying out substantive testing. AU Section 329.02 states, "A basic premise underlying the application of analytical procedures is that plausible relationships among data may reasonably be expected to exist and continue in the absence of known conditions to the contrary."[5] In addition, knowledge of financial statement analysis using ratios is a component of several professional certifications, including the CPA (Certified Public Accountant), CMA (Certified Management Accountant), and CFA (Chartered Financial Analyst) certifications, so clearly critical for any accountant.

Auditors will use ratio analysis to pinpoint potential audit issues by considering how a company's financial statements depart from industry performance, a close competitor, or even the same company's prior-year performance. Competitors might use ratio analysis to understand the vulnerabilities of a competitor. Bond investors might use ratio analysis to see if a bond covenant is violated (e.g., some bond contracts require a borrower to maintain a current ratio above 1.0 to help ensure the loan can be paid off). So, you can quickly see how ratios might be used.

These ratios include the current ratio, the receivables turnover ratio, inventory turnover ratio, asset turnover ratio, profit margin ratio, debt-to-equity ratio, return on assets, and return on equity ratios.

Classes of Ratios

There are basically four types of ratios: liquidity, activity, solvency (or financing), and profitability.

Liquidity is the ability to satisfy the company's short-term obligations using assets that can be most readily converted into cash. Liquidity ratios help measure the liquidity of a company. Liquidity ratios include the current ratio and the acid-test ratio.

Activity ratios are a computation of a firm's operating efficiency. Company activity is often measured by use of turnover ratios reflect the number of times assets flow into and out of the company during the period and serve as a gauge of the efficiency of putting assets to work. Receivables, inventory, and total asset turnover are all examples of activity ratios.

We use *solvency* (or sometimes called *financing*) ratios to help assess a company's ability to pay its debts and stay in business. In other words, we assess the company's financial risk—that is, the risk resulting from a company's choice of financing the business using debt or equity. Debt-to-equity, long-term debt-to-equity, and times interest earned ratios are also useful in assessing the level of solvency.

Profitability ratios are a common calculation when assessing a company. They are used to provide information on the profitability of a company and its prospects for the future.

---

[5]AICPA, AU section 329, http://www.aicpa.org/Research/Standards/AuditAttest/DownloadableDocuments/AU-00329.pdf.

DuPont Ratio Analysis

A popular method to analyze performance and ratios is the use of the **DuPont ratio**. The DuPont ratio was developed by the DuPont Corporation to measure performance as a decomposition of the return on equity ratio in this way.

$$\text{Return on equity (ROE)} = \text{Profit margin} \times \text{Operating leverage (or Asset turnover)} \times \text{Financial leverage}$$

$$= (\text{Net profit/Sales}) \times (\text{Net profit/Sales})(\text{Sales/Average total assets}) \times (\text{Average total assets/Average equity})$$

It decomposes return on equity into three different types of ratios: profitability (profit margin), activity (operating leverage or asset turnover), and solvency (financial leverage) ratios. We illustrate it in Exhibit 8-3 by considering a calculation from some standard XBRL data.

Exhibit 8-3
DuPont Analysis Using XBRL Data

Source: https://www.calcbench.com/xbrl_to_excel.

ticker	year	period	revenue	cost of revenue	profit margin	assets	operating leverage	equity	financial leverage	return on equity
DD	2009	Q2	$7,088,000,000	$5,007,000,000	29.4%	$35,258,000,000	20.1%	$7,474,000,000	471.7%	27.8%
DD	2009	Q3	$6,156,000,000	$4,560,000,000	25.9%	$36,168,000,000	17.0%	$8,083,000,000	447.5%	19.7%
DD	2009	Y	$27,328,000,000	$19,708,000,000	27.9%	$38,185,000,000	71.6%	$7,651,000,000	499.1%	99.6%
DD	2010	Q1	$8,844,000,000	$5,796,000,000	34.5%	$37,986,000,000	29.3%	$8,423,000,000	451.0%	36.2%
DD	2010	Q2	$9,080,000,000	$5,984,000,000	34.1%	$37,712,000,000	24.1%	$9,276,000,000	406.6%	33.4%
DD	2010	Q3	$7,067,000,000	$5,443,000,000	23.0%	$39,918,000,000	17.7%	$9,651,000,000	413.6%	16.8%
DD	2010	Y	$28,899,000,000	$20,574,000,000	28.8%	$40,410,000,000	71.5%	$9,800,000,000	412.3%	84.9%
DD	2011	Q1	$10,059,000,000	$6,831,000,000	32.1%	$42,600,000,000	23.6%	$11,279,000,000	377.7%	28.6%
DD	2011	Q2	$10,493,000,000	$7,191,000,000	31.5%	$47,736,000,000	22.0%	$12,502,000,000	381.8%	26.4%
DD	2011	Q3	$8,303,000,000	$6,345,000,000	23.6%	$47,794,000,000	17.4%	$12,024,000,000	397.5%	16.3%
DD	2011	Y	$34,423,000,000	$21,264,000,000	38.2%	$48,643,000,000	70.8%	$9,208,000,000	528.3%	142.9%
DD	2012	Q1	$10,194,000,000	$6,816,000,000	33.1%	$50,223,000,000	20.3%	$10,427,000,000	481.7%	32.4%
DD	2012	Q2	$10,208,000,000	$5,844,000,000	42.8%	$50,031,000,000	20.4%	$10,645,000,000	470.0%	41.0%
DD	2012	Q3	$7,336,000,000	$4,779,000,000	34.9%	$50,607,000,000	14.5%	$10,711,000,000	472.5%	23.9%
DD	2012	Y	$35,310,000,000	$21,538,000,000	39.0%	$49,859,000,000	70.8%	$10,299,000,000	484.1%	133.7%
DD	2013	Q1	$10,500,000,000	$7,105,000,000	32.3%	$50,564,000,000	20.8%	$12,315,000,000	410.6%	27.6%
DD	2013	Q2	$10,003,000,000	$6,057,000,000	39.4%	$51,349,000,000	19.5%	$13,355,000,000	384.5%	29.5%
DD	2013	Q3	$7,805,000,000	$5,165,000,000	33.8%	$51,990,000,000	15.0%	$13,900,000,000	374.0%	19.0%
DD	2014	Q1	$10,145,000,000	$6,000,000,000	40.9%	$47,800,000,000	21.2%	$16,442,000,000	290.7%	25.2%

You'll note for the Quarter 2 analysis in 2009, for DuPont (Ticker Symbol = DD), if you take its profit margin, 0.294, multiplied by asset turnover of 20.1 percent multiplied by the financial leverage of 471.7 percent, you get a return on equity of 27.8 percent.

The Use of Sparklines and Trendlines in Ratio Analysis

LO 8-3

Explain how to create and read visualizations of financial statement data

By using sparklines and trendlines, financial statement users can easily see the data visually and give meaning to the underlying financial data. We define **sparklines** as a small trendline of graphic that efficiently summarizes numbers or statistics in a graph without axes. Because they generally can fit in a single cell within a spreadsheet, they can easily add to the data without detracting from the tabular results.

For what types of reports or spreadsheets should sparklines be used? It usually depends on the type of reporting that is selected. For example, if used in a digital dashboard that already has many charts and dials, additional sparklines might clutter up the overall appearance. However, if used to show trends where it replaces or complements lots of numbers, it might be used as a very effective visualization. The nice thing about sparklines is they are generally small and just show simple trends rather than all the details regarding the horizontal and vertical axes that you would expect on a normal graph.

Exhibit 8-4 provides an example of the use of sparklines in a DuPont analysis for **Walmart**. It is also part of one of the end-of-chapter labs that details the use of XBRL data and sparklines in ratio analyses.

The DuPont Framework

The DuPont Framework outlines the components that affect return on equity as a combination of asset management and profitability.

Exhibit 8-4
Illustration of the Use
of Sparklines to Show
Trends in the DuPont
Ratio Analysis for
Walmart

Wal Mart Stores Inc

Trend	2014	2015	2016		
	0.20	0.20	0.18	$ 15,080	
				$ 84,774	

Return on equity (ROE)

$$\frac{\text{Net income}}{\text{Average shareholders' equity}}$$

Trend	2014	2015	2016		
	0.04	0.04	0.03	$ 15,080	
				$ 478,614	

Profit margin on sales (PM)

$$\frac{\text{Net income}}{\text{Net sales}}$$

Trend	2014	2015	2016		
	2.32	2.36	2.37	$ 478,614	
				$ 201,536	

Asset turnover (AT)

$$\frac{\text{Net sales}}{\text{Average total assets}}$$

Trend	2014	2015	2016		
	2.50	2.44	2.38	$ 201,536	
				$ 84,774	

Equity multiplier (EM)

$$\frac{\text{Average total assets}}{\text{Average total equity}}$$

DuPont Framework

$ROE = PM \times AT \times EM$

✓ PROGRESS CHECK

4. How might standardized XBRL metrics be useful in comparing the financial statements of **General Motors, Alphabet,** and **Alibaba**?

5. How might sparklines be used to enhance the analysis of Exhibit 8-3 regarding the DuPont analysis? Would you show the sparklines for each component of the DuPont ROE disaggregation, or would you propose it be shown only for the total?

6. Using Exhibit 8-4 as the source of data and using the raw accounts, show the components of profit margin, operating leverage and financial leverage and how they are combined to equal ROE for Q2 2009 for DuPont (Ticker = DD).

TEXT MINING AND SENTIMENT ANALYSIS

LO 8-4

Describe the value of text mining and sentiment analysis of financial reporting

Some data analysis is used to determine the sentiment included in text. For example, Uber might use text mining and sentiment analysis to read all of the words used in social media associated with its driving or the quality of its smartphone app and its services. The company can analyze the words for sentiment to see how the social media participants feel about its services and new innovations, as well as perform similar analysis on its competitors (like Lyft or traditional cab services).

Similar analysis might be done to learn more about financial reports, Securities and Exchange Commission submissions, analyst reports, and other related documents based on the words that are used. They might provide a gauge of the overall tone of the financial reports. This tone might help us to understand management expectations of past or future performance that might complement the numbers and figures in the reports.

To provide an illustration of the use and predictive ability of text mining and sentiment analysis, Loughran and McDonald[6] use text mining and sentiment analysis to predict the stock market reaction to the issuance of a 10-K form by examining the proportion of negative words used in a 10-K report. Exhibit 8-5 comes from their research suggesting that the stock market reaction is related to the proportion of negative words (or inversely, the proportion of positive words). They call this method *overlap*. Thus, using this method to define the tone of the article, they indeed find a direct association, or relationship, between the proportion of negative words and the stock market reaction to the disclosure of 10-K reports.

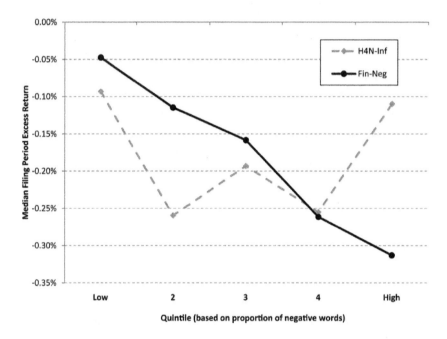

Exhibit 8-5   The Stock Market Reaction (Excess Return) of Companies Sorted by the Proportion of Negative Words.
The lines represent the words from a financial dictionary (Fin-Neg) and a standard English dictionary (H4N-INF).

Source: Tim Loughran and Bill McDonald, "When Is a Liability Not a Liability? Textual Analysis, Dictionaries, and 10-Ks," *Journal of Finance* 66, no. 1 (2011), pp. 35–65.

They measure proportion first by developing a dictionary of 2,337 negative words in the financial context and then counting how many of those words are used as compared to the total words used (called Fin-Neg in Exhibit 8-5). One of their arguments is that a financial dictionary is better than a dictionary created from standard English usage. For that reason, they differentiate their financial dictionary (Fin-Neg) from the negative words used in normal English usage (as shown in Exhibit 8-5 as H4N-Inf). Whereas *cost, expense*, or *liability* might be viewed as negative in normal English, they are not considered to be negative words in the financial dictionary. The most frequent negative words in the financial dictionary include words like *loss, claims, impairment, adverse, restructuring* and *litigation.*

[6]Tim Loughran and Bill McDonald, "When Is a Liability Not a Liability? Textual Analysis, Dictionaries, and 10-Ks," *Journal of Finance* 66, no. 1 (2011), pp. 35–65.

PROGRESS CHECK

7. Which would you predict would have more positive sentiment in a 10-K, the footnotes to the financial statements or the MD&A (management discussion and analysis) of the financial statements?

8. Why would you guess the results between the proportion of negative words and the stock market reaction to the 10-K issuance diverge the Fin-Neg and the H4N-Inf dictionary?

Summary

Data Analytics extends to the financial accounting and financial reporting space.

- By tagging financial elements in a computer readable manner, XBRL facilitates the accurate and timely transmission of financial reporting to all interested stakeholders.
- The XBRL taxonomy provides tags for 19,000 financial elements and allows for the use of company-defined tags when the normal XBRL tags are not suitable.
- XBRL and Data Analytics allow timely analysis of the financial statements and the computation of financial ratios. We illustrated its usage by showing the DuPont ratio framework.
- We introduced and discussed the use of sparklines and trendlines as ways to efficiently and effectively visualize firm performance.
- We concluded the chapter by explaining how sentiment analysis could be used with financial statements, other financial reports, and other financially related information.

Key Words

DuPont ratio analysis (*306*)   Developed by the DuPont Corporation to decompose performance (particularly return on equity [ROE]) into its component parts.

financial statement analysis (*305*)   Used by investors, analysts, auditors, and other interested stakeholders to review and evaluate a company's financial statements and financial performance.

ratio analysis (*305*)   A tool used to evaluate relationships among different financial statement items to help understand a company's financial and operating performance.

sparkline (*306*)   A small trendline or graphic that efficiently summarizes numbers or statistics in a graph without axes.

standardized metrics (*303*)   Metrics used by data vendors to allow easier comparison of company reported XBRL data.

XBRL (*302*)   A global standard for exchanging financial reporting information that uses XML; a global standard for Internet communication among businesses.

XBRL-GL (*303*)   Stands for XBRL-General Ledger; relates to the ability of enterprise system to tag financial elements within the firm's financial reporting system.

XBRL taxonomy (*302*)   Defines and describes each key data element (like cash or accounts payable). The taxonomy also defines the relationships between each element (like inventory is a component of current assets and current assets is a component of total assets).

✓ ANSWERS TO PROGRESS CHECKS

1. By each company providing tags for each piece of its financial data as computer read-able, XBRL allows immediate access to each type of financial statement user, be they financial analysts, investors, lenders, for their own specific use.

2. Standardized metrics allow for comparison of different companies by using similar titles for similar financial elements. While these standardized metrics are determined by a data vendor such as **Calcbench** or **XBRLAnalyst** (among others), they greatly facilitate the use and value of financial reporting provided by XBRL.

3. When journal entries and transactions are made in an XBRL-GL system, there is the pos-sibility of real-time financial reporting. In the author's opinion, income statement infor-mation (including sales, cost of goods sold, and SG&A expenditures) would be useful to financial users on a real-time basis. Any information that does not change frequently would not be as useful. Examples include real-time financial elements, including good-will, long-term debt, and property, plant, and equipment.

4. Standardized metrics are useful for comparing companies because they allow for similar accounts to have the same title regardless of the account names used by the various companies. They allow for ease of comparison across multiple companies.

5. Answers may vary on how to visualize the data. It might depend on the type of reporting that is selected. For example, is it solely a digital dashboard, or is it a report with many facts and figures where more sparklines might clutter up the overall appearance? The nice thing about sparklines is they are generally small and just show simple trends rather than details about the horizontal and vertical axes.

6. Profit margin = (Revenues − Cost of revenue)/Revenues = ($7.088B − $5.007B)/ $7.088B = 29.4%

   Operating leverage = Sales/Assets = ($7.088B / $35.258B) = 20.1%

   Financial leverage = Assets/Equity = $35.258B / $7.474B = 471.7%

   ROE = Profit margin × Operating leverage (or Asset turnover) × Financial leverage = 0.294 × 0.201 × 4.717 = 0.278

7. The MD&A section of the 10-K has management reporting on what happened in the most recent period and what they expect will happen in the coming year. They are usu-ally upbeat and generally optimistic about the future. The footnotes are generally back-ground looking and would be much more factual-based, careful, and conservative. We would expect the MD&A section to be much more optimistic than the footnotes.

8. Accounting has its own lingo. Words that might seem negative for the English language are not necessarily negative for financial reports. For this reason, the results diverge based on whether the standard English usage dictionary (H4N-inf) or the financial dic-tionary (Fin-Neg) is used. The relationship between the excess stock market return and the financial dictionary is what we would expect.

 **connect**

Multiple Choice Questions

1. The DuPont analysis of return on equity (ROE) includes all of the following component ratios *except*:

   a. Asset turnover.

   b. Inventory turnover.

   c. Financial leverage.

   d. Profit margin.

2. XBRL stands for:

   a. Extensible Business Reporting Language.

   b. Extensive Business Reporting Language.

   c. XML Business Reporting Language.

   d. Excel Business Reporting Language.

3. Which term defines and describes each XBRL financial element?

   a. Data dictionary

   b. Descriptive statistics

   c. XBRL-GL

   d. Taxonomy

4. Which stage of the IMPACT model (introduced in chapter 1) would the use of sparklines fit?

   a. Track outcomes

   b. Communicate insights

   c. Address and refine results

   d. Perform test plan

5. What is the name of the output from data vendors to help compare companies using different XBRL tags for revenue?

   a. XBRL taxonomy

   b. Data assimilation

   c. Consonant tagging

   d. Standardized metrics

6. What is the term used to describe the process of assigning XBRL tags internally within a financial reporting/enterprise system?

   a. XBRL tagging

   b. XBRL taxonomy

   c. XBRL-GL

   d. XBRL dictionary

7. What computerized technique would be used to perform sentiment analysis on an annual accounting report?

   a. Text mining

   b. Sentiment mining

   c. Textual analysis

   d. Decision trees

8. What type of ratios measure a firm's operating efficiency?

   a. DuPont ratios

   b. Liquidity ratios

   c. Activity ratios

   d. Solvency ratios

9. What type of ratios measure a firm's ability to pay its debts and stay in business?

   a. DuPont ratios

   b. Liquidity ratios

   c. Activity ratios

   d. Solvency ratios

10. What is considered an essential component of planning an audit and carrying out substantive testing that involves ratio analysis?

   a. Environmental analysis

   b. Competitive analysis

   c. Management integrity analysis

   d. Analytical procedures

Discussion Questions

1. Which would you predict would have more positive sentiment in a 10-K, the financial statements or the MD&A (management discussion and analysis) of the financial statements? More positive sentiment in the footnotes or MD&A? Why?

2. Would you recommend the Securities and Exchange Commission require the use of sparklines on the face of the financial statements? Why or why not?

3. Why do audit firms perform analytical procedures to identify risk? Which type of ratios (liquidity, solvency, activity, and profitability ratios) would you use to evaluate the company's ability to continue as a going concern?

4. Go to https://xbrl.us/data-rule/dqc_0015-lepr/ and find the XBRL element name for Interest Expense and Sales, General, and Administrative expense.

5. Go to https://xbrl.us/data-rule/dqc_0015-lepr/ and find the XBRL element name for Other NonOperating Income and indicate whether XBRL says that should normally be a debit or credit entry.

6. Go to finance.yahoo.com and type in the ticker symbol for **Apple** (AAPL) and click on the statistics tab. Which of those variables would be useful in assessing profitability?

7. Can you think of any other settings, besides financial reports, where tagged data might be useful for fast, accurate analysis generally completed by computers? How could it be used in a hospital setting? Or at your university?

8. Can you think of how sentiment analysis might be used in a marketing setting? How could it be used in a hospital setting? Or at your university? When would it be especially good to measure the sentiment?

Problems

1. Can you think of situations where sentiment analysis might be helpful to analyze press releases or earnings announcements? What additional information might it provide that is not directly in the overall announcement? Would it be useful to have sentiment analysis automated to just get a basic sentiment measure versus the base level of sentiment expected in a press announcement or earnings announcement?

2. We noted in the text that negative words in the financial dictionary include words like *loss, claims, impairment, adverse, restructuring,* and *litigation.* What are other negative words might you add to that list? What are your thoughts on positive words that would be included in the financial dictionary, particularly those that might be different than standard English dictionary usage?

3. You're asked to figure out how the stock market responded to **Amazon**'s announcement on June 16, 2017, that it would purchase **Whole Foods**—arguably a transformational change for **Amazon, Walmart**, and the whole retail industry.

   Required:

   a. Go to finance.yahoo.com, type in the ticker symbol for **Amazon** (AMZN), click on historical data, and input the dates around June 16, 2017. Specifically, see how much the stock price changed on June 16.

   b. Do the same analysis for **Walmart** (WMT) over the same dates, which was arguably most directly affected, and see what happened to its stock price.

4. The preceding question asked you to figure out how the stock market responded to **Amazon's** announcement that it would purchase **Whole Foods**. The question now is if the stock market for **Amazon** had higher trade volume on that day than the average of the month before.

   Required:

   a. Go to finance.yahoo.com, type in the ticker symbol for **Amazon** (AMZN), click on historical data, and input the dates from May 15, 2017, to June 16, 2017. Download the data, calculate the average volume for the month prior to June 16, and compare it to the trading volume on June 16. Any effect on trading volume of the **Whole Foods** announcement by **Amazon**?

   b. Do the same analysis for **Walmart** (WMT) over the same dates and see what happened to its trading volume. Any effect on trading volume of the **Whole Foods** announcement by **Amazon**?

5. Go to Loughran and McDonald's sentiment word lists at https://www3.nd.edu/~mcdonald/Word_Lists.html and download the Master Dictionary. These are what they've used to assess sentiment in financial statements and related financial reports. Give five words that are considered to be "negative" and five words that are considered to be "constraining." How would you use this in your analysis of sentiment of an accounting report?

6. Go to Loughran and McDonald's sentiment word lists at https://www3.nd.edu/~mcdonald/Word_Lists.html and download the Master Dictionary. These are what they've used to assess sentiment in financial statements and related financial reports. Give five words that are considered to be "litigious" and five words that are considered to be "positive."

Answers to Multiple Choice Questions

1. B
2. A
3. D
4. B
5. D
6. C
7. A
8. C
9. D
10. D

Company summary

This lab will pull in XBRL data from *Fortune* 100 companies listed with the SEC. You have the option to analyze a pair of companies of your choice based on your own interest level. This lab will have you compare other companies as well.

Data

The data used in this analysis are XBRL-tagged data from *Fortune* 100 companies. The data are pulled from **FinDynamics**, which in turn pulls the data from the SEC.

Technique

- You will use a combination of spreadsheet formulas and live XBRL data to generate a spreadsheet that is adaptable and dynamic. In other words, you will create a template that can be used to answer several financial statement analysis questions.

Software needed

- Google Sheets (sheets.google.com)
- iXBRLAnalyst script (https://findynamics.com/gsheets/ixbrlanalyst.gs)

In this lab, you will:

Part 1: Identify questions related to the income statement.
Part 2: Analyze a list of calculated financial ratios for a selection of companies.
Part 3: Create a dynamic spreadsheet that pulls in XBRL data.
Part 4: Create formulas to identify the companies based on the ratios.

Part 1: Identify the Questions

Financial statement analysis frequently involves identifying relationships between specific pieces of data. We may want to see how financial data have changed over time or how the composition has changed.

Q1. Select a *Fortune* 100 company, such as **Apple** (AAPL) or **Nike** (NKE), and identify three questions you might want to know about that company's income over the past three years. For example, "What is the trend of operating costs?"

Q2. Form a hypothesis for each of your questions. For example, "I expect **Nike**'s operating costs have gone up."

Part 2: Generate a Request for Data

To create a dynamic spreadsheet, you must first connect your sheet to a data source on the Internet. In this case, you will use Google Sheets because it is hosted online and then add the iXBRLAnalyst script to connect it to **FinDynamics** so you can use formulas to query financial statement elements.

1. Log into Google Sheets (sheets.google.com), and create a new, blank sheet called **XBRL Common**.
2. Click **Tools > Script Editor** from the menu.
3. In a new window, go to findynamics.com/gsheets/ixbrlanalyst.gs.
4. Copy and paste the entire script from the **FinDynamics** page into the **Script Editor** window, replacing any existing text.

5. Click **Save** and name the project **XBRL**.
6. Close the **Script Editor** window and return to your Google Sheet.
7. Reload/refresh the page. If you see a new **iXBRLAnalyst** menu appear, you are now connected to the XBRL data.
8. Test your connection by typing in the following formula anywhere on your sheet: =XBRLFact("AAPL","AssetsCurrent","2017"). If your connection is good, it should return the value 128645000000 for **Apple Inc.**'s 2017 balance in current assets.
9. Delete the formula and continue to the next step.

Note: Once you've added the iXBRLAnalyst script to a Google Sheet, you can simply open that sheet, then go to **File > Make a copy . . . ,** and the script will automatically be copied to the new sheet.

The basic formulas available with the iXBRLAnalyst script are:

=FinValue(company, tag, year, period, member, scale)
=XBRLFact(company, tag, year, period, member, scale, true)
=SharePriceStats(company, date, duration, request)

where:

company = ticker symbol (e.g., "AAPL" for **Apple Inc.**)
tag = XBRL tag or normalized tag (e.g., "NetIncomeLoss" or "[Net Income]")
year = reporting year (e.g., "2017")
period = fiscal period (e.g., "Q1" for 1st Quarter or "Y" for year)
scale = rounding (e.g., "k," "thousands," or "1000" for thousands) [*Note:* There is an error with rounding, so it is suggested to simply divide the formula by the scale instead, e.g. =XBRLFact(c,t,y,p)/scale.]

Because companies frequently use different tags to represents similar concepts (such as the tags ProfitLoss or NetIncomeLoss to identify Net Income), it is important to make sure you're using the correct values. **FinDynamics** attempts to coordinate the diversity of tags by using normalized tags that use formulas and relationships instead of direct tags. Normalized tags must be contained within brackets []. Some examples are given in Lab Table 8-1A.

If you're looking for specific XBRL tags, you can explore the current XBRL taxonomy at xbrlview.fasb.org.

Balance Sheet	Income Statement	Statement of Cash Flows
[Cash, Cash Equivalents and Short-Term Investments]	[Revenue]	[Cash From Operations (CFO)]
[Short-Term Investments]	[Cost of Revenue]	[Changes in Working Capital]
[Accounts Receivable, Current]	[Gross Profit]	[Changes in Accounts Receivables]
[Inventory]	[Selling, General & Administrative Expense]	[Changes in Liabilities]
[Other Current Assets]	[Research & Development Expense]	[Changes in Inventories]
[Current Assets]	[Depreciation (& Amortization), IS]	[Adjustments of Non-Cash Items, CF]
[Net of Property, Plant & Equipment]	[Non-Interest Expense]	[Provision For Doubtful Accounts]
[Long-Term Investments]	[Other Operating Expenses]	[Depreciation (& Amortization), CF]
[Intangible Assets, Net]	[Operating Expenses]	[Stock-Based Compensation]
[Goodwill]	[Operating Income]	[Pension and Other Retirement Benefits]
[Other Noncurrent Assets]	[Other Operating Income]	[Interest Paid]
[Noncurrent Assets]	[Non-Operating Income (Expense)]	[Other CFO]
[Assets]	[Interest Expense]	[Cash from Investing (CFI)]
[Accounts Payable and Accrued Liabilities, Current]	[Costs and Expenses]	[Capital Expenditures]
[Short-Term Borrowing]	[Earnings Before Taxes]	[Payments to Acquire Investments]
[Long-Term Debt, Current]	[Income Taxes]	[Proceeds from Investments]
[Other Current Liabilities]	[Income from Continuing Operations]	[Other CFI]
		[Cash From Financing (CFF)]
		[Payment of Dividends]

Lab Table 8-1A Normalized Accounts Created by FinDynamics for XBRLAnalyst

Balance Sheet	Income Statement	Statement of Cash Flows
[Current Liabilities] [Other Noncurrent Liabilities] [Noncurrent Liabilities] [Liabilities] [Preferred Stock] [Common Stock] [Additional Paid-in Capital] [Retained Earnings (Accumulated Deficit)] [Equity Attributable to Parent] [Equity Attributable to Noncontrolling Interest] [Stockholders' Equity] [Liabilities & Equity]	[Income from Discontinued Operations, Net of Taxes] [Extraordinary Items, Gain (Loss)] [Net Income] [Net Income Attributable to Parent] [Net Income Attributable to Noncontrolling Interest] [Preferred Stock Dividends and Other Adjustments] [Comprehensive Income (Loss)] [Other Comprehensive Income (Loss)] [Comprehensive Income (Loss) Attributable to Parent] [Comprehensive Income (Loss) Attributable to Noncontrolling Interest]	[Proceeds from Sale of Equity] [Repurchase of Equity] [Net Borrowing] [Other CFF] [Effect of Exchange Rate Changes] [Total Cash, Change] [Net Cash, Continuing Operations] [Net CFO, Continuing Operations] [Net CFI, Continuing Operations] [Net CFF, Continuing Operations] [Net Cash, DO] [Net CFO, DO] [Net CFI, DO] [Net CFF, DO]

Lab Table 8-1A (*Continued*)

Part 3: Perform an Analysis of the Data

We will begin by creating a common-size income statement for one company over a three-year period.

10. In your Google Sheet, begin by entering the values for the tags, as shown:

LAB EXHIBIT 8-1A

	A	B
1	Company	AAPL
2	Year	2016
3	Period	Y
4	Scale	1000000

11. Then set up your financial statement using the following normalized tags and periods. *Note:* Because we already identified the most current year in A2, we'll use a formula to find the three most recent years.

LAB EXHIBIT 8-1B

	A	B	C	D
6		=$B2	=B6-1	=C6-1
7	[Revenue]			
8	[Cost of Revenue]			
9	[Gross Profit]			
10	[Selling, General & Administrative Expense]			
11	[Research & Development Expense]			
12	[Other Operating Expenses]			
13	*[Operating Expenses]*			
14	[Operating Income]			
15	[Depreciation (& Amortization), CF]			
16	[Interest Income]			

	A	B	C	D
17	[Earnings before Taxes]			
18	[Income Taxes]			
19	[Net Income]			

12. Now enter the =XBRLFact() formula to pull in the correct values, using relative references (e.g., $A$1) as necessary. For example, the formula in B7 should be =XBRLFact($B$1,$A7,B$6,$B$3)/$B$4.

13. If you've used relative references correctly, you can either drag the formula down and across columns B, C, and D, or copy and paste the cell (not the formula itself) into the rest of the table.

14. Use the formatting tools to clean up your spreadsheet, then take a screenshot (label it 8-1A).

Next, you can begin editing your dynamic data and expanding your analysis, identifying trends and ratios.

15. In your Google Sheet, use a sparkline to show the change in income statement accounts:
    a. In cell E7, type: =SPARKLINE(B7:D7).
    b. Note: The line is trending toward the left.

16. Now perform a vertical analysis in the columns to the right showing each value as a percentage of revenue:
    a. Copy cells B6:D6 into F6:H6.
    b. In F7, type =B7/B$7.
    c. Drag the formula to fill in F7:H19.
    d. Format the numbers as a percentage.
    e. Add a sparkline in Column I.

17. Take a screenshot (label it 8-1B).

Part 4: Address and Refine Results

Now that you have a common-size income statement, replace the company ticker in cell B1 with your selected company's ticker and press Enter. The data on the spreadsheet will update.

Q3. Look at the trends and composition of the income statement, then answer your three questions from Q1.

Q4. How did the actual results compare with your hypothesis?

Q5. Replace the company ticker with a competitor of your company (e.g., MSFT vs AAPL). How do their trends compare with your initial company?

Q6. How could you expand this spreadsheet to include multiple competitors' data on the same sheet for quick analysis?

End of Lab

Lab 8-2 Use XBRLAnalyst to Create Dynamic Common-Size Financial Statements

XBRLAnalyst allows us to easily create common-size financial statements. Using the skills learned in Lab 8-1, now extend the analysis to identify some companies based on their financial performance. The *Fortune* 100 companies listed in Lab Exhibit 8-2A operate in a variety of industries. Their FY2016 revenue and assets appear below:

LAB EXHIBIT 8-2A
Background Information on Selected *Fortune* 100 Companies

Company	Revenue (millions) FY2016	Assets (millions) FY2016
BANK OF AMERICA (BAC), through its subsidiaries, provides various banking and financial products and services for individual consumers, small- and middle-market businesses, institutional investors, corporations, and governments in the United States and internationally.	$80,104	$2,187,702
WALMART (WMT) operates retail stores in various formats worldwide. The company operates in three segments: Walmart U.S., Walmart International, and Sam's Club.	$482,130	$199,581
CISCO (CSCO) designs, manufactures, and sells Internet protocol (IP)–based networking and other products related to the communications and information technology industries worldwide.	$49,247	$121,652
COCA-COLA (KO) is a beverage company engaging in the manufacture, marketing, and sale of nonalcoholic beverages worldwide.	$41,863	$87,270
BOEING (BA) engages in the design, development, manufacture, sale, and support of commercial jetliners, military aircraft, satellites, missile defense, human space flight, and launch systems and services worldwide.	$94,571	$89,997
EBAY (EBAY) provides online platforms, tools, and services to help individuals and merchants in online and mobile commerce and payments in the United States and internationally.	$8,979	$23,847
AMAZON (AMZN) operates as an online retailer in North America and internationally.	$135,987	$83,402
MERCK (MRK) provides various health solutions through its prescription medicines, vaccines, biologic therapies, animal health, and consumer care products worldwide.	$39,807	$95,377
WALT DISNEY COMPANY (DIS) is an entertainment company that operates television and movie studios as well as theme parks.	$55,632	$92,033
MONDELEZ (MDLZ) produces consumer food products, such as Oreo cookies.	$25,923	$61,538

In Lab Exhibit 8-2B, you'll find the common-size ratios for each Lab Exhibit 8-2A company's income statement (as a percentage of revenue) and balance sheet (as a percentage of assets).

	A	B	C	D	E	F	G	H	I	J
As a Percentage of Sales	100.0%	100.0%	100.0%	100.0%	100.0%	100.0%	100.0%	100.0%	100.0%	100.0%
Revenue	100.0%	100.0%	100.0%	100.0%	100.0%	100.0%	100.0%	100.0%	100.0%	100.0%
Cost of Goods Sold	64.9%	37.1%	74.9%	22.4%	9.6%	34.9%	60.9%	4.5%	39.3%	85.4%
Gross Profit	35.1%	62.9%	25.1%	77.6%	90.4%	65.1%	39.1%	95.5%	60.7%	14.6%
Research & Development	0.0%	12.8%	0.0%	12.4%	0.0%	25.4%	0.0%	0.0%	0.0%	4.9%
Selling, General and Administrative Expenses	7.1%	23.2%	20.1%	36.4%	15.7%	24.5%	25.2%	53.8%	36.5%	3.8%
Other Operating Expenses	89.8%	0.5%	0.0%	3.0%	−4.3%	1.6%	3.3%	0.0%	0.0%	0.0%
Total Operating Expenses	96.9%	37.2%	20.1%	51.8%	16.0%	51.6%	29.2%	54.7%	36.5%	8.7%
Operating Income/Loss	3.1%	25.7%	5.0%	25.9%	84.0%	13.5%	9.9%	47.7%	20.6%	6.2%

LAB EXHIBIT 8-2B   Mystery Ratios

	A	B	C	D	E	F	G	H	I	J
As a Percentage of Sales	**100.0%**	**100.0%**	**100.0%**	**100.0%**	**100.0%**	**100.0%**	**100.0%**	**100.0%**	**100.0%**	**100.0%**
Total Other Income/Expenses Net	−0.2%	0.5%	0.0%	0.0%	0.0%	−1.8%	−4.3%	0.6%	−1.4%	0.0%
Interest Expense	0.4%	1.4%	0.5%	0.0%	−0.5%	0.0%	0.0%	12.4%	1.8%	0.3%
Income before Tax	2.8%	26.2%	4.5%	40.7%	26.7%	11.7%	5.6%	31.4%	19.4%	5.9%
Income Tax Expense	1.0%	4.4%	1.4%	−40.5%	9.1%	1.8%	0.5%	9.0%	3.8%	0.7%
Minority Interest	0.0%	0.0%	0.1%	0.0%	0.7%	0.1%	0.0%	0.0%	0.1%	0.0%
Net Income	1.7%	21.8%	3.1%	80.9%	17.6%	9.9%	6.4%	22.4%	15.6%	5.2%
As a Percentage of Assets	**100.0%**	**100.0%**	**100.0%**	**100.0%**	**100.0%**	**100.0%**	**100.0%**	**100.0%**	**100.0%**	**100.0%**
Current Assets	54.9%	64.7%	30.2%	37.2%	18.4%	32.1%	13.8%	0.0%	39.0%	69.4%
Cash	23.2%	6.3%	4.4%	7.6%	5.0%	6.8%	0.0%	6.8%	9.8%	9.8%
Investments	8.0%	47.8%	0.0%	22.4%	0.0%	8.2%	0.0%	8.2%	15.6%	1.4%
Receivables	10.0%	4.8%	2.8%	2.5%	9.8%	7.4%	4.2%	40.9%	4.4%	9.8%
Inventory	13.7%	1.0%	22.3%	0.0%	1.5%	5.1%	4.0%	0.0%	3.1%	48.0%
Other Current Assets	8.0%	52.6%	4.9%	27.1%	6.9%	12.8%	2.7%	0.0%	21.7%	11.5%
Total Current Assets	54.9%	64.7%	30.2%	37.2%	18.4%	32.1%	13.8%	0.0%	39.0%	69.4%
Long-Term Investments	0.0%	3.4%	0.0%	16.6%	4.7%	12.0%	9.1%	13.4%	18.6%	1.5%
Property, Plant and Equipment	34.9%	2.9%	55.2%	6.4%	29.7%	12.6%	13.4%	0.4%	12.2%	14.2%
Goodwill	4.5%	21.9%	8.4%	18.9%	30.2%	19.0%	32.9%	3.2%	12.2%	5.9%
Intangible Assets	0.0%	2.1%	0.0%	0.4%	7.6%	18.1%	29.4%	0.1%	11.2%	2.8%
Amortization	0.0%	0.0%	0.0%	0.0%	0.0%	0.0%	0.0%	0.0%	0.0%	0.0%
Other Assets	5.7%	5.0%	6.3%	20.5%	9.4%	6.1%	1.4%	0.0%	6.8%	6.1%
Long-Term Assets	45.1%	35.3%	69.8%	62.8%	81.6%	67.9%	86.2%	85.0%	61.0%	30.6%
Total Assets	100.0%	100.0%	100.0%	100.0%	100.0%	100.0%	100.0%	100.0%	100.0%	100.0%
Liabilities	76.9%	47.7%	58.1%	55.8%	48.6%	57.7%	59.0%	87.8%	73.4%	99.0%
Current Liabilities	52.5%	20.5%	32.4%	16.1%	18.3%	18.0%	23.4%	0.0%	30.4%	55.7%
Accounts Payable	30.3%	3.7%	29.4%	1.6%	9.9%	6.7%	12.7%	0.0%	10.9%	28.8%
Current Portion of Long-Term Debt	0.0%	0.0%	1.7%	0.0%	4.0%	0.0%	2.4%	7.8%	4.0%	0.0%
Other Current Liabilities	22.2%	13.3%	0.0%	8.4%	4.4%	10.8%	4.3%	57.6%	15.5%	26.5%
Long-Term Debt	9.2%	20.1%	19.1%	31.5%	17.9%	25.5%	0.0%	0.0%	34.0%	0.0%
Other Liabilities	15.1%	6.4%	2.9%	8.2%	12.4%	14.2%	14.1%	0.0%	9.0%	32.7%
Minority Interest	0.0%	0.0%	1.5%	0.0%	4.4%	0.2%	0.1%	0.0%	0.2%	0.1%
Total Liabilities	76.9%	47.7%	58.1%	55.8%	48.6%	57.7%	59.0%	87.8%	73.4%	99.0%
Total Stockholders' Equity	23.1%	52.3%	41.9%	44.2%	51.4%	42.3%	41.0%	12.2%	26.6%	1.0%
Total Liabilities and Stockholders' Equity	100.0%	100.0%	100.0%	100.0%	100.0%	100.0%	100.0%	100.0%	100.0%	100.0%

LAB EXHIBIT 8-2B   (*Continued*)

1. Use a Google Sheet with the iXBRLAnalyst script as well as the normalized accounts in Lab Exhibit 8-2B (or search for XBRL tags in the FASB taxonomy if normalized accounts aren't available) to recreate the ratios above.
2. Take a screenshot (label it 8-2A) of your completed worksheet.

   Q1.   Using the skills learned from your prior financial accounting classes, your ability to extract information from XBRL, and your knowledge of common-size financial statements, match the company names in Lab Exhibit 8-2A with their corresponding ratios in each column of Lab Exhibit 8-2B?

- Column A = _____ which company?
- Column B = _____
- Column C = _____
- Column D = _____
- Column E = _____
- Column F = _____
- Column G = _____
- Column H = _____
- Column I = _____
- Column J = _____

End of Lab

Lab 8-3   Use XBRL to Access and Analyze Financial Statement Ratios—The Use of DuPont Ratios

Financial analysts, investors, lenders, auditors, and many others perform ratio analysis to help review and evaluate a company's financial statements and financial performance. This analysis allows the stakeholder to gain an understanding of the financial health of the company and gives insights to allow more insightful and, hopefully, more effective decision making.

In this lab, you will access XBRL data to complete data analysis and generate financial ratios to compare the financial performance of several companies. Financial ratios can more easily be calculated using spreadsheets and XBRL. You will (1) select an industry to analyze, (2) create a copy of a spreadsheet template, (3) input ticker symbols from three U.S. public companies, and (4) calculate financial ratios and make observations about the state of the companies using these financial ratios.

Data
- Financial Elements from XBRL from SEC Filings

Software needed
- Google Account
- Google Sheets
- Browser connected to Internet

Specifically, you will:

Part 1: Analyze financial changes over a three-year period for a single company.
Part 2: Compare financial metrics across competing companies within one industry for a single period.
Part 3: Identify potential flaws or shortcomings in the data.
Part 4: Understand how XBRL facilitates complex financial analyses.

Part 1: Identify the Problem

Interested stakeholders of the firm need access to real-time, accurate financial data. Since 2011, stakeholders have used XBRL data to meet this need.

Q1. How does XBRL fulfill the need for real-time, accurate financial data?

Q2. Why is it useful to compare multiple companies at once?

Part 2: Master the Data and Prepare for Analysis

To master the data and prepare for analysis, we need to pick which industry and which companies to analyze.

1. Below is a list of 15 *Fortune* 100 companies in five different industries. Each of these companies has attributes and strategies that are similar to and different from its competitors. Choose one industry to analyze.

    Retail: Walmart (WMT), Target (TGT), Costco (Cost)

    Technology: Microsoft (MSFT), Apple (AAPL), Facebook (FB)

    Pharmaceutical: Johnson & Johnson (JNJ), Merck (MRK), Bristol-Myers Squibb (BMY)

    Finance: Citigroup (C), Wells-Fargo (WFC), JPMorgan Chase (JPM)

    Energy: ExxonMobil (XOM), Chevron (CVX), ConocoPhillips (COP)

    Create a copy of a spreadsheet template in the following way:

2. Open a web browser and go to drive.google.com.
3. If you haven't done so already, sign in to your Google account.
4. Go to http://tinyurl.com/xbrlratios. You will see a spreadsheet similar to Lab Exhibit 8-3A.
5. Click **File > Make a copy. . .** as shown in Lab Exhibit 8-3A.
6. Rename your spreadsheet if desired and click **OK** to save a copy to your Drive. A new tab will open with your copy of the spreadsheet. You may now edit the values and formulas.

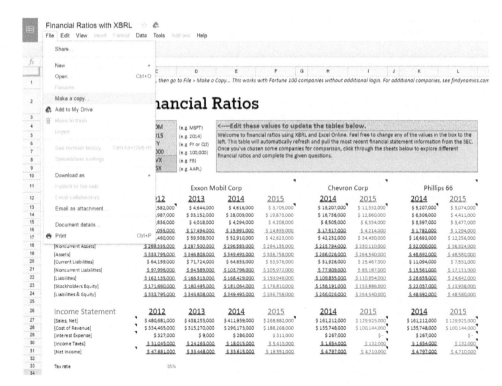

LAB EXHIBIT 8-3A
XBRL Financial Ratios in Google Sheets

Source: Microsoft Excel 2016

Part 3: Input Ticker Symbols

Refer to Lab Exhibit 8-3B for your industry's ticker symbols.

LAB EXHIBIT 8-3B

Input Ticker Symbols

Retail	Technology	Pharmaceutical	Finance	Energy
WMT	MSFT	JNJ	C	XOM
TGT	AAPL	MRK	WFC	CVS
KR	FB	BMY	JPM	PSX

7. Referring to Lab Exhibit 8-3B for your industry's ticker symbols, in the **Main Company Ticker** field, input the ticker of the company you would like to focus your analysis on and press **Enter**. In a moment, the value on the spreadsheet will change to **Loading. . .** and then show your company's financial figures.

8. In the **Most Recent Year** field, enter the most recent reporting year. It may be the current year or the previous year.

9. In the **Period** field, enter either **FY** for a fiscal year or **Q1** for 1st quarter, etc.

10. In the **Round to** field, choose the rounding amount. 1,000 will round to thousands of dollars; 1,000,000 will round to millions of dollars.

11. In the **Comparable 1 Ticker** field, input the ticker of a second company you would like to compare with your first company.

12. In the **Comparable 2 Ticker** field, input the ticker of a third company you would like to compare with your first company.

13. Take a screenshot (label it 8-3A) of your figure with the financial statements of your chosen companies.

Part 4: Analyze the Financial Ratios

First, review the Facts sheet (or tab) to determine whether there are any values missing for the companies you are analyzing. Describe what impact (if any) the missing data have on the ratios. Once you have determined whether any data are missing, you have a chance to find some interesting trends and comparisons in the data. You will click through the sheets at the bottom to review the ratios. To aid in this analysis, the template also includes sparklines that provide a mini-graph to help you quickly visualize any significant values or trends.

Q3. Review the 14 financial ratios and make some conclusions or judgments about the values, trends, or comparisons with the other companies. For example, if one company has a significantly higher debt-to-equity ratio than the other two, what might be driving this?

Q4. Has the company you are analyzing seen any major changes in its ratios in the past three years? Which of the three companies is most liquid in the most current year?

Q5. How has your company managed short-term liabilities over the last three years?

Q6. Analyze liquidity, profitability, financing (leverage), and activity for your company. Where is it strong?

Q7. Consider the DuPont framework to interpret the results and make sure you make a judgment about your company's financial position based upon the data.

End of Lab

Lab 8-4 Use SQL to Query an XBRL Database

Company summary

As the chapter mentioned, there are 19,000 tags in the XBRL taxonomy, which doesn't even include the custom tags that organizations have created for themselves. The normalized tags XBRLAnalyst provides can be helpful, but sometimes you will need to find a more specific tag. One way that you can do this is by using SQL to query an XBRL database for all tags that are similar to the normalized tag you are working with.

Data

We have provided a subset of the XBRL database in the Access database file XBRL.accdb. We have used the Arelle open-source XBRL platform to build our subset, which in turn pulls the data from the SEC.

Technique

- You will use SQL to query the database.

Software needed

- Microsoft Access

In this lab, you will:

Part 1: Identify questions related to XBRL tags and taxonomy.
Part 2: Analyze tags and then do more in-depth querying.

Part 1: Identify the Questions

One of the aspects that querying the XBRL database can be most helpful for is quickly viewing a list of tags that are similar or for quickly viewing a list of companies that have something in common over the years or even during a specific filing period.

> Q1. Identify three questions that would be interesting regarding finding commonalities in XBRL tags or in filtering the data to view a subset based on similar criteria.

> Q2. If you didn't know how to use SQL to query an XBRL database, how would you go about trying to answer the three questions you identified in Q1?

The questions we will answer are the following:

1. To see another way of working with the data to filter down to only seeing companies that meet a certain type of criteria, what large accelerated filers filed last March?
2. To help us identify how many different iterations there are within one type of financial statement data element, we will create a query to show us all of the XBRL tags that contain "cash" in their description.

Part 2: Master the Data

The XBRL database in full is a very large database. Our subset is a bit easier to manage. Lab Exhibit 8-4A is a database schema of the tables, attributes, and relationships in the Access database that you will work with in this lab. The database schema in full can be found at this URL: http://arelle.org/wordpress/wp-content/uploads/2014/07/sql_diagram.png if you are interested.

Lab Exhibit 8-4B, describes the most common table functions.

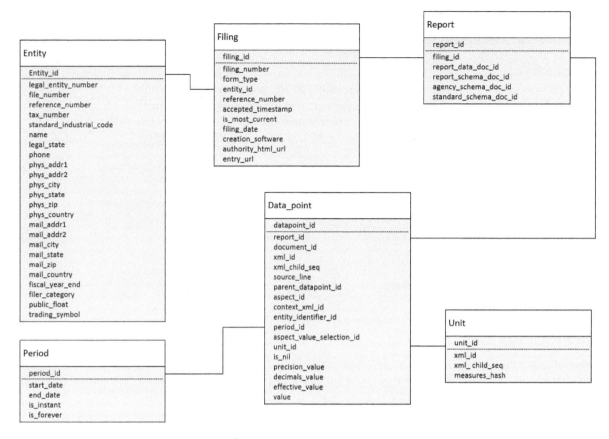

LAB EXHIBIT 8-4A XBRL Database Schema—Subset

LAB EXHIBIT 8-4B
Table Explanations

Table Name	Description
Entity	Information on the entity that submitted the filing
Filing	Information about individual filings
Report	Link from the information *about* the filing to the information *in* the filing
Period	Date information
Unit	To what degree any observation was recorded

Q3. Looking through the database schema, identify the tables you will need to retrieve data from to answer the two questions we'll work through in this lab.

Part 3: Perform an Analysis of the Data

3. In Access, create the query to identify the number of large, accelerated filers last March.
4. Take a screenshot (label it 8-4A) that includes the first rows that are in your output, as well as the bottom corner that indicates how many total rows were in the query results.
5. In Access, create the query to identify the different tags that contain the word *Cash* in them.
6. Take a screenshot (label it 8-4B) that includes the first rows that are in your output, as well as the bottom corner that indicates how many total rows were in the query results.

Part 5: Address and Refine Results

Based on the massive amount of tags that contain the word *cash* in them, we may decide to be more specific with the query.

7. This time, refine the query to show only the tags that *begin* with the word *Cash*.
8. Take a screenshot (label it 8-4C) that includes the first rows that are in your output, as well as the bottom corner that indicates how many total rows were in the query results.

    Q4.   How would you further drill down into the first question about the large filers?

    Q5.   Do you think the number of outputs you got for the different types of tags with the word *Cash* is reasonable? What recommendation would you have regarding the numerous elements in the taxonomy?

End of Lab

Glossary

A

Audit Data Standards (ADS) *(193)*   The Audit Data Standards define common tables and fields that are needed by auditors to perform common audit tasks. The AICPA developed these standards.

B

Balanced Scorecard *(252)*   A particular type of digital dashboard that is made up of strategic objectives, as well as KPIs, target measures, and initiatives, to help the organization reach its target measures in line with strategic goals.

Benford's law *(100)*   An observation about the frequency of leading digits in many real-life sets of numerical data. The law states that in many naturally occurring collections of numbers, the leading significant digit is likely to be small.

big data *(4)*   Datasets that are too large and complex for businesses' existing systems to handle utilizing their traditional capabilities to capture, store, manage, and analyze these datasets.

C

causal modeling *(95)*   A data approach similar to regression, but used when the relationship between independent and dependent variables where it is hypothesized that the independent variables cause or are associated with the dependent variable.

classification *(9, 95)*   A data approach used to assign each unit in a population into a few categories potentially to help with predictions.

clustering *(10, 94)*   A data approach used to divide individuals (like customers) into groups (or clusters) in a useful or meaningful way.

co-occurrence grouping *(10, 94)*   A data approach used to discover associations between individuals based on transactions involving them.

composite primary key *(42)*   A special case of a primary key that exists in linking tables. The composite primary key is made up of the two primary keys in the table that it is linking.

computer-assisted audit techniques (CAATs) *(212)*   Computer-assisted audit techniques (CAATs) are automated scripts that can be used to validate data, test controls, and enable substantive testing of transaction details or account balances and generate supporting evidence for the audit.

continuous data *(142)*   One way to categorize quantitative data, as opposed to discrete data. Continuous data can take on any value within a range. An example of continuous data is height.

D

Data Analytics *(4)*   The process of evaluating data with the purpose of drawing conclusions to address business questions. Indeed, effective Data Analytics provides a way to search through large structured and unstructured data to identify unknown patterns or relationships.

data dictionary *(14, 43)*   Centralized repository of descriptions for all of the data attributes of the dataset.

data reduction *(11, 94)*   A data approach used to reduce the amount of information that needs to be considered to focus on the most critical items (i.e., highest cost, highest risk, largest impact, etc.).

data request form *(45)*   A method for obtaining data if you do not have access to obtain the data directly yourself.

data warehouse *(193)*   A data warehouse is a repository of data accumulated from internal and external data sources, including financial data, to help management decision making.

decision boundaries *(104)*   Technique used to mark the split between one class and another.

decision tree *(104)*   Tool used to divide data into smaller groups.

declarative visualizations *(143)*   Made when the aim of your project is to "declare" or present your findings to an audience. Charts that are declarative are typically made after the data analysis has been completed and are meant to exhibit what was found in the analysis steps.

descriptive analytics *(212)*   Descriptive analytics summarize activity or master data elements based on certain attributes.

descriptive attributes *(42)*   Attributes that exist in relational databases that are neither primary nor foreign keys. These attributes provide business information, but are not required to build a database. An example would be "Company Name" or "Employee Address."

diagnostic analytics *(212)*   Diagnostic analytics looks for correlations or patterns of interest in the data.

digital dashboard *(252)*   An interactive report showing the most important metrics to help users understand how a company or an organization is performing. Often created using Excel or Tableau.

discrete data *(142)* One way to categorize quantitative data, as opposed to continuous data. Discrete data are represented by whole numbers. An example of discrete data is points in a basketball game.

DuPont ratio analysis *(306)* Developed by the DuPont Corporation to decompose performance (particularly return on equity [ROE]) into its component parts.

E

ETL *(44)* The extract, transform, and load process that is integral to mastering the data.

exploratory visualizations *(143)* Made when the lines between steps **P** (perform test plan), **A** (address and refine results), and **C** (communicate results) are not as clearly divided as they are in a declarative visualization project. Often when you are exploring the data with visualizations, you are performing the test plan directly in visualization software such as Tableau instead of creating the chart after the analysis has been done.

F

financial statement analysis *(305)* Used by investors, analysts, auditors, and other interested stakeholders to review and evaluate a company's financial statements and financial performance.

flat file *(41, 193)* A means of storing data in one place, such as in an Excel spreadsheet, as opposed to storing the data in multiple tables, such as in a relational database.

foreign key *(42)* An attribute that exists in relational databases in order to carry out the relationship between two tables. This does not serve as the "unique identifier" for each record in a table. These must be identified when mastering the data from a relational database in order to extract the data correctly from more than one table.

fuzzy match *(102)* A computer-assisted technique of finding matches that are less than 100 percent perfect by finding correspondencies between portions of the text of each potential match.

fuzzy matching *(218)* Fuzzy matching finds matches that may be less than 100 percent matching by finding correspondences between portions of the text or other entries.

H

heterogeneous systems approach *(193)* Heterogeneous systems represent multiple installations or instances of a system. It would be considered opposite of a homogenous system.

homogenous systems approach *(193)* Homogenous systems represent one single installation or instance of a system. It would be considered opposite of a heterogeneous system.

I

interval data *(142)* The third most sophisticated type of data on the scale of nominal, ordinal, interval, and ratio; a type of quantitative data. Interval data can be counted and grouped like qualitative data, and the differences between each data point are meaningful. However, interval data do not have a meaningful 0. In interval data, 0 does not mean "the absence of" but is simply another number. An example of interval data is the Fahrenheit scale of temperature measurement.

K

key performance indicator (KPI) *(252)* A particular type of performance metric that an organization deems the most important and influential on decision making.

L

link prediction *(10, 95)* A data approach used to predict a relationship between two data items.

M

mastering the data *(40)* The second step in the IMPACT cycle; it involves identifying and obtaining the data needed for solving the data analysis problem, as well as cleaning and preparing the data for analysis.

monetary unit sampling (MUS) *(213)* Monetary unit sampling allows auditors to evaluate account balances. MUS is more likely to pull accounts with large balances (higher risk and exposure) because it focuses on dollars, not account numbers.

N

nominal data *(141)* The least sophisticated type of data on the scale of nominal, ordinal, interval, and ratio; a type of qualitative data. The only thing you can do with nominal data is count, group, and take a proportion. Examples of nominal data are hair color, gender, and ethnic groups.

normal distribution *(142)* A type of distribution in which the median, mean, and mode are all equal, so half of all of the observations fall below the mean and the other half fall above the mean. This phenomenon is naturally occurring in many datasets in our world, such as SAT scores and heights and weights of newborn babies. When datasets follow a normal distribution, they can be standardized and compared for easier analysis.

O

ordinal data *(141)* The second most sophisticated type of data on the scale of nominal, ordinal, interval, and ratio; a type of qualitative data. Ordinal can be counted and categorized like nominal data and the categories can also be ranked. Examples of ordinal data include gold, silver, and bronze medals.

P

performance metric *(252)* Any calculation measuring how an organization is performing, particularly when that measure is compared to a baseline.

predictive analytics *(212)* Predictive analytics attempt to find hidden patterns or variables that are linked to abnormal behavior.

predictor (or independent or explanatory) variable *(9)* A variable that predicts or explains another variable, typically called a predictor or dependent variable.

prescriptive analytics *(212)* Prescriptive analytics use machine learning and artificial intelligence for auditors as decision support to assist future auditors find potential issues in the audit.

primary key *(41)* An attribute that is required to exist in each table of a relational database and serves as the "unique identifier" for each record in a table.

production or live systems *(193)* Production (or live systems) are those active systems that collect and report and are directly affected by current transactions.

profiling *(10, 94)* A data approach used to characterize the "typical" behavior of an individual, group or population by generating summary statistics about the data (including mean, standard deviations, etc.).

proportion *(141)* The primary statistic used with quantitative data. Proportion is calculated by counting the number of items in a particular category, then dividing that number by the total number of observations.

Q

qualitative data *(141)* Categorical data. All you can do with such data is count and group; in some cases, you can rank the data. Qualitative data can be further defined in two ways: nominal data and ordinal data. There are not as many options for charting qualitative data because they are not as sophisticated as quantitative data.

quantitative data *(142)* More complex than qualitative data. Quantitative data can be further defined in two ways: interval and ratio. In all quantitative data, the intervals

between data points are meaningful, allowing the data to be not just counted, grouped, and ranked, but also to have more complex operations performed on it such as mean, median, and standard deviation.

R

ratio analysis *(305)* Tool used to evaluate relationships among different financial statement items to help understand a company's financial and operating performance.

ratio data *(142)* The most sophisticated type of data on the scale of nominal, ordinal, interval, and ratio; a type of quantitative data. Such data can be counted and grouped just like qualitative data, and the differences between each data point are meaningful like with interval data. Additionally, ratio data have a meaningful 0; in other words, once a dataset approaches 0, 0 means "the absence of." An example of ratio data is currency.

regression *(9)* A data approach that attempts to estimate or predict, for each unit, the numerical value of some variable using some type of statistical model.

regression *(95)* A data approach used to estimate or predict, for each unit, the numerical value of some variable using some type of statistical model.

relational database *(41)* A means of storing data in order to ensure that the data are complete, not redundant, and to help enforce business rules. Relational databases also aid in communication and integration of business processes across an organization.

response (or dependent) variable *(9)* A variable that responds to, or is dependent, on another.

S

similarity matching *(10)* A data approach that attempts to identify similar individuals based on data known about them.

similarity matching *(95)* A data approach used to identify similar individuals based on data known about them.

sparklines *(306)* A small trendline or graphic that efficiently summarizes numbers or statistics in a graph without axes.

standard normal distribution *(142)* A special case of the normal distribution used for standardizing data. The standard normal distribution has 0 for its mean (and thus, for its mode and median, as well), and 1 for its standard deviation.

standardization *(142)* The method used for comparing two datasets that follow the normal distribution. By using a formula, every normal distribution can be transformed into the standard normal distribution. If you standardize both datasets, you can place both distributions on the same chart and more swiftly come to your insights.

standardized metrics *(303)*   Metrics used by data vendors to allow easier comparison of company reported XBRL data.

structured data *(98)*   Data that are organized and reside in a fixed field with a record or a file. Such data are generally contained in a relational database or spreadsheet and are readily searchable by search algorithms.

supervised approach/method *(94)*   Approach used to learn more about the basic relationships between independent and dependent variables that are hypothesized to exist.

support vector machines *(106)*   A discriminating classifier that is defined by a separating hyperplane that works first to find the widest margin (or biggest pipe).

Systems translator software *(193)*   Systems translator software maps the various tables and fields from varied ERP systems into a consistent format.

T

test data *(104)*   A set of data used to assess the degree and strength of a predicted relationship established by the analysis of training data.

training data *(104)*   Existing data that have been manually evaluated and assigned a class, which assists in classifying the test data.

U

unsupervised approach/method *(94)*   Approach used for data exploration looking for potential patterns of interest.

X

XBRL (eXtensible Business Reporting Language) *(102, 302)* A global standard for exchanging financial reporting information that uses XML; a global standard for Internet communication among businesses.

XBRL taxonomy *(302)*   Defines and describes each key data element (like cash or accounts payable). The taxonomy also defines the relationships between each element (like inventory is a component of current assets and current assets is a component of total assets).

XBRL-GL *(303)*   Stands for XBRL general ledger; relates to the ability of enterprise system to tag financial elements within the firm's financial reporting system.

Index

Note: Page numbers followed by *n* indicate source notes or footnotes.